BEAT THE FEDS IN COURT

BEAT THE FEDS IN COURT

A SELF-HELP LEGAL RESOURCE FOR EVERY AMERICAN

EDWARD AARON HARVEY SR.

WAYNE, MICHIGAN

Copyright © 2017
Edward Harvey
All rights reserved
Including the right of reproduction
In whole or in part in any form
Published by Edward Harvey
Wayne, Michigan

Library of Congress Control Number:
2016914880

ISBN: 9781530581092

LEGAL DISCLAIMER

BEAT THE FEDS IN COURT by Edward Harvey. All rights reserved. No part of this Manifesto may be reproduced in any form except where express written permission is granted, nor may any part of this Manifesto be reproduced by any electronic means, including information storage systems and retrieval systems, without permission in writing from the author, except by a reviewer who may quote brief passages in a review.

This publication is designed to provide you with accurate and authoritative information in regard to the subject matter covered. It is sold with the understanding that the publisher, and/or author, is not engaged in rendering legal or other professional advice or services. This publication is not a substitute for the advice of an attorney. If legal or other expert advice or assistance is required, you should seek the services of a competent professional. The information, ideas, and suggestions contained herein have been developed from sources believed to be reliable; at the same time no guarantees are made either expressly or by implication. Moreover, because of the technical nature of the materials contained herein, the assistance of a qualified Counselor/Attorney at Law, or other professional is heartily recommended.

DEDICATION

For my beloved Mother, Brenda ("G.H.S.")
My loving wife and partner in life, Paula
our children,
Michael
Ashli
Eddie
Amanda
Stephanie and Cindy
our Grandchildren,
Ryan
Brett
Stacie
Lindsey
Kylie
and
Abigail
My Father and master of wisdom, Dan
and my beloved Mema and Papa, I will meet you
there
With love.

INTRODUCTION

Dear Citizen,

I hope and trust you will find *Beat the Feds In Court* extremely enlightening. Although I am not the most eloquent writer, the law contained within is spot-on. It is not based on any Sovereign Citizen propaganda, the Uniform Commercial Code, nor any alleged invalidity of Title 18 U.S.C. Rather, it will show you in the law, as it is written today, (beside the fact that the majority of federal inmates have not committed a federal crime at all), the following:

1) The "United States" (Federal Government) can no more prosecute felonies as necessary and proper under the guise of regulating interstate commerce than they can prosecute felonies that occur on their own lands as necessary and proper without cession and acceptance of jurisdiction (unless the land is purchased by the consent of the particular state). If they could, jurisdiction would not need to be ceded and accepted, as provided for under Article I, § 8, cl. 17, U.S. Constitution.

2) The "United States" cannot "punish" felonious crimes as necessary and proper where the power to "punish" is not delegated in the Constitution, because it is enumerated in four other provisions (which enumeration proves it is delegated), and the Tenth Amendment states that undelegated powers are reserved to the States or to the People. As the Supreme Court has stated time and again, "Enumeration presupposes something not enumerated."

3) The United States District Courts do not have jurisdiction over the place of the crime just because it is alleged to have occurred within their respective Judicial Districts. This is proven by Title 40 U.S.C. § 3112(c) [Federal jurisdiction], which states: "Presumption. It is conclusively presumed that jurisdiction has not been accepted until the Government accepts jurisdiction over <u>land</u> as provided in this section."

4) Without cession of jurisdiction, or the delegated (enumerated) power to "punish", the Federal

Courts do not have subject-matter jurisdiction, i.e., no "Offense against the laws of the United States" has been made out. Title 18 U.S.C. § 3231.

5) Almost all federal crimes codified under Title 18 U.S.C., Title 21 U.S.C., and Title 26 U.S.C., including "interstate commerce" and R.I.C.O. crimes, are written to occur on lands where the several 50 Union states have ceded territorial jurisdiction (exclusive legislation) to the Federal Government. The crimes written to occur outside of these areas, for example, counterfeiting and felonies committed on the high Seas, must be supported by a constitutional foundation, such as the power to "punish".

It is my sincere hope that you will be able to utilize this "self-help legal resource" to spread awareness and free yourself and others from the legal tyranny that grips our great nation. I am also urging Citizens and others to demand their particular State's Governor, Mayors, Attorney General, and District Attorneys bring criminal charges against, and arrest the Federal

Judges and U.S. Attorneys that practice within the State's territorial jurisdiction. And, that your State Supreme Court suspends each U.S. Attorney's State Bar membership, which allows them to practice in the State, pending an investigation. It is evident, at least to me, that the Federal Courts and U.S. Attorneys have been committing treason against the Constitution, perjuring their sworn oaths, and violating the People's rights in order to secure and maintain unconstitutional convictions (which amount to crimes against the People). In fact, a Federal Public Defender recently confirmed that is exactly what they are doing.

Knowledge is power. Patriots, welcome to "The Awakening".

Sincerely,
Edward Harvey, President
Beat Feds Book

PREFACE

In this Manifesto, I will explain, in detail, exactly how the United States Federal Government is indicting, prosecuting, and incarcerating American Citizens, and others, in violation of the U.S. Constitution (Our Supreme Law), under the guise of regulating "interstate commerce."

Because many have been raised from birth to believe that the U.S. Federal Government has this inherent power, and most people trust their Government, their personal understanding is analogous to being brainwashed. Because of this misunderstanding you will most likely have to read through the material several times before you begin to see it clearly for yourself. As Will Rodgers correctly stated, "The problem isn't what we don't know, the problem is what we believe to be so and isn't so."

The U.S. Federal Government will probably seek to indict and prosecute me for writing this book. There goes our right to free speech reserved under the First

Amendment to the U.S. Constitution. They may even try to convince you that this is just another conspiracy theory. I have news for them, however: It is not a "theory" if it can be proven with facts, by utilizing their own laws, as I have done. Those of you who have been fighting and filing in court will soon learn why you cannot get any relief, or why it feels like you are being railroaded through the federal court system—you are.

Logically it is highly unlikely that a conspiracy of such magnitude is happening or, if so, has continued to succeed for decades. Especially when we try to reason that not one Federal Judge or U.S. Attorney has had any conscience to confess what is happening, even from their deathbed. Conspiracy or not it is happening, has been happening, and will continue to happen until something is done to change it.

While one person's voice may not be heard, it is the hope of this writer that the voices of the many will become deafening. I implore you to tell others about this Manifesto and encourage them to purchase their own copy so that they will have the knowledge necessary to vindicate themselves from legal tyranny. While I do not advocate violence, it has been said that it may take cartel and mafia hit men to remedy the situation by targeting the U.S. Federal District Court Judges and U.S. Attorneys. I absolutely cannot recommend this action. I cannot prevent it either. As Abraham Lincoln stated, "The people are the masters of both Congress and the courts, not to overthrow the Constitution, but to overthrow the men who would pervert it!"

In this Manifesto you will learn how the U.S. Federal Government "United States district courts," [sic][1] are not authorized to hear the vast majority of cases before them; how the U.S. Constitution has been manipulated to make it appear that this authority to hear your prosecution exists under it; how the Federal Judges and U.S. Attorney's (including your attorney), are complicitly aware of this or are ignorant of the law (which is no defense) and completely incompetent; and how the U.S. Supreme Court has been spurning

---

[1] sic. [Latin "so, thus"] Spelled or used as written. Black's Law Dictionary, Seventh Edition, page 1385.

their duty to uphold the Constitution by turning a blind eye to these unconstitutional prosecutions, convictions, and incarcerations (leaving helpless those whose rights they are supposed to be protecting). All this while allegedly swearing an oath to uphold the Constitution[2] (and perjuring that oath). They conspire together to commit treason against the Constitution they have sworn to uphold, and crimes against the people, for their own personal and financial interests.

The answers that you have sought for so long are here in this Manifesto. It is the only source in the world which will provide you with those answers. Good Luck and God Bless.

---
[2] Article VI, cl. 3

TABLE OF CONTENTS

A LITTLE HISTORY 16
NOTHING BUT THE TRUTH 18
THE CONSTITUTION 22
THE POWER TO PUNISH 54
THE COURTS 190
THE JUDGES 299
HOW IT'S DONE 317
IT'S IN THE LAW 353
SUBSTANTIAL EFFECTS TEST? 426
WHAT HAVE WE LEARNED? 493
PRETRIAL REMEDY 506
AFTER ARRAIGNMENT 511
AFTER JUDGMENT 511
PROPER PROCEDURE IN 12 STEPS 513
A HELPFULL HINT 524
SUE THEM 537
SOMETHING TO CONSIDER 542
APPENDIX i
RON PAUL FAREWELL SPEECH ii
INSPIRATIONAL QUOTES xxxix
OTHER INFORMATIVE DEFINITIONS xlvi
Magna Carta Translation xlviii
Transcript of Declaration of Independence (1776) lxvii

Transcript of Articles of Confederation (1777) lxxxi
The Constitution of the United States: A Transcription ... xciv
Amendments to the Constitution of the United States of
America cxii
The Kentucky Resolutions of 1798 cxxviii
The Kentucky Resolutions of 1798-99 cxxxix
Virginia Resolution of 1798 cxliii
The Judiciary Act of 1789 cxlvi
The Judiciary Act of 1801 clxvii
The Judiciary Act of 1802 clxxxviii
Establishment of the U.S. Circuit Courts of Appeals, 1891 ccix
OPINION OF HON. WILLIAM. H. H. MILLER, OF INDIANA ccxvii
OPINION OF HON. A.H. GARLAND ccxviii
OPINION OF HON. RICHARD OLNEY ccxix
JOINT RESOLUTION ccxx

A LITTLE HISTORY

The fight for personal liberties (freedom) is an age old fight stemming back since the beginning of time. In the United States of America this fight stems back to the Magna Charta. That document was obtained by the Barons, from King John of England, at the point of a sword, in AD 1215 at a field named Runnymede. This "bill of rights" reserved rights that the Barons and citizens were unwilling to surrender. It also eased the tyranny of King John against the people.

After America was founded, the people here found themselves in a similar situation with England. To remedy their situation, they declared themselves to be independent sovereigns and separate from England. This historic event is forever memorialized in "The Declaration of Independence" of July 4, 1776. Like all who wish to be free from tyrannical rule, they must fight to keep it. So comes the "Revolutionary War".

The "Articles of Confederation", the first Constitution, was drafted over the next two years and ratified between the years 1778 and 1781.[3] However, because of its apparent flaws, a new Constitution was written. While much controversy surrounded the proposed new Constitution it was, nevertheless, drafted and ratified on September 17, 1787, resulting in the current "U.S. Constitution". Fast forward to today.

---

[3] "After the Declaration of Independence the United Colonies, through delegates appointed by each of the colonies, considered articles of confederation, which were debated from day to day, and from time to time, for two years, and were on July 9, 1778, ratified by ten States; by New Jersey on November 26 of the same year; by Delaware on the 23rd of February, 1779, and by Maryland on March 1, 1781." Missouri v. Illinois, 180 US 208, 219-220 (1901)

NOTHING BUT THE TRUTH

The belief put forward by the U.S. Federal Government ("United States"), is that under the commerce clause, Article I, § 8. cl. 3, they can "punish" felonious crimes. The contention, which everyone believes, is that if a person transports, or causes to be transported, anything across State lines, which is "interstate commerce", then that activity can be regulated through the imposition of felonious criminal statutes. This is simply not true.

I will show you how this is being accomplished through the manipulation of the law. I will show how Congress has written the "law" to allow this unconstitutional end to be achieved through obfuscation; how your ignorance of the Law is being used against you to achieve this; how, through that ignorance, the Supreme Court has sanctioned unconstitutional prosecutions, convictions, and incarcerations; and how they are directly benefiting by milking the taxpayers of their hard earned money to keep you illegally incarcerated for years.

That is how they make their money. That is what the "United States" (Federal Government) has decided is "for your own good". The question is, since they have gone to all this trouble to perpetrate this fraud on the American People, and others, on such a grand scale, how then do we know what other fraudulent schemes are being unleashed upon us (such as the "Federal Reserve" and the "I.R.S.")? [Please read, "The Creature From Jekyll Island", by G. Edward Griffin for more information.]

More importantly, if this power to "punish" under the guise of regulating interstate commerce was the will of the people, why then was the Constitution not amended? How did this usurpation of power and jurisdiction not belonging to the Federal Government happen? The only answer is that those in power the people entrusted to represent us, by voting them into their positions, have utilized their positions to manipulate, and directly benefit themselves financially by preying upon those very people who voted for them. They literally make their living off the backs of the ignorant—the ones who trusted them. They have betrayed their country and their people, committing treason, to satisfy their own personal greed and lust for power.

I am going to lay this Manifesto out somewhat like a court pleading utilizing the U.S. Constitution, a wealth of Supreme Court precedent (standing case law), a limited amount of appellate cases from a couple of Circuits, one or two District Courts, positive law (Supreme Law enacted by Congress), and Federal Rules of Procedure governing court cases. It may feel overwhelming at times, but do not be discouraged. Your perseverance will pay off in the end. The lights will start turning on, as they did for me, and you will be absolutely amazed and dumbfounded how this "system" has managed to gain such a foothold.

For those of you who are currently incarcerated, have already served your time in Federal prison, have lost a loved one while in prison, are waiting for a loved one to be released from prison, are currently serving life sentences, my heart and compassion goes out to you. You will have to decide what to do because the courts will not listen. There is no one to help you except for yourself, others similarly situated, and the People. The Federal Government will not. What will you do to make them listen? For those of you currently being prosecuted, look at the U.S. Attorney, the Judge, and your Attorney. They are all working against you. They are all on the same team. Your prosecution and conviction is how they make their money. The only interest your Attorney has is getting you to plead guilty (pleading you out). That will become painfully clear as you read through, and learn from, this Manifesto. Anyway, without further ado, let's get started.

THE CONSTITUTION

There are a growing number of people who put forth the belief that the Constitution is, in reality, a contract, because its establishment bears some semblance to the way contracts are formed, and are therefore not bound by it. This is untrue. While it is true we are not the "People" but rather the "Posterity", if you go to other countries and break their laws you will be prosecuted and sent to their prisons, even though you were not a party to the ratification of their Constitution either. Nowhere in any court opinion will you find the court opining that the U.S. Constitution is a contract (an agreement between people, parties, *etc.*), as opposed to a compact (an agreement between governments). See for example Article I, § 10, cl. 3, U.S. Constitution. You will also not find any dictionary defining the U.S. Constitution as a contract. The U.S. Constitution specifically states exactly what it is:

>We the People of the United States, in Order to form a more

perfect Union, establish Justice, insure domestic Tranquility, provide for the common defense, promote the general Welfare, and secure the Blessings of Liberty to ourselves and our Posterity, do ordain and establish <u>this Constitution</u> for the United States of America. <u>Preamble</u>, U.S. Constitution

A "constitution" is defined as:

> The fundamental and organic <u>law</u> of a nation or state. <u>Black's Law Dictionary</u>, Eighth Edition, page 330.
>
> fundamental law. The organic law that establishes the governing principes of a nation or state; esp., CONSTITUTIONAL LAW.

Black's Law Dictionary, Eighth Edition, page 697.

Constitutional Law. The body of law deriving from the U.S. Constitution and dealing primarily with government powers, civil rights, and civil liberties. Black's Law Dictionary, Eighth Edition, page 331.

In the United States of America ("U.S.A."), the U.S. Constitution is the Supreme Law of the land and includes supreme law enacted by Congress. Those Supreme Laws of Congress are conditioned upon their being made pursuant to the Constitution. All laws that are contrary to the Constitution, whether written that way, or carried out so as to reach a prohibited end, are unconstitutional. This includes laws that are "void for vagueness". See Article VI, cl. 2, U.S. Constitution:

> This Constitution, and the Laws of the United States which shall be made in Pursuance thereof; and all Treaties made, or which shall be made, under the Authority of the United States, shall be the supreme Law of the Land.

Additionally, the Supreme Court has stated that:

> [T]he Constitution itself is in every real sense a law—the lawmakers being the people themselves, in whom under our system all political power and sovereignty primarily resides, and through whom such power and sovereignty primarily speaks. It is by that law, and not otherwise, that the legislative, executive, and judicial agencies which it created exercise such political authority as

they have been permitted to possess.

The framers of the Constitution ... provided explicitly-This Constitution, and the Laws of the United States <u>which shall be made in pursuance thereof</u>; ... shall be the supreme Law of the Land; ...." The supremacy of the Constitution as law is thus declared without qualification. That supremacy is absolute; <u>the supremacy of a statute enacted by Congress is not absolute</u> but conditioned on its being made in pursuance of the Constitution. <u>Carter v. Carter Coal Co.</u>, 298 US 238, 296 (1936)

The Constitution also mandates that, "[A]ll executive and judicial Officers, both of <u>the United States</u>

and of the several States, shall be bound by Oath or Affirmation, to support this Constitution."[4] The Supreme Court has explained that the Constitution of the United States, with all powers conferred by it on the General Government, and surrendered by States, was the voluntary act of the People of the several States, deliberately done, for their own protection and safety against injustice from one another, and their anxiety to preserve it in full force, in all its powers, and to guard against resistance to or evasion of its authority, is proved by the provision of Article VI, cl. 3, which requires that members of the State Legislatures, and all executive and judicial officers, of the several States as well as those of the General Government, shall be bound by oath or affirmation, to support the Constitution.[5] The Supreme Court has also made clear that:

> Ignorance of the law is no excuse for men in general. It is less an excuse for men whose special

---

[4] Article VI, cl. 3

[5] Ableman v. Booth, 62 US 506, 21 How 506, 524 (1859)

duty is to apply it, and therefore to know and observe it.

When they enter such a domain in dealing with the citizen's rights, they should do so at their peril, whether that be created by state or federal law. For their sworn oath and their first duty are to uphold the Constitution. Screws v. United States, 325 US 91, 129-130 (1944)

The Tenth Amendment to the U.S. Constitution is very clear that, "The powers not delegated to the United States by the Constitution ... are reserved to the States respectively, or to the people." Under Article I, § 8, cl. 3 Congress is authorized to regulate commerce. Regulate is defined as: "To fix, establish, or control; to adjust by rule, method, or established mode; to direct by rule or restriction. Regulate means to govern or direct according to rule."[6] Rule is defined

---

[6] Black's Law Dictionary, Sixth Edition, page 1286

as: "An established standard, guide, or regulation."[7] As can be seen by the legal definitions, the terms regulation and rule are synonymous. This is also the interpretation of Congress. In the Code of Federal Regulations ("C.F.R."), "Regulation and rule have the same meaning."[8]

In the seminal case of Gibbons v. Ogden,[9] Chief Justice Marshall, speaking for the Supreme Court, stated that:

> Commerce, undoubtedly ... is regulated by prescribing rules for carrying on that intercourse.
>
> What is this power? It is the power to regulate; that is, to prescribe the rule by which commerce is to be governed.

---

[7] Black's Law Dictionary, Sixth Edition, page 1331
[8] Title 1 C.F.R. §1, Definitions
[9] Gibbons v. Ogden, 9 Wheat 1, 189-190, 196 (1824)

Clearly, pursuant to the aforementioned legal definitions, and Supreme Court authority, "commerce" is regulated by prescribing "regulations (rules)," not felony criminal statutes. However, pursuant to <u>Article I, § 8. cl, 18</u> (the Necessary and Proper clause), Congress is authorized, "To make all Laws which shall be necessary and proper for carrying into Execution the foregoing Powers...." This is, perhaps, the most misunderstood and obfuscated clause in the Constitution. It has been construed as a grant of power when it is not. What is the power the "United States" (Federal Government) purports the necessary and proper clause grants? The power to "punish," of course. The Supreme Court has stated otherwise:

> The last paragraph of the section which authorizes Congress to make all laws which shall be necessary and proper for carrying into execution the foregoing powers, and all other powers vested by this Constitution in the government of the United States, or

> in any department or officer thereof, <u>is not the delegation of a new and independent power</u>, but simply provision for making effective the powers theretofore mentioned. <u>Kansas v. Colorado</u>, 206 US 46, 88 (1907)

The Constitution contains only four provisions wherein the Framers delegated to Congress the power to punish (only three which are of concern): counterfeiting the Securities and current Coin of the United States, Piracies and Felonies committed on the high Seas and offenses against the Law of Nations, and Treason.[10]

I will explain this power to "punish" a little later. For now, let's return to the "necessary and proper clause", also called the "sweeping clause."[11] Taking a common sense approach, we can clearly see that

---

[10] <u>Article I, § 8, cl. 6</u>; <u>Article I, § 8, cl. 10</u>; and <u>Article III, § 3, cl.2</u>, respectively.

[11] <u>Article I, § 8, cl. 18</u>

Congress is authorized, "To make all Laws which shall be necessary and proper for carrying into Execution the foregoing Powers ...."[12] However, unlike the counterfeiting clause and the high Seas clause,[13] the power to <u>punish</u> is not a "foregoing power" under the Commerce Clause.[14] It is an <u>undelegated</u> power which is "reserved to the States respectively, or to the people."[15] In a recent Supreme Court Opinion Chief Justice Roberts, concurring, stated that:

> [T]he Necessary and Proper Clause authorizes congressional action incidental to [an <u>enumerated</u>] power ... no great substantive and independent power can be implied as incidental to other powers, or used as a means of executing them. The enumeration presupposes

---

[12] <u>Article I, § 8, cl. 18</u>

[13] <u>Article I, § 8, cl. 6</u>; <u>Article I, § 8, cl. 10</u>, respectively

[14] <u>Article I, § 8, cl. 3</u>

[15] <u>Tenth Amendment</u>

something not enumerated. United States v. Kebodeaux, 186 Led2d 540 (2013) (citations and quotation marks omitted)

A recent Supreme Court dissent by Justice Thomas, with whom Justice Scalia joined except for footnote 2, from the denial of certiorari, states that:

This Court has consistently recognized that the Constitution imposes real limits on federal power. The powers of the legislature are defined, and limited; and that those limits may not be mistaken, or forgotten, the constitution is written. **It follows from the enumeration of specific powers that there are real boundaries to what the Federal Government may do.** The enumeration presupposes something not enumerated. The Constitution withhold[s] from Congress a plenary police power that would authorize enactment of every type of legislation. <u>Carroll v. United States</u>, 178 Led2d 799 (2011) (citations and internal quotation marks omitted)

<u>Article I, § 8, cl. 3</u>, "To <u>regulate</u> Commerce with foreign Nations, and among the several States, and with the Indian Tribes"

<u>Article I, § 8, cl. 5</u>, "To coin Money, <u>regulate</u> the Value thereof, and of foreign Coin, and fix the Standards of Weights and Measures"

<u>Article I, § 8, cl. 6</u>, "To provide for the **Punishment** of counterfeiting the Securities and current Coin of the United States"

<u>Article I, § 8, cl. 10</u>, "To define and **punish** Piracies and Felonies committed on the high Seas, and Offences against the Law of Nations"

<u>Article III, § 3, cl. 2</u>, "The Congress shall have Power to declare the **Punishment** of Treason, but no Attainder of Treason shall work Corruption of Blood, or Forfeiture except during the Life of the Person attained"

<u>Article IV, § 3 cl. 2</u>, "The Congress shall have Power to dispose of and make <u>all</u> needful Rules and <u>Regulations</u> respecting the Territory or other Property belonging to the United States; and nothing in this Constitution shall be so construed as to Prejudice any Claims by the United States, or of any particular State"

In fact, the Anti-federalists objected that the Necessary and Proper Clause would allow Congress, inter alia, to "constitute new Crimes, . . . and extend [its] Power as far as [it] shall think proper; so that the State Legislatures have no Security for the Powers now presumed to remain to them; or the People for their

Rights." Hamilton responded that these objections were gross "misrepresentation[s]." He termed the Clause "perfectly harmless," for it merely confirmed Congress' implied authority to enact laws in exercising its enumerated powers. Gonzales v. Raich, 545 US 1, n5 (2005)

Since the "necessary and proper clause" is not a grant of power, but simply a provision for carrying into execution the foregoing powers, how then does it grant the power to punish where that power has not been delegated? Is the Federal Government not a government of delegated,[16] limited, and enumerated[17] powers? As the Supreme Court explained:

---

[16] Delegation. The act of entrusting another with authority or empowering another to act as an agent or representative. Black's Law Dictionary, Seventh Edition, page 438.

[17] Enumerated power. A political power specifically delegated to a governmental branch by a constitution. – Also termed express power. Black's Law Dictionary, Seventh Edition, page 1189.

The Constitution is the supreme Law of the land ordained and established by the people. All legislation must conform to the principles it lays down.

The question is not what power the Federal Government ought to have but what powers in fact have been given by the people.

When a Law for carrying into Execution the Commerce Clause violates the principle of state sovereignty reflected in the various constitutional provisions we mentioned earlier, it is not a Law proper for carrying into Execution the Commerce Clause, and is thus merely <u>an act of usurpation</u> which deserves to be treated as such. <u>Printz v. United States</u>, 521 US 898, 923-924 (1997)

How then does the United States (Federal Government) Department of Justice ("DOJ"), purport to punish under the guise of regulating commerce when the power to punish is not even a delegated power under the commerce clause? The truth is that the power to punish felonies comes from other provisions in the Constitution which I will address later. The prevention of commingling powers granted with powers not granted is exactly the reason why the Tenth Amendment was written.

> From the accepted doctrine that the United States is a government of delegated powers, it follows that those not expressly granted, or reasonably to be implied from such as are conferred, are reserved to the states or to the people. To forestall any suggestion to the contrary, the Tenth Amendment was adopted. The same proposition, otherwise stat-

ed, is that <u>powers not granted are prohibited</u>.

It is an established principle that the attainment of a prohibited end may not be accomplished under the pretext of the exertion of powers which are granted.

"Should Congress, in the execution of its powers, adopt measures which are prohibited by the Constitution; or should Congress, under the pretext of executing its powers, pass laws for the accomplishment of objects not entrusted to the government; it would be the painful duty of this tribunal, should a case requiring such a decision come before it, to say that such an act was not the law of the land."

"Congress can<u>not</u>, under the pretext of executing delegated power, pass laws for the accomplishment of objects not entrusted to the Federal Government. And we accept as established doctrine that any provision of an act of Congress ostensibly enacted under power granted by the Constitution not naturally and reasonably adapted to the effective exercise of such power but solely to the achievement of something plainly within the power reserved to the States, is invalid and cannot be enforced." United States v. Butler, 297 US 1, 67-69 (1936)(citations omitted)

The Supreme Court has further explained that:

> The general rule with regard to the respective powers of the national and the state governments

under the Constitution is not in doubt. The states were before the Constitution; and, consequently, their legislative powers antedated the Constitution. Those who framed and those who adopted that instrument meant to carve from the general mass of legislative powers, then possessed by the states, only such portions as it was thought wise to confer upon the federal government; and in order that there should be no uncertainty in respect of what was taken and what was left, the national powers of legislation <u>were not aggregated but enumerated</u>—with the result that what was not embraced by the enumeration remained vested in the states without change or impairment. Thus "when it was found necessary to establish a national government for national purposes," this court said in <u>Munn. v. Illinois</u>, 94 US 113, 124, "a part of the powers of the States and of the people of the States was granted to the United States and the people of the United States. This grant operated as a further limitation upon the powers of the States, so that now the governments of the States possess all the powers of the Parliament of England, except such as have been delegated to the United States or reserved by the people."

While the states are not sovereign in the true sense of that term, but only quasi-sovereign, yet in respect of all powers reserved to them they are supreme—"as independent of the general government as that government within its sphere is independent of the States." <u>Col-</u>

lector v. Day (Buffington v. Day), 11 Wall 113, 124. And since every addition to the national legislative power to some extent detracts from or invades the power of the states, it is of vital moment that, in order to preserve the fixed balance intended by the Constitution, the powers of the general government be not so extended as to embrace any not within the express terms of the several grants or the implications necessarily to be drawn therefrom. It is no longer open to question that the general government, unlike the states, Hammer v. Dagenhart, 247 US 251, 275, possesses no inherent power in respect of the internal affairs of the states; and emphatically not with regard to legislation. The question in respect of the inherent power of that government as to the external affairs of the nation and in the field of international law is a wholly different matter which it is not necessary now to consider. [citing cases]

The determination of the Framers Convention and the ratifying conventions to preserve complete and unimpaired state self-government in all matters not committed to the general government is one of the plainest facts which emerges from the history of their deliberations. And adherence to that determination is incumbent equally upon the federal government and the states. State powers can neither be appropriated on the one hand nor abdicated on the other. As this court said in Texas v. White, 7 Wall 700, 725—"the preservation of the States, and the maintenance of their governments, are as much within the design and care of the Constitution as the preservation of the Union and the maintenance of the National Government. The Constitution, in all its provisions, looks to an indestructible Union, composed of indestructible States." Every journey to a forbidden end begins with the first step; and the danger of such a step by the federal government in the direction of taking over the powers of the states is that the end of the journey may find the states so despoiled of their powers, or—**what may amount to the same thing**—so relieved of the responsibilities which possession of the powers necessarily enjoins, as to reduce them to little more than geographical subdivisions of the national domain. It is safe to say that if, when the Constitution was under consideration, it had been thought that any such danger lurked behind its plain words, it would never have been ratified. Carter v. Carter Coal Co., 298 US 238, 294-296 (1936)

If that were not clear enough, and it is, the Supreme Court 29 years earlier stated that:

"The government, then, of the United States, can claim no powers which are not granted to it by the Constitution, and the powers actually granted must be such as are expressly given or given by necessary implication." "The government of the United States is one of delegated, limited, and enumerated powers."

[I]t is still true that no independent and unmentioned power passes to the national government or can rightfully be exercised by the congress. Kansas v. Colorado, 206 US 46, 87-88 (1907)

Sovereignty is defined as: "Supreme dominion, authority, or rule. The supreme political authority of an independent state. The state itself."[18] Dominion is defined as: "Control, possession. Sovereignty".[19] In Pollard v. Hagan [20] the Supreme Court explains that:

> [T]he United States never held any municipal sovereignty, jurisdiction, or right of soil in and to the territory, of which Alabama, or

---

[18] Black's Law Dictionary, Seventh Edition, page 1402

[19] Black's Law Dictionary, Seventh Edition, page 502

[20] Pollard v. Hagan, 3 How (US) 212, 221-224, 11 Led 565 (1845)

any of the new States were formed.

[T]he United States have no constitutional capacity to exercise municipal jurisdiction, sovereignty, or eminent domain, within the limits of a State or elsewhere, <u>except</u> in cases in which it is <u>expressly</u> granted. [*Cf.* <u>Article I, § 8, cl. 17</u>].[21]

The provision of the Constitution above referred to shows that no such power can be exercised by the United States within a State. Such a power is not only <u>repugnant</u> to the Constitution, but it is inconsistent with the spirit and <u>intention</u> of the deeds of cession.[22]

---

[21] My note

[22] Cession. The act of relinquishing property rights. <u>Black's Law Dictionary</u>, Seventh Edition, page 221.

Although the Constitution created a system of dual sovereigns, each Union State retained sovereignty (supreme dominion) over their land (territory), except where concurrent or exclusive legislative (territorial) jurisdiction has been expressly relinquished in accordance with the Constitution. The Federal Government ("United States") exercises sovereignty relinquished to them over the District of Columbia, and other like places via Article I, § 8, cl. 17. The Federal Government also exercises jurisdiction (authority) concurrent with the Union States as to the enumerated powers delegated to them. The authority to carry into execution their delegated powers within the Union States is analogous to territorial jurisdiction. However, as we will learn, territorial jurisdiction over land remains with each Union State until ceded. Therefore, as the Framers of our Constitution explained, the Federal Government's "jurisdiction extends to certain enumerated objects only, and leaves to the several States a residuary and inviolable sovereignty over all other objects." The Federalist Papers, No. 39.

When the Federal Government exercises undelegated powers reserved to the several 50 Union States under the guise of carrying into execution delegated powers then they are exercising exclusive legislation, a sort of "police power". Of course it is not truly a "police power" because their ability to exercise exclusive legislation is derived from the consent of the Union States which are quasi-sovereign, the true sovereigns being the People. For example, because the Federal Government has no territorial jurisdiction within the Union States (accept where relinquished through consent to purchase or cession, and acceptance), they can only exercise the powers delegated to them. When they exercise an undelegated power to "punish" felonious crimes under the guise of carrying into execution their "Commerce Clause" power they are exercising exclusive legislation which must occur within lands under their concurrent or exclusive jurisdiction per Article I, § 8, cl. 17, U.S. Constitution. The Supreme Court explained that:

> All powers which properly appertain to sovereignty, which have not been delegated to the Federal government, belong to the states and the people. United

States v. Illinois Central R. Co., 154 US 225, 241 (1894) (quoting New Orleans v. United States, 10 Peters 662, 737, 30 US 662 (1836)); and that

[T]itle, jurisdiction, and sovereignty, are <u>inseparable</u> incidents, and remain so till the State makes some <u>cession</u>. A cession of territory is essentially a cession of jurisdiction. <u>The State of Rhode Island v. The State of Massachusetts</u>, 12 Peters 657, 733, 37 US 657 (1838); and that

[T]he proposition that there are legislative powers affecting the Nation as a whole which belong to, although not expressed in that grant of powers, is in direct conflict with the doctrine that this is a government of enumerated powers.

This natural construction of the original body of the Constitution is made absolutely certain by the Tenth Amendment. This amendment, which was seemingly adopted with prescience of just such contention as the present, disclosed the widespread fear that the National Government might, under the pressure of a supposed general welfare, attempt to exercise powers which had not been granted. With equal determination the framers intended that no such assumption should ever find justification in the organic act [Constitution], and that if in the future further powers seemed necessary they should be granted by the people in the manner they had provided for amending that act Carter v. Carter Coal Co., supra at 293

(quoting Kansas v. Colorado, supra at 89)

THE POWER TO PUNISH

Before proceeding further, you need to know what the power to "punish" actually is. The enumerated power to "punish" delegated in the Constitution is a grant of power to punish felonies nationwide. This is very apparent in Article I, § 8, cl. 10, (the high Seas clause), by simply reading the clause without the word Piracies: "To define and punish ... Felonies ...." I will explain in more detail as we proceed through this Manifesto. For now, keep in mind that the power to punish felonies is united with whoever is sovereign over the land. This power was not surrendered except in those 3 aforementioned provisions: counterfeiting, Piracies and Felonies committed on the high Seas, and offenses against the Law of Nations, and Treason.[23] Moving on, the proposition often advanced is that the power of Congress to regulate "interstate commerce" contains an implied power to "punish" and can be utilized whenever they deem it "necessary and proper". I will prove otherwise. I will show you what

---

[23] Article I, § 8, cl. 6; Article I, § 8, cl. 10; and Article III, § 3, cl. 2, respectively.

the United States (Federal Government) does not want you to know and has hidden from you for so long.

Implication of the power to "punish" under the commerce clause, by and through the necessary and proper clause, is not favored nor appropriate. Congress can<u>not</u> grant themselves jurisdiction or an undelegated power to "punish" felonies, pursuant to their delegated power to regulate interstate commerce, whenever they deem it "necessary and proper" because jurisdiction "cannot be acquired tortuously by disseisin of the State,"[24] and because "it [is] a fundamental precept that the rights of sovereignty are <u>not</u> to be taken away by implication."

---

[24] Fort Leavenworth R.R. Co. v. Lowe, 114 US 525, 538-539 (1885)

Tortious. Wrongful; of the nature of a tort. Black's Law Dictionary, Sixth Edition, page 1,489.

Disseisin. Dispossession; a deprivation of possession; a privation of seisin; a usurpation of the right of seisin and possession, and an exercise of such powers and privileges of ownership as to keep out or displace him to whom these rightfully belong. Black's Law Dictionary, Sixth Edition, page 472.

Seisin. Possession of real property under claim of freehold estate. Black's Law Dictionary, Sixth Edition page 1,358.

Id.__25__ As Chief Justice Marshall stated, "It is a rule of construction, acknowledged by all, that the exceptions from a power mark its extent." <u>Gibbons v. Ogden</u>, 9 Wheat 1, 189-191 (1824)

In other words, the fact that the power to "punish" has been delegated, by enumeration, in other provisions of the Constitution, yet has not been delegated, by enumeration, under the commerce clause, is proof on its face that it is a power not delegated to Congress in aid of their commerce clause powers. A very recent Supreme Court opinion, rendered by Chief Justice Roberts himself, clearly states that:

> The enumeration of powers is also a limitation of powers, **because "[t]he enumeration <u>presupposes</u> something not enumerated."** The Constitution's express conferral of some

---

[25] Id. Abbr. [Latin idem] The same. Id. Is used in a legal citation to refer to the authority cited immediately before. <u>Black's Law Dictionary</u>, Seventh Edition, page 748.

powers makes clear that it does not grant others. And the Federal Government "can exercise only the powers granted to it."

If no <u>enumerated power</u> authorizes Congress to pass a certain law, that law may not be enacted, even if it would not violate any of the express prohibitions in the Bill of Rights or elsewhere in the Constitution. <u>National Federation of Indep. Bus. v. Sebelius</u>, 183 Led2d 450, 465-466 (2012) (citations omitted)

James Madison, the Father of the Constitution, stated, in regard to the power to punish treason, that:

As treason may be committed against the United States, **the authority of the United States**

ought to be enabled to punish it. But as new-fangled and artificial treasons have been the great engines by which violent factions, the natural offspring of free government, have usually wreaked their alternate malignity on each other, the convention have, with great judgment, opposed a barrier to this peculiar danger, **by inserting a constitutional definition of the crime**, and fixing the proof necessary for conviction of it, and restraining the Congress, even in punishing it, from extending the consequences of guilt beyond the person of its author. The Federalist Papers, No. 43 (Madison); and that

The powers delegated by the proposed Constitution to the federal government are few and defined. Those which are to remain in the State governments are numerous and indefinite. The former will be exercised principally on external objects, as war, peace, negotiation, and foreign commerce; with which last the power of taxation will, for the most part, be connected. The powers reserved to the several States will extend to all the objects which, in the ordinary course of affairs, concern the lives, liberties, and properties of the people, and the internal order, improvement, and prosperity of the State. <u>The Federalist Papers</u>, No. 45 (Madison)

If the power to <u>regulate</u> allowed Congress to <u>punish</u>, by and through the necessary and proper clause, then there would have been no reason to delegate, by enumeration, the power to <u>punish</u> counterfeiting the securities and current coin of the United States[26] in aid of their power to coin money and <u>regulate</u> the value thereof under the Constitution.[27] The power to punish counterfeiting was delegated to Congress because counterfeiting devalues legal tender and undermines our economy. Remember, their power is to regulate the <u>value</u> of the coin.

> The authority of the existing Congress is restrained to the regulation of coin struck by their own authority, or that of the respective States. It must have been seen at once that the proposed uniformity in the value of the current coin might be destroyed by subjecting that of foreign coin to different regulations of different States.

---

[26] Article I, § 8, cl. 6
[27] Article I, § 8, cl. 5

> The punishment of counterfeiting ... the current coin, is submitted of course ... to secure the <u>value</u>.... <u>The Federalist Papers</u>, No. 42

Clearly, the power to punish counterfeiting was delegated in aid of Congress' power to regulate the value of the money they coin. They did not inherently have this power. The Framers of the Constitution would not have delegated to Congress an enumerated power to punish if they already had this power whenever they deemed it "necessary and proper," nor would they have done so if this power to punish could be implied pursuant to their delegated and enumerated power to regulate.

The Framers would have never delegated the power to punish in certain provisions, and then delegate the power to regulate in other provisions, if the power to punish and the power to regulate were synonymous. Instead, they carefully chose the language used. For example, in <u>Article I, § 8, cl. 10</u>, the Framers would have more easily stated "to <u>regulate</u> the high Seas and offenses against the Law of Nations" instead of the "to define and punish Piracies and Felonies" language. The power to regulate commerce is the power to prescribe the rule (regulation) by which commerce is to be governed. Chief Justice Marshall stated this twice in Gibbons v. Ogden.[28]

I know you are probably thinking to yourselves what if you break the rules? The answer is coming. For now, know that the Constitution limits the places (geographical locations), where Congress can impose sanctions for violating these regulations of commerce, depending on whether the sanction is civil, a misdemeanor, or a felony.

The power to "punish" felonies is inherent in the rights of sovereignty. This was well known when the Constitution was written. Each of the then 13 States that ratified the Constitution retained all the powers not delegated by enumeration to the "United States" (Federal Government). Of these powers retained was the right to punish the people who committed crimes within their own territorial boundaries. This is called

---

[28] Gibbons v. Ogden, 9 Wheat 1, 189-190, 196 (1824)

"territorial jurisdiction." Territorial Jurisdiction is defined as: "the <u>sovereign jurisdiction</u> that a state has <u>over the land</u> within its limits ... and <u>over all persons</u> and things within those areas subject to its control.[29]

> "Every independent state has as one of the incidents of its <u>sovereignty</u> the right of municipal legislation over all persons within its <u>territory</u>."
>
> [N]o sovereignty can extend its jurisdiction beyond its own <u>territorial</u> limits. <u>United States v. Wong Kim Ark</u>, 169 US 690 (1898)

Obviously this power to punish people within the territorial limits of any State was not delegated to Congress (except in the 3 aforementioned provisions). If Congress already had this power, there

---

[29] <u>Webster's Third New International Dictionary</u>, unabridged (1981), page 2,361

would have been no need to delegate the power to "punish" (especially in light of the alleged power to "regulate"), and more importantly, there would have been no need to have specifically authorized the several States to cede jurisdiction over property (land) purchased by the Federal Government. See Article I, § 8, cl. 17, commonly known as the "enclave clause." I prefer to call it the "exclusive legislation clause," because the term "Federal enclave" has been used deceptively to lawfully prosecute certain crimes while still, in other cases, exercising "exclusive legislation" to prosecute other crimes without any "exclusive jurisdiction" or lawful authority to "punish" under the Constitution to do so.[30] As the Supreme Court explained:

> "Exclusive legislation" is consistent only with exclusive jurisdiction.

---

[30] exclusive legislation is simply the ability to enact laws and carry out undelegated powers within the exterior territorial boundaries of any ONE OF the several 50 Union States, *i.e.*, powers which they otherwise have no authority under the Constitution to carry out (except within these specific geographical locations and their own territories not yet Union States).

"[F]or if exclusive jurisdiction and exclusive legislation do not import the same thing, the states could not cede or the United States accept, for the purposes enumerat- enumerated in this clause, any exclusive jurisdiction." Surplus Trading Co. v. Cook, 281 US 647, 654 (1928), citing United States v. Cornell, 2 Mason, 60, Fed. Cas. No. 14,867 (Mr. Justice Story, at Circuit)

It should be noted that if the Federal Government purchases property with the consent of the State, then exclusive jurisdiction automatically vests in the "United States" (the name of our Federal Government), until they cease to own the land. In Fort Leavenworth,[31] the Supreme Court stated that, "If the United States ... had the right of exclusive legislation ... they

---

[31] Fort Leavenworth R.R. Co. v. Lowe, 114 US 525 (1885)

would also have exclusive jurisdiction."[32] The Supreme Court also explained that:

> Crimes are thus cognizable— "when committed within or on lands reserved or acquired for the exclusive use of the United States, and under the exclusive jurisdiction thereof, or any place purchased or otherwise acquired by the United States by consent of the legislature of the State." Bowen v. Johnston, 306 US 19, 22 (1939)

In other words, if you, or anyone else for that matter, own land within any ONE OF the several 50 Union States,[33] then the Federal Government cannot provide for the punishment of felonious crimes within

---

[32] Id. at 538

[33] Union. A popular term in America for the United States. Black's Law Dictionary, Sixth Edition, page 1,532.

the exterior boundaries of those lands (except where the power to punish has been delegated, as in the 3 constitutional provisions). This is because they have no territorial jurisdiction and the power to punish is not delegated by enumeration elsewhere in the Constitution. Keep in mind that the original 13 Union States[34] that drafted and ratified the Constitution were sovereign over all the land and waters each within their own territorial limits. The Federal Government had no land. They had no sovereignty to punish anyone anywhere. This is why Virginia and Maryland ceded exclusive jurisdiction over land not exceeding 10 miles square (which comprises the District of Columbia), to the Federal Government in the Constitution.[35] With this cession of jurisdiction to legislate exclusively, Congress could write laws to protect themselves and "exercise like Authority over all <u>places</u> purchased by the <u>Consent</u> of the Legislature of the State"[36] (and

---

[34] "North Carolina and Rhode Island were the last to ratify the Constitution." <u>Twining v. New Jersey</u>, 211 US 78, 108-109 (1908). North Carolina was the 12th State that ratified the Constitution on November 21, 1789. Rhode Island was the 13th State that ratified the Constitution on May 29, 1790.

[35] <u>Article I, § 8, cl. 17</u>

[36] Id.

by <u>Cession</u> of particular States, and the Acceptance of Congress). It should be noted that the Federal Government owns <u>all</u> the land in the District of Columbia. People own the property on that land, but they do not own the land itself. This is because if the Federal Government were to sell any of the land so ceded, the jurisdiction over that land sold would immediately revert back to the particular Union State (Maryland or Virginia).

This power to legislate exclusively is jurisdiction,[37] which is necessary to enforce criminal legislation (felonies). This is because the power to punish people is united with whoever is sovereign over the land, *i.e.*, "place", wherein those people reside. Likewise, a sovereign can punish if an activity done outside of their territorial jurisdiction affects their land. For example, setting a fire on land adjacent to land under their territorial jurisdiction that spreads onto their land. When the Federal Government acquires land within a Union State and jurisdiction is subsequently relin-

---

[37] Jurisdiction. A government's general power to exercise authority over all persons and things within its <u>territory</u>. <u>Black's Law Dictionary</u>, Seventh Edition, page 855. Compare "Territorial Jurisdiction, " *supra* at note 29.

quished through consent to purchase or cession, with acceptance, they become sovereign over that land. It is these <u>places</u> where Congress can exercise powers outside of those enumerated elsewhere in the Constitution. This is what <u>Article I, § 8, cl. 17</u>, allows Congress to do within the exterior territorial boundaries of any ONE OF the several 50 States which comprise the Union.

The power to "punish" is analogous to a cession of concurrent jurisdiction under <u>Article I, § 8, cl. 17</u>, U.S. Constitution (absent the requirement to own the property). Although analogous to a cession of concurrent jurisdiction it is not a cession of, and does not cede any, territorial jurisdiction. The Federal Government is simply authorized to "punish", feloniously or otherwise, those specific crimes where the power to "punish" is delegated, by enumeration, within the legislative (territorial) jurisdiction of any ONE OF the particular Union States. Whenever Territories (New States) join the Union, they agree to be bound by these specific grants of the punishing power. Nothing short of an Amendment to the Constitution could change this in order to grant Congress nationwide power to "punish" other felonious crimes.

First, I will simply state, in my opinion, the reason no amendment was drafted or ratified to allow this is because the several States each jealously guarded their sovereignty. Under the Constitution three-fourths of the States cannot surrender tortuously, by disseisin, the sovereignty of the other one-fourth of the States by delegating to the Federal Government the power to "punish" other felonious crimes against the people within their territorial (legislative) jurisdictions. This is, again, because jurisdiction, which is necessary to "punish" felonies, is united with whoever is sovereign over the land which, under the Constitution, can only be ceded.

If this were allowed it would cause conflict among the Union States. It would allow 3/4 of the Union States to decide what will be a crime in the other 1/4 of the Union States. In essence this would allow the Federal Government to implement arbitrary control and power over the Citizens of those 1/4 Union States. We can be certain that the Union States would never have entered into such a compact with each other if that could have been done because it would have defeated the independence of each Union State. Such a power would be analogous to that exercised by the King of England against the Colonies, something we can rest assured the newly Free States would never have allowed and, in fact, did not allow. Historically, what would follow would be similar to when the slaves were freed after ratification of the thirteenth Amendment, which lead to the Southern states seceding from the Union and ultimately the Civil War.

Upon admission into the Union each of the several States had to agree, by ratifying the Constitution, to surrender the punishing power where it is delegated by enumeration. This is why no Amendment has been added to the Constitution authorizing Congress to define and "punish" felonious crimes pursuant to their power to regulate commerce between the several Union States. This means the Federal Government is usurping this "punishing" power. The Supreme Court has explained that:

> [W]e are of the opinion that the right of exclusive legislation within the territorial limits of any State can be acquired by the United

States only in the mode pointed out in the Constitution, <u>by purchase</u>, <u>by consent</u> of the Legislature of the State in which the same shall be for the erection of forts, magazines, arsenals, dockyards, and other needful buildings.

The essence of that provision[38] is that the State shall freely <u>cede</u> the particular <u>place</u> to the United States for one of the specific and enumerated objects. This jurisdiction cannot be acquired tortuously by disseisin of the State; much less can it be acquired by mere occupancy, with the implied or tacit consent of the State ...." <u>Fort Leavenworth</u>, *supra* at 538-539

---

[38] <u>Article I, § 8, cl. 17</u>

The only way to pass such an amendment would be to get all the States to pass it (like when all 13 States ratified the Constitution). Obviously Congress could never pass such an amendment now, even if all the several 50 Union States agreed, because it would be proof on its face to the layman that they never had this power. However, I would like to suggest that the following amendment would have sufficed: Amendment- "To define and punish felonies committed in interstate commerce".

It would not be necessary to extend this amendment to foreign commerce because of Article I, § 8, cl. 10.[39] The Constitution, then, under Article I, § 8, cl. 17,[40] is the only other mode the Federal Government ("United States") can utilize to punish felonious crimes by allowing the States to cede jurisdiction over land,

---

[39] Article I, § 8, cl. 10, "To define and punish Piracies and Felonies committed on the high Seas, and Offenses against the Law of Nations."

[40] Article I, § 8, cl. 17, "To exercise exclusive Legislation in all Cases whatsoever, over such District (not exceeding ten Miles square) as may, by Cession of particular States, and the Acceptance of Congress, become the Seat of the Government of the United States, and to exercise like Authority over all Places purchased by the Consent of the Legislature of the State in which the Same shall be, for the Erection of Forts, Magazines, Arsenals, dock-Yards, and other needful Buildings."

or to consent to the purchase of land, with the requisite acceptance of Congress. It should be noted that, "Since 1940 Congress has required the United States to assent to the transfer of jurisdiction over property, however it may be acquired." Paul v. United States, 371 US 245, 264 (1963)

Because the power to "punish" is not delegated to Congress in aid of their power to regulate interstate commerce, the exercise of such power within the several 50 Union States is "exclusive legislation," which "can be acquired by the United States only in the mode pointed out in the Constitution, ... ,"[41] (Article I, § 8, cl. 17).

Near the beginning of our Republic, Chief Justice Marshall, speaking for the Supreme Court, stated that:

> What, then, is the extent of jurisdiction which a state possesses?

---

[41] Fort Leavenworth, *supra* at 538-539

We answer, without hesitation, **the jurisdiction of a state is co-extensive with its territory**; co-extensive with its legislative power.

The place described is unquestionably within the original territory of Massachusetts. It is then within the jurisdiction of Massachusetts, unless that jurisdiction has been ceded to the United States.

It is observable that the power of exclusive legislation (which is jurisdiction) is united with cession of territory."[42]

---

[42] United States v. Bevans 16 US (3 Wheat) 336, 4 LEd 404 (1818)

Obviously, if "exclusive legislation" (Article I, § 8, cl. 17), is jurisdiction, then the United States (Federal Government) has zero jurisdiction except where jurisdiction has been ceded. They can only exercise the powers delegated to them by the States under the Constitution. This is, again, because jurisdiction is united with the land. That is jurisdiction. Indeed, the Supreme Court has stated that "in a criminal case ... a person convicted by a court without jurisdiction over the place of the crime could be released from restraint by *habeas corpus*." The Supreme Court also stated that, "The consent of the state legislature is by the very terms of the Constitution ... a virtual surrender and cession of its sovereignty over the place."[43] Chief Justice Marshall, with regard to the necessary and proper clause, observed that:

> Congress may pass all laws which are necessary and proper for giving the most complete effect to this power. Still, the

---

[43] United States v. Williams, 341 US 58, 66-67 (1951) ; Surplus Trading Co. v. Cook, 281 US 647, 654 (1928)

> general jurisdiction over the place [of the crime], ... adheres to the territory, as a portion of sovereignty not yet given away. United States v. Bevans, 16 US (3 Wheat) 336, 389, 4 LEd 404 (1818)

The Supreme Court, quoting Justice Story's Commentaries on the Constitution in People v. Godfrey,[44] more than 65 years later, stated in Fort Leavenworth R.R. Co.,[45] that, "If there has been no cession by the State of the place ... the State jurisdiction still remains complete and perfect." In People v. Godfrey,[46] the New York Supreme Court stated that:

> The jurisdiction of the courts of the United States must be de-

---

[44] People v. Godfrey, 17 Johns. 225 (1819)
[45] Fort Leavenworth R.R. Co. v. Lowe, 114 US 525, 538 (1885)
[46] People v. Godfrey, 17 Johns. 225 (1819)

rived under the eighth section of the first article and seventeenth paragraph of the Constitution of the United States, which gives to Congress "exclusive legislation over all places purchased by the consent of the legislature of the State in which the same shall be for the erection of forts, magazines, arsenals, dock-yards, and other needful buildings."

To oust this state of its jurisdiction to support and maintain its laws, and to punish crimes, it must be shown that an offence committed within the acknowledged limits of the state, is clearly and exclusively cognizable by the laws and courts of the United States. In the case already cited, Chief Justice Marshall observed, that to bring the offence within the jurisdiction of the courts of the union, it <u>must</u>

have been committed out of the jurisdiction of any state; <u>it is not</u> (he says,) <u>the offence committed, but the place in which it is committed</u>, which <u>must</u> be out of the jurisdiction of the state.

The Federal Government would have you believe that "out of the jurisdiction of the state" means between states during interstate commerce. Wow! This is an outright fabrication. Remember that jurisdiction is united with <u>places</u>. There is no such thing as jurisdiction over <u>places</u> in between states. That is ridiculous. The several 50 Union States butt up against each other (except Alaska and Hawaii). To the average person,[47] who is ignorant of the law, this concept sounds plausible. The Supreme Court, however, observing what <u>places</u> are "out of the jurisdiction of the state", stated that:

---

[47] Layman. One of the people, and not one of the clergy; one who is not of a particular profession (*i.e.* non-lawyer). <u>Black's Law Dictionary</u>, Sixth Edition, page 888.

Of course, we exclude from the present consideration forts, arsenals, and like <u>places</u> within the exterior limits of a state, but over which exclusive jurisdiction has been <u>ceded</u> to the United States, because <u>they are regarded not as part of a state, but as excepted out of it</u>. <u>Southern Surety Co. v. Oklahoma</u>, 241 US 582, 586 (1915)

"If there be a common jurisdiction, the <u>crime</u> can<u>not</u> be punished in the courts of the Union."[48] This is because, "Federal Courts have no common law jurisdiction in <u>criminal</u> cases."[49] *Cf.* Title 18 U.S.C. <u>Crimes</u> and Criminal procedure. The reason the Federal Government has no common law jurisdiction in felonious criminal cases is because they are <u>not</u> sovereign

---

[48] <u>Wayne v. United States</u>, 21 US 234, 24 (1910)

[49] <u>Tennessee v. Davis</u>, 100 US 257, 282 (1880)

over any land within the several 50 Union States <u>except</u> where jurisdiction has been ceded under the Constitution. In other words, they have no "territorial jurisdiction." They were created by the express assent of the People of the Union States. This is why the Federal Government "can claim no powers which are not granted to it by the Constitution."[50] Therefore, because the power to punish is not granted under the commerce clause the Federal Government cannot claim this power. Instead, they are usurping it. As the Supreme Court explained:

> "Each State in the Union is sovereign as to all the powers reserved. It must necessarily be so, because the United States have no claim to any authority but such as the States have surrendered to them." <u>United States v. Lopez</u>, 514 US 549, 584 (1995)

---

[50] <u>Kansas v. Colorado</u>, 206 US 46 (1907)

(quoting Chisholm v. Georgia, 2 Dall 419, 435 (1793)

This principle of law, that jurisdiction is united with cession of territory, *i.e.*, whoever is sovereign over the land, is supported by literally hundreds of cases. The Supreme Court, 127 years ago, explained that:

> Upon admission of a state into the Union, the state doubtless acquires general jurisdiction, [51] civil and criminal ... except where it has ceded exclusive jurisdiction to the United States. The rights of local sovereignty ... vest in the State, and not in the United States. Van Brocklin v. Anderson, 117 US 151, 167-168 (1886)

---

[51] general jurisdiction. A court's authority to hear a wide range of cases, civil or criminal, that arise within its geographic area. Black's Law Dictionary, Seventh Edition, page 856. Compare note 80 *infra*.

The Supreme Court again, quoting Bevans,[52] 73 years later, reiterates that:

> The jurisdiction of a State is coextensive with its territory; coextensive with its legislative power. The place described is unquestionably within the original territory of Massachusetts. It is then within the jurisdiction of Massachusetts, unless that jurisdiction has been ceded to the United States. Manchester v. Commonwealth of Massachusetts, 139 US 240, 263 (1891)

"Without the State's 'consent' the United States does not obtain the benefits of Art I § 8, cl 17."[53] The

---

[52] United States v. Bevans, 16 US (3 Wheat) 336, 4 Led 404 (1818)

Ninth Circuit, quoting Justice Field in United States v. Smiley *et* el.,[54] 69 years later, stated that:

> It is a general rule of criminal law that the crime must be committed within the sovereignty seeking to try the offense in order to give that sovereign jurisdiction.
>
> "The criminal jurisdiction of the government of the United States— that is, its jurisdiction to try parties for offenses committed against its laws ... [T]he criminal jurisdiction of the United States is necessarily limited to their own territory ... Their actual territory is coextensive with their possessions." Yenkichi Ito v. United

---

[53] Paul v. United States, 371 US 245, 264 (1963)

[54] United States v. Smiley et al., 27 Fed Case page 1132, No. 16317 (1864)

States, 64 F2d 73, 74 (9th Cir. 1933)

Even though the Federal Government is a sovereign, they have no sovereignty, *i.e.*, dominion,[55] over the land (territory) within the several 50 Union States, <u>except</u> where legislative (territorial) jurisdiction has been obtained through consent to purchase or by cession. That same year (1933), the Supreme Court stated that, "It is <u>true</u> that the criminal jurisdiction of the United States [Federal Government][56] is in general <u>based on the territorial principle</u>."[57] *Cf.* <u>18 U.S.C. § 7</u>, Territorial jurisdiction of the United States defined. In the year 2006, the United States district court for the Judicial District of Northern California, stated that:

---

[55] Dominion. Control, possession. Sovereignty. <u>Black's Law Dictionary</u>, Seventh Edition, page 502.

[56] my note

[57] <u>United States v. Flores</u>, 289 US 137, 155 (1933)

> In order for a federal court to exercise jurisdiction over a criminal action, the offense must have occurred within: [L]ands reserved or acquired for the use of the United States, and under the exclusive or concurrent jurisdiction thereof ... by consent of the legislature of the State...." United States v. Perez, at III. LEGAL STANDARD, LEXIS 75086, No. CR-06-0001-MAG (MEJ) (N.D. Ca. 2006)

The Supreme Court, some 133 years after Ex Parte Watkins,[58] quoted that:

> "An imprisonment under a judgment cannot be unlawful, unless that judgment be an absolute nullity; and it is not a nullity if the

---

[58] Ex Parte Watkins, 3 Pet 193, 7 Led 650 (1830)

> <u>court has general jurisdiction</u> of the subject ...." <u>Fay v. Noia</u>, 372 US 391, 450 (1963)

A Federal court only has **general jurisdiction** over the subject-matter in the following types of cases: (1) Felonies-within Federal Territories, ceded lands, un-ceded lands pursuant to the power to "punish" (Article III courts only), and the high seas; (2) Misdemeanors-Federal Territories, ceded lands, un-ceded lands pursuant to a delegated power (Article III courts only), and the high seas. The Supreme Court in <u>New Orleans v. United States</u>,[59] now standing for 177 years and reaffirmed 58 years later,[60] stated that:

> **Congress can<u>not</u> by legislation, enlarge the Federal jurisdiction**, nor can it be en-

---

[59] <u>New Orleans v. United States</u>, 35 US 662, 10 Pet 662, 736-737, 9 Led 573 (1836)

[60] <u>United States v. Illinois Central R. Co.</u>, 154 US 225, 239-241 (1894)

larged by the treaty-making power.

Special provision is made in the Constitution for the cession of jurisdiction from States over places where the federal government shall establish forts or other military works. **And it is only in these places**, or in the territories of the United States, **where it can exercise a general jurisdiction**.

The state of Louisiana was admitted into the Union on the same footing as the original states. Her rights of sovereignty are the same, and, by consequence, no jurisdiction of the federal government, either for purposes of police or otherwise, can be exercised over this public ground, which is not common to the United States.[61]

The Supreme Court, just 13 years ago, quoting Chief Justice Marshall in Cohens v. Virginia,[62] standing for nearly 200 years, stated that, "[I]t is 'clear. . . that **congress can<u>not</u> punish felonies <u>generally</u>**."[63] See "<u>only in these places</u>", New Orleans, *supra*.[64] Except of course, the 3 provisions wherein the power to "punish" is delegated, by enumeration, in the Constitution.

Felony is defined as, "A serious crime usually punishable by <u>imprisonment for more than one year</u>."[65]

---

[61] It should be noted that for purposes of the 3 provisions in the Constitution which delegate, by enumeration, the power to "punish", Congress can punish, feloniously, those specific crimes, even though the ground is not common. The ground (land) becomes <u>common</u> only when purchased or obtained by consent of the Legislature of the particular State, or by cession of jurisdiction, with the acceptance of Congress.

[62] <u>Cohens v. Virginia</u>, 6 Wheat 264, 426, 428, 5Led 257 (1821)

[63] <u>United States v. Morrison</u>, 52 US 598, 618 (2000)

[64] *Supra*. [Latin "above"] Earlier in this text; used as a citational signal to refer to a previously cited authority. <u>Black's Law Dictionary</u>, Seventh Edition, page 1454.

[65] <u>Black's Law Dictionary</u>, Sixth Edition, page 633

See also Federal Rules of Criminal Procedure, Rule 7(a)(1)(B), (2). In Logan v. United States,[66] now standing for 121 years, the Supreme Court stated that:

> **The Constitution contains <u>no</u> <u>grant</u>, general or specific, to Congress of the power to provide for the punishment of crimes**, <u>except</u> piracies and felonies committed on the high seas, offenses against the law of nations, treason, and counterfeiting the securities and current coin of the United States.

These crimes are the same <u>exact</u> crimes wherein the 3 constitutional provisions delegate to Congress the power to "punish". The "no grant, general or specific", axiomatically excludes the commerce clause

---

[66] Logan v. United States, 144 US 263, 283 (1892)

and the necessary and proper clause (wherein the power to "punish" is **not** delegated to Congress). I would just like to explain, because there seems to be some confusion surrounding the entire statement, which states that:

> Although the Constitution contains no grant, general or specific, to Congress of the power to provide for the punishment of crimes, except piracies and felonies committed on the high seas, offenses against the law of nations, treason, and counterfeiting the securities and current coin of the United States, no one doubts the power of Congress to provide for the punishment of all crimes and offenses against the United States, whether committed within one of the states of the Union, or within territory over

which Congress has plenary and exclusive jurisdiction.

The Supreme Court was not saying that the Constitution contains no grant to Congress of the power to provide for the punishment of crimes except where the power to punish has been delegated in the Constitution, and then saying that they could still punish other crimes regardless of those limited grants. Such a statement would be considered an "oxymoron". The Supreme Court was speaking about "Crimes" (felonies) and "offenses" (felonies and misdemeanors), and their implementation within the restrictions the Constitution imposes. This distinction between felonies and misdemeanors, and their implementation within the Union States, as they relate to the power to "punish" and the necessary and proper clause, is elaborated in detail a little further into this Manifesto. However, suffice it to say that if the Federal Government ("United States") supposes to punish felonious or misdemeanor crimes in excess of the limitations imposed by the Constitution then it is not a crime or offense against the laws of the United States.

While Congress may legislate in respect to all arid lands within limits of territories, it has no legislative control over states, and must, so far as they are concerned, be limited to authority over property belonging to the "United States" within their limits.[67] States have no power to directly enlarge or contract federal jurisdiction.[68] Congress has legislated the same way.

> (c) Presumption. It is <u>conclusively</u> presumed that jurisdiction has <u>not</u> been accepted <u>until</u> the Government accepts <u>jurisdiction over land</u> as provided in this section. 40 U.S.C. § 3112, Federal jurisdiction

Clearly, if the Federal Government already had this jurisdiction then they would not need to "accept" it. Consequently, this is in perfect alignment with the

---

[67] <u>Kansas v. Colorado</u>, *supra* at 92

[68] <u>Duchek v. Jacobi</u>, 646 F2d 415 (9th Cir. 1981)

requirement in the Constitution, "To exercise exclusive Legislation in all Cases whatsoever, ... as may, by Cession of particular States, <u>and the acceptance of Congress</u>, ..."[69] The Supreme Court, 134 years ago, stated that:

> Courts possess no jurisdiction over crimes and offenses committed against the authority of the United States, <u>except</u> what is given them by the power that <u>created</u> them; nor can they be invested with any such jurisdiction beyond what the power <u>ceded</u> to the United States by the Constitution authorizes Congress to confer. Congress may provide for the punishment of counterfeiting the securities and current coin of the United States, and may pass laws to define and punish pira-

---
[69] <u>Article I, § 8, cl. 17</u>

> cies and felonies committed on the high seas, and offenses against the law of nations, [and treason].[70] United States v. Hall, 98 US 343, 345-346 (1879)

Unless and until notice and acceptance of jurisdiction has been given, Federal courts are without jurisdiction to punish under criminal laws of the United States an act committed on lands acquired by the United States, as provided by 40 U.S.C.S. § 3112 (former 40 U.S.C. § 255). Unless and until the United States has so filed and published acceptance of jurisdiction it is to be <u>conclusively</u> presumed that no such jurisdiction has been accepted.[71] The Supreme Court has explained that if the court is without jurisdiction then it would not matter if found guilty by a jury 100 times. See Maxfield's Lessee v. Levy, 4 US 330, 4 Dall 330 (1797).

---

[70] my note

[71] Adams v. United States, 319 US 312 (1943)

Apparently the misconception that Congress can punish felonious crimes under the commerce clause came into being beginning sometime in the late 19th century (1800's). A case heavily relied on by the courts to advance their deception is <u>Champion v. Ames</u>, 188 US 321 (1903). The courts and the government will both claim that the Supreme Court in <u>Champion</u> acknowledged that the commerce clause allows Congress to regulate by means of punishment imposed through criminal statutes. This is patently false.

In <u>Champion</u> the petitioner insisted that the carrying of lottery tickets from one state to another state did not constitute, and could not by any act of Congress be legally made to constitute, commerce among the states within the meaning of the commerce clause. He claimed that Congress could not make his conduct an offense at all. He stated that, "Congress could not make it an offense to cause such tickets to be carried from one state to another."[72]

---

[72] <u>Champion v. Ames</u>, 188 US 321, 325-345 (1903), [Eighteen sections (326-344) are missing from the official opinion. These sections contain the arguments of counsel].

In Champion the Court states that the commerce clause power has "the same restrictions on the exercise of the power as are found in the Constitution of the United States."[73] Again, the Court states that this power is "subject only to such limitations as the Constitution imposes upon the exercise of the powers granted by it."[74] Here, the Supreme Court is acknowledging the fact that the Commerce Clause power has restrictions and limitations. As we have already learned, the "United States" (Federal Government) is exercising an undelegated power to "punish", a police power reserved to the several 50 Union States, under the guise of regulating interstate commerce.

Curiously enough, the Champion Court then states that "we know of no authority in the courts to hold that the means devised is not appropriate and necessary,"[75] to prevent Congress from making carrying of lottery tickets from one state to another a "criminal offense." This is obviously the passage the deception

---

[73] Champion, *supra* at 347

[74] Champion, *supra* at 353

[75] Champion, *supra* at 358

hinges on. When I tell you the basis this unconstitutional law and conviction was allowed to stand, you will not believe it. The one thing you will be wondering is, why did the Supreme Court not prevent this legislative encroachment by the Federal Government on the jurisdiction and sovereignty of the States, in violation of the Tenth Amendment, and upon this victims due process rights as secured in the Fifth Amendment to the Constitution? The Supreme Court will answer stating that they presume that Congress legislates constitutionally and, based on this presumption, will refuse to address the constitutionality of any act of Congress unless they feel they have no choice.

In Champion,[76] the Court states that:

> [T]he power of Congress to regulate commerce among the states, although plenary[77] ... is subject to

---

[76] *Supra* at 362-364

[77] Plenary. Full, entire, complete, absolute, perfect, unqualified. Black's Law Dictionary, Sixth Edition, page 1154.

Continued on next page.

such limitations or restrictions as are prescribed in the Constitution.[78] This power therefore, may

---

Plenary powers. Authority and power as broad as is required in a given case. Black's Law Dictionary, Sixth Edition, page 1154.

Do not be confused by these definitions. As Chief Justice Marshall stated twice in Gibbons v. Ogden, 9 Wheat 1, 189-190, 196 (1824), commerce is regulated by prescribing rules. The power to exact a certain "punishment" for violating those rules, whether a misdemeanor or felony, is limited by the Constitution. Under the necessary & proper clause, misdemeanors can be enforced throughout the territorial jurisdiction of the several Union States as long as the prohibited conduct alleged is connected to the execution of the delegated power to regulate commerce among them (interstate commerce). Felonies, on the other hand, can only be prosecuted within the territorial jurisdiction of the "United States" (land under the concurrent or exclusive legislative jurisdiction of the Federal Government). The only exception is that where the power to "Punish" is delegated, by enumeration, in the Constitution, Congress can enforce misdemeanor & felony prohibitions within the territorial (legislative) jurisdiction of the several Union States

---

[78] The "exclusive legislation clause," Article I, § 8, cl. 17, and the Tenth Amendment, both operate as limitations, or restrictions, on the exercise of the "commerce clause" power granted. This is because the power to "punish" is not enumerated under the commerce clause which proves it is not delegated there. This also means Congress cannot provide for the prosecution of felonies within the territorial (legislative) jurisdiction of the several Union States under the guise of regulating interstate commerce. Any legislation enacted by Congress which assumes to prosecute felonies under the guise of regulating interstate commerce is exclusive legislation (because the power to "punish" is not delegated under the Commerce Clause) and therefore can only be Continued on next page.

not be exercised so as to infringe rights secured or protected by that instrument.

It would not be difficult to imagine legislation that would be justly liable to such an objection as that stated, and be hostile to the objects for the accomplishment of which Congress was invested with the general power to regulate commerce among the several states. But as often said, the possible abuse of a power is not an argument against its existence. There is probably no governmental power that may not be exerted to the injury of the public. If what is done by Congress is manifestly in excess of

---

lawfully executed if the alleged criminal conduct occurs within ceded lands under the concurrent or exclusive legislative (territorial) jurisdiction of the "United States" (Federal Government) and their own territories not yet Union States. There are other limitations and restrictions elsewhere in the Constitution which is of no concern because they have no bearing on our issue.

the powers granted to it, <u>then upon the courts will rest the **duty** of adjudging that its action is neither legal nor binding upon the people</u>.

The whole subject is too important, and the questions suggested by its consideration are too difficult of solution, to justify any attempt to lay down a rule for determining in advance the <u>validity</u> of every statute that may be enacted under the commerce clause.

We decide <u>nothing more</u> in the present case than that lottery tickets are subjects of traffic among those who choose to sell or buy them; that the carriage of such tickets by independent carriers from one state to another is therefore interstate commerce; that under its power to regulate commerce among the several states Congress - <u>subject to the limitations imposed by the Constitution upon the exercise of the powers granted</u> - has plenary authority over such commerce, and may <u>prohibit</u> the carriage of such tickets from state to state; and that <u>legislation to that end</u>, <u>and of that character</u>, <u>is not inconsistent with any limitation or restriction imposed upon the exercise of the powers granted</u> to Congress.

Clearly, the Supreme Court, 110 years ago, did <u>not</u> do its duty to determine whether such punishment was appropriate under the limits imposed by the Constitution. It is equally clear that for the first 116 years after the Constitution was drafted and ratified, "the first Congresses did <u>not</u> enact nationwide punishments for <u>criminal</u> conduct under the Commerce Clause."[79] The Supreme Court has stated that:

> Article I of the Constitution grants Congress broad power to legislate in certain areas. **Those legislative powers are, however, limited** not only by the Framer's affirmative delegation, but also **by the principle "that they may not be exercised in a way that violates other specific provisions of the Constitution."** <u>Saenz v. Roe</u>, 526 US 489, 508 (1999)

Cf. <u>Article I, § 8, cl. 17</u>, and the <u>Tenth Amendment</u>, as "other specific provisions of the Constitution." So, why did the Supreme Court not decide the <u>validity</u> of the statute in <u>Champion</u>? Because the petitioner in

---

[79] <u>United States v. Morrison</u>, 529 US 598, 618-619 (2000)

that case did not raise the issue as to whether imposition of a felonious criminal statute was an appropriate exercise of Congress' power under the commerce clause in his case. That's right: it was not an issue before the Court. It is most likely that the petitioner would have had to show how the felony statute was not a valid exercise of Congress' power under the commerce clause, obviously not being able to rely on the Supreme Court or the Government to protect his rights.

Remember what the issue he raised was? That Congress could not make his conduct an offense at all. In other words, Congress could not prohibit what he was doing. So the Court simply decided "nothing more" than that Congress could prohibit that conduct. Amazing!

The Constitution delegates no such power to "punish" felonious crimes under the commerce clause. Even if it were true that the commerce clause allowed Congress to "punish" felonies generally, [80] Congress

---

[80] "It is 'clear...that congress can<u>not</u> punish felonies generally. United States v. Morrison, *supra*.

Continued on next page.

has not legislated this way. The Supreme Law of Congress under Title 18 U.S.C., prohibits only the transportation of certain things in "interstate commerce" between places, *i.e.* federal lands under the concurrent or exclusive jurisdiction of the "United States" (Federal Government), and other like places, *i.e.*, federal lands under the concurrent or exclusive jurisdiction of the "United States" (Federal Government). I will cover this in detail and show you explicitly where in the law this is spelled out. You will also see clearly how forced constructions of the law have allowed this unconstitutional system to prosper through its vagueness. For now, let's continue.

The Federal Government, and Federal Courts, would have you believe that Congress' power to regulate interstate commerce provides an implied power allowing Congress to "punish" felonious crimes whenever they deem it "necessary and proper."

"Special provision is made in the Constitution for the cession of jurisdiction over places... And it is only in these places, ... where it [the Federal Government] can exercise a general jurisdiction." New Orleans v. United States, *supra*.

As I pointed out previously, the power to "punish" cannot be implied because it is enumerated (delegated) in 3 other provisions in the Constitution (<u>not</u> under the commerce clause).

It is not the power to regulate that is drawn into question but, rather, the power to "punish" felonies within the territorial boundaries of any ONE OF the several 50 Union States wherein jurisdiction has not been ceded. The Supreme Court has explained in <u>Butler</u>,[81] that Congress can<u>not</u> attain a prohibited end by executing an undelegated power to "punish" felonies (a power reserved to the States), under the pretext of executing their delegated power to regulate commerce among the several 50 Union States ("interstate commerce").

The <u>Tenth Amendment</u> reserves all powers not delegated to the "United States" (Congress/Federal Government), to the States respectively, or to the people. Because the power to "punish" is not delegated, by enumeration, in aid of Congress' commerce clause power, the <u>places</u> wherein Congress can regu-

---

[81] *supra*

late interstate commerce through the imposition of felonious criminal statutes is limited by the Constitution.

The Supreme Court has stated time and again that, "The Federal Government has <u>nothing</u> approaching a police power".[82] This is because, "The police power of the States was <u>not</u> surrendered when the people of the United States conferred upon Congress the general power to regulate commerce with foreign nations and between the several States."[83] "Police Power" is defined as:

> <u>The inherent power of a government to exercise reasonable control over persons</u> and property <u>within its jurisdiction</u> in the interests of the general security, health, safety, morals, and welfare except where legally prohibited (as by constitutional

---

[82] <u>United States v. Lopez</u>, 514 US 549, 584-585 (1995)

[83] <u>Patterson v. Kentucky</u>, 97 US 501, 505 (1879)

provision. [84] <u>Webster's Third New International Dictionary</u>, unabridged (1981), page 1,754.

Obviously Congress has no jurisdiction within any ONE OF the several 50 Union States except where it has been obtained through consent to purchase the land or where jurisdiction has been <u>ceded</u> over land they own. This is why they cannot exercise a police power. The Supreme Court, clearly showing that the "police power" is analogous to the suppression of "violent crime," stated that:

> Indeed, we can think of no better example of the <u>police power</u>, which the Founders denied the National Government and reposed in the States, than the suppression of <u>violent crime</u>.

---

[84] Cf. <u>Article I, § 8, cl. 17</u> and the <u>Tenth Amendment</u>

"The Constitution ... withhold[s] from Congress a plenary police power." [W]e always have rejected readings of the Commerce Clause and the scope of federal power that would permit Congress to exercise a police power and noting that **the first congresses did not enact nationwide punishments for criminal conduct under the Commerce Clause.**

Until this Court replaces its existing Commerce Clause jurisprudence with a standing more consistent with the original understanding, we will continue to see Congress appropriating state police powers under the guise of regulating commerce. United States v. Morrison, 529 US 598, 618 (2000)

We can obviously draw a very reasonable conclusion that a violent crime falls within the meaning of felony, which we defined earlier as, "A serious crime usually punishable by imprisonment for more than one year."[85] Title 18 U.S.C. also defines violent crime:

>The term "crime of violence" means—
>
>(a) an offense that has an element the use, attempted use, or threatened use of physical force against the person or property of another, or
>
>(b) any other offense that is a felony and that, by its nature, involves a substantial risk that physical force against the person or property of another may be used in the course of committing

---
[85] Black's Law Dictionary, Seventh Edition, page 633

> the offense. 18 U.S.C. § 16,
> Crime of violence defined

Now that we know a violent crime is a felony (but obviously not all felonies, and obviously not misdemeanors), we can see that the "police power," which was withheld from the Federal Government, is the power to punish felonies (or enact other legislation in excess of, and inconsistent with, their delegated and enumerated powers). And we already showed that "the Federal Government has nothing approaching a police power,"[86] because they have no jurisdiction. It should be noted that although Congress has made many non-violent crimes felonies, this does not change the limitations imposed by the Constitution upon the exercise of the police power.

> Infamous crime. These crimes are treason, felony, and the crimen falsi. It is not the charac-

---
[86] United States v. Lopez, *supra*.

ter of the crime but the nature of the punishment which renders the crime 'infamous' [a felony].[87] **Whether an offense is infamous depends on the punishment which may be imposed therefore, <u>not</u> on the punishment which was imposed.** Black's Law Dictionary, Sixth Edition, page 371.

As is apparent, it is not whether the crime is "violent" or "nonviolent" that makes it a felony. It is the potential punishment you are exposed to. If the potential punishment is imprisonment for "more than one year"[88] then it is a felony, even if you are sentenced to one year or less.

At this point you should be able to see a very clear pattern emerging that Congress' power to punish felonious crimes within the territorial (legislative)

---

[87] my note

[88] Black's Law Dictionary, Seventh Edition, page 633, "felony."

jurisdiction of any ONE OF the several 50 Union States is limited to those crimes where the power to "punish" has been delegated by enumeration. It is also limited to places within any ONE OF the several 50 Union States wherein jurisdiction has been ceded and to their own territories not yet Union States. They have no constitutional authority to exercise municipal sovereignty/municipal jurisdiction, a/k/a "police power" to punish felonies within the territorial (legislative) jurisdiction of any ONE OF the several 50 Union States (except over places where jurisdiction has been obtained through consent to purchase, or has been ceded, and accepted). *Cf.* Pollard v. Hagan, *supra* (footnote 20). Although Congress is authorized to feloniously punish counterfeiting and treason, no exclusive jurisdiction is needed in order to carry into execution those delegated powers.

There are many popular unfounded beliefs that the meaning of the Constitution has changed or changes as society changes. One such popular unfounded belief is that certain "Amendments" allow the Federal Government to punish crime under the commerce clause. This is untrue. When pressed on the issue no one can point out which amendment has done so. As far as the meaning of the Constitution changing, the Supreme Court has stated that:

> In the construction of the Constitution we must look to the history of the times and examine the state of things existing when it was framed and adopted to ascertain the old law, the mischief, and the remedy. <u>The State of Rhode Island v. The State of Massachusetts</u>, 12 Pet 657, 723, 9 LEd 1233 (1838).

The Supreme Court then reiterates, 57 years later, that "<u>We are bound to</u> interpret the Constitution in the light of the law as it existed at the time it was adopted."[89] Again, the Supreme Court explains, 10 years later, that:

---

[89] <u>Mattox v. United States</u>, 156 US 237, 243 (1895)

The Constitution is a written Instrument. As such <u>its meaning does not alter</u>. That which it meant when it was adopted, it means now. Any other <u>rule of construction</u> would abrogate the judicial character of this court, and make it the reflex of the popular opinion or passion of the day.

To determine the <u>extent</u> of the grant of power, we must, therefore, place ourselves in the position of the men who framed and adopted the Constitution, and inquire what they must have understood to be the meaning and scope of those grants. <u>South Carolina v. United States</u>, 199 US 437, 448-450 (1905)

I am certain that Thomas Jefferson, Founding Father, Creator and signer of the Declaration of

Independence, and former President of the United States, understood <u>exactly</u> what the Constitution truly "meant when it was adopted." In fact, in a document authored by him entitled, "<u>The Kentucky Resolutions of 1798</u>,"[90] reprinted in "The Portable Thomas Jefferson," 281, 282 (Merrill Peterson ed., 1979), he stated as follows in the 1st Resolved Clause: that "[W]hensoever the general government assumes undelegated powers, its acts are unauthoritative, void, and of no force." And in the 2nd Resolved Clause that:

> [T]he Constitution of the United States, having delegated to Congress the power to <u>punish</u> treason, counterfeiting the securities and current coin of the United States, piracies, and felonies committed on the high seas, and

---

[90] This document, "<u>The Kentucky Resolutions of 1798</u>," can be found on the internet through a simple <u>Google.com</u> search, and is available at no charge (free). It has also been included in the Appendix of this Manifesto.

offenses against the law of nations, <u>and no other crimes whatsoever</u>; and it being true as a general principle, and one of the amendments to the Constitution having so declared,[91] that "the powers not delegated to the United States by the Constitution, nor prohibited by it to the States, are reserved to the States respectively, or to the people," therefore ... **all their other acts which assume to create, define, or punish crimes, other than those so enumerated in the Constitution, <u>are altogether void and of no force</u>**; and that the power to create, define, and punish such other crimes is reserved, and, of right, appertains solely and exclusively to the re-

---

[91] The <u>Tenth Amendment</u>

spective States, <u>each within its own territory</u>."

Well, there are those <u>crimes</u> again; the ones where the power to "punish" has been delegated by enumeration. Did you notice that the Founding Father specifically mentioned "...the power to <u>punish</u>"? And that the Constitution delegates to Congress "...no other <u>crimes</u> whatsoever"? He then states that all of Congress' "....other acts which assume to create, define, or <u>punish crimes</u>, ... are altogether <u>void</u>, and <u>of no force</u>." It should be noted that the terms "crime" and "misdemeanor", properly speaking, are synonymous terms. However, in common usage, as when the Constitution was written, and in the same sense Thomas Jefferson was speaking, the word "crime" denotes offenses of a more serious nature, like felonies, than those designated as misdemeanors, which were referred to as transgressions or trespasses.

The power to "punish," as explained by Thomas Jefferson, is the delegation, by enumeration, of the power to punish felonies (which includes misdemeanors as incidental to this power). The power to punish felonies may <u>not</u> be implemented as necessary and proper, where it is not delegated by enumeration, because it is specifically delegated by enumeration in other provisions of the Constitution. The power to prosecute misdemeanors, on the other hand, is a common-law power and may be implemented as necessary and proper to carry into execution any delegated power. To hold otherwise would mean that the United States (Federal Government) would be powerless to enforce the observance of laws written and enacted pursuant to their other delegated powers where the power to "punish" is <u>not</u> delegated by enumeration. Unlike felonies, certain misdemeanors (transgressions, trespasses, *etc.*), can be prosecuted by citizens, against other citizens, as civil actions. See <u>Black's Law Dictionary</u>, Sixth and Seventh Editions, "Crime" and "Felony", pages 370 and 633, respectively.

Lastly, Mr. Jefferson states that the power to <u>punish</u> other crimes is <u>reserved</u> "... solely and exclusively to the respective <u>States</u>, each within its own <u>territory</u>." He directly connects the power to "punish" other crimes to the States. He even uses the language in the <u>Tenth Amendment</u>, explaining that where this power to "punish" is not delegated, by enumeration, it is <u>reserved</u> to the States, each within their own <u>territory</u>. Can you see the direct connection to "punish" other crimes is united with whoever has territorial jurisdiction (sovereignty over the land)?

Remember, the Supreme Court stated that "...no sovereignty can extend its jurisdiction beyond its own <u>territorial</u> limits."[92] That "...this jurisdiction cannot be acquired tortuously by disseisin of the State."[93] That "...the consent of the state legislature is by the very terms of the Constitution a virtual surrender and <u>cession</u> of its <u>sovereignty over the place</u>."[94] And that "...if there has been no <u>cession</u> by the State of the <u>place</u> ... the state jurisdiction still remains <u>complete and perfect</u>."[95]

We then have the Supreme Court stating that, "It is <u>true</u> that the criminal jurisdiction of the United States

---

[92] <u>United States v. Wong Kim Ark</u>, *supra*

[93] <u>Fort Leavenworth R.R. Co.</u>, *supra* at 538-539, See also note 24

[94] <u>Surplus Trading Co. v. Cook</u>, *supra*

[95] <u>Fort Leavenworth R.R. Co.</u>, *supra* at 538

is in general based on the territorial principle." [96] Congress has defined the term "United States" in a territorial sense,[97] for all of Title 18 U.S.C., as places subject to the jurisdiction of the United States. Congress defines these territorial places at 18 U.S.C. § 7, "Territorial jurisdiction of the United States defined."

When we examine the Constitution, the territorial jurisdiction of the "United States"[98] (Federal Government) becomes very apparent. First, we see that they have territorial jurisdiction over land (sovereignty) within the several 50 Union States wherever they purchase land with the consent of the legislature of that particular Union State. We can also see that where land is purchased without consent, jurisdiction can be

---

[96] United States v. Flores, *supra*

[97] 18 U.S.C. § 5, United States defined

[98] Black's Law Dictionary, Sixth Edition, page 1533, "United States".

The term "United States" may be used in any one of several senses. It may designate territory over which the sovereignty of the United States extends. Hooven & Allison Co. v. Evatt, 324 US 652, 671 (1945)

ceded. The Federal Government must also accept all cessions of jurisdiction.[99]

This "Federal jurisdiction" only remains as long as they maintain ownership over the land. Once their ownership over the land ceases, jurisdiction automatically reverts back to the particular Union State. The Federal Government also has territorial jurisdiction over their own territories not yet Union States pursuant to the "property clause."[100] The Constitution also grants the Federal Government Special Maritime jurisdiction over the high Seas. However, that jurisdiction (although analogous to territorial jurisdiction over land), is concurrent with the Union States. This is because the high Seas within 12 nautical miles of the baselines of any ONE OF the several 50 Union States, nor within the additional 12 miles (the contiguous zone), is not territory or other property belonging to the Federal Government ("United States"), within the meaning of the property clause. This is self-evident because that clause (Article I, § 8, cl.10) names the "high Seas" (a specific place), and be-

---

[99] Article I, § 8, cl. 17; 40 U.S.C. § 3112

[100] Article IV, § 3, cl. 2

cause of the delegation of the enumerated power to define and "punish"[101] felonies. See, "territorial waters": waters under state's jurisdiction, esp. part of sea within stated distance of shore. Oxford Color Dictionary, page 683. The high Seas clause differs from the 2 other specific provisions wherein the power to punish has been delegated[102] (which do not grant any territorial jurisdiction), because no place is named in those 2 clauses, and because the power to "punish" is limited to specific crimes.

If the Federal Government contends for the power to prosecute felonious crimes outside of their concurrent or exclusive legislative (territorial) jurisdiction they must prove an extra-territorial application of the statute in question as well as a constitutional foundation supporting the same. Absent this showing, no federal prosecution can be commenced for offenses committed outside their concurrent or exclusive legislative (territorial) jurisdiction.

---

[101] Article I, § 8, cl. 10

[102] Article I, § 8, cl. 6, counterfeiting; Article III, § 3, cl. 2, Treason

Congress can<u>not</u> grant themselves territorial jurisdiction (which under the Constitution can only be ceded), to punish felonious crimes, whenever they deem it necessary and proper. Neither can they obtain territorial jurisdiction under the guise of regulating commerce, because, "Congress cannot by legislation, enlarge the Federal jurisdiction."[103] If Congress could expand their territorial jurisdiction to punish felonious crimes whenever they deemed it necessary and proper, or whether under the guise of regulating interstate commerce or, more noticeably, when regulating the value of the current coin, simply by writing laws (legislating), there would have been no need for the Framers of the Constitution to delegate the enumerated power to "punish" where it is delegated.[104] Likewise, there would be no need to cede territorial jurisdiction over land under the "exclusive legislation clause."[105]

The power to punish felonious crimes comes from other provisions of the Constitution. Not from regula-

---

[103] New Orleans v. United States, *supra*

[104] Article I, § 8, cl. 6; Article I , § 8, cl. 10; Article III, § 3, cl. 2

[105] Article I, § 8, cl. 17

tory or necessary and proper powers. See, for example, the counterfeiting clause, the high Seas clause, the exclusive legislation clause, the treason clause, and the property clause (territories not yet Union States).[106] Note the Supreme Court's admission as to the limit & extent of power:

> Congress is expressly authorized "to provide for the punishment of counterfeiting the securities and current coin of the United States, and to define and punish piracies and felonies committed on the high seas and offenses against the laws of nations." It is also empowered to declare the punishment of treason, and provision is made for impeachments. <u>This is the extent of power to punish crime expressly conferred.</u> Knox

---

[106] Article I, § 8, cl. 6; Article I, § 8, cl. 10; Article I, § 8, cl. 17; Article III, § 3, cl. 2; Article IV, § 3, cl. 2

v. Lee and Parker v. Davis, 79 US 457, 535-536 (1871)

"Preventing and dealing with crime is much more the business of the States than it is of the Federal Government."[107] The Supreme Court has stated that:

> The proposition, often advanced and as often discredited, that the power of the federal government inherently extends to purposes affecting the nation as a whole with which the states severally cannot deal or cannot adequately deal, and the related notion that Congress, entirely apart from those powers delegated by the Constitution, may enact laws to promote the general welfare, have <u>never</u> been accepted but

---

[107] Patterson v. New York, 432 US 197, 201 (1977)

<u>always</u> definitely rejected by this court. Mr. Justice Story, as early as 1816, laid down the cardinal rule, which has ever since been followed-that the general government "can claim no powers which are not granted to it by the Constitution, and the powers actually granted, must be such as are expressly given, or given by necessary implication." <u>Martin Hunter</u>, 1 Wheat. 304, 326, 4 LEd 97, 102.

In the Framer's Convention, the proposal to confer a general power akin to that just discussed was included in Mr. Randolph's resolutions, the sixth of which, among other things, declared that the National Legislature ought to enjoy the legislative rights vested in Congress by the Confederation, and "moreover to legislate in all cases to which the separate

States are incompetent, or which harmony of the United States may be interrupted by the exercise of individual Legislation."

The convention, however, declined to confer upon Congress power in such general terms; instead of which it carefully limited the powers which it thought wise to entrust to Congress by specifying them, thereby denying all others not granted expressly or by necessary implication. It made no grant of authority to Congress to legislate substantively for the general welfare, United States v. Butler;[108] and no such authority exists, save as the general welfare may be promoted by the exercise of the powers which are granted. Compare Jacobsen v.

---

[108] United States v. Butler, *supra*

Massachusetts.[109] Carter v. Carter Coal Co., *supra* at 291-292 (1936)

Mr. Justice Harlan, in a different and dissenting Supreme Court opinion, stated that:

> The idea prevails with some—indeed, it found expression in arguments at the bar—that we have in this country substantially or practically two national governments; one to be maintained under the Constitution, with all its restrictions; the other to be maintained by Congress outside and independently of that instrument, by exercising such powers as other nations of the earth are ac-

---

[109] Jacobson v. Massachusetts, 197 US 11, 22 (1905)

customed to exercise. It is one thing to give such a latitudinarian construction to the Constitution as will bring the exercise of power by Congress, upon a particular occasion or upon a particular subject, within its provisions. It is quite a different thing to say that Congress may, if it so elects, proceed outside of the Constitution.

The glory of our American system of government is that it was created by a written constitution which protects the people against the exercise of arbitrary, unlimited power, and the limits of which instrument may not be passed by the government it created, or by any branch of it, or even by the people who ordained it, except by amendment or change of its provisions. "To what purpose," Chief Justice Marshall said in <u>Marbury v. Madison</u>, 1 Cranch, 137, 176, 2 LEd 60, 73, "are powers limited, and to what purpose is that limitation committed to writing, if these limits may, at any time, be passed by those intended to be restrained? The distinction between a government with limited and unlimited powers is abolished if those limits do not confine the persons on whom they are imposed, and if acts prohibited and acts allowed are of equal obligation."

The wise men who framed the Constitution, and the patriotic people who adopted it, were unwilling to depend for their safety upon what, in the opinion referred to, is described as "certain principles of natural justice inherent in Anglo-Saxon character, which need no expression in constitutions or statutes to give them effect or to secure dependencies against legislation manifestly hostile to their real interests." They proceed upon the theory—the wisdom of which experience has vindicated—that the only safe guaranty against governmental oppression was to withhold or restrict the power to oppress. They well remembered that Anglo-Saxons across the ocean had attempted, in defiance of law and justice, to trample upon the rights of Anglo-Saxons on this continent, and had sought, by military force, to establish a government that could at will destroy the privileges that inhere in liberty. They believed that the establishment here of a government that could administer public affairs according to its will, unrestrained by any fundamental law and without regard to the inherent rights of freemen, would be ruinous to the liberties of the people by exposing them to the oppressions of arbitrary power. Hence, the Constitution enumerates the powers which Congress and the other departments may exercise, — leaving unimpaired, to the states or to the people, the powers not delegated to the national government nor prohibited to the states. That instrument so expressly declares in the 10th Article of Amendment. It will be an evil day for American liberty if the theory of a government outside of the supreme law of the land finds lodgment in our constitutional jurisprudence. No higher duty rests upon this court than to exert its full authority to prevent all violation of the principles of the Constitution. Downes v. Bidwell,

182 US 244, 380-382, 45 LEd 1088 (1901)

This is exactly what has happened. Congress has written the laws to reach a constitutional end, but so vaguely that no person of reasonable intelligence could interpret them correctly. When you are indicted by the Federal Government for any offense occurring within the exterior territorial boundaries of any ONE OF the several 50 Union States the Federal courts <u>always</u> proceed as though you have committed the crime on Federal land under their concurrent or exclusive jurisdiction, a/k/a "United States", regardless of whether or not the statute contains the words "within the special maritime and territorial jurisdiction of the United States". There are serious problems that result from this. First, without jurisdiction over the place of the crime, Federal courts do not have subject-matter jurisdiction because no "offense against the laws of the United States" has been committed. Second, any judgement rendered by a court without subject-matter jurisdiction would violate the Fifth Amendment (due process) and be void ab initio ["from the beginning"]. That is why the presumption is always against Federal jurisdiction.

Instead of the judges assuring themselves that the crime occurred within the concurrent or exclusive legislative (territorial) jurisdiction of the "United States" (Federal Government), or that the statute in question applies extra-territorially to have effect outside of the "United States" and a constitutional foundation supporting the same, the judges proceed as if the Judicial Districts were actually Federal land under their concurrent or exclusive legislative (territorial) jurisdiction. Actually, that is technically what is happening. What they want us to perceive is happening is the fraudulent assumption that they are lawfully exercising a power to "punish" felonies by implication under their "Commerce Clause" powers as "necessary and proper."

What the Federal Government is doing is proceeding under "color of law". This simply means that because they have authority to do certain things they misuse that authority to do something that in reality they have no such authority to do. For example, if a County Sheriff pulls you over while driving your car and gives you a traffic citation ("ticket"), he appears to have the authority to do so. This is because he has a police car with flashing lights, a police uniform, a badge, and guns. What if that County Sheriff was from a different county? The ticket he gave would then be void for lack of jurisdiction (authority) because he had no legal right to ticket drivers traveling through a county other than his own. It appeared that he had this authority because he is a police officer when in reality he had no such authority. That is "color of law" and is exactly what the Federal Government is doing by prosecuting felonious crimes under the guise of regulating "interstate commerce."

Instead of the Federal courts protecting your rights they condone this illegal activity by the Executive branch. If you file a motion for relief utilizing the issues and law contained in this Manifesto the judges will continually deny them as "frivolous" or "without merit". That is especially true if you are already incarcerated. What they are saying, in other words, is that the Constitution, laws of Congress, rules of procedure (written by the Supreme Court), their own circuit precedent, the opinions of the other circuits, and the opinions of the Supreme Court, all of which they are bound by, utilized in your motion for relief, are all frivolous and meritless. This is because their jobs, as well as the jobs of tens of thousands of others, such as the Drug Enforcement Agency ("D.E.A."), the Federal Bureau of Investigation ("F.B.I."), and the Bureau of Prisons ("B.O.P."), are dependent on these unconstitutional, illegal, prosecutions. They must continue to indict and prosecute you without any lawful authority under the Constitution to do so. The Federal Public Defenders are also financially dependent on these prosecutions. This is how they all make their money. They milk the tax-payers of their hard earned money to pay for these illegal prosecutions and incarcerations. This is why people are sentenced to years for non-violent crimes (some for more time than murderers receive in the State). This is why it feels like you are being railroaded through court—you are.[110] This is why you never had a chance. This will become very apparent as you continue to read through this Manifesto and learn what the law really is. Let's continue.

---

[110] Kangaroo court. Term descriptive of a sham legal proceeding in which a person's rights are totally disregarded and in which the result is a foregone conclusion because of the bias of the court or other tribunal. Black's Law Dictionary, Sixth Edition, page 868.

There are two views that need to be explained. One view is that Congress can enact other criminal laws outside of those specifically enumerated in the Constitution, *i.e.*, where the power to "punish" has been delegated by enumeration. Remember what Justice Harlan of the Supreme Court stated in his dissenting opinion in <u>Downes v. Bidwell</u>?[111] That:

> [We] have in this country substantially or practically <u>two national governments</u>; one to be maintained under the Constitution, with all its restrictions; the other to be maintained by Congress outside and independently of that instrument... <u>Downes v. Bidwell</u>, *supra* (1901).

Congress can enact felonious criminal laws outside of those specifically enumerated powers to

---

[111] <u>Downes v. Bidwell</u>, *supra* (1901)

"punish," but only on their own ceded lands under the "exclusive legislation clause."[112] Congress can also enact whatever criminal legislation they wish within their own territories (which have not ousted the Federal Government of the power to do so by becoming a Union State, *Cf.* the "property clause").[113]

The limitations imposed by the Constitution on Congress' ability to carry out their delegated powers within the several 50 Union States and their ability to exercise undelegated powers (exclusive legislation) within ceded lands and their own territories not yet Union States, are the "two national governments" Mr. Justice Harlan was speaking of.[114] This is the line that has been blurred. This is where the law has been obfuscated. This is where the sovereignty and jurisdiction of the Union States has been usurped under the guise of regulating interstate commerce.

The following view, along with the People's ignorance of the law in general, have allowed this

---

[112] Article I, § 8, cl. 17

[113] Article IV, § 3, cl. 2

[114] Downes v. Bidwell, *supra* (1901) (Mr. Justice Harlan, dissenting).

arbitrary, and tyrannical, vigilante criminal "justice" system to thrive. This second view is that Congress surely must be able to enact criminal legislation if someone were to interfere with their ability to carry out their enumerated powers, such as stealing the mail or setting fire to a United States Post Office. This is *conditionally* true. Where Congress has concurrent or exclusive jurisdiction, or where the power to "punish" has been delegated, Congress can enact and carry out <u>felonious</u> criminal legislation. Where Congress does <u>not</u> have concurrent or exclusive jurisdiction, or where the power to "punish" has <u>not</u> been delegated, Congress can enact and carry out civil or misdemeanor legislation, but <u>only</u> if it has some relation to the execution of a delegated power.

The following case has been utilized by the Federal Government, for years, as their authority to prosecute felonious crimes under the guise of carrying out delegated powers where the power to "punish" has <u>not</u> been delegated, such as the power to regulate interstate commerce. However, as the old saying goes, "the devil is in the details." Here is where ignorance of the law comes into play. Ironically, the Federal Government just happens to be in charge of the Board of Education (please read "The Deliberate Dumbing Down of America," by Charlotte Iserbyt). Chief Justice Marshall explained that:

> So with respect to the whole penal code of the United States: whence arises the power to punish in cases not prescribed by the Constitution? All admit that the government may, legitimately punish any violation of its laws; and yet, this is not among the enumerated powers of Congress. The right to enforce the observance of law, by punishing its infraction, might be denied with more plausibility because it is expressly given in some cases.
>
> The good sense of the public has pronounced, without hesitation, that the power of punishment appertains to **sovereignty**, and may be exercised whenever the sov-

ereign has a right to act, as incidental to his constitutional powers. It is a means for carrying into execution all sovereign powers, and may be used, although not indispensably necessary. It is a right incidental to the power, and conductive to its beneficial exercise. <u>McCulloch v. The State of Maryland *et* al.</u>, 4 Wheat 316, 416-418, 4 LEd 579 (1819)

One has to keep in mind that, at that time, when our Constitution was still in its infancy, it was well understood. Its provisions had not been obfuscated and blurred into undelegated grants of power as they have been today. Even Congress knows this and legislates this way accordingly. Because of what I can only describe as an outright usurpation of power, sovereignty, and jurisdiction not delegated, by those who seek to cover up this major weakness of the Federal Government, whether well intended or for personal and financial reasons, it cannot, and does not, cure the unconstitutionality of it (which is a nice way of saying it is illegal because it is not authorized by the Constitution which is the Supreme Law of the Land). This malfeasance[115] is conspiracy to commit treason against the Constitution, and perjury of their sworn oaths to uphold it, with malice[116] against the People. This is the will of the few and not of the People. If it were the will of the People, the Constitution would have been amended. Who can possibly argue with that?

---

[115] Malfeasance. Evil doing; ill conduct. The commission of some act which is positively unlawful; the doing of an act which is wholly wrongful and unlawful; the doing of an act which person ought not to do at all or the unjust performance of some act which the party had no right or which he had contracted not to do. Black's Law Dictionary, Sixth Edition, page 956.

[116] Malice. The intentional doing of a wrongful act without just cause or excuse, with intent to inflict an injury or under circumstances that the law will imply an evil intent. A condition of mind which prompts a person to do a wrongful act willfully, that is, on purpose, to the injury of another, or to do intentionally a wrongful act toward another without justification or excuse. A conscious violation of the law (or the prompting of the mind to commit it) which operates to the prejudice of another person. A condition of the mind showing a heart regardless of social duty and fatally bent on mischief. Malice in the law is not necessarily personal hate or ill will, but it is that state of mind which is reckless of law and of the legal rights of the citizen. Black's Law Dictionary, Sixth Edition, page 956.

Congress legislates to reach constitutional ends, but they do so in such a way that allows the limits imposed by the Constitution to be disregarded. This allows arbitrary and capricious powers not granted to be wielded by those intended to be restrained. Because of this obfuscation, which allows the laws enacted by Congress to be carried out so as to reach a prohibited end, they are void for vagueness and unconstitutional. This is because no person of reasonable intelligence could possibly figure this out, especially when it (the system), is being upheld on presumptions, deceit, false beliefs, and outright lies. As Chief Justice Marshall so explicitly stated:

> To what purpose are powers limited, and to what purpose is that limitation committed to writing, if these limits may, at any time, be passed by those intended to be restrained? The distinction between a government with limited and unlimited powers is abolished if those limits do not

> confine the persons on whom they are imposed, and if acts prohibited and acts allowed are of equal obligation. Marbury v. Madison, 1 Cranch (US) 137, 176-178, 2 LEd 60 (1803)

While Congress can enact all laws necessary and proper in aid of carrying out their enumerated powers, they cannot enact, as necessary and proper, felonious criminal legislation where the power to punish has not been delegated or where jurisdiction over land has not been ceded. That right is reserved to the States respectively, or to the People. Congress can enact civil and misdemeanor offenses in aid of their delegated and enumerated powers where the power to punish has <u>not</u> been delegated by enumeration. To address this, let's take another look at McCulloch,[117] wherein Chief Justice Marshall stated that:

---

[117] McCulloch v. Maryland, *supra* at 422 (1819).

> The power to "make all needful rules and regulations respecting the territory or other property belonging to the United States," is not more <u>comprehensive</u> than the power "to make all laws which shall be necessary and proper for carrying into execution" the powers of the government.

Comprehensive is defined as: "Broad in scope or content."[118] What Chief Justice Marshall said, in other words, is that the necessary and proper clause carries with it no more authority than the property clause. Keeping that in mind, and the fact that jurisdiction is united with whoever is sovereign over the land, which is necessary to punish felonious crimes (except where the power to "punish" has been delegated by enumeration in the Constitution) let's take another look at the property clause, which states that:

---

[118] <u>Webster's New Riverside University Dictionary</u>, (1982), page 292.

> The Congress shall have the Power to make all needful Rules and Regulations respecting the **Territory or other Property** belonging to the United States; and nothing in this Constitution shall be so construed as to Prejudice any Claims of the United States, or of any particular State. Article IV, § 3, cl. 2

The Supreme Court, explaining the limitations the Constitution imposes on Congress under the Property Clause, stated that:

> We have noted, for example, that the Property Clause gives Congress the power over the public

land[119] "to control their occupancy and use, **to protect them**

---

[119] public land. Unappropriated land belonging to the federal or a state government; the general public domain. Black's Law Dictionary, Seventh Edition, page 882.

Public domain. Government-owned land. Black's Law Dictionary, Seventh Edition, page 1,243.

Public Lands, in a strict legal sense are lands owned by the Federal Government (a/k/a "United States"), that have not been purchased with the consent of the Legislature of the particular State, or where jurisdiction has not been ceded The Supreme Court explained that:

The United States has large bodies of public lands. These properties are used for forests, parks, ranges, wildlife sanctuaries, flood control, and other purposes which are not covered by Clause 17. Collins v. Yosemite Park & C. Co., 304 US 518, 529-530 (1938)

The Supreme Court has also explained that:

It is not unusual for the United States to own within a state lands which are set apart and used for public purposes. Such ownership and use without more do not withdraw the lands from the jurisdiction of the state. On the contrary, the lands remain part of her [the state's] territory and within the operation of her laws save that the latter cannot affect the title of the United States or embarrass it in using the lands or interfere with its right of disposal.

[T]he State undoubtedly may cede her jurisdiction to the United States and may make the cession either absolute or qualified as to her may appear desirable, provided the qualification ... is accepted by the United States. And where such a cession is made and accepted it will be determinative of the jurisdiction of both the United States and the State. Surplus Trading Co. v. Cook, 281 US 647, 650-652 (1928)

from **trespass** [120] and **injury** [121] and to prescribe the conditions upon which others may obtain rights in them..."

Absent consent [to purchase][122] or cession a State undoubtedly retains jurisdiction over federal lands within its territory.

The Federal Government does not assert exclusive jurisdiction over public lands ... and the State is free to enforce its criminal and civil laws on those lands. Kleppe

---

[120] trespass. An unlawful act committed against the person or property of another; esp., wrongful entry on another's real property. At common law, a legal action for injuries resulting from an unlawful act of this kind. Archaic—**MISDEMEANOR.**

"Before the word "misdemeanor' became well established the old writers tended to use the word 'trespass' to indicate an offense below the grade of a felony." Black's Law Dictionary, Seventh Edition, page 1,508.

[121] Injury. The violation of another's legal right, for which the law provides a remedy; a wrong or injustice. Harm or damage. Black's Law Dictionary, Seventh Edition, page 789.

[122] my note

v. New Mexico, 426 US 529, 543 (1976)

As we can clearly see from this Supreme Court opinion, Congress can protect Federal lands (owned by the "United States")[123] from <u>trespass</u> and <u>injury</u> (remember those terms). In the definition of felony (which is defined as a serious crime punishable by imprisonment for more than one year), it is explained that:

> The other, and lesser, crimes were known as "transgressions" or "**trespasses**," and did not obtain <u>their present name of misdemeanors</u> until a much later

---

[123] The Federal Government is called the "United States", because Congress is made up of representatives from each of the Union States. They are also referred to as, "THE UNITED STATES OF AMERICA" in some legal pleadings.

It should be remembered that the Federal Government (a/k/a/ "United States") does <u>not</u> own all the land which comprise the several 50 Union States. Far from it, although they do own an enormous amount of land.

date. Black's Law Dictionary, Seventh Edition, page 633.

So lesser crimes, such as a "trespass" are misdemeanors, which are defined as:

> A crime that is less serious than a felony and is usu. punishable by fine, penalty, forfeiture, or confinement (usu. for a brief term) in a place other than prison (such as a county jail). Blacks Law Dictionary, Seventh Edition, page 1,014.

Remember Kleppe v. New Mexico, *supra*? Under the "property clause," as explained by the Supreme Court,[124] Congress can provide for the prosecution of misdemeanors. They cannot "punish" felonies except

---

[124] Kleppe v. New Mexico, *supra*.

where they have purchased the land by consent of the Legislature of the particular Union State, or where concurrent[125] or exclusive jurisdiction has been <u>ceded</u> over land owned by the Federal Government ("United States"). The Federal Government must also accept all <u>cessions</u> of jurisdiction. What does this tell us about the necessary and proper clause? Its authority is no more broad in scope, *i.e.*, "comprehensive," than Congress' power under the property clause.[126]

Obviously if the Necessary and Proper Clause, or the power to regulate, allowed Congress to provide for the punishment of felonies then there would be no need for the Union States to cede legislative (territorial) jurisdiction over land owned by the "United States" (Federal Government) since under the Property Clause Congress is authorized to "make <u>all</u> needful

---

[125] It should be noted that a grant of concurrent jurisdiction is qualified by the terms of the cession. Just because concurrent jurisdiction is <u>ceded</u>, does not mean that Congress can prosecute felonies that occur on that land.

Do not forget that if you or anyone else owns the land, the "United States" (Federal Government) can<u>not</u> prosecute felonies therein, <u>except</u> where the power to "<u>punish</u>" (those specific offenses), has been <u>delegated</u>, by enumeration, in the Constitution.

[126] *Confer* Chief Justice Marshall in <u>McCulloch</u>, *supra*.

Rules and Regulations respecting the Territory or other Property" belonging to them. Such an erroneous construction of the Constitution would mean that Congress could feloniously punish any crime they wish, like murder for example, without the need for jurisdiction to be ceded. It would also not be necessary for Congress to specify that the crime of murder must occur within the special maritime and territorial jurisdiction of the United States. See 18 U.S.C. §§ 1111, 1112, murder and manslaughter, respectively.

By Analyzing Congress' power to regulate Federal lands under the property clause we can clearly see the limitations on the exercise of that power absent the delegation of the enumerated power to "punish". Utilizing this information we can better understand Chief Justice Marshall's analogy of the power to "make all needful rules and regulations respecting the territory or other property belonging to the United States" and the "necessary & proper clause" as it relates to the power to regulate commerce among the several States, i.e., "interstate commerce". Because the Federal Government ("United States") does not have territorial (legislative) jurisdiction over the land, Congress cannot utilize an undelegated power to "punish" as necessary & proper for carrying into execution their power to regulate interstate commerce; because doing so is "exclusive legislation" which requires "exclusive jurisdiction," the power to "punish" being an undelegated police power reserved to the several States respectively, or to the people. The Supreme Court explained that:

> [O]ur Federal government is one of enumerated powers.
>
> The control by Congress over interstate commerce cannot authorize the exercise of authority not entrusted to it by the Constitution.
>
> In interpreting the Constitution it must never be forgotten that the nation is made up of states to which are entrusted the powers of local government. And to them and to the people the powers not expressly delegated to the national government are reserved.

<u>Hammer v. Dagenhart</u>, 247 US 251, 275 (1918)

What if the U.S. Congress passed a law stating that whoever commits murder is guilty of a felony punishable by twenty years to life imprisonment? Would that be applicable to someone who murdered another person in any Union State even though the statute did not contain the special maritime and territorial jurisdiction language? If not, then why or how is it that other felonious crimes are being punished even though the Constitution limits the felonious crimes the Federal Government can prosecute to only three provisions, i.e., where the power to "punish" has been delegated by enumeration? It is because what we believe to be so is not so, therefore allowing our ignorance of the law to be utilized to our deprivation of life, liberty, the pursuit of happiness, and other inalienable rights, some of which have been specifically secured under the Constitution and some of which have not, yet nevertheless are retained by We the People. See the Ninth Amendment, "The enumeration in the Constitution, of certain rights, shall not be construed to deny or disparage others retained by the people."

As previously discussed, the power to punish felonies is united with whoever has sovereignty over the land. Think of it this way; if you committed a murder within any ONE OF the several 50 Union States, are you guilty of murder in Australia? How about China? Obviously not, because you were not in Australia or China. The same is true for crimes that occur within any ONE OF the several 50 Union States. Because the Union States are not "territories" belonging to the Federal Government, Congress cannot provide for the prosecution of felonies within any ONE OF those Union States. The only exceptions to this rule are found in the U.S. Constitution. Do you remember what those constitutional exceptions are? Other than where the power to "punish" has been delegated (which is a grant of authority to punish feloniously only those specific offenses), Congress cannot provide for the punishment of other felonies. This is because they have no territorial jurisdiction over the place where the crime occurs.

Other than their own territories, like Puerto Rico for example, the Union States have to cede territorial jurisdiction over the land owned by the "United States" (Federal Government), unless that land is purchased with the consent of the legislature of the particular State. Congress must also accept all cessions of jurisdiction otherwise jurisdiction would remain in the state. For example, if you commit a murder in Ohio the crime cannot be lawfully prosecuted in New York or any other Union State. Although you may be guilty of an offense against the laws of Ohio, you are not guilty of an offense against the laws of New York. This is because New York has no territorial (legislative) jurisdiction over the place where the crime occurred (Ohio). If there were no such thing as territorial jurisdiction, then New York, or any other Union State for that matter, could prosecute you for the murder committed in Ohio (likewise, Virginia and Maryland would be prosecuting State crimes within the District of Columbia). Each Union State is sovereign over the land and waters within its territorial boundaries. Territorial (legislative) jurisdiction then is the right of each sovereign to enact and carry into execution laws throughout its own territory (a/k/a "police power"). The reason why the Federal Government has nothing approaching a "police power," is because they are not sovereign over the land comprising the several 50 Union States. They can only legislate as authorized under the compact which is memorialized in the U.S. Constitution, our supreme Law.

Because Ohio has territorial (legislative) jurisdiction over the crime of murder occurring within its geographical boundaries, you are (f)actually innocent of an offense against the laws of any other Union State. No matter how far outside the record the government of New York (or any other Union State) goes, it is impossible for them to prove you are guilty of an offense against their laws. That is how to prove actual innocence under the law utilizing territorial (legislative) jurisdiction. As the Supreme Court explained:

> Actual innocence means factual innocence, not mere legal insufficiency. In other words, the Government is not limited to the existing record to rebut any showing that petitioner might make. Bousley v. United States, 523 us 614, 623-624 (1998)

Legal insufficiency simply means that the record evidence is insufficient to establish your guilt. This entitles you to a new trial but is not actual innocence because the government is able to prove you are guilty of a crime against their laws by utilizing evidence not contained in the record.

Because the Union States are not "territories" belonging to the Federal Government, ("United States") they have no territorial jurisdiction (general jurisdiction) over the place where the crime occurs, and therefore the Federal courts do not have subject-matter jurisdiction to hear the prosecution of the alleged criminal offense. Like Australia and China, no offense against the laws of the "United States" (Federal Government) has been committed, because you were not in the "United States," *i.e.* places where they are sovereign over the land (their own territories not yet Union States, and where concurrent or exclusive jurisdiction has been obtained through consent to purchase or ceded, and accepted). The term "jurisdiction" means "... the court's statutory or constitutional power to adjudicate the case," and objections to subject-matter jurisdiction "may be raised at any time".[127] The Federal courts have zero "statutory or constitutional power" (subject-matter jurisdiction) to adjudicate[128] felonious criminal cases if the crime occurs outside of the territorial places (geographical locations) under the concurrent or exclusive legislative jurisdiction of the "United States" (Federal Government). The Supreme Court has explained that:

> [S]ubject-matter jurisdiction, because it involves a court's power to hear a case, can never be forfeited or waived. Consequently, defects in subject-matter jurisdiction require correction regardless of whether the error was raised in district court. United States v. Cotton, 535 US 625, 630 (2002)

---

[127] United States v. Cotton, 535 US 625, 630 (2002); Henderson v. Shinseki, 131 SCt 1197 (2011)

[128] Adjudicate. To rule upon judicially. Black's Law Dictionary, Seventh Edition, page 42.

Again, if the felonious crime has not occurred in these places, the Federal courts have zero subject-matter jurisdiction to adjudicate the prosecution of the alleged criminal offense.[129] The courts are then constitutionally required to correct the "defect" in jurisdiction. They have to let you go. The Federal courts are obligated under the Constitution, because the due process rights secured under the Fifth Amendment require it, to take notice *sua-sponte* [130] as to whether they have subject-matter jurisdiction over the crime (constitutional authority), or not. If the felony prosecution is not pursuant to a crime where the power to "punish" has been delegated, by enumeration, in the Constitution, then the crime must have occurred within land (or affecting land) under the concurrent or exclusive legislative (territorial) jurisdiction of the Federal Government ("United States") in order for the federal courts to have subject-matter jurisdiction to adjudicate the case. For example, you

---

[129] With the single exceptions being where the power to "punish has been delegated".

[130] Sua Sponte. [Latin "of one's own accord; voluntarily"] Without prompting or suggestion; on its own motion <the court took notice sua sponte that it lacked jurisdiction over the case>. Black's Law Dictionary, Seventh Edition, page 1,437

discharge a firearm near federal land and it kills someone on federal land. Otherwise, the federal courts have zero subject-matter jurisdiction to adjudicate the case because no felony "offense against the laws of the United States" has been committed. As the Supreme Court explained:

> [C]ourts, including this Court, have an independent <u>obligation</u> to determine whether subject-matter jurisdiction exists, even in the absence of a challenge from any party. <u>Arbaugh v. Y & H Corp.</u>, 163 Led2d 1092, 1101 (2006) [citations omitted]

The federal courts, however, <u>never</u> take notice on their own motion in criminal cases when they lack subject-matter jurisdiction. They <u>always</u> claim that they have subject-matter jurisdiction under <u>18 U.S.C.</u>

§ 3231,[131] but they <u>know</u> that they do <u>not</u>. They cannot have it, because there is no "offense against the laws of the United States" for the courts to take subject-matter jurisdiction of if the felonious crime occurs outside the "territorial" <u>places</u> (land) under the concurrent or exclusive jurisdiction of the Federal Government ("United States").[132]

The court is already divided against you because they know they have no subject-matter jurisdiction to adjudicate felonious criminal prosecutions in the majority of those cases (especially in so-called "interstate commerce" cases, for example, drugs, computers, mail, *etc.*). It is you against the court and the prosecuting United States Attorney (who has also knowingly conspired to deprive you of your rights under the Constitution, by having you fraudulently indicted, knowing that the alleged criminal activity did

---

[131] "The <u>district courts of the United States</u> shall have original jurisdiction, exclusive of the <u>courts of the States</u>, of all offenses against the laws of the United States.

Nothing in this title shall be held to take away or impair the jurisdiction of the <u>courts of the several States</u> under the laws thereof." 18 U.S.C. § 3231

[132] With the single exceptions being where the power to "punish" has been delegated.

not occur in these "territorial" places). The court then appoints you a Federal Public Defender to feed you to the wolves. You obviously could not have proven this until you read this Manifesto. There is more to learn, so let's continue.

Unlike felonies, Congress does not need territorial jurisdiction to prosecute misdemeanors. Any act which interferes with Congress' ability to carry out their delegated powers can be properly made a misdemeanor offense against the United States. As the Supreme Court explained:

> There is no doubt of the competency of Congress to provide, by suitable penalties, for the enforcement of all legislation necessary or proper to the execution of powers with which it is entrusted.
>
> Any act, committed with a view of evading the legislation of Congress passed in the execution of

any of its powers, or of fraudulently securing the benefit of such legislation, may properly be made an offense against the United States.

But an act committed within a State, whether for a good or bad purpose, or whether, with an honest or criminal intent, cannot be made an offense against the United States, unless it have some relation to the execution of a power of Congress, or to some matter within the jurisdiction of the United States. An act not having any such relation is one in respect to which the State alone can legislate. <u>United States v. Fox</u>, 95 US 670, 672 (1878)

That passage is extremely confusing for the uneducated, helpless victim, indicted by the Federal Government. Even those trained in the law are confused by this passage because of the "brain washing" from birth. We believe what we see and hear is correct because this has been happening our entire lives, even since before we were born. We, including our children, are not taught what the law really is so that this "system" can be forced upon us. The truth has been purposely hidden in order to deprive us of our freedom, other liberties, and rights secured under the Constitution. This tyranny mimics exactly the same tyranny the Colonists endured from England which lead to the Declaration of Independence and the Revolutionary War.[133] The federal employees feel entitled

---

[133] The history of the present King of Great Britain is a history of <u>repeated injuries and usurpations,</u> <u>all having in direct object the establishment of an absolute tyranny over these States</u>. To prove this, let Facts be submitted to a candid world.

> He has made Judges dependent on his Will alone, for the tenure of their offices, and the amount and payment of their salaries.

> He has erected a multitude of New Offices [Confer the Internal Revenue Service ("I.R.S."), Federal Bureau of Investigation ("F.B.I."), Drug Enforcement Agency ("D.E.A."), and Department of Justice ("D.O.J."), for example], and sent hither swarms of Officers to harass our people, and eat out their substance.

> He has combined with others to subject us to <u>a jurisdiction foreign to our constitution</u>, and unacknowledged by our laws; giving his Assent to <u>their Acts of pretended Legislation</u>:

Continued on next page.

to do what they are doing to us because they work for, and are getting paid by, the Federal Government. Just like the Soldiers felt entitled to do to the Colonists what they were doing. After all they were sent over and getting paid by the King, his Royal Majesty himself. The only difference between what was done to the Colonists then, and what is being done to us now, is that it is our own government doing it to us instead of the King of England. If such an implied power to punish under the commerce clause truly existed under the law, then ask yourself why the law is not written this way? Why do they have to continuously lie, perjure their sworn oaths to uphold the Constitution, and commit treason, to do what they are doing?

> For transporting us beyond Seas [far away places] to be tried for pretended offences:
>
> For abolishing the free System of English Laws in a neighboring Province, establishing therein an Arbitrary government, and enlarging its Boundaries so as to render it at once an example and fit instrument for introducing the same absolute rule into these Colonies:
>
> For taking away our Charters, abolishing our most valuable Laws, and altering fundamentally the Forms of our Governments:
>
> For suspending our own Legislatures, and declaring themselves invested with power to legislate for us in all cases whatsoever." Declaration of Independence, July 4, 1776.

It appears that we are more apt to continue to suffer the evils that men do, so long as they are sufferable, rather than right the wrong, just as the Declaration of Independence states.

Congress can create misdemeanor and felony offenses against the "United States" (Federal Government). Where those offenses can be lawfully prosecuted under the limits imposed by the Constitution is an altogether different matter. Do you remember what Justice Field stated in Fox, *supra*, about "suitable penalties" being "properly" made an "offense" against the United States? Justice Field was just stating the obvious. That Supreme Court opinion is not granting any power, one way or the other, to the Federal Government to punish felonious crimes if the offensive conduct has some relation to the execution of a delegated power. Only Congress alone can legislate,[134] which is restricted to the limitations imposed by the Constitution. Whether an offense against the United States is properly made a felony or misdemeanor is dependent on the limitations imposed by

---

[134] "All legislative Powers herein granted shall be vested in a Congress of the United States," Article I, § 1, U.S. Constitution.

the Constitution. As one of our most prominent jurists warned us decades ago:

> Experience should teach us to be most on guard to protect liberty when the government's purposes are beneficent. The greatest dangers to liberty lurk in insidious encroachment by mean of zeal, well meaning but without understanding. <u>Olmstead v. United States</u>, 277 US 438, 479 (1928) (Brandeis, J., dissenting)

In their desire to suppress crime, their road to injustice, like the road to Hell, is often paved with good intentions. Again, the <u>places</u> where felonies and misdemeanors can be lawfully made an offense against the laws of the United States (Federal Government) is limited by the Constitution. As I have previously stated, if Congress already had jurisdiction to punish felonies, whenever they deemed it "necessary and proper," there would be no need for the Union States to <u>cede</u> jurisdiction to Congress, and no need for Congress to <u>accept</u> those cessions of jurisdiction.[135] Chief Justice Marshall, speaking with regard to the necessary and proper clause, observed that:

> Congress may pass all laws which are <u>necessary and proper</u> **for giving the most complete effect** to this power.[136] Still, the

---

[135] "To exercise exclusive Legislation in all Cases whatsoever ... by Cession of particular States, <u>and the acceptance of Congress</u>, ... and to exercise like Authority over all Places purchased by the Consent of the Legislature of the State," <u>Article I, § 8. cl. 17</u>, U.S. Constitution.

"Presumption. It is <u>conclusively</u> presumed that jurisdiction has <u>not</u> been accepted <u>until</u> the Government <u>accepts jurisdiction over land</u> as provided in this section." <u>40 U.S.C. § 3112</u>

[136] The judicial power extending to "all Cases of admiralty and maritime Jurisdiction" power. <u>Article III, § 2</u>, U.S. Constitution

Do not be confused that he is speaking of this particular power which does not delegate the power to punish. The Chief Justice's necessary and proper clause analysis applies to all powers delegated to Congress. If the power to punish is delegated then Congress can punish felonies pursuant to those specific provisions. Otherwise the "<u>general jurisdiction</u>" over the place of the crime has to be <u>ceded</u> by the particular Union State. Confer note 80, *supra*.

Continued on next page.

general **jurisdiction over the place** [of the crime], ... **adheres to the territory**, as a portion of sovereignty [137] not yet given away. United States v. Bevans,

---

The Bevans case dealt with a murder on board the Federal ship of war, "Independence," by a marine in the Boston harbor in waters of sufficient depth at all times of tide for ships of the largest size, and to which there is at all times a free and unobstructed passage to the sea or ocean. It was not on the high Seas. Had it been, Congress could have punished the felony under the high Seas clause at Article I, § 8, cl. 10, where the power to punish has been delegated.

It was held that Congress could have provided for the punishment of the murder because it occurred on board their own ship which would have been out of the jurisdiction of the State where the ship was docked (under International Law a ship is considered under the jurisdiction of the sovereign whose flag it flies, including when docked in a foreign country, and is also subject to the foreign country's jurisdiction it enters). However, no statute had been enacted by Congress to do so. Therefore the place where the crime occurred was in the State. The grant to the United States in the Constitution of all cases of admiralty and maritime jurisdiction, does not extend to a cession of the waters in which those cases may arise, or of general jurisdiction over the same.

The exclusive jurisdiction which the United States have in forts and dock-yards ceded to them, is derived from the express assent of the States by whom the cessions are made. It could be derived in no other manner; because without it, the authority of the State would be supreme and exclusive therein.

[137]Sovereignty. Supreme dominion, authority, or rule. The Supreme political authority of an independent state. The State itself. Black's Law Dictionary, Seventh Edition, page 1,402.

16 US (3 Wheat) 336, 4 Led 404 (1818)

Even before Chief Justice Marshall, the Supreme Court stated that:

> In relation to <u>crimes and punishments</u>, the objects of the delegated power of the United States <u>are enumerated and fixed</u>. **Congress may provide for the punishment of counterfeiting the securities and current coin of the United States; and may define and punish felonies committed on the high seas, and offenses against the laws of nations. Art. 1. s. 8. And, so, likewise Congress may make all laws which shall be <u>necessary and proper</u>, for carrying into execution the powers of the general government. But here is <u>no reference to a com-</u>**

mon law authority: Every power is a matter of definite and positive grant; and the very powers that are granted cannot take effect until they are exercised through the medium of the law.

Peters, Justice. Whenever a government has been established, I have always supposed, that a power to preserve itself, was a necessary, and inseparable, concomitant. But the existence of the Federal government would be precarious, it could no longer be called an independent government, if, **for the punishment of offenses of this nature, tending to obstruct and pervert the administration of its affairs**, an appeal must be made to the State tribunals, or the offenders must escape with absolute impunity. **The power to punish misdemeanors** is originally and

strictly a common law power; of which, I think, the United States are constitutionally possessed.

It might have been exercised by Congress in the form of a Legislative act; but, it may, also, in my opinion be enforced in a course of Judicial proceeding. **Whenever an offence aims at the subversion of any Federal institution, or at the corruption of its officers, it is an offence against the well-being of the United States.** The United States v. Worrall, 2 U.S. (Dall.) 384, 391, 395 (1798)

As stated, the Necessary & Proper Clause contains no reference to a common law authority, like the power to "punish", for example. Therefore it can only be utilized to carry into execution the delegated (enumerated) powers. Because the power to "punish" is a definite and positive grant of power delegated (enumerated) in certain provisions of the Constitution, it cannot be utilized as necessary and proper to carry into execution other delegated powers.

It should be perfectly clear by now that Congress can provide for the punishment of felonies within any ONE OF the several 50 Union States where the power to punish has been delegated in the Constitution. Congress can also punish felonies in their own territories and over land they own within any Union State where concurrent or exclusive jurisdiction has been ceded. Once again, exclusive jurisdiction automatically vests to Congress when they purchase the land with the consent of the particular Union State. Congress must also accept all cessions of jurisdiction.[138]

Where the power to punish has not been delegated, or jurisdiction ceded, Congress can, pursuant to the necessary and proper clause, prosecute misdemeanors if it has some relation to the execution of a

---

[138] Presumption. It is conclusively presumed that jurisdiction has not been accepted until the Government accepts jurisdiction over land as provided in this section. Title 40 U.S.C. § 3112, Federal jurisdiction.

delegated power, or within land they own. This is because, as an independent sovereign, the "United States" (Federal Government) is already constitutionally possessed with the common law power to punish misdemeanor offenses in order to enforce the observance of their laws. Otherwise it would not be an independent government because it would have no choice but to rely on the governments of the several Union States to enforce compliance with their laws. That would defeat the purpose of creating the "United States" (Federal Government) as the several Union State governments, and for the most part the people, could willfully ignore federal laws with impunity. Where jurisdiction has not been ceded, the Supreme Court explains:

> The <u>consent</u> of the States to the <u>purchase</u> of lands within them for the special purposes named is, however, <u>essential</u>, under the Constitution, to the transfer to the General Government, with the title, of political jurisdiction and

dominion. Where lands are acquired without such consent, the possession of the United States, <u>unless</u> political jurisdiction be <u>ceded</u> to them in some other way, is simply that of an <u>ordinary proprietor</u>.

Where, therefore, lands are acquired in any other way by the United States within the limits of a State than by purchase with her consent, they will hold lands subject to this qualification: that if upon them forts, arsenals, or other public buildings are erected for the uses of the General Government, such buildings, with their appurtenances, as instrumentalities [139] for the execution of its powers, will be free from any

---

[139] Instrumentality. A thing used to achieve an end or purpose. A means or agency through which a function of another entity is accomplished, such as a branch of a governing body. <u>Black's Law Dictionary</u>, Seventh Edition, page 802.

such interference and jurisdiction of the State as would destroy or impair their effective use for the purposes designed.

Such is the law with reference to all instrumentalities created by the General Government. Their exemption from state control is essential to the independence and sovereign authority of the United States within the sphere of their delegated powers. But, when not used as such instrumentalities, the legislative power of the State over places acquired will be as full and complete as over any other places within her limits. Fort Leavenworth R.R. Co. v. Lowe, 114 US 525, 530-531, 539 (1885)

Because the Federal Government is not sovereign over the land, Congress cannot provide for the punishment of felonies within the exterior territorial boundaries of any ONE OF the several 50 Union States without concurrent or exclusive jurisdiction.[140] Those matters, *i.e.*, the power to "punish" felonies, are left to the particular Union State.

---

[140] With the single exceptions being where the enumerated power to "punish" has been delegated.

THE RULES

Keeping in mind all of the aforementioned supporting documentation on jurisdiction to punish felonies, let's take a look at <u>Federal Rules of Criminal Procedure</u>, Rule 1(a)(1), 1(b)(9), 26, and 54. Rule 1(a)(1) states that, "These rules govern the procedure in <u>all</u> criminal proceedings in the United States district court<u>s</u>"; Rule 1(b)(9), Definitions. The following definitions apply to these rules, "'State', includes the District of Columbia, and any commonwealth, territory, or possession of the United States"; Rule 26, Advisory Committee Notes, paragraph 2, states that, "[A]ll Federal Crimes are statutory and all criminal prosecutions in the Federal courts are based on <u>acts of Congress</u>"; Rule 54, (transferred, not repealed or abrogated), paragraph (c), states that, "As used in these rules the following terms have the designated meanings. <u>'Act of Congress'</u> includes any act of Congress locally applicable to and in force in the District of Columbia, in Puerto Rico, in a territory or in an insular possession."

Did you notice that "...all criminal prosecutions in the Federal courts are based on <u>Acts of Congress</u>"? That those "Acts of Congress" include only acts applicable to the District of Columbia, Puerto Rico, territories and insular possessions? The Supreme Court has expressly held that:

> [I]n construing a statute, the rule of ejusdem generis—that where particular words of description are followed by general terms, the latter will be regarded as referring to persons or things of a like class with those particularly described—will, like other words of statutory construction, be applied to give effect to, but not to subvert or defeat, the legislative intent or purpose in enacting the statute.

The Supreme Court has likewise held that in construing a statute, the rule of noscitur a sociis—that a word is known by the company it keeps—will, like other rules of statutory construction, be applied to ascertain the meaning of words otherwise obscure or doubtful only where the result of such application of the rule is consistent with the legislative intent. Supreme Court Annotations, 46 LEd2d 879, Ejusdem Generis-Noscitur A Sociis, § 2, Summary.

[T]he Supreme Court noted that noscitur a sociis is a rule of construction applicable to all written instruments, whereby if any particular word, taken by itseif, is obscure or of doubtful meaning, its obscurity or doubt may be removed by reference to associated words. Supreme Court Annotations, 46 LEd2d

879, Ejusdem Generis-Noscitur A Sociis, § 4, General principles governing application of noscitur a sociis rule.

In the following case[], the rule of ejusdem generis was applied by the Supreme Court in construing criminal statutes. Holding that a ship was not "any other place" within the meaning of the federal statute providing "that if any person or persons shall, within any fort, arsenal, dockyard, magazine, or in any other place, or district of country, under the sole and exclusive jurisdiction of the United States, commit the crime of willful murder, such person or persons, on being thereof convicted, shall suffer death," the Supreme Court in United States v. Bevans, (1818) 16 US 336, 4 LEd 404, reasoned that in view of the fixed and territorial nature of the places specifically enumerated by the statute, the construction seemed irresistible that the words "other place" were intended to mean another place of a similar character to those previously enumerated. Supreme Court Annotations, 46 LEd2d 879, Ejusdem Generis-Noscitur A Sociis, § 5, criminal statutes, [a] Rule held applicable.

So, in ascertaining the meaning of words like commonwealth, territory, and insular possession that are doubtful or otherwise obscure, we can utilize the rule of Ejusdem Generis or Noscitur a Sociis which inform us that they take on the same meaning as the words District of Columbia and Puerto Rico. That is, they are places under the concurrent or exclusive legislative (territorial) jurisdiction of the "United States" (Federal Government).

In the year 2002, Federal Rules of Criminal Procedure ("FRCrP"), Rule 54, was transferred to Rule 1.

The definition of "Act of Congress" was removed. The reason given was that the restyled rules instead use the self-explanatory term "federal statute".[141] However, *confer* FRCrP, Rule 1(b)(9), *supra*. See also Title 28 U.S.C. § 2072(b), "All laws in conflict with such rules shall be of no further force or effect after such rules have taken effect." All federal crimes are based on statutes (Acts of Congress) which criminal prosecutions are applicable only in places under the concurrent or exclusive jurisdiction of the "United

---

[141] Rule 1 is entirely revised and expanded to incorporate Rule 54, which deals with the application of the rules. Consistent with the title of the existing rule, the Committee believed that a statement of the scope of the rules should be placed at the beginning to show readers which proceedings are governed by these rules. The committee also revised the rule to incorporate the definitions found in Rule 54(c) as a new Rule 1(b).

Rule 1(b) is composed of material currently located in Rule 54(c), with several exceptions. First, the reference to an "Act of Congress" has been deleted from the restyled rules; instead the rules use the self-explanatory term "federal statute." FRCrP, Applicability of Rules, Rule 1, Scope; Definitions, History; Ancillary Laws and Directives, Notes of Advisory Committee on 2002 amendments, paragraphs 1 & 4.

Certain provisions in current Rule 54 have been moved to revised Rule 1 as part of a general restyling of the Criminal Rules to make them more easily understood and to make style and terminology consistent throughout the rules. Other provisions in Rule 54 have been deleted as being unnecessary. FRCrP, Rule 54, [Transferred], History; Ancillary Laws and Directives, Notes of Advisory Committee on 2002 amendments.

States" (Federal Government). That is what the rules tell us. I will explain why the rules tell us this as we continue through this Manifesto.

It is a cardinal rule of statutory construction that words or phrases omitted from a statute by Congress were <u>intended</u> to be left out. It is also a maxim of law. The Courts, therefore, have a duty not to read words or phrases into the legislation of Congress that are not there.[142] The obvious reason is because in doing so the courts would be legislating for Congress which they have no power to do. This rule obviously stems from <u>Article I, § 1</u>, U.S. Constitution, which vests Congress with "<u>All</u> legislative powers."

---

[142] Inclusio unius est exclusio alterius. The inclusion of one is the exclusion of another. The certain designation of one person [or place (my note)] is an absolute exclusion of all others. This doctrine decrees that where law expressly describes particular situation to which it shall apply, an irrefutable inference <u>must</u> be drawn that what is <u>omitted</u> or excluded was <u>intended</u> to be omitted or excluded. <u>Black's Law Dictionary</u>, Sixth Edition, page 763.

[Law Latin] A canon of construction holding that to express or include one thing implies the exclusion of the other, or of the alternative. <u>Black's Law Dictionary</u>, Eighth Edition, page 620.

See for example <u>Hohn v. United States</u>, 526 US 236, 250 (1998) and <u>Keene Corp. v. United States</u>, 508 US 200, 208 (1993)

Clearly the several States are not even mentioned in the definition of "Act of Congress." When Congress intends to include all, or any ONE OF, the several 50 Union States, they do so explicitly. For example, compare Title 18 U.S.C. § 836, ¶4, "As used in this section, the term 'State' includes the several States, Territories, and possessions of the United States, and the District of Columbia"; and Title 18 U.S.C. § 891(8), "The term 'State' includes the District of Columbia, the commonwealth of Puerto Rico, and territories and possessions of the United States." The "several States" are not automatically included as is clear from these particular definitions of "State."

And see, for example, Title 26 U.S.C. § 3121(e), Definitions, History; Ancillary Laws and Directives, Amendments:

> In 1960, P.L.[143] 86-624, Sec. 18(c), deleted "Hawaii," in para. (e)(1), effective 8/21/59.

---

[143] Public Law ("P.L.")

Prior to amendment, subsec. (e) read as follows:

(e)(1) State.-The term "State" includes **Hawaii**, the District of Columbia, Puerto Rico, and the Virgin Islands.

In 1959, P.L. 86-70, Sec. 22(a), deleted "<u>Alaska</u>," in para. (e)(1), effective 1/3/59.

The territories of Alaska and Hawaii were removed from the definition of "State" after they became ONE OF the several Union States on January 3, 1959, and March 18, 1959, respectively. Remember, the Supreme Court previously explained that:

> Upon admission of a state into the Union, the state doubtless acquires <u>general jurisdiction</u>, civil and criminal ... <u>except</u> where it has <u>ceded</u> exclusive jurisdiction

to the United States. The rights of local <u>sovereignty</u> ... vests in the State, and <u>not</u> in the United States. <u>Van Brocklin v. Anderson</u>, 117 US 151, 167-168 (1886) (citing cases)

If the Federal Government already had territorial jurisdiction (general jurisdiction) within the several 50 Union States it would not have been necessary to remove Alaska and Hawaii from the definition of "State". As the Supreme Court explained above in Van Brocklin, the State (not the Federal Government) acquires general (legislative/territorial) jurisdiction when a Federal Territory joins the Union (becoming the new State).

THE COURTS

Thomas Jefferson, Founding Father, Creator & signer of the Declaration of Independence, and former President of the United States, stated regarding the courts, that:

> At the establishment of our Constitution, the judiciary bodies were supposed to be the most helpless and harmless members of the government. Experience, however, soon showed in what way they were to become the most dangerous; that the insufficiency of the means provided for their removal gave them a freehold and irresponsibility in office, that their decisions, seeming to concern individual suitors only, pass silent and unheeded by the public at large, that these decisions nevertheless become law

by precedent, sapping by little and little the foundations of the Constitution and working its change by construction before any one has perceived that that invisible and helpless worm has been busily employed in consuming its substance. In truth, man is not made to be trusted for life if secured against all liability to account.—Thomas Jefferson to A Coray, 1823, ME 15:486, "The Writings of Thomas Jefferson" (memorial edition), Lipscomb & Bergh, editors; and that

This member of the government ... has proved that the power of declaring what the law is, *ad libitum*, by sapping and mining, slyly, and without alarm, the foundations of the Constitution, can do what open force would not dare to attempt.—Thomas Jefferson to Edward Livingston, 1825,

> ME 16:114, "The Writings of Thomas Jefferson" (memorial edition), Lipscomb & Bergh, editors

In the Federal judicial system there are two types of criminal courts. Constitutional courts "ordained and established" under Article III, of the U.S. Constitution, via Article I, § 8, cl. 9, which are inferior to the Supreme Court, and "legislative" courts created under Article I, § 8, cl.17, and Article IV, § 3, cl. 2. The courts created under Article I § 8, cl.17 and Article IV, § 3, cl. 2, are also referred to as "congressional" and/or "territorial" courts. The Supreme Court explained that:

> The Constitution nowhere makes reference to "legislative courts." The power given Congress in Art 1, § 8, cl. 9, "To constitute Tribunals inferior to the Supreme Court," plainly relates to the "infe-

rior Courts" provided for in Art 3, § 1; it has <u>never</u> been relied on for establishment of any other tribunals.

The concept of a legislative court derives from the opinion of Chief Justice Marshall in <u>American Ins. Co. v. Canter</u>, (US) 1 Pet 511, 7 Led 242, dealing with courts established in a territory.

"These Courts, then, <u>are not constitutional Courts, in which the judicial power conferred by the Constitution on the general government, can be deposited. They are incapable of receiving it. They are legislative Courts</u>, created in virtue of the general right of sovereignty which exists in the government, or in virtue of that clause [Article IV, § 3, cl. 2] which enables Congress to make all needful rules and regulations, respecting the territory belonging to the United States." <u>Glidden v. Zdanok</u>, 370 US 530, 543-544 (1962)

Every federal court not created under Article III of the U.S. Constitution is a legislative court. Their subject-matter jurisdiction is limited to matters occurring within the concurrent or exclusive legislative (territorial) jurisdiction of the "United States" (Federal Government). Their subjects of jurisdiction are defined by statutes created by Congress for these courts. Because legislative courts are not constitutional courts created under Article III, they are incapable of extending the judicial power under that Article to the subjects of jurisdiction enumerated there in section 2 (although they are exercising <u>legislative</u> judicial power). The Supreme Court in <u>Glidden v. Zdanok</u>, *supra*, speaks of Congress' power to assign specified jurisdiction to administrative agencies and "tribunal[s] having every appearance of a court and composed of judges enjoying statutory assurances of life tenure and undiminished compensation." Id at 550.

Constitutional courts on the other hand, are authorized to extend the judicial power under Article III of the U.S. Constitution to the subjects of jurisdiction enumerated there in section 2. This includes all felony offenses against the laws of the United States occurring within the territorial (legislative) jurisdiction of any particular Union State where the power to "punish" has been delegated, by enumeration, in the Constitution. It also includes all misdemeanor offenses against the laws of the United States, occurring within the territorial (legislative) jurisdiction of any particular Union State, if the alleged conduct is connected to the execution of a delegated power. If Congress enacts a law in excess of the limitations imposed by the Constitution, these courts will strike it down as unconstitutional. Likewise, these courts should also strike down as unconstitutional any law carried out in such a way so as to reach a prohibited (unconstitutional) end, regardless of whether the law is constitutionally valid on its face (as written). As the Supreme Court explained:

Constitutional power is merely the first hurdle that must be overcome in determining that a federal court has jurisdiction over a particular controversy [or case]. It is a fundamental precept that federal courts are courts of limited jurisdiction. The limits upon federal jurisdiction, whether imposed by the Constitution or Congress, must be neither disregarded nor evaded. Owen Equipment & Erection Co. v. Kroger, 437 US 365, 372, 374 (1978)

What I am about to present to you throughout this section is perhaps the only circumstantial evidence surrounding whether the current federal "United States district courts" are constitutional courts "ordained & established" under Article III or are legislative courts created by Congress pursuant to their "exclusive legislation" powers under Article I, § 8, cl. 17. It is my opinion that there is sufficient evidence to draw a very reasonable conclusion that they are the latter. Whether legislative or Article III courts, the level of corruption within the federal court system is unparalleled, to say the least, with a majority of decisions being arbitrary, capricious, and contrary to law. If they are legislative courts, as proposed, this would at least provide some reasonable explanation why the judges thereof consistently violate your rights, their sworn oaths to uphold the Constitution, and the separation of powers by acting as the executive branch. However, you must decide for yourself what to believe. A "legislative" court is defined as:

> **A court created by a statute**, as opposed to one created by a constitution. Black's Law Dictionary, Eighth Edition, page 382.

Obviously the Supreme Court is created by the Constitution itself. When Congress "ordains & establishes" inferior Article III constitutional courts, they are created by the Constitution which delegates that power to Congress. Congress also has authority to establish legislative courts throughout the several 50 Union States under their "Enclave Clause" (Article I, § 8, cl. 17) powers.

When Congress establishes new courts they do so in an Act which is a statute. If Congress fails to clarify in those Acts a court's status as "ordained & established under Article III," how do we know the courts are not legislative courts? It appears the answer is determined by a court's physical location. However, this is not always true. Obviously a court sitting in a territory is a legislative court. The argument that a court's status is determined by its physical location fails when applied to the several 50 Union States. If Congress can establish Article III courts within the District of Columbia, why can't they establish legislative courts throughout the Union States in making all "needful Rules and Regulations" respecting the millions of acres of land under their concurrent or exclusive legislative (territorial) jurisdiction? On that note we turn to the Federal Rules of Evidence which state that:

These various provisions do <u>not</u> in <u>terms</u> [144] describe the same courts [and] in congressional[145] usage the phrase "<u>district courts of the United States</u>," without further qualification, traditionally has included the district courts established by Congress in the States <u>under Article III</u> of the Constitution, which are "constitutional" courts, and has <u>not</u> included the <u>territorial courts</u> created under <u>Article IV, Section 3, clause 2</u>, which are "legislative" courts.[146]

<u>Federal Rules of Evidence</u>, Rule 1101, Applicability of Rules,

---

[144] Term. A word or phrase; an expression; particularly one which possesses a fixed and known meaning in some science, art, or profession. Black's Law Dictionary, Sixth Edition, page 1,470.

[145] Congressional powers. The authority vested in the Senate and House of Representatives to enact laws, etc. as provided in U.S. Const., Art. 1. Black's Law Dictionary, Sixth Edition, page 301.

[146] <u>Hornbuckle v. Toombs</u>, 85 US 648, 21 Led 966 (1873)

notes of Advisory Committee on Rules, paragraph 2.

The Supreme Court explained that:

> The words "district court of the United States" [in their historic, technical sense], commonly describe constitutional courts created under Article 3 of the Constitution, not the legislative courts which have long been the courts of the Territories. International L. & W. U. v. Juneau Corp., 342 US 237, 241 (1952).

If the words "district court of the United States" describes constitutional courts created under Article III, then we know that the "U.S. Court of International Trade" is not a "district court of the United States" because of its name, even though it is a constitutional court established under Article III. Likewise, we know that the "United States district courts" are not the constitutional "district courts of the United States" established under Article III because of their name. If the current "United States district courts" are clearly not the former "district courts of the United States", then what are they? In a Ninth Circuit case it was stated that:

> The <u>United States district court</u> for the Territory of Hawaii may <u>not</u>, for all purposes, be considered a <u>District Court of the United States</u>, but it has the jurisdiction of a District Court of the United States and is by law required to proceed in the same manner as a District Court of the United States. <u>Mookini et al. v. United States</u>, 92 F2d 126 (9th Cir. 1937)

Just because a territorial "United States district court", or any other legislative court, is vested with jurisdiction (subject-matter jurisdiction), to hear the same kinds of cases as an Article III court (see Article III, § 2, subjects of jurisdiction), it does not mean their jurisdiction comes from Article III. On certiorari to review the Mookini case, the Supreme Court explained that:

> The term "District Court of the United States," [in its historic and proper sense] ... has its historic significance. It describes the constitutional courts created under article 3 of the Constitution.
>
> Courts of the Territories are legislative courts, properly speaking, and are not District Courts of the United States. We have often held that **vesting a territorial court with jurisdiction similar to that vested in the District Courts of the United States does not make it a "District Court of the United States"**

[numerous citations omitted]. Mookini v. United States, 303 US 201, 205 (1938)

As we proceed from this point forward, several important issues will be discussed. For instance, the government will purport that the term, words, or phrase "district courts of the United States" is describing the "United States district courts" sitting throughout the several 50 Union States as if they were one and the same court established under Article III. This is subterfuge[147] and you have the right to know it and use it as a defense. The character of a federal court within the several 50 Union States is not dependent on its physical location. Constitutional

---

[147] subterfuge. deception by artifice or stratagem in order to conceal, escape, or evade. A deceptive device or stratagem. Webster's Ninth New Collegiate Dictionary, (1991), page 1,177.

artifice. An artful stratagem: TRICK. Webster's Ninth New Collegiate Dictionary, (1991), page 106.

stratagem, an artifice or trick in war for deceiving and outwitting the enemy. A cleverly contrived trick or scheme for gaining an end. Skill in ruses or trickery. Webster's Ninth New Collegiate Dictionary, (1991), page 1,165.

courts are "ordained & established" under Article III, U.S. Constitution and "legislative" courts, also called "congressional" and "territorial" courts, are created by statutes pursuant to other congressional powers.

The Federal Government will argue that the statutes codified at Title 28 U.S.C. § 132 ("Creation and composition of district courts"), creating (constituting/ establishing) "United States district courts" within the several 50 Union States are creating Article III constitutional courts, that the "United States district courts" it creates in the Territories, such as Puerto Rico, are legislative "territorial" courts (which they definitely are), and that the "United States district court" it creates within the District of Columbia is an Article III court (having authority not only over local laws applicable solely within the district, but also over all those controversies, civil and criminal, arising under the Constitution and the statutes of the United States and having nationwide application, because of the special character of the District of Columbia being made up from Union States). The claim that a court's physical location, at least within the 50 Union States, is determinative of its status as either an Article III court or legislative court, is untrue. Exactly how do we determine the status of the "United States district courts" when Congress has cleverly established them in a statutory scheme that appears to clearly create a "United States district court" in each of the established judicial districts? Notwithstanding the fact that the words "ordained & established" and "Article III" are nowhere to be found declaring their status, the definition of "district court of the United States" at 28 U.S.C. § 451 encompassing every "United States district court" within each Judicial District is only applicable to Title 28 U.S.C. and not to other Titles of the United States Code, such as 18 U.S.C. § 3231. Remember, the phrase "district courts of the United States" describes constitutional courts established under Article III, not the phrase "United States district courts".

We learned earlier that the power to create legislative courts comes from Article I, § 8, cl. 17 (Exclusive Legislation Clause), when established within the Union States, and Article IV, § 3, cl. 2 (Property Clause), when established in a Territory. We also learned that the power to establish Article III constitutional courts comes from Article I, § 8, cl. 9. The Supreme Court reaffirmed this stating that:

It is equally true that Article I, § 8, cl 9, which provides that Congress may "constitute Tribunals inferior to the supreme Court," does not explicitly say, Tribunals under Article III, below." Yet, this power "plainly relates to the 'inferior Courts' provided for in Article III, § 1; it has never been relied on for establishment of any other tribunals." Freytag v. Commissioner, 501 US 858 (1991) citing Glidden v. Zdanok

Since there are three distinct and separate provisions in the Constitution relied on to create either constitutional courts or legislative courts, we can deduce that those powers cannot therefore be combined into a single statute which creates all of the courts. A standing Supreme Court opinion regarding courts created in the District of Columbia states that:

Pursuant to its Clause 17 authority, Congress has from time to time enacted laws that compose the District of Columbia Code. The 1970 Reorganization Act amended the Code by creating the Superior Court of the District of Columbia and the District of Columbia Court of Appeals, the courts being expressly "established pursuant to article I of the Constitution." This title makes clear (section 11-101 [DC Code]) that the District of Columbia Courts (the District of Columbia Court of Appeals, and the Superior Court of the District of Columbia) are <u>Article I courts, created pursuant to Article I, section 8, clause 17</u> of the United States Constitution, and are not Article III courts. The authority under which the local courts are established has not been statutorily provided in prior law; the Supreme Court of the United States has not declared the local system to be either Article I or Article III courts, decisions having indicated that the District of Columbia courts are, in this respect, both fish and fowl. **This expression of the intent** by Congress **clarifies the status** of the local courts.

The case before us is a far cry from O'Donoghue [289 US 516 (1933)]. Here Congress has expressly created two systems of courts in the District. One of them is made up of the United States district court for the District of Columbia and the United States Court of Appeals for the District of Columbia Circuit, which are constitutional courts manned by Art III judges to which the citizens of the District must or may resort for consideration of those constitutional and statutory matters of general concern which so moved the Court in O'Donoghue. The other system is made up of strictly local courts, the Superior Court and the District of Columbia Court of Appeals. These courts were expressly created pursuant to the plenary Art I power to legislate for the District of Columbia ... and to exercise the "powers of ... **a State** government in all cases where legislation is possible."

It is apparent that neither this Court nor Congress has read the Constitution as requiring every federal question arising under the federal law, or even every criminal prosecution for violating an Act of Congress, to be tried in an Art III court before a judge enjoying lifetime tenure and protection against salary reduction. Rather, both Congress and this Court have recognized that **state courts** are appropriate forums in which federal questions and federal crimes may at times be tried. Palmore v. United States, 411 US 389, 406-408 (1973)

We can see from the above opinion that the Supreme Court is reluctant to declare the status of the federal courts in the District of Columbia absent express congressional intent. This is obviously due to the special character of the District of Columbia being made up from Union States where exclusive legislative jurisdiction has been ceded. Because of this special characteristic, Congress is authorized to establish both legislative courts as well as constitutional courts. However, in order to be certain of the status of those courts, Congress must clearly express their intention by clarifying the power utilized to establish them.

The current Judiciary Act makes no declaration of congressional intent under which the current United States district court for the District of Columbia or the United States Court of Appeals for the District of Columbia Circuit were established. The Supreme Court in Palmore, *supra*, however, states that both courts are Article III courts. This is obviously contrary to what they stated in the opinion, *i.e.*, that they are reluctant to declare the status of the District of Columbia courts absent express congressional intent.

For example, 28 U.S.C. § 171(a), states that, "The court [of Federal Claims] is declared to be a court established under article I of the Constitution." To those unlearned at law, this statement seems to imply that this court is created under Article I, § 8, cl. 9, of the Constitution. As we have shown, that provision (Article I, § 8, cl. 9) is utilized to establish only article III courts and not article I courts. The source of power to create legislative courts on or for ceded lands within the several 50 Union States comes from Article I, § 8, cl. 17 (Enclave Clause), and from Article IV, § 3, cl. 2 (Property Clause) for courts in the Territories of the "United States" (Federal Government).

It should be noted that the Court of Federal Claims has no creation statute. However, Congress originally declared it to be a court established under Article III. In 1982 Congress changed its status by expressly declaring the court to be established under Article I.

The power to establish Article III courts comes from the Constitution itself, (which is the supreme Law of the Land), via Article I, § 8, cl 9, "To constitute Tribunals inferior to the supreme Court." All Congress needs to do is declare that a court is ordained and established under Article III and it immediately is. They can memorialize this in an Act of Congress and establish how many judges will sit in that court, clerks, its judicial boundaries (or geographic reach), as well as limit the subjects of jurisdiction under Article III that the court will adjudicate, *etc.*

If a territorial legislature, like Puerto Rico or even the District of Columbia, enacts legislation that creates (establishes/ constitutes) courts there, then they are not constitutional courts. If Congress itself establishes courts for these places then they are legislative (territorial) courts if established in a federal territory, like Puerto Rico. If they are established in the District of Columbia then Congress must clarify the status of those courts by declaring the constitutional authority under which they are created. I propose the possibility that the "United States district courts" currently sitting throughout the several 50 Union States are legislative courts established under Congress' Article I, § 8, cl. 17 powers to hear cases that occur on the massive amounts of federal land under their concurrent or exclusive legislative jurisdiction situated within each of the Union States.

Another possibility is that, if they are Article III courts, then the judges, acting in concert with the United States Attorneys, are purposely misconstruing the law because they believe the National Legislature ought to enjoy the right "to legislate in all cases to which the separate States are incompetent, or of which the harmony of the United States may be interrupted by the exercise of individual legislation", Carter v. Carter Coal Co., *supra* at 291-292 (1936). That is a power the Framers declined to confer upon Congress. Perhaps they are "those who wish it to be believed that man cannot be governed but by a rod of iron", The Kentucky Resolution of 1798.

Whatever the status of the courts, clearly there is something amiss. The Supreme Court has stated that, "the true test lies in the power under which the court was created and in the jurisdiction conferred", Ex Parte Bakelite Corp., 279 US 438, 458-460 (1929). Chapter 85 of Title 28 U.S.C., District Courts, Jurisdiction, lists civil, admiralty, maritime, patent, bankruptcy, *etc.*, and does not once list, mention, or describe any criminal jurisdiction whatsoever. Just as we have shown in the Federal Rules of Evidence, the Supreme Court has expressly held that:

> The term **district court of the United States** standing alone includes only the constitutional courts. Such words describe courts created under Article III of the Constitution.
>
> [T]he term 'district court' or 'district court of the United States' is commonly considered as referring to constitutional courts.

> The words 'district court of the United States' commonly describe constitutional courts created under Article III of the Constitution. <u>United States v. King</u>, 119 F. Supp. 398, 401-403 (9th Circuit, District Court, Alaska Third Division, Anchorage, 1954) (citations omitted)

The current Judiciary Act states at 28 U.S.C. § 132(a) that, "There shall be in each judicial district a district court which shall be a court of record known as the **United States district court** for the district". The Judiciary Act also states that:

> The provisions of title 28, Judiciary and Judicial Procedure, of the United States Code, set out in section 1 of this Act, with respect to the organization of each of the several courts therein provided

for ... **shall be construed as continuations of existing law.... No loss of rights, interruption of jurisdiction,** or prejudice to matters pending in any such courts on the effective date of this Act **shall result from its enactment.** 28 U.S.C., other provisions, Continuation of organization of court.

None of the Judiciary acts prior to our current Judiciary Act even mention "United States district court" as opposed to "district court of the United States." I have included the following in the Appendix: "The Judiciary Act of 1789", September 24, 1789, "An Act to establish the Judicial Courts of the United States"; "The Judiciary Act of 1801", February 13, 1801, "An Act to provide for the more convenient organization of the Courts of the United States"; "The Judiciary Act of 1802", April 29, 1802, "An Act to amend the Judicial System of the United States"; "Establishment of the U.S. Circuit Courts of Appeals", March 3, 1891, "An

Act to establish circuit courts of appeals and to define and regulate in certain cases the jurisdiction of the courts of the United States, and for other purposes"; "The Judicial Code of 1911 (excerpted)", March 3, 1911.

How exactly is the current Judiciary Act a continuation of existing law if the district courts established by it are "United States district courts" as opposed to "district courts of the United States" with no name change provision as was done for the United States Courts of Appeal? What we have here is a vague & ambiguous provision of law surrounding the establishment of our current federal district courts. We can clearly see that the term "district courts of the United States" is standing alone, without further qualification, in the Jurisdiction and Venue provision for federal crimes in Title 18 U.S.C.:

> The **district courts of the United States** shall have original jurisdiction, exclusive of the courts of the States, of all offens-

es against the laws of the United States.

Nothing in this title shall be held to take away or impair the jurisdiction of the <u>courts of the several States</u> under the laws thereof. Title 18 U.S.C. § 3231

The following legal maxims, i.e., doctrines of law (cannons of construction), state that:

Expression unius est exclusion alterius. The mention of one is the exclusion of another, *i.e.*, when certain persons or things are specified in a document, an intention to exclude all others from its operation may be inferred.

Expressum facit cessare tacitum. What is expressed makes what is silent to cease, *i.e.*, where we find an express declaration we should not resort to implication. <u>The Law Dictionary</u>, Copyright ©2002 Anderson Publishing Co.

In other words, the mention of the "district courts of the United States" as specified in 18 U.S.C. § 3231, intentionally excludes the "United States district courts", which we are not to resort to by implication. The definition of "district courts of the United States" in <u>Title 28 U.S.C. § 451</u>, which includes the term "United States district court" in that definition, does not make those courts applicable to the term "district courts of the United States" in <u>Title 18 U.S.C. § 3231</u>. *Confer*, "As used in <u>this title</u>", <u>Title 28 U.S.C. § 451</u>.

The definition of "district courts of the United States" as used in Title 28 U.S.C. § 451 also includes the "United States district court" for the territory of Puerto Rico in that definition. Congress uses both terms interchangeably throughout Title 28 U.S.C. which in and of itself, if not for the sole purpose to sow confusion, defies logic. If the term, words, or phrase "district courts of the United States", as used in Title 18 U.S.C. § 3231 included the "United States district courts" in Title 28 U.S.C., it would not have been necessary for Congress to state, "As used in this title". Congress would have presumably stated, "As used in all titles" or more easily omitted the, "As used in this title" language altogether. It is elementary that all of the words used in a legislative act are to be given force and meaning, otherwise they would be superfluous having been enough to have written the act without the words. The Supreme Court explained that:

> It is our duty to give effect, if possible, to every clause and word of a statute. [D]escribing this rule as a cardinal rule of statutory construction. [A] statute ought, upon the whole, to be so construed that, if it can be prevented, no clause, sentence, or word shall be superfluous, void, or insignificant. We are thus reluctant to treat statutory terms as surplus-

age in any setting. <u>Duncan v. Walker</u>, 533 US 167, 174 (2001)(citations omitted)

If indeed the federal district courts are legislative courts, as opposed to constitutional courts, that would mean that the judges of those courts could not lawfully render judgment against you without violating your due process rights secured under the <u>Fifth Amendment</u>, U.S. Constitution, unless the civil action or crimes (misdemeanors and felonies alike) occur on land under the concurrent or exclusive legislative (territorial) jurisdiction of the United States (Federal Government). However, this <u>would</u> allow Congress to control the court and punish felonious crimes under the guise of regulating interstate commerce, usurping the sovereignty and jurisdiction of the Union States, in a scheme that condones the exercise of an undelegated power to "punish" by the Executive branch while at the same time eliminating the Judicial branch (Article III courts) from interfering with the encroachment on the sovereignty of the several Union States and the outright violation of the People's inalienable rights.

The Supreme Court, explaining that the authority granted to legislative courts is judicial power, but is not that judicial power granted by § 1 and defined by § 2[148] of Article III of the Constitution; but rather is derived from the property clause,[149] stated that:

> [J]udicial power apart from that article [Article III, U.S. Constitution] [150] may be conferred by Congress upon legislative courts, as well as upon constitutional courts,[151] is plainly apparent from

---

[148] § = section; ¶ = paragraph.

[149] The Congress shall have Power to dispose of and make all needful Rules and Regulations respecting the Territory or other Property belonging to the United States; and nothing in this Constitution shall be so construed as to Prejudice any Claims of the United States, or of any particular State. Article IV, § 3, cl. 2

[150] my note

[151] Congress can confer jurisdiction outside of Article III on constitutional courts, ordained and established under Article III, that sit in places under their exclusive or concurrent jurisdiction within the Union States. For example, the Supreme Court for the District of Columbia was declared to be a constitutional court of the Continued on next page.

the opinion of Chief Justice Marshall in <u>American Ins. Co. v. 356 Bales of Cotton</u>, 1 Pet. 511, 546, 7 LEd 243, 256 , dealing with the territorial courts.

"The jurisdiction," he said, "with which they are invested, is <u>not</u> a part of that <u>judicial power</u> which is defined in the 3d article of the Constitution, but is conferred by Congress, in the execution of those general powers which that body possesses <u>over the territories</u> of the United States."

That is to say (1) that the courts of the territories (**and, of course, other legislative courts**) are invested with judicial power, but (2) that this power <u>is not</u> conferred

---

United States ordained and established under Article III. This was discussed at length in <u>O'Donoghue v. United States</u>, 289 US 516 (1933).

by the third article of the Constitution, but by Congress in the execution of other provisions of that instrument.

Congress cannot vest any portion of the judicial power granted by § 1 and defined by § 2 of the third article of the Constitution in courts not ordained and established by itself. <u>Williams v. United States</u>, 289 US 553, 566 (1933)

Under the property clause,[152] Congress has authority over their own Territories "or <u>other Property</u>." Congress can also, under the exclusive legislation clause,[153] "... exercise like Authority over all <u>places</u> purchased by the Consent of the Legislature of the

---

[152] <u>Article IV, § 3, cl. 2</u>

[153] <u>Article I, § 8, cl. 17</u>

State;" and also over all places where concurrent[154] or exclusive jurisdiction has been ceded.

Congress can provide for the adjudication of crimes in legislative courts if they occur on their own property within any ONE OF the Union States, where they have concurrent or exclusive jurisdiction. You have the right to be tried in a constitutional Article III court for crimes that occur on land where jurisdiction has not been ceded or relinquished to Congress through consent to purchase. This right cannot be knowingly and intelligently waived by you or your attorney on your behalf because you cannot vest jurisdiction on a court even by pleading guilty. The Supreme Court has stated that:

> [C]ases are legion holding that a party may not waive a defect in subject-matter jurisdiction or invoke federal jurisdiction simply by

---

[154] The authority of the Federal Government over their own property under a grant of concurrent jurisdiction is limited by the terms of the cession.

consent. This must be particularly so in cases in which the federal courts are entirely without Article III power to entertain the suit. <u>Pennsylvania v. Union Gas Co.</u>, 491 US 1, 26 (1989) (citing cases)

As we reviewed, all of the Judiciary Acts prior to the current one (enacted in 1948) make no mention of "United States district court" but only "district courts of the United States". The term, words, or phrase "United States district court" appears to reflect courts created in federal territories, like Puerto Rico, the Northern Mariana Islands, and Hawaii (before becoming a Union State). The Supreme Court explained that:

> The **United States district court** **is** **not** **a true United States Court established under Article III of the Constitution** to admin-

ister the judicial power of the United States therein conveyed. **It is created...under Article IV, Section 3** ... [in] making all <u>needful rules and regulations respecting the territory belonging to the United States</u>. The resemblance of its jurisdiction to that of true United States courts ... does not change its character as <u>a mere territorial court</u>. <u>Balzac v. Porto Rico</u>, 258 US 298, 312 (1921)[155]

And see, for example the Ninth Circuit, in *pari materia*[156] stating that:

---

[155] The words "Puerto Rico" were substituted on the authority of Act May 17, 1932, ch 190, 47 Sat. 158, which is classified as 48 USCS § 732a, and which designated the name of the island Porto Rico as Puerto Rico. <u>Title 48 U.S.C. § 864</u>, History; Ancillary Laws and Directives, Explanatory notes.

[156] in *pari materia*. [Latin "in the same matter"]. On the same subject; relating to the same matter. <u>Black's Law Dictionary</u>, Seventh Edition page 794.

> [T]he United States district court for the Northern Mariana Islands as a court established under Article IV of the United States Constitution, shall have the same jurisdiction as other United States district courts. Armstrong et al. v. Commonwealth, 576 F3d 950, 952 (9th Cir. 2009)

As we have reviewed, Chapter 85 of Title 28 U.S.C., District Courts, Jurisdiction, lists civil, admiralty, maritime, patent, bankruptcy, *etc.*, and does not once list, mention, or describe, any criminal jurisdiction whatsoever. To reiterate, it appears that traditionally, courts named "United States district court" are legislative courts and courts named "district court of the United States" are Article III courts. The following passage states that:

> The (then called) Supreme Court and Court of Appeals of the District of Columbia are

constitutional courts of the United States, ordained and established under article III of the Constitution ... and also **changed the name** of the Supreme Court of the District of Columbia **to "district court of the United States for the District of Columbia**." Title 28 U.S.C. § 88, District of Columbia, History, Ancillary Laws and Directives, Prior Law and revision, paragraphs 2-3.

As we can clearly see from the above passage, district courts ordained and established under Article III are constitutional courts of the United States named "district court of the United States." The following passage paints a similar picture for "United States district court" which states that:

> The <u>United States district court</u> for the <u>District</u> of Hawaii **established by and existing under title 28 of the United States Code** shall thenceforth be a <u>court of the United States</u> with judicial power <u>derived</u> from Article III, section 1, of the Constitution of the United States. <u>28 U.S.C. § 91</u>, Historical And Statutory Notes, Court of the United States; District Judges

This passage appears to be conveying that the "United States district court" for the District of Hawaii is a constitutional "court of the United States" with Article III jurisdiction. I first turn your attention to the fact that the passage states that the court is "established by and existing under title 28 of the United States Code", the same as the court for Puerto Rico. It does <u>not</u> specify that the court is "ordained & established under Article III". Second, the reference that the court "shall thenceforth be a court of the United States" is technically correct even if it is not a constitutional court "ordained & established" under Article III. In Title 28 U.S.C. it states that:

> As used in <u>this</u> title:
>
> The term "court of the United States" includes the Supreme Court of the United States, courts of appeals, district courts constituted by chapter 5 of this title [28 USCS §§ 81 *et seq.*], including the Court of International Trade and **<u>any court created by Act of Congress</u> the judges of which are entitled to hold office during good behavior**.
>
> The terms "district court" and "district court of the United States" means the courts consti-

tuted[157] by chapter 5 of this title [28 USCS §§ 81 *et seq.*]. Title 28 U.S.C. § 451.

What Congress has done in Title 28 U.S.C.[158] is redefine the terms "court of the United States" and "district court of the United States" to include not only courts created under Article III, but also legislative courts created under Article I, and Article IV.[159] For example, the "United States district court" for Puerto Rico. Prior to Hawaii becoming a Union State, "The courts in Hawaii and Puerto Rico [were defined as] district courts of the United States under definitive section 451 of this title." 28 U.S.C. § 753, History; Ancillary Laws and Directives, Prior law and revision. Bankruptcy courts are not included in that provision because their judges are only "appointed for a term of

---

[157] Constitute. Archaic: CONSTITUTED, ESTABLISHED. Webster's Third New International Dictionary, unabridged (1981), page 486.

[158] See "As used in this title." 28 U.S.C. & 451.

[159] Legislative courts within the Union States are all established under the Enclave Clause (Article I, & 8, cl. 17), and legislative courts in the territories (territorial courts) are established under the Property Clause (Article IV, & 3, cl. 2).

fourteen years," 28 U.S.C. § 152 (a)(1). Addressing this very issue, the Ninth Circuit explained that:

> Long before 1932 ... the phrase "court of the United States" had been given a definite and restricted meaning by the Supreme Court. The phrase, without more, means solely courts created by Congress under Article III of the Constitution and not territorial courts. International L. & W. U. v. Wirtz, 170 F2d 183, 185 (9th Cir. 1948)

Clearly the phrase "court of the United States" can be viewed in the name "district court of the United States for the northern district of California" as opposed to "United States district court," for example.

The following Supreme Court case concerning a writ of *habeas corpus*[160] states that it:

> ...issued October 2, 1895, by the **district court of the United States for the northern district of California**. <u>United States v.</u>

---

[160] *Habeas corpus*. Latin. (You have the body.) The name given to a variety of writs (of which these were anciently the emphatic words), having for their object to bring a party before a court or judge. In common usage, and whenever these words are used alone, they are usually understood to mean the *habeas corpus ad subjiciendum* (see *infra*). <u>United States ex rel Bilokumsky v. Tod</u>, 263 US 149, 158 (1923). The primary function of the writ is to release from unlawful imprisonment. The office of the writ is not to determine prisoner's guilt or innocence, and only issue which it presents is whether prisoner is restrained of his liberty by due process.

A form of collateral attack. An independent proceeding instituted to determine whether a defendant is being unlawfully deprived of his or her liberty. It is not an appropriate proceeding for appeal-like review of discretionary decisions of a lower court. For federal *habeas corpus* procedures, see 28 U.S.C.A. § 2241 et seq. <u>Black's Law Dictionary</u>, Sixth Edition, page 708.

Habeas corpus ad subjiciendum. A writ directed to the person detaining another, and commanding him to produce the body of the prisoner, or person detained. This is the most common form of *habeas corpus* writ, the purpose of which is to test the legality of the detention or imprisonment; not whether he is guilty or innocent. This writ is guaranteed by U.S. Const. Art. I, § 9, and by state Constitutions. <u>Black's Law Dictionary</u>, Sixth Edition, page 709.

Wong Kim Ark, 169 US 690 (1898)

As we have shown, Congress has redefined the term "court of the United States" which, standing alone in a statute without further qualification, means only constitutional courts created under Article III.[161] As the Ninth Circuit explained:

> Congress, when it intends to include territorial courts in the phrase "court of the United States" does so expressly. International L. & W. U. v. Wirtz, supra at 186

Even though Congress has included territorial (legislative) courts in the definition of "court of the United

---

[161] See American Ins. Co. v. 356 Bales of Cotton, 1 Pet 511, 546, 7 Led 242 (1828); and many other cases summarized in McAllister v. United States, 141 US 174, 183 (1890).

States," this does not make them constitutional Article III courts. The Supreme Court has stated that:

> Doubtless, the courts of a territory are not, strictly speaking, courts of the United States. <u>United States v. McMillan</u>, 165 US 504 (1897)

In fact, the following passages from the <u>Federal Rules of Criminal Procedure</u>, show us that territorial courts are named "United States district court" which are legislative courts:

> paragraph 6, Hawaii- Hawaii has a dual system of courts. <u>The United States district court</u> for the Territory of Hawaii, <u>a legislative court</u>, has the jurisdiction of district courts of the United States.

paragraph 9, Canal Zone- In the Canal Zone there is a United States district court for the Canal Zone, a legislative court. FRCrP, Rule 54, [Transferred], History, Ancillary Laws and Directives, Other Provisions, Notes of Advisory Committee on Rules.

In fairness, the previous passages are referring to territorial courts which are always legislative courts. However, we can clearly see the connection the references make between "United States district courts" and federal territories.

Now there is another passage from that section I want to mention that is meant to confuse us. It is paragraph 7, Puerto Rico, which states that, "Puerto Rico has a dual, system of courts. The "District Court of the United States" for Puerto Rico, a legislative court, has jurisdiction of all cases cognizable in the district courts of the United States and proceeds 'In the same manner,' 48 U.S.C. § 863." There never was an Article III "District Court of the United States" for Puerto Rico. It has always been a "legislative" court and is a "District Court of the United States" in name only.[162] This is because Congress is not authorized under the Constitution to establish Article III Courts in the Territories, like Puerto Rico, because that Article (III) is not applicable to the Territories. Courts in the Territories are created under Article IV § 3, cl. 2; unlike the "district court of the United States for the District of Columbia," which was an Article III court. As we have reviewed, Congress can establish Article III Courts there because the District of Columbia is made up from Union States. The First Circuit explained that:

> The courts of the United States are those Congress is authorized to establish under article 3, § 1, of the Constitution of the United

---

[162] The "United States district court for the District of Puerto Rico" was substituted for "District Court of the United States for Puerto Rico" on the authority of Act June 25, 1948, ch 646, § 1, **62 Statute 895**, which appears as **28 USCS §§ 132(a)** and 119, and which provide respectively, that there shall be a district court of record in each judicial district known as the United States district court for that district and that Puerto Rico shall comprise one judicial district. Title 48 U.S.C. § 864, History; Ancillary Laws and Directives, Explanatory notes.

States, and by section 2 of that article ... whereas the federal District Court for Puerto Rico is <u>not</u> a court of the United States, but <u>a legislative court created under article 4, § 3, cl. 2</u> of the Constitution. <u>Sanfeliz v. Bank of Nova Scotia</u>, 74 F2d 338 (1st Cir. 1934)

The purpose of a court's name containing the phrase "court of the United States" was supposed to inform us that the court was established under Article III. For example, the former "circuit courts of the United States" were established under Article III. These were the courts of Appeal, hence the name "<u>circuit court of the United States.</u>" They are not our current courts of Appeal. The "circuit courts of Appeal" were established by § 2 of the Act of March 3, 1891, 26 Statutes at Large 826, chap. 517.[163]

---

[163] <u>Textile Mills Sec. Corp. v. Comr. Of Int. Rev.</u>, 314 US 326 (1941). See also <u>United States v. Stone & D. Co.</u>, 274 US 225, Continued on next page.

"In 1911, Congress abolished the circuit courts of the United States."[164] The Judicial Code (Act of March 3, 1911, chap. 231, 36 Statutes at Large 1087), accomplished this. Next, the 3rd section of the then twenty year old Act of March 3, 1891, made the circuit judges "competent to sit as judges of the circuit courts

---

232 (1927) (By the Act of [March 3], 1891, creating circuit courts of appeal (26 Stat. at L. 826, chap. 517, § 6))

The circuit court of appeals is a constitutional court under the definition of such courts as given in the Bakelite Corp. Case, *supra*, and a case or controversy may come before it, provided it involves neither advisory nor executive action by it. Old Colony Trust Co. v. Commissioner of Int. Rev., 279 US 716, 724 (1929) However, the Bakelite case does not specify the status of the circuit courts of appeal. Instead, it recognizes that there is a difference between "whether [a] court is a statutory or constitutional court." Ex Parte Bakelite Corp., 279 US 438, 456 (1929) Fifteen years later the Supreme Court states that:

The circuit courts of appeal are creatures of statute. No original jurisdiction has been conferred on them. "... courts created by statute must look to the statute as the warrant for their authority; certainly they cannot go beyond the statute, and assert an authority with which they may not be invested by it, or which may be clearly denied to them." This circuit has never departed from the view that circuit courts of appeal are statutory courts having no original jurisdiction but only appellate jurisdiction. Hazel-Atlas Glass Co. v. Hartford-Empire Co., 322 US 238, 258 (1944)

Again, four years later, the Supreme Court states that, "The Circuit Courts of Appeal are statutory courts and must look to a statutory basis for any jurisdiction they exercise. Price v. Johnston, 334 US 266, 300 (1948)

[164] Jett v. Dallas Ind. School Dist., 491 US 701, 730 (1989)

of appeals within their respective circuits."[165] In other words, the judges of the "circuit courts of the United States" became ex officio[166] judges of the respective "circuit courts of appeals" when the "circuit courts of the United States" were abolished. Lastly, in 1948 the names of the "circuit courts of Appeal" were changed to the current "United States Courts of Appeal" that we all know today.[167]

To paraphrase, the Article III "circuit courts of the United States" were in existence since shortly after the U.S. Constitution was adopted and ratified. In the year 1891, Congress created the "circuit courts of Appeal." Twenty years later, in 1911, Congress abolished the "circuit courts of the United States." A provision of the 1891 act (then 20 years old) made the

---

[165] Textile Mills Sec. Corp. v. Comr. of Int. Rev, *supra*.

[166] ex officio. By virtue or because of an office <the Vice President serves ex officio as president of the Senate>. Webster's Ninth New Collegiate Dictionary (1991), page 435.

[167] Act June 25, 1948, ch 646, § 2 (b), 62 Stat. 869, provided that each of the circuit court of appeals should, after Sept. 1, 1948, be known as a "United States Court of Appeals", but that the enactment of act June 25, 1948, should in no way entail any loss of rights, interruption of jurisdiction, or prejudice to matters pending in any such courts on Sept. 1, 1948. Title 28 U.S.C. § 43, History; Ancillary Laws and Directives, Other provisions: Change of name of court.

judges of the recently abolished "circuit courts of the United States" judges of the "circuit courts of Appeal." Then, in 1948, Congress changed the name of the "circuit courts of Appeal" to "United States Courts of Appeal." The Constitution does vest Congress with authority to establish Article III appellate courts although not immediately obvious. See <u>Article III, § 2, cl. 2</u>, "In all the other Cases before mentioned, the supreme Court shall have appellate jurisdiction, both as to Law and Fact, with such Exceptions, and under such Regulations as the Congress shall make." One such exception could be that an inferior Article III court must first review the case before proceeding to the Supreme Court on Appeal.

Unlike the Article III "circuit courts of the United States," Congress never expressly abolished the Article III "district courts of the United States." Instead, in 1948, Congress enacted <u>Title 28 U.S.C.</u> which created a "United States district court" in each of the judicial districts. These courts then took over the functions of the Article III "district courts of the United States" which are currently vacant. The obvious reason Congress did not expressly abolish the former "district courts of the United States" is because the

Federal Government is purporting that the current "United States district courts" are those courts. If Congress were to have expressly abolished the "district courts of the United States," as they did the former "Circuit Courts of the United States," it would be prima facie evidence to the layman that the two courts are not the same courts. More deceptively, the "United States district courts" were quietly slipped in and then assumed the role of the Article III "district courts of the United States," and all right under the noses of the Union States. Remember, the Federal Rules of Evidence clearly utilize the words, term, or phrase "United States district courts" in several passages. They then state that, "These various provisions do not in terms describe the same courts." They then go on to explain that the phrase "district courts of the United States," without further qualification, traditionally includes only district courts established in the Union States under Article III, which are constitutional courts, and has not included legislative courts.

The last paragraph describing the "United States district court" for the Judicial District of Hawaii (28 U.S.C. § 91), states that its judicial power is derived from Article III, section 1, of the Constitution. It appears from this passage that the court is a constitutional Article III court although there is no mention that it is "ordained & established" under Article III as opposed to "established by and existing under title 28 of the United States Code." There is also no similar provision regarding the other "United States district courts." The presumption proffered is that the "United States district courts" established within the several 50 Union States are Article III constitutional courts. It is apparent that the Supreme Court in Palmore, *supra*, is assuming the same regarding the "United States district court" and the "United States Court of Appeals" for the District of Columbia. We already know that it is impossible for the "United States district court" for the Judicial District of Puerto Rico to be an Article III court, although Congress has included it in the definition of "Court of the United States" and "district court of the United States" as used in Title 28 U.S.C. and defined at section 451.

The current Judiciary Act is the first and only Judiciary Act to establish "United States district courts" in the Union States. Every Judiciary Act prior to the current one established "district courts of the United

States" and only within the Union States. With the exception of the current Judiciary Act, "United States district courts" were traditionally created by either congressional legislation establishing a Federal Territory, by legislation later enacted by Congress, or the legislature of and for a particular Federal Territory. Our current Judiciary Act creates "United States district courts" for not only Federal Territories, but also the several 50 Union States.

Even if the "United States district courts" in the Union States are constitutional courts "ordained & established" under Article III, of which there is no proof that they are, unless we consider the location where they sit as the only possible proof (which is not proof positive), this does not explain the difference in the "phraseology" of the two distinctly different terms describing the courts as continuations of existing law, *i.e.*, "United States district courts" and "district courts of the United States."

Obviously Congress could have established "district courts of the United States" instead of "United States district courts." This would have rendered it unnecessary to define the "United States district courts" as "district courts of the United States" at 28 U.S.C. § 451, which also limits those definitions to that particular title of the United States Code by stating "as used in this Title." Congress could have then easily defined the term "district court of the United States," as used in Title 28 U.S.C., to include the Article III "district courts" established in each of the judicial districts and the "United States district court" for either the Judicial District of Columbia, Puerto Rico, or both. Provided, however, that section 132 stated that:

> There shall be in each judicial district, except the judicial district of Puerto Rico, a district court of the United States which shall be a court of record ordained & established under Article III.

Congress could add the Judicial District of Columbia to that exception if they did not wish to establish an Article III "district court of the United

States" there. Can you see how much simpler that would have been? Can you see how it would have also resolved the statutory ambiguity surrounding the two courts? Especially as this ambiguity relates to the criminal jurisdiction statute at 18 U.S.C. § 3231. Obviously Congress could have amended the Judiciary Act codified in Title 28 U.S.C. to establish Article III "district courts of the United States". However, they have not done so, even after more than 65 years. The purpose of the "United States district courts" is clear. This was not some mistake or accident, this was done purposefully.

It is reasonable to draw the conclusion that this was done to cover something up. I am going to go out on a limb here and state that the reason was to usurp the sovereignty and jurisdiction of the Union States by exercising an undelegated power to "punish" under the guise of regulating "interstate commerce." It is much easier for Congress to control judges who are dependent on their will than those who are free from control and domination of the other branches of government, because the latter receive constitutional guarantees of lifetime tenure and undiminishable salary, as opposed to statutory grants of these benefits, which are not guaranteed.

The proposition just offered should really come as no surprise when we consider it. It appears there has always been an attempt to control the courts. This is no stretch of the imagination considering Thomas Jefferson and James Madison stated, via the Kentucky Resolutions and Virginia Resolution, that as early as 1798 the Federal Government was already attempting to enlarge its powers beyond the limits imposed upon them by the Constitution. That is only 11 years after its ratification. Not to mention the Thomas Jefferson letters stating that they soon learned how the courts would be the most dangerous, sapping the foundations of the Constitution, by declaring what the law is *ad libitum* (at pleasure). How far do you think the Federal Government has been able to enlarge their powers beyond the limits imposed upon them by the Constitution after 227 years, more than two centuries—especially when the People no longer understand the Constitution (our Supreme Law) and the limits imposed on the Federal Government under it? How about as far as punishing felonies under the guise of regulating interstate commerce?

In order to alleviate any doubt as to the true status of our current "United States district courts" as either legislative or constitutional courts, I would like to present for your consideration the Federal Rules of Criminal Procedure which limit the reach of not only felonious "interstate commerce" violations, but also misdemeanor "interstate commerce" violations, to lands under the concurrent or exclusive legislative jurisdiction of the "United States" (Federal Government). Although the limitation to punish felonious "interstate commerce" violations is proof that no such power exists under the Constitution to do so within the several 50 Union States, the key here is the limitation to punish misdemeanor violations affecting "interstate commerce." If the "United States district courts" were Article III constitutional courts then they would be able to adjudicate misdemeanor cases occurring within the legislative (territorial) jurisdiction of the several 50 Union States pursuant to any of the enumerated powers delegated to them, regardless of the absence of the punishing power or cession of jurisdiction. This is explained in detail further into this Manifesto. Under Title 18 U.S.C.

> The district courts of the United States shall have original jurisdiction, exclusive of the courts of the States, of all offenses against the laws of the United States.
>
> Nothing in this title shall be held to take away or impair the jurisdiction of the courts of the several States under the laws thereof. Title 18 U.S.C. § 3231

Remember what the Supreme Court stated in Mookini?[168] "We have often held that vesting a territorial court with jurisdiction similar to that vested in the District Courts of the United States does not make it a 'District Court of the United States.'" The definition of "district court of the United States," in Title 28 U.S.C. § 451, which includes not only the "United States district courts" in the Union States but also the undeniably legislative "United States district court" for the Judicial District of Puerto Rico in that definition,

---
[168] Mookini v. United States, 303 US 201, 205 (1938)

does not make those courts applicable to the term "district court of the United States" in 18 U.S.C. § 3231, which term, standing alone, and without further qualification, commonly describes only the constitutional courts established under Article III. *Confer*, "As used in this title," Title 28 U.S.C. § 451. This is clearly another obfuscation attempt by Congress to fraudulently conceal the Article III "district courts of the United States," and to create the false impression that they have been re-defined as, replaced by, and/ or rendered synonymous with, the "United States district courts."

It is axiomatic that the term "district courts of the United States", as used in 18 U.S.C. § 3231, is referring to constitutional courts "ordained & established" under Article III. The term "courts of the States" is referring to not only legislative courts in the Union States, but also those on federal property under the concurrent or exclusive legislative (territorial) jurisdiction of the Federal Government within them, like the District of Columbia, for example, and those within federal territories, like Puerto Rico. The term "courts of the several States" includes every non-federal Union State Court within each of the several 50 Union States. The Supreme Court explained that:

> [U]ntil 1875 Congress refrained from providing the lower federal courts with general federal question jurisdiction. Until that time, the **state courts** provided the only forum for vindicating many important federal claims. Even then, with exceptions, the state courts remained the sole forum for trial of federal cases not involving the required jurisdictional amount, and for the most part retained concurrent jurisdiction of federal claims properly within the jurisdiction of the lower federal courts.
>
> It was neither the legislative nor judicial view, therefore, that trial and decision of all federal questions were reserved for Art III

judges. Nor, more particularly, has the enforcement of federal criminal law been deemed the exclusive province of federal Art III courts. **Very early in our history, Congress left the enforcement of selected federal criminal laws to <u>state courts</u>** and to state court judges who did not enjoy the protections prescribed for federal judges in Art III. <u>Palmore v. United States</u>, 411 US 389, 410-411 (1973)

We can clearly see from this Supreme Court opinion that at one time Union State courts were adjudicating certain federal civil and criminal cases that occurred within each of their particular legislative (territorial) jurisdictions. Keep in mind, however, that all of the Union States today, except the original thirteen, were at one time federal territories. Therefore, it was not necessary for Congress to provide Article III courts rather than legislative courts. That said, I would like to elaborate further regarding the term "district courts of the United States" as used in the jurisdiction provision at 18 U.S.C. § 3231. I would also like to propose for your consideration the possibility that the current "United States district courts" are, in reality, the legislative "courts of the States" in that same provision. The Fifth Circuit, citing the Supreme Court and the Ninth Circuit, regarding the rules of statutory construction, stated that:

> In construing statutes, words are to be given their natural, plain, ordinary and commonly understood meaning unless it is clear that some other meaning was intended, and where Congress has carefully employed a term in one place and excluded it in another, it should not be implied where excluded.
>
> By the same reasoning, words in statutes should not be discarded as "meaningless" and "surplus-

age" when Congress specifically and expressly included them, particularly where words are excluded in other sections of the same act. United States v. Wong Kim Bo, 472 F2d 720, 722 (5th Cir., 1972)

As we reviewed, the term "district courts of the United States" is standing alone in 18 U.S.C. § 3231, without further qualification and, as such, historically describes constitutional courts created under Article III. Since that term is not qualified further by definition to specifically include any of the "United States district courts," that silence compels us to adopt the ordinary and commonly understood meaning of that term, phrase, or those words. The Supreme Court, in *pari materia*, explained that:

> The term "interest" is not specifically defined in the RICO statute. This silence compels us to "start

with the assumption that the legislative purpose is expressed by the ordinary meaning of the words used." Russelio v. United States, 464 US 16, 21 (1983)(citation omitted)

As we have shown, the term "district courts of the United States", as used in the criminal jurisdiction statute (18 U.S.C. § 3231), can only be given its ordinary meaning because "United States district courts" are clearly not included in that term. Because Congress has not defined the term "district courts of the United States" at 18 U.S.C. § 3231 to include "United States district courts," as was done for Title 28 U.S.C. § 451, see, "As used in this title", those courts cannot be made applicable to that particular provision of Title 18 U.S.C. Confer, United States v. King, *supra*, "This title, as used in said section 451, must refer to Title 28." The Supreme Court's views regarding the "Rule of Lenity" as a cannon of statutory construction, states that:

> If the legislative intent is unclear, doubt will be resolved in favor of the defendant. In this context, the rule of lenity may be no more than a restatement of the ancient maxim that criminal statutes are to be strictly construed.
>
> [T]he court has frequently emphasized, the touchstone of the rule of lenity is statutory ambiguity. <u>Supreme Court Annotations</u>, 62 LEd2d 827, Rule of Lenity

A point that should be clarified further is the fact that the government will purport the term, words, or phrase "district court<u>s</u> of the United States" is the plural for "United States district court." Not only is this untrue, it is not even proper English grammar. In fact they are two very different courts. This cannot be overemphasized. The following cannon of construction prevents the commingling of the Article III "constitutional" "district court<u>s</u> of the United States"

[sic], with the, "United States district court<u>s</u>" [sic]. This rule of statutory construction states that:

> In determining <u>any</u> Act of Congress, unless the context indicates otherwise—words importing the singular include and apply to several persons, parties, or things; words importing the plural include the singular. <u>Title 1 U.S.C. § 1</u>, Rules of Construction, Words denoting number, gender, and so forth.

In other words, the singular words "United States district court" include several "United States district court<u>s</u>" and the singular words "district <u>court</u> of the United States" include several "district court<u>s</u> of the United States." Likewise, the plural words "United States district court<u>s</u>" include the singular "United States district court" and the plural words "district court<u>s</u> of the United States" include the singular "district court of the United States." Therefore we see two phrases for each court. The singular and plural for the "United States district court(s)" and the singular and plural for the Article III "district court(s) of the United States".

The proper plural for "United States district court" is located in several places.[169] Please note three of

---

[169] United States district court<u>s</u>. Federal Rules of Criminal Procedure ("FRCrP"), Rule 1(a)(1); and Federal Rules of Evidence ("FREv"), Rule 1101, Applicability of Rules, notes of Advisory Committee on Rules, paragraphs 1, 3, and 5.

Title 26 U.S.C. § 7402, Jurisdiction of district courts:

(a) To issue orders, processes, and judgments. The **district courts of the United States** at the instance of the United States shall have such jurisdiction to make and issue in civil actions, writs and orders of injunction, and of *ne exeat republica*, orders appointing receivers, and such other orders and processes, and to render such judgments and decrees as may be necessary or appropriate for the enforcement of the internal revenue laws. The remedies hereby provided are in addition to and not exclusive of any and all other remedies of the United States in such courts or otherwise to enforce such laws.

(b) To enforce summons. If any person is summoned under the internal revenue laws to appear, to testify, or to produce books, papers, or other data, the **district court of the United States** for the district in which such a person resides or may be found shall have jurisdiction by appropriate process to compel such attendance, testimony, or production of books, papers, or other data.

(c) For damages to United States officers or employees. Any officer or employee of the United States acting under authority of this title, or any person acting under or by authority of any such officer or employee, receiving any injury to his person or property
Continued on next page.

the four phrases in the following statute, Title 26 U.S.C. § 7402, which shows the singular words "district court of the United States," the plural words "district courts of the United States," and the plural words "United States district courts," all in the same statute which makes my Manifesto's point clear. The Supreme Court clearly explained that:

---

in the discharge of his duty shall be entitled to maintain an action for damages therefor, in the **district court of the United States**, in the district wherein the party doing the injury may reside or shall be found.

(d) Repealed

(e) To quiet title. The **United States district courts** shall have jurisdiction of any action brought by the United States to quiet title to property if the title claimed by the United States to such property was derived from enforcement of a lien under this title.

(f) General jurisdiction. For general jurisdiction of the **district courts of the United States** in civil actions involving internal revenue, see section 1340 of title 28 of the United States Code.

---

ne exeat republica. [Latin "let him not go out of the republic"]. A writ restraining a person from leaving the republic. A chancery writ ordering the person to whom it is addressed not to leave the jurisdiction of the court or the state. Ne exeat writs—no longer widely used—are usu. issued to ensure the satisfaction of a claim against the defendant.—Often shortened to ne exeat.— Also termed writ of ne exeat; ne exeat regno. Black's Law Dictionary, Seventh Edition, page 1,054.

260

> It is well settled that where Congress includes particular language in one section of a statute but omits it in another section of the same Act, it is generally presumed that Congress acts intentionally and purposely in the disparate inclusion or exclusion. <u>Duncan v. Walker</u>, 533 US 167, 173 (2001)(citing cases)

Several statutes in the Act of June 25, 1948, Title 18 of the United States Code, entitled "Crimes and Criminal Procedure", include either the term "district court of the United States", "United States district court", or both. I list the following as examples:

§ 156,	"United States district court"
§ 216,	"United States district court"
§ 402,	"district court of the United States"
§ 1965,	"district court of the United States"
§ 2076,	Clerk of United States district court,

	"district court of the United States"
§ 3231,	"district court of the United States"
§ 3511(a)(c),	"United States district court"
	"district court of the United States"

It is a well established rule that statutes conferring jurisdiction on federal courts are to be strictly construed and doubts are resolved against federal jurisdiction. See Russell v. New Amsterdamm Casualty Co., 325 F2d 996, 998 (8th Cir., 1964); Phillips v. Osborne, 403 F2d 826, 828 (9th Cir., 1968); General Atomic Co. v. United Nuclear Corp., 655 F2d 968, 968-69 (9th Cir., 1981), cert. denied, 455 US 948 (1982); F&S Construction Co. v. Jenson, 337 F2d 160, 161 (10th Cir., 1964).

Because the term, phrase, or words, "district courts of the United States" have been specifically and expressly employed in the criminal jurisdiction statute (18 U.S.C. § 3231), and are excluded in other sections of the same Act (Title 18 U.S.C.), as listed above, that term, phrase, or those words, should not be discarded as "meaningless" and "surplusage". Since the term, phrase, or words, "United States district courts" have been excluded from 18 U.S.C. § 3231, yet have been explicitly included in other statutes of Title 18 U.S.C., as previously shown, they should not be implied where excluded. *Confer* <u>United States v. Wong Kim Bo</u>, *supra*. This follows our strict statutory construction rule.

We can clearly see that creating "United States district courts", as opposed to "district courts of the United States", has caused an onslaught of statutory ambiguity. For example, 18 U.S.C. § 3006A(j) states that, "As used in this section, the term 'district court' means each <u>district court of the United States</u>, created by chapter 5 of title 28 [28 USCS §§ 81 et seq.]...." As we have reviewed, 28 U.S.C. § 132 creates a "United States district court" in each judicial district, <u>not</u> a "district court of the United States". Congress has simply redefined the term "district court of the United States" at 28 U.S.C. § 451 to mean the "United States district courts" created by section 132 as those terms are used in Title 28 U.S.C. When Congress wishes to include legislative (territorial) courts, like the "United States district court" for the Judicial District of

Puerto Rico, for example, in the phrase "district court of the United States" they do so expressly. *Confer*, International L. W. U. v. Wirtz, *supra* at 186.

I believe the reason for all of the statutory ambiguity is clear, and that reason is to usurp the sovereignty and jurisdiction of the Union States by exercising an undelegated power to "punish" under the guise of regulating interstate commerce. Clearly the power to "punish" is not enumerated under the Interstate Commerce Clause, which proves that power is not delegated there.

Keeping that in mind, I would like to draw your attention to the fact that 18 U.S.C. § 3006A admits that "each" court is "created by chapter 5 of title 28 [28 USCS § 81 et seq.]." This simply means they are created by the statutes codified there naming the judicial districts via section 132. If Congress were to establish a new judicial district, anywhere in the world, section 132 of Title 28 U.S.C. would immediately create a "United States district court" within it. *Confer*, "legislative court," *supra*, *i.e.*, "A court created by a statute." Black's Law Dictionary, Eighth Edition, page 382. The Supreme Court explained that:

[O]ther articles invest Congress with powers in the exertion of which it may create inferior courts and clothe them with functions deemed essential or helpful in carrying those powers into execution. But there is a difference between the <u>two classes of courts</u>. Those established under the specific power given in § 1 of article 3 are called constitutional courts. They share in the exercise of the judicial power defined in that section, can be invested with no other jurisdiction, and have judges who hold Office during good behavior, with no power in Congress to provide otherwise. On the other hand, those created by Congress in the exertion of other powers are called <u>legislative courts</u>. Their functions always are directed to the execution of one or more of such powers and are prescribed by Congress independently of § 2 of article 3; and their judges hold for such term as Congress prescribes, whether it be a fixed period of years or during good behavior. Ex Parte Bakelite Corp., 279 US 438, 449 (1929)

Deprivation of Article III courts and the right to adjudication before the Judges thereof with protections from that article are significant and cannot be overstated. Common sense tells us that if there were no significant difference in the courts Congress established it would have not been done at all. Congress would not have had to redefine the term, or words, "district court of the United States" to mean "United States district court" and then commingle those two very different terms throughout the United States Code if they were in truth and in fact one and the same court. The very fact that Congress has gone through all of this trouble invites suspicion because it defies logic and common sense. Common sense tells me that the reason it was done was to make us believe the two very different courts are the same court. More precisely, it was done to make us believe that the "United States district courts" are constitutional courts "ordained & established" under Article III. We know they are not because no name change provision has been provided as was done for the "Circuit Courts of Appeal," now the "United States Courts of Appeal."

However, the fact that Congress created "Circuit Courts of Appeal" in 1891 to replace the Article III "circuit courts of the United States," which they expressly abolished twenty years later in 1911, invites suspicion in and of itself. If the constitutional "circuit courts of the United States" were hearing appeals from the Article III "district courts of the United States," as the Judiciary Acts reveal, why did Congress go through all of this trouble to replace them? One reason we can entertain is that the Article III "circuit courts of the United States" were also hearing original jurisdiction cases, the same as the Article III "district courts of the United States" did. Therefore cases adjudicated originally in the "circuit courts of the United States" were going directly to the Supreme Court on appeal. The excuse given is the Supreme Court's docket was becoming increasingly backed-up.

That excuse does not rest well with me since Congress could have easily redefined the jurisdiction of the Article III "circuit courts of the United States" to hear only appeals from the Article III "district courts of the United States", thus removing their original jurisdiction to hear cases instead of creating new and completely different courts altogether.

Another reason is that, if the purpose was to usurp the sovereignty and jurisdiction of the Union States, by exercising an undelegated power to "punish" felonious crimes under the guise of regulating interstate commerce, and case law reveals that it started between 1895 and 1903, then Congress would first have to replace the Article III appellate courts with legislative appellate courts before replacing the Article III district courts with legislative district courts. This is because, if the Article III district courts were replaced with legislative district courts first, the Article III appellate courts would overturn those cases on appeal for lack of subject-matter jurisdiction.

That is another issue I will not delve into deeper in this Manifesto. It does provide a very interesting and thought provoking topic for debate since Congress went to all the trouble to create the "Circuit Courts of Appeal," now "United States Courts of Appeal," and since they are created in the same manner as our current "United States district courts". Taking all of the aforementioned into consideration, the Supreme Court opined in 1948 (the same year our current Judiciary Act was enacted into positive law) that:

> The Circuit Courts of Appeal are statutory courts and must look to a statutory basis for any jurisdiction they exercise. Price v. Johnson, 334 US 266, 300 (1948)

In the year 1976 the Supreme Court reiterated that, "The courts of appeals are statutory courts", Taylor v. McKeithen, 407 US 191, 195 (1976); and that:

[Mr. Chief Justice Burger]

> [C]ircuit courts of appeal were authorized in the Judiciary Act of [February 13,] 1801, [2 Statute 89]; however, after the election of Thomas Jefferson, that statute was repealed the following year. [N]early a century passed before such courts were finally created [o]n [March 3,] 1891, [26 Statute 826]; they exist today as the <u>United States Courts of Appeals</u> for the 11 Circuits. <u>Brown Transport Corp. v Atcon, Inc.</u>, 439 US 1014 (1978)(Mr. Justice White, with whom Mr. Justice Blackmun joins, dissenting from the denial of certiorari)

The Supreme Court is clearly informing us that the "Circuit Courts of Appeal," which are now our current "United States Courts of Appeal," are "statutory" courts. However, the Supreme Court at one time stated in the year 1929 that, "The circuit court of appeals is a constitutional court." Old Colony Trust Co., supra at 724 (citing Bakelite Corp., 279 US 438 (1929)). In Bakelite the Supreme Court recognized that there is a difference between "whether [a] court is a statutory court or a constitutional court." Id. at 456. Fifteen years later the Supreme Court states that "circuit courts of appeal are statutory courts," Hazel-Atlas Glass, supra at 258. Four years later the Supreme Court reiterates that, "The Circuit Courts of Appeal are statutory courts," Price v. Johnston, supra at 300. It is apparent that we have conflicting Supreme Court opinions surrounding the status of our current "United States Courts of Appeal" with the majority of those opinions stating that the "United States Courts of Appeal" are "statutory courts". The following Supreme Court opinion provides fuel for the proposition and debate that the "United States Courts of Appeal" are legislative courts by clearly relating "statutory" courts to Territorial Courts, as opposed to "constitutional courts," in reference to the appointment of judges, stating that:

judges of Territorial (<u>statutory</u>) courts; judges of the Supreme Court and Court of Appeals for the District of Columbia (<u>statutory courts</u>), appointed to serve "during good behavior" .... circuit and district (constitutional) courts. <u>Myers v. United States</u>, 272 US 52, 181-182 (1926)(The separate opinion of Mr. Justice McReynolds)

Notwithstanding the aforementioned documentation, in the year 1911 the judges of the Article III "circuit courts of the United States" were made ex officio judges of the then twenty year old "Circuit Courts of Appeal". It should not escape our notice that, in 1913, two years after the constitutional "circuit courts of the United States" were abolished, the Federal Reserve and I.R.S. were created. That same year Congress ratified the Sixteenth Amendment giving them power to tax the citizenry's income from whatever source derived. Twenty years later, in 1933,

Congress declared bankruptcy and converted our lawful gold & silver monetary system to the unconstitutional fiat monetary system we are under today. See House Joint Resolution (H.J.R.) 192.

Of major significance is the fact that, since the enactment of our current Judiciary Act, people are being continuously found guilty of Federal crimes they are not guilty of committing, and/ or of which the current "United States district courts" have no authority to adjudicate. For example, "interstate commerce" and "firearms" crimes. I know how that sounds at first blush, but for a law to be effective, jurisdiction must exist. The Supreme Court explained that, "Jurisdiction is power to declare the law, and when it ceases to exist, the only function remaining to the [tribunal] is that of announcing the fact and dismissing the cause," and that, "[W]ithout jurisdiction the court cannot proceed at all in any cause."[170] As the Article III "circuit court of

---

[170] Union Specific R.R. v. Brotherhood, 175 Led2d 428, 445 (2009), citing Steele Co. v. Citizens for Better Env., 523 US 83, 94 (1998), quoting Ex parte McCardle, 7 Wall 506, 514 74 US 506 (1869); see also Ruhrgas AG v. Marathon Oil Co., 526 US 574, 577 (1999)

the United States" for the District of Massachusetts stated:

> A question has been made by the learned counsel for prisoner, as to the jurisdiction of the court. This is, in its nature, a <u>preliminary</u> question; for if the court have not jurisdiction of the offense alleged in the indictment, it would be superfluous to proceed in the inquiry relative to the guilt or innocence of the prisoner. The objection rests on the terms of the <u>cession</u>, by the commonwealth to the United States, of the ground occupied for a navy yard. <u>United States v. Travers</u>, 28 F.Cas 204 (1814)

Legislative courts (non Article III courts) have no subject-matter jurisdiction over offenses that occur outside of Federal Territories or other property under the concurrent or exclusive jurisdiction of the Federal Government. Article III courts, on the other hand, are simply authorized to take jurisdiction of the subject-matter. They extend the judicial power of the United States to all cases and controversies arising under the Constitution and Laws of the United States occurring within the several Union States, including the high seas. This, of course, is qualified by the limitations on the powers granted contained in the Constitution. As the Supreme Court recently stated, "[A] law beyond the power of Congress, for any reason, is no law at all." <u>Carol Anne Bond v. United States</u>, 131 SCt 2355 (2011)(internal quotation marks omitted). Keeping that in mind, the Supreme Court has stated that:

> A Judiciary free from control by the Executive and the Legislative is <u>essential</u> if there is a right to have claims decided by judges who are free from potential domination by other branches of

government. <u>United States v. Will</u>, 449 US 200, 217-18 (1980).

We cannot be free from control of the Executive and Legislative branches of the Federal Government, <u>if</u> the courts we are being prosecuted in are legislative courts (non Article III courts), and the prosecutor is from the Executive branch of the Federal Government. The union of legislative and judicial powers is pronounced to be, in the words of Mr. Madison, "The very definition of tyranny," Federalist No. 47; or as Thomas Jefferson says, "Precisely the definition of a despotic government." (Notes on Virginia, 195).

The Supreme Court established the general principle that parties to a case or controversy in a federal forum are <u>entitled</u> to have the cause determined by judges with salary and tenure guarantees under Article III. The <u>Marathon</u> Court cataloged three limited exceptions to that general principle: territorial courts, military tribunals, and "public rights" cases.[171]

In cases involving a criminal defendant, Article III protections should be most zealously regarded because individual liberty is at stake and the Legislative and Executive branches are currently making **federal** criminals of people who have committed no federal crimes. Justice Douglas of the Supreme Court, in a dissenting opinion, emphasized this important function of Article III when he wrote:

> The safeguards accorded Art. III judges were designed to protect litigants with unpopular or minority cases or litigants who belong to despised or suspect classes; Kurland, The Constitution and the Tenure of Federal Judges: some notes from History, 36 U. Chi. L. Rev. 665, 698 (1969) (life tenure

---

[171] Northern Pipeline Constr. Co. v. Marathon Pipeline Co., 458 US 50, 64-70 (1982)

of Federal judges "not created for the benefit of the judges but for the benefit of the judged"). Palmore v. United States, 411 US 389, 412 (1973).

The Ninth Circuit, enunciating that non-Article III judges can prosecute criminal cases under Article I, § 8, cl. 17, stated that:

> "When Congress legislates with respect to the District of Columbia and federal enclaves it acts as a state government with all powers of a state government." See id.; Paul v. United States, 371 US 245, 263 (1963)
>
> In Palmore,[172] the Supreme Court established "whether a defendant charged with a felony under the

---

[172] United States v. Palmore, 411 US 389, 390-91 (1973)

District of Columbia Code may be tried by a judge who does not have protection with respect to tenure and salary under Art. III of the Constitution." Id. at 390. The Court held that under clause 17 Congress could provide that such a defendant be tried before a non-Article III judge [a judge who does not have protection with respect to tenure and salary under Art. III of the Constitution].[173] Id. at 390-391.[174]

---

[173] my note

[174] It is also true that throughout our History, Congress has exercised its power under Art IV to "make all needful Rules and Regulations respecting the Territory or other Property belonging to the United States" by creating territorial courts and manning them with judges appointed for a term of years. These courts have not been deemed subject to the strictures of Art III, even though they characteristically enforced not only the civil and criminal laws of Congress applicable throughout the United States [lands under the concurrent or exclusive jurisdiction of the Federal Government], but also the laws applicable only within the boundaries of the particular territory. United States v. Palmore, 411 US 389, 402-403 (1973). An example of "laws applicable only within the boundaries of [a] particular territory" are the laws of Puerto Rico. The Laws of Puerto Rico cannot be Continued on next page.

[C]lause 17 does not distinguish between the District of Columbia and other federal enclaves. See Paul v. United States, 371 US at 263 ("The power of Congress over federal enclaves that come within the scope of Art. I, § 8, cl. 17, is obviously the same as the power of Congress over the District of Columbia"). Under clause 17 Congress acts as a State government with total legislative, executive and judicial power. Palmore, 411 US at 397.

Thus, the requirements of Article III are consistent with the establishment by Congress of **non-Article III courts to enforce federal criminal laws in special geographic areas where, pur-**

---

lawfully applied to land owned by the United States, under their concurrent or exclusive legislative jurisdiction.

suant to clause 17, it functions as a state government.

See Marathon Pipe Line Co., 102 SCt at 2874 (emphasizing Congress' unique power under Article I, § 8, cl. 17, to legislate in certain geographic areas).

Did you notice that under Article I, § 8, cl. 17, Congress operates as a "State" government with all the same powers that they can exercise within the District of Columbia and their own territories not yet Union States? Now do you understand why the definition of "State" in the Federal Rules of Criminal Procedure, Rule 1(b)(9), does not list any of the several 50 Union States? And that under positive law at Title 28 U.S.C. § 2072(b), "All laws in conflict with such rules shall be of no further force or effect after such rules have taken effect"? It is because "commerce ... is regulated by prescribing rules"[175] and the Constitution does not

---

[175] Commerce, undoubtedly ... is regulated by prescribing rules for carrying on that intercourse.

Continued on next page.

delegate the power to "punish" felonies under the commerce clause. This also explains why the alleged legislative "United States district courts" are sitting throughout the several 50 Union States instead of Article III "district courts of the United States." The presumption, as I have previously stated earlier in this Manifesto, is that the alleged felonious "interstate commerce" crime has occurred on Federal land under the concurrent or exclusive jurisdiction of Congress. If it has not occurred on such land there is no felonious federal crime. Only the Union State could prosecute such crimes—if they have so legislated.

This conspiracy to usurp the sovereignty and jurisdiction of the Union States, the Tenth Amendment to the U.S. Constitution, and your rights secured under it, was a well thought out and executed plan with its implementation taking 57 years (between 1891 to 1948). We can only speculate who the real criminals were that started us down this destructive path, but there is no question as to who perpetuates this tyran-

---

What is this power? It is the power to regulate; that is, to prescribe the rule by which commerce is to be governed. Gibbons v. Ogden, 9 Wheat 1, 189-190, 196 (1824) (Chief Justice Marshall)

ny by denying nearly every appeal and petition for redress of grievances a convicted "felon" submits. The Eighth Circuit explained that:

> [T]he existence of a criminal conspiracy or a defendant's participation in that scheme need not be proven by direct evidence. "A fraudulent scheme ... may be and usually is established by circumstantial evidence; by inferences from the evidence of relationship of the parties and by overt acts, conduct and other probative circumstances."
>
> Moreover, once the government has established the existence of a conspiracy, even slight evidence connecting a particular defendant to the conspiracy may be substantial and therefore sufficient proof of the defendant's involvement in the scheme.

> If a defendant's participation in a conspiracy has been established, then the defendant is culpable for everything said, written or done by any of the other conspirators in furtherance of the common purpose of the conspiracy.
>
> Even if the defendant joined the conspiracy subsequent to its original formation, he may be held responsible for acts committed by other conspirators in furtherance of the conspiracy before he joined it. <u>United States v. Overshon</u>, 494 F2d 894, 895-896 (CA8, 1974) (citations omitted)

Obviously if Article III "district courts of the United States" were still in place along with the alleged legislative "United States district courts," we would already all know their differences and why. In order to pull off the subterfuge, both courts could not exist at the same time. This usurpation of the sovereignty and jurisdiction of the Union States was all done in order to prosecute felonies under the guise of regulating "interstate commerce." This of course is big business, siphoning capital away from the Union States, making them weak, dependent, and inferior while making the Federal Government strong, independent, and superior by milking the tax-payers of $6.6 billion every year just to house 219,000 federal inmates for 1 year. This number grows by 6,000 inmates per year[176] and does not include the costs of investigations, prosecutions, public defender appointments for the indigent, grand

---

[176] In an article written by Walter Pavlo for Forbes, it stated that there are currently 219,000 federal inmates growing at a rate of over 6,000 per year. That while state prison populations have declined, mostly due to budget concerns, the federal inmate population continues to grow each year. More inmates mean more dollars. In 1980 there were 25,000 federal inmates [and 10,000 B.O.P. employees], and the Bureau of Prisons had an annual budget of about $330 million. Today's inmate population of 219,000 inmates [and over 36,000 B.O.P. employees], requires a budget of $6.6 billion per year [$6,600,000,000.00 dollars]. There is no parole with prisoners receiving only 54 days of good conduct time which begins after their first year. According to FedCure.org chairman Mark Varca, if the Congress would change (amend) the 54 days/ year to 128 days/year, it would save the U.S. government [and taxpayers] $1.2 billion per year [$1,200,000,000.00 dollars]. See also Federal Register, Volume 80, No. 45, Monday, March 9, 2015, Notices, page 12523, Department of Justice, Bureau of Prisons, Annual Determination of Average Cost of Incarceration, stating that, "The fee to cover the average cost of incarceration for Federal inmates in Fiscal Year 2014 was $30,619.85 ($83.89 per day)".

jury proceedings, jury trials, or transportation of prisoners by bus and plane (which requires expensive jet fuel). Notably, the Union States could be keeping and utilizing for themselves all of the drug money and other tangible property confiscated from lawful prosecutions for job employment and other budget concerns. According to the Bureau of National Affairs ("BNA") Criminal Law Reporter, Vol. 98, No. 10, the Department of Justice ("DOJ") collected more than $23 Billion dollars in civil and criminal cases in Fiscal Year 2015 alone.

Worth mentioning is the fact that most of the Federal inmates are non-violent offenders serving more time than many violent criminals and murderers are doing in the Union States. Even though it should be void for vagueness, Congress has written the law to reach a constitutional end, it is simply that the Federal United States Attorneys and Federal Courts are not following it. They are parasites feeding off the People's ignorance of the law. The Supreme Court has explicitly stated that:

Even if punishment of the "guilty" were society's highest value—and procedural safeguards denigrated to this end—in a Constitution that a majority of the Members of this Court would prefer, that is not the ordering of priorities under the Constitution forged by the Framers, and this Court's sworn duty is to uphold that Constitution and not frame its own. The procedural safeguards mandated in the Framers' Constitution are not admonitions to be tolerated only to the extent they serve functional purposes that ensure that the "guilty" are punished and the "innocent" freed; rather; every guarantee enshrined in the Constitution, our basic charter and the guarantor of our most precious liberties, is by it endowed with an independent vitality and value, and this

Court is not free to curtail those constitutional guarantees even to punish the most obviously guilty. To sanction disrespect and disregard for the Constitution in the name of protecting society from lawbreakers is to make the government itself lawless and to subvert those values upon which our ultimate freedom and liberty depend. [I]t is "a less evil that some criminals should escape than that the Government should play an ignoble part." Stone v. Powell, 428 US 465, 523 (1976)

It is apparent that the Supreme Court of the United States is also involved in this conspiracy to deprive us of our rights under the Constitution. It is unimaginable that the Supreme Court is unaware of the fact that alleged legislative "United States district courts" are sitting throughout the Union States as opposed to Article III "district courts of the United States." In fact, the Supreme Court, in what can only be described as a brazen effort to deceive the people, attempted to conceal the Article III "district courts of the United States" by fraudulently conveying that they have been replaced by, are the same as, or have been rendered synonymous with "United States district courts," by recently, and purposefully misquoting another Supreme Court decision standing for 75 years:

> Moreover, we do not read the designation statute without regard for the "historic significance" of the term "United States district court" used in Title 28. Mookini v. United States, 303 US 201, 205 (1938). "[W]ithout an addition expressing a wider connotation," that term ordinarily excludes Article IV territorial courts, even when their jurisdiction is similar to that of a United States district court created under Article III.

Ibid. Nguyen v. United States, 539 US 69, 76 (2003).

Now compare what the Mookini case really stated:

> The term "**District Court of the United States**," as used in the rules, without an addition expressing a wider connotation, has its historic significance. It describes the constitutional courts created under article 3 of the Constitution. Courts of the Territories are legislative courts properly speaking, and are not District Courts of the United States. We have often held that vesting a territorial court with jurisdiction similar to that vested in the District Courts of the United States does not make it a "District

Court of the United States." Mookini v. United States, 303 US 201, 205 (1938)

Did you notice the Supreme Court in Mookini refers to the "historic significance" of the term "District Court of the United States" which describes Article 3 courts? The Supreme Court in Nguyen intentionally misquoted Mookini referring instead to the "historic significance" of the term "United States district court" blatantly putting forth the fraud that the "United States district courts" are the former "district courts of the United States" created under Article III. Congress has also legislated, by subterfuge, in order to put forth the deception that legislative "United States district courts" [sic], are Article III courts, under the Bankruptcy Courts provision in Title 28 U.S.C., which states that:

> Bankruptcy judges shall serve as judicial officers of the United States district court established

under Article III of the Constitution. 28 U.S.C. § 152 (a) (1)

Obviously the bankruptcy judges in the federal Territories are not serving in Article III, United States district courts. Again, Congress has zero authority to establish Article III courts in federal Territories because they are <u>not</u> Union States. This is why Article III <u>does not</u> apply to those geographic land areas (places). The power of Congress to establish courts in the Territories comes from the Property Clause (Article IV, § 3, cl. 2). It can come from no other source (such as Article I, § 8, cl. 9). Period!

There are also old Supreme Court decisions, which, in my opinion have either been altered to make it appear that the "district courts of the United States" and the "United States district courts" are one and the same or the latter term was coined by a judge in the early days of our Republic. They do this by referring back and forth to allegedly the same court, which in and of itself defies logic and common sense. Whatever the truth is, whether the term "United States district court" [sic] was fabricated to perpetuate the fraud & treason we currently face or not, that term does <u>not</u> appear in <u>any</u> of the judiciary acts until 1948, our current judiciary act. For example, the following Supreme Court opinion continuously refers back and forth between the two distinctly different terms, stating that:

> Thus it will be seen that this record or proceeding in the State Court, was introduced into the <u>United States district court</u> by D'Arbel himself, as the grounds upon which he claimed a right to have his cause tried in a court of the United States. It was therefore evidence offered by him originally in the <u>District Court of the United States</u>, and it does not lie with him now to say that that record was not duly authenticated, when introduced by him into the <u>United States district court</u>. This record, as offered to the Circuit Court on the trial of this

cause, came from the <u>District Court of the United States</u>, and the proceedings and oath relied upon, were then introduced by D'Arbel himself. <u>Urtetegui v. D'Arbel</u> *et al.*, 9 LEd 276, 9 Peters 692. (1835)

To reiterate, the first 100 years of Judiciary Acts do not even mention "United States district courts" and consistently refer to "district courts of the United States" only, thereby proving the "United States district courts" are not, and never were, the same court, *i.e.*, "district courts of the United States" created under Article III. This is furthered by the fact that the Supreme Court for the District of Columbia's name was changed to "district court of the United States" for the District of Columbia in order to reflect its status as a constitutional court of the United States "ordained and established" under Article III, as we showed earlier. Common sense also tells us that Congress would not, and did not, ordain and establish "United States district courts" under Article III and create others under Articles I & IV, and then refer to the ones created under Article III as "district courts of the United States" to help everyone else figure it out.

Even if it were true that there once were "United States district courts" ordained & established under Article III (which none of the Judiciary Acts reflect), it is clear that all of the "United States district courts" existing today are created by the statutes naming the Judicial Districts via the statute currently codified at Title 28 U.S.C. § 132, *i.e.*, chapter 5 of title 28 [28 USCS §§ 81, et seq.]. It is impossible for the U.S. Attorneys to prove otherwise. There is absolutely no proof available in the law for them to utilize to prove the current "United States district courts" are "ordained & established" under Article III or that they are the former constitutional "district courts of the United States", which burden of proof is on them as the asserter that jurisdiction exists. The presumption is against jurisdiction until positive proof appears in the record and doubts are resolved against it. To reiterate:

> Federal courts are courts of limited jurisdiction. They possess

only that power authorized by Constitution and statute, which is not to be expanded by judicial decree. It is to be presumed that a cause lies outside this limited jurisdiction and the burden of establishing the contrary rests upon the party asserting jurisdiction. <u>Kokkonen v. Guardian Life Ins. Co.</u>, 511 US 375, 377 (1994)

Utilizing a "follow the money" approach, we can draw a very reasonable conclusion that the ones responsible for this subterfuge are those who stand to directly benefit from it, *i.e.*, Congress, the U.S. Attorneys, and other legislative and executive branch employees. Again, <u>none</u> of the "United States district courts" are the former Article III "district courts of the United States". Obviously the term, or phrase, "United States district court(s)" is <u>not</u> the term, or phrase, "district court(s) of the United States" which, standing alone, and without further qualification, describes <u>only</u> constitutional courts created under Article III.

This is prima facie evidence that the Supreme Court has been corrupted, is not upholding the Constitution, and is conspiring with the Legislative and Executive Branches of the Federal Government to deprive us of our great inalienable rights secured under it. In essence, the 3 branches of the Federal Government (Legislative, Executive, and Judicial), have combined together, joining forces to usurp the sovereignty and jurisdiction of the several 50 Union States in violation of the <u>Tenth Amendment</u>, and several other provisions of the Constitution, with blatant disregard for the Supreme Law of the Land, their sworn oaths to uphold it, and our vital rights secured under it. They provide nothing more than lip service to the public when in reality their hearts are far from the Constitution.

We are now a Nation ruled by Democracy instead of a constitutional Democratic-Republic. A democracy is where the vote of half plus one can quash the rights of all the rest, but in a democratic-republic the majority cannot take away the inalienable rights of anyone. The Constitution mandates that:

> The United States shall guarantee to every State in this Union a Republican Form of Government, and shall protect each of them against Invasion. Article IV, § 4, U.S. Constitution

How, exactly, is the United States protecting the Union States from invasion when they are the ones doing the invading? How can we rely on decisions of the Supreme Court when those decisions can be ignored at will and there is no remedy under the law? If the doctrine of stare decisis has any meaning at all, it requires that people in their everyday affairs be able to rely on decisions of the U.S. Supreme Court and not be needlessly penalized for such reliance. United States v. Mason, 412 US 391, 399-400 (1973).

THE JUDGES

Although Congress has included a lifetime tenure during good behavior provision in Title 28 U.S.C. for judges of the "United States district courts", this does not indicate that guarantee comes from Article III, nor does it indicate that the courts are Article III courts. That guarantee also applies to the territorial "United States district court" for the Judicial District of Puerto Rico. The Supreme Court has stated that:

> The view that courts in the territories are legislative courts, as distinguished from courts of the United States, [is not] weakened by the circumstance that Congress, in a few of the Acts providing for territorial courts, fixed the terms of the office of the judges of those courts during "good behavior." McAllister v. United States, 141 US 174, 184-185 (1891)

Confer Title 28 U.S.C. § 134(a), Tenure and Residence of district judges, "The district judges shall hold office during good behavior." Repeal that statute and the district judge's tenure during good behavior is no longer "guaranteed" unless the court is a constitutional court "ordained & established" under Article III. The judicial power of the United States under Article III is vested in courts established under that Article.

In creating the district courts, Congress provided (28 U.S.C. § 132): "There shall be in each judicial district a district court..." and "the judicial power of a district court ... may be exercised by a single judge...." This last provision should be noticed; it is fundamental that a district judge has no judicial power individually; his power is exercised as the representative of a court. "Jurisdiction is lodged in a court, not in a person. The judge, exercising the jurisdiction, acts for the court."[177] United States v. Roberts, 618 F2d 530, 546 (9th Cir. 1979)(Wyatt, Senior District Judge, dissenting)

See Article III, § 1, U.S. Constitution:

The judicial Power of the United States, shall be vested ... in such inferior Courts as the Congress may from time to time ordain and establish. The Judges ... of the ... inferior Courts, shall hold their Offices during good Behavior...

---

[177] In re Brown, 346 F2d 903, 910 (5th Cir. 1965), quoted with approval in United States v. Teresi, 484 F2d 894, 898 (7th Cir. 1973)

Even though Circuit and United States district court judges are appointed by the President, by and with the advice and consent of the Senate, like Supreme Court Justices, such Presidential appointments do <u>not</u> make them Article III judges or mean that the courts to which they are appointed are Article III courts. The Constitution states that the President:

> ...shall nominate, and by and with the Advice and Consent of the Senate, shall appoint ... Judges of the supreme Court, and all other Officers of the United States, whose Appointments are not herein provided for, and which by Law vest the Appointment of such inferior Officers, as they think proper, in the President alone, in the Courts of Law, or in the Heads of Departments. <u>Article II, § 2, cl. 2</u>, U.S. Constitution

The following statutes vest the President with power to appoint Circuit Judges and "United States district court" Judges:

> The President shall appoint, by and with the advice and consent of the Senate, circuit judges for the several circuits. Title 28 U.S.C. § 44(a), Appointment, tenure, residence and salary of circuit judges.
>
> The President shall appoint, by and with the advice and consent of the Senate, district judges for the several judicial districts. Title 28 U.S.C. § 133(a), Appointment and number of district judges.

This appointment of district judges also includes the appointment of judges to the "United States district court" for the judicial district of Puerto Rico (a legislative/ territorial court). As the Supreme Court explained:

> The judges of the Supreme Court of the Territory are appointed by the President under Act of Congress, but this does not make the courts they are authorized to hold courts of the United States [Article III courts]. McAllister v. United States, 141 US 174, 182 (1891)

The Supreme Court has stated that legislative court "... judges hold for such term as Congress prescribes, whether it be a fixed period of years or during good behavior."[178] The Ninth Circuit has also opined that:

---

[178] Ex Parte Bakelite Corp., 279 US 438, 449 (1929)

The Supreme Court has recognized that Congress may establish "legislative courts" whose judges <u>do not</u> enjoy Article III guarantees. Such courts have been upheld when <u>their jurisdiction is limited to the territories</u>, to local matters arising in the District of Columbia, and to limited subject matter. The Court has indicated, however, that "inherently judicial" tasks <u>must</u> be performed by Article III judges. <u>United States v. Saunders</u>, 641 F2d 659, 663 (CA9, 1980)(citing cases)

Like the "United States district court" judges, Congress has established a similar tenure provision for judges of the "Court of International Trade" at <u>Title 28</u>

U.S.C. § 252.[179] I believe this has been done to sow confusion. That court is an Article III court. The immediate thought that comes to mind is that if Congress has provided a lifetime tenure provision for the Article III Court of International Trade then the "United States district courts" must be Article III courts also, because they have a lifetime tenure provision during good behavior. This, of course, would mean that the "United States district court" for the judicial district of Puerto Rico is an Article III court also, which we already know is not. The Supreme Court explained that Congress has previously assigned jurisdiction "to tribunal[s] having every appearance of a court and composed of judges enjoying statutory assurances of life tenure and undiminished compensation." Gliddon v. Zdanok, 370 US 530, 550 (1962)

Likewise, Congress has provided a lifetime tenure during good behavior provision for the "United States Courts of Appeal" Title 28 U.S.C. § 44(b), "Circuit judges shall hold their office during good behavior."

---

[179] Title 28 U.S.C. § 252, "Judges of the Court of International trade shall hold office during good behavior."

Unlike legislative "United States district courts," for example, Puerto Rico, the repeal of the Court of International Trade's tenure provision would not affect the judges thereof. This is so because, "The Court is a court established under article III of the Constitution of the United States."[180] The Court of International Trade has no creation statute. Instead, Congress surreptitiously inserted this information in with the "Appointment and number of judges; offices" provision.

It should be noted that no such tenure provision is provided for the Supreme Court of the United States, which is obviously an Article III court.[181] The information that the Court of International Trade is an Article III court is enough to inform anyone that its judges have lifetime tenure and salary protections under that Article.

---

[180] Title 28 U.S.C. § 251(a), Appointment and number of judges; offices, "The President shall appoint, by and with the advice and consent of the Senate, nine judges who shall constitute a court of record to be known as the United States Court of International Trade. Not more than five of such judges shall be from the same political party. **The court is a court established under article III of the Constitution of the United States."**

[181] Title 28 U.S.C., Chapter 1, Supreme Court.

We can clearly see that the Supreme Court has not resisted encroachment on the Judicial Branch by the Legislative Branch because they continuously render opinions on cases that come before them from the lower district courts with no jurisdiction over the subject-matter. The Supreme Court continuously fails to take notice "*sua-sponte*" of the lower courts lack-of jurisdiction over the subject-matter and subsequently their own lack-of jurisdiction to decide the merits of the case. Every single opinion rendered by the Supreme Court from the federal district and appellate courts throughout the Union States where the felonious "interstate commerce crime" did not occur on land under the concurrent or exclusive jurisdiction of the United States (Federal Government) is null and void for lack-of jurisdiction over the subject-matter. Remember, the Supreme Court stated that:

> When the lower federal court lacks jurisdiction, we have jurisdiction on appeal, not of the merits but merely for the purpose of correcting the error of the low-

er court in entertaining the suit. Steel Co. v. Citizens for Better Env., 523 US 83, 89-101 (1998)

It appears the reason a tenure provision was provided for the Court of International Trade may have been to mislead us concerning the true status of the "United States district courts" and the "United States Courts of Appeal".

It should be clear by now that legislative courts are <u>not</u> constitutional courts. Their authority in criminal cases is <u>limited</u> to the territories or other property belonging to the United States wherein they have sovereignty. They cannot adjudicate criminal cases, whether misdemeanors or felonies, that occur outside of these places, regardless of where the power to punish is delegated in the Constitution. Within the boundaries of the several 50 Union States this authority is limited to land (places) wherein jurisdiction has been <u>ceded</u> through consent to purchase or cession. Although they are given jurisdiction similar to that of courts established (created) under Article III, this does not make them "constitutional" "courts of the United States."[182]

On the other hand, courts established under Article III are "constitutional" "courts of the United States" vested with the judicial Power of the United States. They can adjudicate felony and misdemeanor criminal

---

[182] These courts, then, are not constitutional courts, in which the judicial power conferred by the Constitution can be deposited. They are incapable of receiving it. They are legislative courts, created in virtue of the general right of sovereignty which exists in the government, or by virtue of that clause which enables Congress to make all needful rules and regulations respecting the territory belonging to the United States. The jurisdiction with which they are invested is not a part of that judicial power which is defined in the third article of the Constitution, but is conferred by Congress, in the execution of those general powers which that body possesses over the Territories of the United States. In legislating for them, Congress exercises the combined powers of the general and of a state government.

[T]he distinction between the federal and state jurisdictions, under the Constitution of the United States, has no foundation in these territorial governments; that "they are legislative governments, and their courts legislative courts, Congress, in the exercise of its powers in the organization and government of the Territories, combining the powers of both the federal and state authorities." Again, after citing the judicial clause of the Constitution (art.3, sec.1), the court said: "Congress must not only ordain and establish inferior courts within a State, and prescribe their jurisdiction, but the judges appointed to administer them must possess the constitutional tenure of office before they can become invested with any portion of the judicial power of the Union. There is no exception to this rule in the Constitution." McAllister v. United States, 141 US 174, 181-183 (1891.

cases where the power to punish has been delegated in the Constitution and also under Article I, § 8, cl. 17. They can also adjudicate misdemeanor criminal cases where the alleged activity has some relation to a delegated power (even where the power to punish has not been delegated or jurisdiction ceded). Obviously if a legislative court is overseeing the prosecution of criminal cases it cannot extend the judicial power under Article III to any of those cases. Do you understand the danger of comingling legislative, executive, and judicial powers? The Framers of Our Constitution did. This is what they had to say:

> The accumulation of all powers, legislative, executive, and judiciary, in the same hands, whether of one, a few, or many, and whether hereditary, self-appointed, or elective, may justly be pronounced <u>the very definition of tyranny</u>.
>
> [I]t may be clearly inferred that in saying, "There can be no liberty

where the legislative and executive powers are united in the same person, or body of magistrates," or, "if the power of judging be not separated from the legislative and executive powers."

[W]here the whole power of one department is exercised by the same hands which possess the whole power of another department, the fundamental principles of a free constitution are subverted.

"When the legislative and executive powers are united in the same person or body," ... "there can be no liberty, because apprehensions may arise lest the same monarch or senate should enact tyrannical laws to execute them in a tyrannical manner." Again: **"Were the power of judging joined with the legisla-**

tive, the life and liberty of the subject would be exposed to arbitrary control, <u>for the judge would then be the legislator</u>. Were it joined to the executive power, the judge might behave with all the violence of an oppressor." <u>The Federalist Papers</u>, No. 47.

The Supreme Court has also opined that:

> The federal judicial power, then, must be exercised by judges who are independent of the Executive and the Legislature in order to maintain the checks and balances that are crucial to our constitutional structure.
>
> The Framers also understood that a principle benefit of the separation of the judicial power

from the legislative and executive powers would be the protection of individual litigants from decision makers susceptible to majoritarian pressures. <u>Northern Pipeline Co. v. Marathon Pipeline Co.</u>, 458 US 50, 57-58 (1982)

A judge wielding judicial power in a legislative court with an Executive branch officer prosecuting criminal cases is completely arbitrary, capricious, oppressive, [183] and the very definition of tyranny. It

---

[183] Arbitrary. Not done or acting according to reason or judgment; depending on the will alone; absolutely in power; capriciously; tyrannical; despotic. <u>Black's Law Dictionary</u>, Sixth Edition, page 104.

Arbitrary and capricious. Characterization of a decision or action taken by an administrative agency or inferior court meaning willful and unreasonable action without consideration or in disregard of facts or law or without determining principle. <u>Black's Law Dictionary</u>, Sixth Edition, page 105.

Arbitrary power. Power to act according to one's own will. <u>Black's Law Dictionary</u>, Sixth Edition, page 105.

Despotism. That abuse of government where the sovereign power is not divided, but united and unlimited in the hands of a single man, whatever may be his official title. It is not, properly, a form of government.

Continued on next page.

appears that our constitutional form of government has been, and still is currently being, stolen from us in clandestine[184] style. The 219,000 current Federal inmates, those who have already served their time in prison, and those who are currently being indicted and prosecuted for alleged felonious "interstate com-

---

"Despotism" is not exactly synonymous with "autocracy," for the former involves the idea of tyranny or abuse of power, which is not necessarily implied by the latter. Every despotism is autocratic; but an autocracy is not necessarily despotic. Black's Law Dictionary, Sixth Edition, page 448.

Autocracy. The name of an unlimited monarchical government. A government at the will of one man (called an "autocrat"), unchecked by constitutional restrictions or limitations. Black's Law Dictionary, Sixth Edition, page 134.

Oppression. The misdemeanor committed by a public officer, who under color of his office, wrongfully inflicts upon any person any bodily harm, imprisonment, or other injury. An act of cruelty, severity, unlawful exaction, or excessive use of authority. An act of subjecting to cruel and unjust hardship; an act of domination. Black's Law Dictionary, Sixth Edition, page 1,093.

Oppressor. A public officer who unlawfully uses his authority by way of oppression. Black's Law Dictionary, Sixth Edition, page 1,093.

Tyranny. Arbitrary or despotic government; the severe and autocratic exercise of sovereign power, either vested constitutionally in one ruler, or usurped by him by breaking down the division and distribution of governmental powers. Black's Law Dictionary, Sixth Edition, page 1,519.

[184] Clandestine. Secret, hidden, concealed; usually for some illegal or illicit purpose. For example, a clandestine marriage is one contracted without observing the conditions precedent prescribed by law, such as publication of banns, procuring a license, or the like. Black's Law Dictionary, Sixth Edition, page 248.

merce" crimes, are the collective victims of this treachery.

HOW IT'S DONE

Congress has established a total of 13 Circuits and numerous judicial districts throughout each of the Union States. As we have shown, statutes codified in Title 28 U.S.C., create a United States Court of Appeals and a "United States district court", in each Circuit and judicial district. Of major significance is the fact that the judicial districts throughout the Union States are <u>not</u> the same as the judicial District of Columbia or the judicial district of Puerto Rico, because Congress does <u>not</u> have exclusive jurisdiction[185] over all the land within the Union States like they do over the District of Columbia and Puerto Rico. The District of Columbia was <u>ceded</u> by Maryland and Virginia to Congress under the Constitution and Puerto Rico is a territory not admitted as a Union State.

I can only speculate that Congress created these judicial districts in order to more easily identify places

---

[185] Exclusive jurisdiction. That power which a court or other tribunal exercises over an action or over a person to the exclusion of all other courts. That forum in which an action must be commenced because no other forum has the jurisdiction to hear and determine the action. <u>Black's Law Dictionary</u>, Sixth Edition, page 564.

(land) where a federal crime is committed. This also enabled Congress to establish limits on the geographical boundaries applicable to each "United States district court" in civil actions and criminal cases wholly within those judicial districts. In other words, the "United States district" being places within a judicial district under their exclusive or concurrent jurisdiction (territorial jurisdiction). However, only Article III "district courts of the United States" are authorized under the Constitution to extend the judicial power of the United States to civil controversies and criminal cases occurring within any judicial district where jurisdiction has not been obtained through consent to purchase or cession.

It is apparent that the establishment of these judicial districts only helped to further the ruse[186] that Congress has nationwide jurisdiction to punish felonies under the commerce clause when they do not. Take, for example, drug crimes. There is nothing stopping a Union State from criminalizing the transportation of drugs in or out of its territory. Instead, the

---

[186] ruse. A wily subterfuge. Syn See TRICK. Webster's Ninth New Collegiate Dictionary (1991), page 1,032.

Union States have criminalized drug possession and sales. We do not need the Federal (Central) Government to police the entire country, under the guise of regulating interstate commerce, because criminals are capable of committing a felonious crime in one Union State and then escaping into another Union State. The Framers never delegated such a power to the Federal Government. Instead, the Constitution provides that:

> A person charged in any State with Treason, Felony, or other Crime, who shall flee from Justice, and be found in another State, shall on demand of the executive Authority of the State from which he fled, be delivered up, to be removed to the State having jurisdiction of the Crime. Article IV, § 2, cl. 2, U.S. Constitution.

In order to pull off the fraud that Congress can punish felonies under the guise of regulating interstate commerce, the United States Attorneys indict as if the entire judicial districts in each of the Union States were actually under the exclusive or concurrent jurisdiction of the Federal Government. We know they are not because they do not own all the land within each of the judicial districts. They also insist that there is an implied power to "punish" under the commerce clause and can be utilized as necessary and proper to the execution of not only that power but all of their powers. That is not merely subterfuge but, rather, malicious fraud.

KEY CONSTITUTIONAL & LOGICAL PROOF

The following paragraph clearly and logically illustrates undisputable constitutional proof beyond any reasonable doubt that felonies cannot be punished as necessary and proper pursuant to any enumerated power where the power to "punish" is not delegated (enumerated). With this passage we can more easily understand the relationship between the "Necessary and Proper Clause" and the "Property Clause" that Chief Justice Marshall was referring to in McCulloch

v. Maryland, supra. Because the Constitution does not authorize Congress to "punish", as necessary and proper, murders (or other felonies) that occur on federal land without cession of jurisdiction, we can clearly see the lack of authority to punish felonies, as necessary and proper, pursuant to other enumerated powers (such as the Commerce Clause, etc.), that occur on or over land (places) absent cession of jurisdiction to the "United States" (Federal Government) by the particular Union State.

To reiterate, if the Necessary and Proper Clause, or the power to regulate, allowed Congress to provide for the punishment of felonies by implication (because we can clearly see that the power to punish is not enumerated there, which proves it is not delegated), then it would not be essential for the Union States to cede legislative (territorial) jurisdiction over land owned by the "United States" (Federal Government), or consent to its purchase, under Article I, § 8, cl. 17, since under the Property Clause Congress is authorized to "make all needful Rules and Regulations respecting the Territory or other Property" belonging to them. The erroneous construction of the Constitution presently being construed by the courts pursuant to the Commerce Clause power to <u>regulate</u>, would also mean that under the Property Clause Congress could feloniously punish as necessary and proper any crime they wished, like murder for example, without the need for concurrent or exclusive legislative (territorial) jurisdiction to be ceded. It would also not be necessary for Congress to specify that the crime of murder must occur "within the special maritime and territorial jurisdiction of the United States." See <u>18 U.S.C. §§ 1111, 1112</u>, murder and manslaughter, respectively. Two excellent cases supporting this proposition of law are <u>United States v. Tully</u>, 140 F. 899 (9th Cir. September 23, 1905) [Circuit Court, D. Montana]; and <u>United States v. Watkins</u>, 22 F2d 437 (U.S.D.C., N.D. California, S.D., October 18, 1927).

In <u>Tully</u>, a man who had committed murder on federal land was released because the court found that the Federal Government had not obtained jurisdiction over the parcel of land where the homicide was committed. The right to punish the felonious crime, therefore, resided with the state.

In <u>Watkins</u>, a man who had committed murder on federal land was convicted, the court finding that jurisdiction over the parcel of land where the homicide was committed had been obtained by the Federal Government. The right to punish the felonious crime, therefore, resided the "United States (Federal Government).

See also <u>Adams v. United States</u>, 319 US 312 (1943), unless and until notice and acceptance of jurisdiction has been given, Federal courts are without jurisdiction to punish under criminal laws of the United States an act committed on lands acquired by the United States, as provided by 40 U.S.C. § 3112 (former 40 U.S.C. § 255).

It cannot be stressed enough that ALL of Title 18 U.S.C. is written to occur within the special maritime and territorial jurisdiction of the United States (Federal Government), unless a statute clearly conveys that it is meant to apply extra-territorially (which must be supported by a constitutional foundation, such as the power to "punish"). This is why the "United States" is defined in a "territorial sense" at 18 U.S.C. § 5, as places subject to their jurisdiction (which places are defined at 18 U.S.C. § 7). This statutory definition created by Congress of the "United States" is explained further into this Manifesto.

Moreover, the "United States" (Federal Government) cannot even adopt laws of the Union States under Title 18 U.S.C. § 13, with respect to crimes committed in places, although they may be owned by the "United States" (Federal Government), that are not subject to its exclusive or concurrent jurisdiction. Obviously, if the "United States" (Federal Government) already had concurrent jurisdiction over the several 50 Union States, it would be impossible for any ONE OF the several Union States to cede concurrent jurisdiction to the Federal Government ("United States"). As revealed by Title 18 U.S.C. § 13, "areas within Federal jurisdiction" are provided in section 7 [18 U.S.C. § 7].

Like the Union States, the Federal Government can punish felonies that occur within their own lands but only those lands which are under their exclusive or concurrent jurisdiction. These places are where the Federal Government has territorial jurisdiction (general jurisdiction).[187] When a felony or misdemeanor "interstate commerce" offense is committed wholly within one or more of these specific places, it is punished the same as a Union State would punish intrastate commerce crimes (commerce crimes wholly within the State). When someone commits a felony or misdemeanor offense in those ceded places and completes that felony or misdemeanor offense in another like place, Congress defines it as "interstate commerce" which can be prosecuted in either of the judicial districts ("United States district") in which such activity occurred. It is apparent that the sole purpose of creating felonious "interstate commerce" crimes was to deceive us into believing that their commerce clause power allows them to do so. This is how these tyrants usurp the sovereignty and jurisdiction of the Union States through our ignorance of the law. It is by exercising an undelegated power to "punish" under the delegated power to "regulate" commerce among the Union States (interstate commerce). Under the U.S. Constitution:

---

[187] see note 80, *supra*.

> The trial of all Crimes, except in Cases of Impeachment, shall be by Jury; and such Trial shall be held in the State where the said Crimes shall have been committed; **but when not committed within any State, the trial shall be at such Place or Places as the Congress may by Law have directed.** Article III, § 2, cl. 3, U.S. Constitution.

Remember what places the Supreme Court said is not considered part of a State?

> Of course, we exclude ... places within the exterior limits of a state ... over which exclusive jurisdiction has been ceded to the United States, because they are regarded not as part of a state, but as excepted out of it. Southern Sure-

ty Co. v. Oklahoma, 241 US 582, 586 (1915).

As we learned earlier in this Manifesto, Congress can provide for the nationwide punishment of felonious crimes where the power to "punish" has been delegated by enumeration in the Constitution. We also learned that because the power to "punish" is delegated, by enumeration in other provisions of the Constitution, it presupposes that where the power to "punish" is not delegated by enumeration, it is not delegated. However, only Article III courts have jurisdiction of the subject-matter over offenses that occur within land (places) where concurrent or exclusive jurisdiction has not been relinquished through purchase by consent or cession, and acceptance. Legislative courts only have subject-matter jurisdiction over offenses that occur on land under the exclusive or concurrent jurisdiction of the United States (Federal Government).

By proceeding under the fraudulent assumption that a federal crime has occurred on federal land under the exclusive or concurrent jurisdiction of the

Federal Government (for all intents and purposes a "United States district"),[188] the U.S. Attorney's, working in concert with the judges of the "United States district courts," continuously conspire together to fundamentally alter our constitutional republican form of government (which is treason). They do so in order to prosecute us in violation of the Constitution for federal crimes we are not guilty of committing and/or which these courts have no subject-matter jurisdiction to adjudicate. Without jurisdiction over the place of the crime (or the delegation of the punishing power), no felonious federal crime has been committed. They deprive us of our inherent inalienable rights secured under the Constitution with absolute impunity while at the same time perjuring their sworn oaths to uphold it. There is no excuse for this because, "Trial judges are presumed to know the law and to apply it in making

---

[188] A "United States district" differs from an ordinary "judicial district," in that, under the law, the former is describing places under the exclusive or concurrent jurisdiction of Congress while the latter is not. What congress has done is include the United States districts of Columbia and Puerto Rico as judicial districts. This only aids their subterfuge to usurp the sovereignty and jurisdiction of the Union States by obfuscating the very serious difference under our Constitution between land under their exclusive or concurrent jurisdiction and land that is not.

their decisions." <u>Walton v. Arizona</u>, 497 US 639, 653 (1990).

For example, the following case demonstrates the tyranny we all face today through a twisting of the law beyond its constitutional limitations:

> Obrient Webb, appearing pro se, appeals his conviction to possess with intent to distribute cocaine, in violation of 21 U.S.C. §§ 841(a)(1) and 846. Webb first contends that the district court lacked jurisdiction...; that Texas is not a State of the United States...; that he was not arrested within the territorial jurisdiction of the United States; and that his Fourth and Fifth Amendment rights were violated by the purported lack of jurisdiction
>
> Webb's jurisdictional arguments are frivolous. ...Texas is plainly a state of the United States within the territorial jurisdiction of the

United States, see United States v. 1,078.27 Acres of Land, 446 F2d 1030, 1039 (5th Cir. 1971). Webb's contentions **based on 18 U.S.C. § 7** are without merit. United States v. Webb, 220 Fed.Appx. 293 (5th Cir. 2007) (per curium, *i.e.*, "by the court") (non-precedential)

Clearly Webb's contention that Texas is not a "State of the United States" is absolutely correct. If Texas were a "state of the United States within the territorial jurisdiction of the United States" it would be impossible for Texas to cede any concurrent or exclusive jurisdiction to the Federal Government (United States) under Article I, § 8, cl. 17, U.S. Constitution, as defined in Title 18 U.S.C. § 7(3), in order for lands to be within the territorial jurisdiction of the "United States" (Federal Government). As we can see, the judge twisted the law thereby arbitrarily and capriciously denying Webb's inalienable Fifth Amendment due process right secured under the Constitution his sworn duty is to uphold.

We shouldn't have to know the law. That job belongs to the judges and attorneys. Because the majority of the populace is ignorant of the law the Federal Judges and United States Attorneys utilize that ignorance to deny your rights and provide themselves and others careers. They are keenly aware that we do not know or understand what the law really is, and that our understanding of the law is based on what we believe or perceive it to be. Based on their "awareness" of our ignorance of the law they treat us as if we are therefore stupid enough to believe whatever they say is true, not what really is true. For example, if they told you the sun was the color green, and you had a color wheel that proved the sun was the color orange, they would just refuse to admit that you are correct and continue to put forward the lie that the sun is green, and expect you to believe and accept it, whether you like it and agree with it or not. They don't care!

When we review the case relied on by the court we can see Texas was admitted into the Union on December 29, 1845, and after <u>ceding</u> certain property to the "United States" (Federal Government) for the public defense, retained "all vacant and unappropriated lands lying within its limits." Remember, the joining of the Territory of Texas to the Union ousts the "United States" (Federal Government) of general jurisdiction both civil and criminal, except where it <u>cedes</u> concurrent or exclusive legislative (territorial) jurisdiction to them.

It is possible the Federal Employees, or at least some of them, have been told that what I have shown you is a "loophole" in the Constitution and believe they are performing some sort of patriotic duty by concealing it. If there are such people, they have been lied to and made into criminals by their own government, not patriots. The Constitution provides for amending it in order to fix any "loopholes." However, this has not been done. Instead, they usurp this power by acting outside of the law We the People ordained and established, under the guise that they are carrying out lawfully delegated powers, to the detriment and deprivation of our lives, liberty, property and pursuit of happiness. It appears that the "loophole" being exploited is the People's ignorance of the law.

That is what they utilize while tirelessly working to overthrow our lawful form of government. If the Supreme Court would just do their sworn duty to uphold the Constitution, by overturning all of the cases that come before them without jurisdiction over the subject-matter, this tyranny would end. As the Supreme Court stated:

> [It should never] be lost sight of, that the government of the United States is one of limited <u>and</u> enumerated powers, and that a departure from the true import and sense of its powers is pro tanto the establishment of a new Constitution. It is doing for the people what they have not chosen to do for themselves. It is usurping the functions of a legislator, and deserting those of an expounder of the law. Arguments drawn from impolicy or inconvenience ought here to be of no

weight. The <u>only</u> sound principle is to declare, ita lex scripta est ["so the law is written"], to follow, and to obey. <u>Myers v. United States</u>, 272 U.S. 52, 182-183 (1926)

Next, the "United States Courts of Appeal," working as a link in the chain conspiracy, simply deny almost all of the appeals and applications for relief that come before them. Further, the Supreme Court of the United States, now bottle-necked with approximately 6,000 petitions for writ of certiorari review per year, summarily deny the vast majority of those petitions. They, admittedly, grant oral argument in only 1% (about 60) of those 6,000 petitions. How is our right to petition for redress of grievances upheld if we cannot obtain meaningful review of those grievances?

The Supreme Court has consistently stated that if the lower courts did not have jurisdiction then they do not have jurisdiction to reach the merits of the issues we present for certiorari review and can only decide that the lower court erred in hearing the case.[189] They have also explained that:

---

[189] Subject-matter jurisdiction [means], *i.e.* the court's statutory or constitutional power to adjudicate the case.

The Ninth Circuit has denominated this practice—-which it characterizes as "assuming" jurisdiction for the purpose of deciding the merits—the "doctrine of hypothetical jurisdiction."

We decline to endorse such an approach because it carries the courts beyond the bounds of authorized judicial action and thus offends fundamental principles of separation of powers. This conclusion should come as no surprise, since it is reflected in a long and venerable line of our cases. "Without jurisdiction the court cannot proceed at all in any cause. Jurisdiction is power to declare the law, and when it ceases to exist, the only function remaining to the court is that of announcing the fact and dismissing the cause." "On every writ of error or appeal, the first and fundamental question is that of jurisdiction, first, of this court, and then of the court from which the record comes. This question the court is bound to ask and answer for itself, even when not otherwise suggested, and without respect to the relation of the parties to it." The requirement that jurisdiction be established as a threshold matter "springs from the nature and limits of the judicial power of the United States" and is "inflexible and without exception."

This Court's insistence that proper jurisdiction appear begins at least as early as 1804.

Every federal appellate court has a special obligation to satisfy itself not only of its own jurisdiction, but also that of the lower courts in a cause under review, even though the parties are prepared to concede it. And if the record discloses that the lower court was without jurisdiction <u>this court will notice the defect, although the parties make no contention concerning it</u>. When the lower federal court lacks jurisdiction, we have jurisdiction on appeal, not of the merits but merely for the purpose of correcting the error of the lower court in entertaining the suit.

Continued on next page.

Before considering the questions raised by the petition for certiorari, the jurisdiction of the federal court ... <u>must</u> be determined. <u>Treinies v. Sunshine Mining Co.</u>, 308 US 66, 70 (1940)

How then does the Supreme Court grant certiorari review in those 1% of cases knowing that the lower Federal courts did not have jurisdiction to render judgment of conviction in so-called felonious "interstate commerce" crimes unless the alleged criminal

---

While some of the above cases must be acknowledged to have diluted the absolute purity of <u>the rule</u> that Article III jurisdiction is <u>always</u> an antecedent question, none of them even approaches approval of a doctrine of "hypothetical jurisdiction" that enables a court to resolve contested questions of law when its jurisdiction is in doubt. Hypothetical jurisdiction produces nothing more than a hypothetical judgment—which comes to the same thing as an advisory opinion, disapproved by this court from the beginning. Much more than legal niceties are at stake here. The statutory and (especially) constitutional elements of jurisdiction are an <u>essential</u> ingredient of separation and equilibration of powers, restraining the courts from acting at certain times, and even restraining them from acting permanently regarding certain subjects. <u>Steel Co. v. Citizens for Better Env.</u>, 523 US 83, 89-101 (1998)

activity occurred within places (lands) under their exclusive or concurrent legislative (territorial) jurisdiction? It is apparent that not being able to get justice at the lowest level possible almost entirely eliminates the possibility altogether.

The Supreme Court is obviously an essential link in the chain to defraud the American People and usurp the sovereignty and jurisdiction of the Union States. It is manifestly transparent that this treason could not continue if the Justices were not willing participants. The fact that the Supreme Court authored the Rules of Procedure (see Title 28 U.S.C. § 2072(a)), and is still rendering opinions on the merits of felonious "interstate commerce" cases that come before them from the lower federal courts, without any jurisdiction over the subject-matter, is further proof of the Supreme Court's active roll to commit treason against the Constitution, deprive us of our inalienable rights, perjure their sworn oaths, and the willful failure of the Justices to "hold their Offices during good Behavior." As the Supreme Court stated:

That by the Constitution of the United States, the government thereof is divided into three distinct and independent branches, and that it is the **duty** of each to abstain from, **and to oppose**, encroachments on either. Musk- rat v. United States, 219 US 346, 352 (1911)

Can anyone point out how exactly the Supreme Court has opposed the encroachments on the Judicial branch by staying silent on the issue, to the point of allowing, (1) Congress to maintain unconstitutionally vague laws surrounding "interstate commerce" crimes, (2) Congress to establish "United States district courts" (which every Judiciary Act prior to the current Judiciary Act does not mention and which are historically recognized as territorial courts), and then perpetrate the fraud (which the Supreme Court condones and joins) that they are continuations of existing law, i.e., the former constitutional "district courts of the United States" ordained and established under Article III, and (3) the Executive branch to continuously prosecute felonious criminal "interstate commerce" cases in violation of the Constitution and our inalienable rights secured under it (which the Supreme Court consistently fails to notice sua-sponte their lack of subject-matter jurisdiction and instead continuously renders decisions on the merits of these cases that come before them from the lower federal courts anyway)?

Does the fact that every executive and judicial officer must continuously perjure their sworn oaths to uphold the Constitution in violation of Article VI, cl. 3 in order to maintain this treasonous fraud on the People raise an eyebrow? Does the fact that every federal court is not following the laws of Congress and instead are allowing felonious criminal prosecutions to be carried out by the executive branch while refusing to acknowledge that the Constitution does not delegate to Congress the power to "punish" under the "Commerce Clause" speak volumes? When this is all made public & the people in each of the Union States realize what has happened there will either be swift reforms & justice or bloodshed. I predict that there will be bloodshed before reforms are implemented. As Thomas Jefferson stated:

> The tree of liberty must be refreshed from time to time, with the blood of the patriots and tyrants. It is its natural manure.[190] Thomas Jefferson, Founding Father, Creator and signer of the Declaration of Independence, and former President of the United States.

Is this not the remedy, *i.e.*, the law, to tyranny and oppression that our Founding Father is pointing out? It was sure the remedy he and the Colonists used in the Revolutionary War. Even before them it was the remedy used by the Barons on the field of Runny-

---

[190] Taken from a private letter to William Smith in 1787 prior to the adoption of the Constitution of the United States which in Article V made provision for amendment, whereby our form of government could be changed in a peaceful manner. Confer United States v. Lightfoot, 228 F2d 861, 867 n. 5 (7th Cir. 1956)

mede to obtain the Magna Charta in AD 1215. This "right of revolution" is defined as:

> The inherent right of a people to cast out their rulers, change their polity, or effect radical reforms in their system of government or institutions, by force or general uprising, when the legal and constitutional methods of making such changes have proved inadequate or are so obstructed as to be unavailable. Black's Law Dictionary, Eighth Edition, page 1,350.

I would like to state that the reason the constitutional and procedural remedies are inadequate is because the Federal Government is too big. The Framers knew what big government would do to liberty. That is exactly why they kept the governments small and close to the people creating 50 individual sovereignties each with their own separate laws instead of joining into one individual sovereignty all under the same exact laws. This is our unique form of government. Like 50 different and totally independent countries. We therefore have 50 Union State jurisdictions and federal jurisdiction, for a total of 51 jurisdictions. The enormity of the Federal Government was never intended by the Framers. This is why their powers to tax were limited to certain subjects. They would petition the Union States for the taxes needed to carry out their delegated powers. However, the ratification of the 16th Amendment gave Congress the ability to tax the citizenry's income and use those taxes for any purpose whatsoever. This provided zero transparency, allowing the government to spend that money however they see fit, even to bribe corrupt officials, *etc.* It also allowed the "United States" (Federal Government) to develop into the tyranny it is today. That provides a reasonable explanation why so much money mysteriously vanishes and is unaccounted for. For example, a similar occurrence happened with the Troubled Asset Relief Program ("TARP") established under the Emergency Economic Stabilization Act of 2008 (EESA)(Pub.L. 110-343; 122 Stat. 3765), see

Title 31 C.F.R. § 30.1, where several hundred million dollars were allegedly "misappropriated".

It is no secret that the Federal Government is effectively encroaching upon, eroding and outright denying, our inalienable rights secured under the Constitution more and more as its power grows beyond the People's control. For example, our Fourth Amendment rights, Fifth Amendment due process rights, privacy rights, *etc.*, and the list continues to grow. See Ninth Amendment, U.S. Constitution:

> The enumeration in the Constitution, of certain rights, shall not be construed to deny or disparage others retained by the people.

The Framers, while expounding the Constitution, stated that:

> If the federal government should overpass the just bounds of its

authority and make a tyrannical use of its powers, the people, whose creature it is, must appeal to the standards they have formed, and take such measures to redress the injury done to the Constitution as the exigency may suggest and prudence justify.
The Federalist Papers, No. 33

Assuming Americans wake up to the real causes of their unhappiness, there is sure to be bloodshed. My heart grieves over the indiscriminant loss of life in Egypt, Israel, Libya, Gaza, Syria, Iraq, Ukraine, *etc.* I can't bear the thought of such in my country! Those who drew and continue to draw first blood should be the only ones to pay! Wouldn't that reduce any un-necessary blood shed? Now I will show you a better way.

Article V of the Constitution is a provision for amending the Constitution in order to change our form of government peacefully. I suggest the following amendments:

The power to regulate commerce among the several States does NOT allow Congress to Punish felonies. Such power to Punish, being a grant of authority to Punish felonies concurrently with the several Union States, is expressly reserved to the several Union States via the Tenth Amendment.

This Constitution contains no grant, general or specific, to the Congress of the power to provide for the punishment of felonious crimes, except where the power to Punish is expressly delegated by enumeration. The Punishment of all other felonious crimes is reserved to the several Union States, regardless of an activities connection to a delegated power, except where jurisdiction has been ceded as provided under the seventeenth clause of the eighth section of the first Article.

The Congress may provide for the Punishment of Misdemeanors as necessary and proper ONLY if it has a direct connection to the execution of a delegated power. The power to regulate shall not extend to any activity wholly within any ONE OF the several Union States, regardless of its potential to substantially affect commerce among the several Union States.

Amendment XXVIII

The Congress shall not establish legislative courts within the several Union States or the District of Columbia (the seat of the Government), and shall only Ordain and Establish constitutional Article III courts within the several Union States, including all Federal land within them, and expressly declare them to be so Ordained and Established, except that Congress shall be authorized to vest the District of Columbia courts with additional jurisdiction not found under Article III, concerning local matters.

Amendment XXIX

The trial or prosecution of all civil, misdemeanor, and felony Offenses against the Laws of the United States (Federal Government, including the District of Columbia and other like property within any particular Union State), shall ONLY be by Judges of constitutional Article III courts, having lifetime tenure and salary protections guaranteed under that Article, unless expressly waived by the Defendant in writing and orally upon the record in open court, which Defendant may then be tried by a Magistrate Judge of that Article III court. <u>Amendment XXX</u>

The establishment of any legislative Federal court within the several Union States or the District of Columbia shall be considered an attempt to overthrow Our constitutional Republican form of government and to fundamentally alter this Constitution, and deemed to be Treason Punishable by Life imprisonment or Death, by both the several Union States and Congress. <u>Amendment XXXI</u>

The courts of the several States shall have Power to issue Writs of *Habeas Corpus* in all cases of illegal and unconstitutional restraint by the United States (Federal Government), each within their own territorial boundaries, after first petitioning and denial by the Federal trial court, the Federal appellate court, the Federal local court (if different from the trial court), and the Supreme Court of the United States. In no case shall the granting or denial by each court take longer than 60 days. All grants or denials of relief shall state their findings of fact and conclusions of law on the merits of the petitioner's claim. Amendment XXXII

The several States shall have Power to Punish all violations of the Constitution and the Rights secured under it that occur within each of their territorial boundaries, regardless of whether it occurs upon Federal Land under the exclusive or concurrent jurisdiction of the United States (Federal Government). Amendment XXXIII

The Sixteenth Amendment is hereby REPEALED and the Congress shall not have power to lay a direct tax within the several Union States, except over land under their concurrent or exclusive jurisdiction. In all cases the Congress shall purchase the land as proprietors. The failure to utilize such land for military purposes or the housing of civilians upon such land (other than the District of Columbia), shall forfeit all grants of jurisdiction which shall immediately revert back to the particular Union State. Amendment XXXIV

The Congress shall have Power to lay proportionate taxes throughout the several Union States, based upon the number of each particular Union States Citizens, in accordance with the first clause of the eighth section of the first Article. Amendment XXXV

The Federal Reserve and Internal Revenue Service is hereby declared to be unconstitutional and forthwith abolished. Congress shall only coin or print Money backed by Gold, Silver, and Platinum. The Congress shall not delegate this power, or the collection of taxes, to independent private agencies. Amendment XXXVI

The Treaty making Power does NOT allow Congress to Punish felonies or misdemeanors within any ONE OF the several Union States. Amendment XXXVII

The Congress shall NOT have the power to regulate Education among the several Union States. Amendment XXXVIII

The Congress shall NOT have power to provide for Public Welfare and Medical Care of the indigent, or others, within the several Union States. This in no way affects the ability of a particular Union State to receive assistance during recovery from natural disasters. <u>Amendment XXXIX</u>

The aforementioned Amendments would substantially secure our freedom and constitutional Republican form of government. However, we must always be ever mindful and vigilant to protect our freedom and personal liberties.

IT'S IN THE LAW

As we learned earlier in this Manifesto, Congress has no delegated power or authority to provide for the punishment of felonies under their power to regulate interstate commerce among the several Union States. The power to regulate being the power to prescribe rules. Congress can provide for the punishment of felonies among the several Union States where the power to punish has been delegated by enumeration in the Constitution, and where they have exclusive or concurrent jurisdiction. We also learned earlier that when a felony or misdemeanor is committed within land under the concurrent or exclusive jurisdiction of the United States (Federal Government), and is completed in another like place, Congress defines that activity as "interstate commerce."

Utilizing the people's ignorance of the Law, Congress refers to places subject to their jurisdiction as the "United States."[191] For example, <u>Title 18 U.S.C. § 5</u>, which defines the term "United States" for all of that title, states that:

> The term "United States," as used in this title in a <u>territorial</u> sense, includes <u>all places</u> and waters, continental or insular, <u>subject to the jurisdiction of the United States</u> [Federal Government][192]

Remember, the Supreme Court has stated that, "It is <u>true</u> that the <u>criminal jurisdiction</u> of the United States [Federal Government][193] is in general[194] based on the <u>territorial</u> principle."[195] The <u>territorial places</u> subject to the jurisdiction of the United States are de-

---

[191] Confer note 98, *supra*.

[192] my note. Confer note 192, *supra*.

[193] my note.

[194] *Confer* note 80, *supra*.

[195] <u>United States v. Flores</u>, 289 US 137, 155 (1933)

fined at Title 18 U.S.C. § 7, Special Maritime and **Territorial jurisdiction of the United States** defined, and includes:

> (3) Any lands, reserved or acquired for the use of the United States, and under the exclusive or concurrent jurisdiction thereof, or any place purchased or otherwise acquired by consent of the legislature of the State.

Notice that this provision is identical in scope to Article I, § 8, cl. 17, in the U.S. Constitution. The definition Congress has provided us, defining the "United States," together with the special maritime and territorial jurisdiction of the United States defined, completes the full statutory definition of the United States. The several Union States are not even mentioned. If the several Union States were already subject to the jurisdiction of Congress, section 7(3) would be superfluous.[196] Likewise, 40 U.S.C. § 3112, would be superfluous as well.[197]

In many Title 18 U.S.C. statutes, dealing with the "Crimes and Criminal Procedure" of the Federal Government, we see a definition of "State" or that certain crimes must occur in or affecting "interstate commerce." For example, the following Racketeering statutes contain definitions of "racketeering activity," "enterprise," "State," and also make specific reference to "interstate or foreign commerce":

As used in this section—

> (a) "racketeering activity" has the meaning set forth in section 1961 of this title [18 USCS § 1961]; and
>
> (b) "enterprise" includes any partnership, corporation, association,

---

[196] superfluous. Exceeding what is sufficient or necessary. Webster's Ninth New Collegiate Dictionary (1991), page 1,184.

[197] *Confer* note 135, *supra*.

or other legal entity and any union or group of individuals associated in fact although not a legal entity, **which is engaged in, or activities of which affect, interstate or foreign commerce**. 18 U.S.C. § 1959

(2) "State" means any State of the United States, the District of Columbia, the Commonwealth of Puerto Rico, any territory or possession of the United States, any political subdivision, or any department, agency, or instrumentality [198] thereof. 18 U.S.C. § 1961

---

[198] *Confer* note 139, *supra*.

In other Title 18 U.S.C. statutes we see no reference to the "United States"[199] nor to "State." For example, Title 18 U.S.C. §§ 641, 642, relating to theft or embezzlement of public money, property or records; and tools and materials for counterfeiting purposes; respectively. The essential ingredient of those two provisions is that each carries a sentence of up to ten years imprisonment, *i.e.*, they are felonies. Remember, Congress cannot punish felonies generally, *confer* "only in these [ceded] places", footnote 80, *supra*. The Supreme Court has continuously explained that:

> Legislation is presumptively territorial and confined to limits over which the lawmaking power has jurisdiction. All legislation is prima facie territorial. New York Central R. Co. v. Chisholm, 268 US 29, 31-32 (1925) (citations

---

[199] See 18 U.S.C. § 5, *supra*, "United States," defined.

and internal quotation marks omitted)

Another Supreme Court opinion rendered twenty-seven years later states that:

> The cannon of construction which teaches that legislation of Congress, unless a contrary intent appears, is meant to apply only within the territorial jurisdiction of the United States is a valid approach whereby unexpressed congressional intent may be ascertained. **Words having universal scope, such as** 'Every contract in restraint of trade', '<u>Every person</u> who shall monopolize', ***etc.*, will be taken as a matter of course to mean only everyone subject to such legislation, not all that the legislator**

subsequently may be able to catch. Steele v. Bulova Watch Co., 344 US 280, 290 (1952) (citations omitted) [*Confer* "any person", 21 U.S.C. § 801 *et seq.*, Drug Crimes]

Nearly 60 years after Steele v. Bulova, *supra*, the Supreme Court again explained that:

> It is a longstanding principle of American law that legislation of Congress, unless a contrary intent appears, is meant to apply only within the territorial jurisdiction of the United States. When a statute gives no clear indication of an extraterritorial application, it has none. Morrison v. National Australia Bank LTD, 177 Led2d 535, 547 (2010)

Congress has clearly defined the <u>territorial jurisdiction</u> of the United States (Federal Government) at Title 18 U.S.C. § 7, pursuant to the limits imposed upon them by the Constitution. Also, the definition of "Extraterritorial" is defined as, "Beyond the geographic limits of a particular jurisdiction." <u>Black's Law Dictionary</u>, Eighth Edition, page 625. For an excellent example of a statute that gives a clear indication of its extraterritorial application see <u>18 U.S.C. § 470</u>, "Counterfeit acts committed outside the United States."

As we proceed from this point, we will begin to see how Congress, acting in concert with the Supreme Court, conspired together, so that the usurpation of the Union State's sovereignty and jurisdiction could be (and was) achieved.

Legislating to reach a constitutional end (although void for vagueness), Congress and the Supreme Court have completely obfuscated that constitutional end. This has been done in order to fundamentally alter our constituted, lawful, form of government, usurp the sovereignty and jurisdiction of the Union States, and deprive us of our inherent, inalienable, rights secured under the Constitution. This is also big business. By prosecuting State Crimes under the guise that a federal crime has been committed, Congress is able to filter away from the States billions of dollars each year.

As we have learned in this Manifesto, the Commerce Clause[200] power does not grant Congress the ability to "punish" felonies by implication. This is because the power to "punish" felonies is united with cession of territory,[201] *i.e.*, whoever has sovereignty

---

[200] Article I, § 8, cl. 3, U.S. Constitution.

[201] When the Framers delegated the power to "punish" in the Constitution, where enumerated, it was, and still is, analogous to a cession of concurrent jurisdiction (without the need to own the land), but only for those very specific and limited crimes. Although analogous to a cession of concurrent jurisdiction, it is not a grant of, and does not grant any, territorial jurisdiction. The Federal Government is simply authorized to do those things within the sovereign jurisdiction of any ONE OF the several Union States. The reason they cannot "punish" under the commerce clause is because that power is not delegated by enumeration there, and they have no territorial jurisdiction. When new States join the Union they are automatically bound by those provisions. This power to punish is essential in order to authorize the Federal Government ("United States") to punish felonious crimes over land in which they are not sovereign (where territorial jurisdiction has not been relinquished through consent to purchase or cession). The only other way for Congress to punish felonious crimes within any ONE OF the several 50 Union States, is the mode authorized in the Constitution, *i.e.*, by consent to purchase land, or cession, with acceptance of jurisdiction, over land owned by the United States (Federal Government).

(territorial jurisdiction) over the land. Because the Framer's did not delegate to Congress, by enumeration,[202] the power to "punish" under the commerce clause, jurisdiction must be ceded as provided under Article I, § 8, cl. 17, of the Constitution. The "United States district courts" proceed under the assumption that a crime has been committed on federal land under the concurrent or exclusive jurisdiction of Congress. The law is written that way because those are the places where they have jurisdiction over crimes. Of course, if you bring this up, they will refuse to admit it. They will even continue to put forth the lie that they really have power to "punish" felonies under the commerce clause and that they really are the constitutional "district courts of the United States" ordained and established under Article III. They are not and you know they have no such power. In order to uphold the fraud, they must continue to conceal the truth at all costs.

---

[202] "The government of the United States is one of delegated, limited, and enumerated powers." Kansas v. Colorado, 206 US 46, 87 (1907)

Legislative court judges are dependent on the will of Congress for their tenure and salary. In other words, since Congress can remove them from their positions, at will (by repealing their tenure statute), they render judgments based on the goal of the legislature. For example, to control the flow of drugs Con-Congress has deemed legal. The constitutional court Justice's tenure and salary are guaranteed <u>under Article III</u> regardless of whether they render a judgment in line with the will of Congress. They are an <u>independent</u> branch of government. They have no fear of being removed from their positions and therefore render judgments in line with the Constitution. The following opinion from Chief Judge Daugherty of the United States district court for the Judicial District of Western Oklahoma illustrates the absolute necessity for constitutional courts.

On March 15, 1977 Defendant Peggy McDaniel entered a plea of guilty to the offense of distributing approximately 1/10 gram of heroin in violation of, 21 U.S.C. §

841(a)(1). She has filed herein a Motion in Arrest of Judgment on the ground that this Court lacked jurisdiction of the Defendant and the subject-matter involved in the instant case. Defendant contends that the crime alleged against Defendant is a State crime, involving a local defendant, a local police officer and a purely local Situation; that this Court lacks jurisdiction to intervene in a purely local matter...and that the act under which Defendant is charged, the Comprehensive Drug Abuse Prevention and Control Act of 1970, 21 U.S.C. § 801 *et seq.*, cannot be applied to activities that are not connected with interstate commerce. In this regard, Defendant asserts that the federal Court's intervention in this case raises significant questions of interference with the

Ninth and Tenth Amendments to the United States Constitution and to the due process rights of the Defendant.

An examination of the Indictment in the instant case discloses that it charges an offense following the language of the statute involved and contains sufficient allegations to fairly notify the Defendant of the charge against her. In view of this, the Indictment conforms to Rule 7(c), Federal Rules of Criminal Procedure. As the Indictment charges Defendant with violating the laws of the United States within this District, this Court has jurisdiction of the offense charged. 18 U.S.C. § 3231. Where the Indictment clearly charges an offense of which this Court has jurisdiction, Defendant's Motion in Arrest of Judgment must be denied. <u>United</u>

States v. Peggy McDaniel, 75 FRD 454 (1977) (citations omitted)

The Chief Judge failed to notice that the crime is only made out when it occurs within the concurrent or exclusive legislative (territorial) jurisdiction of the "United States" (Federal Government). The Fifth Circuit explained that:

> [I]t is axiomatic that the prosecution must always prove territorial jurisdiction over a crime in order to sustain a conviction therefor, and thus territorial jurisdiction and venue are "essential elements" of any offense in the sense that the burden is on the prosecution to prove their existence. United States v. White, 611 F2d 531, 536 (CA5, 1980)(citations omitted)

The Chief Judge also failed to notice, *sua-sponte*, that the court does not have subject-matter jurisdiction because no "offense against the laws of the United States" had been committed by the Defendant. Instead of protecting the rights of the Defendant, the court, via the Chief Judge himself, undertook to deprive her of her rights because she could not point out the law, and did not understand it. This is the problem we currently face with the "United States district courts". For example, the Chief Judge stated that, "An examination of the Indictment in the instant case discloses that it charges an offense following the language of the statute involved." There is no excuse for the Chief Judge's action. Judges are presumed to know the law and to apply it in making their decisions. See Walton v. Arizona, 497 US 639, 653 (1990). The Fifth Circuit explained that:

> An indictment or information in the language of the statute is sufficient except where the words of the statute do not contain all of

the <u>essential elements</u> of the offense. The Sixth Amendment of the federal constitution requires that in every criminal prosecution the accused shall be informed of the nature and cause of the accusation against him. This means that he shall be so fully and clearly informed of the charge against him as not only to enable him to prepare his defense [but also] not be taken by surprise at the trial.

<u>United States v. Cruikshank</u>, 92 US 542, 557-559, deals with the right of the accused to be informed of the nature and cause of the accusation against him. [E]very ingredient of which the offense is composed must be clearly and accurately alleged.

A constitutional defect in an indictment or information is <u>not</u> cured by the verdict. <u>Sutton v.</u>

United States, 157 F2d 661 (CA5, 1946)

On the other hand, the following opinion from a constitutional court illustrates how they undertake to protect the rights of the accused.

> The eighth section of the first article of the constitution of the United States, in the seventeenth clause, gives the right of exclusive legislation to the United States, to exercise authority over all places purchased by the consent of the legislature of the state in which the same shall be for the erection of forts, magazines, arsenals, dock-yards, and other needful buildings. The purchase of lands for the United States, for public purposes, does not of itself oust the jurisdiction of such state

over the lands purchased. The constitution prescribes the only mode by which they can acquire land as a sovereign power; and therefore they hold only as an individual when they obtain it in any other manner. If there be no cession by a state, the state jurisdiction still remains.

It seems too plain for doubt, much as we may regret the fact in this particular case, that this court has no jurisdiction in the premises. <u>United States v. Penn</u>, 48 F 669 (Circuit Court, E.D. Virginia, 1880)

The above illustrations clearly show how "United States district court" judges, as opposed to constitutional court justices, make a conscious effort to deprive you of your rights if you do not know or understand the law. I would like to explicitly point out, just to make sure you did not miss it, that in <u>McDaniel</u>, *supra*, Chief Judge Daugherty states that the Indictment is sufficient because it follows the language of the statute. However, the Sutton court makes it clear that the Indictment or information is sufficient except where the words of the statute do not contain all of the essential elements of the offense. Finally, the court in White, *supra*, opined that territorial jurisdiction and venue are essential elements of any offense. Therefore Peggy McDaniel's indictment was insufficient and did not charge an offense against the laws of the United States, because it did not contain the essential element of territorial jurisdiction, *i.e.*, that the offense alleged occurred within the special maritime and/ or territorial jurisdiction of the United States. It should be noted here that venue can be waived while jurisdiction, territorial or otherwise, can never be forfeited or waived.

It should also be noted that a defect in an indictment does not deprive the court of its jurisdiction to adjudicate the case but, rather, goes only against the United States. See United States v. Cotton, 535 US 625, 631 (2002). However, this is assuming that the trial court would still have jurisdiction over the place of the crime. Without jurisdiction over the place of the crime, the court has no subject-matter jurisdiction of the proceedings to determine the merits of the case.

In the Comprehensive Drug Abuse Prevention and Control Act, 21 U.S.C. § 801 et seq., the drug statutes do not mention the essential element of their territorial reach (territorial jurisdiction). The provisions that limit the territorial reach of the drug statutes are discussed a little further into this Manifesto. The point is that if a felonious federal crime is committed anywhere within the territorial jurisdiction of any Union State pursuant to a delegated power where the power to "punish" is <u>not</u> delegated (enumerated) under the Constitution then the charging instrument (complaint, information, or indictment), must specify that the alleged crime occurred "within the territorial jurisdiction of the United States". *Confer* <u>18 U.S.C. § 7</u>.

If a felonious federal crime has occurred pursuant to a provision in the Constitution where the power to "punish" is enumerated (delegated) then the charging instrument does not need to specify that it occurred "within the territorial jurisdiction of the United States". However, it must allege that the offense occurred within the continental United States, *i.e.*, any Judicial

District other than the District of Columbia and Puerto Rico. Same for misdemeanor offenses committed pursuant to any of the Federal Government's enumerated (delegated) powers.

What the government is doing is charging people with felonious crimes pursuant to enumerated (delegated) powers where the power to "punish" is not delegated, for example, the "Commerce Clause," and more recently the "Treaty Clause," and leaving out the fact that the alleged crime must occur within the "territorial jurisdiction of the United States." As I mentioned, other provisions limit the territorial reach of drug and other federal crimes. I bet you can guess why they omit this "essential element". In order to usurp the sovereignty & jurisdiction of the several 50 Union States by prosecuting felonious crimes under the guise of regulating interstate commerce. In other words, to trick people into believing the Constitution authorizes them to "punish" felonious crimes by implication as "necessary & proper" in order to regulate commerce among the Union States.

The foregoing defects amount to failure to inform you of the nature of the charge against you. See Federal Rules of Criminal Procedure, Rule 7(c). That is prejudicial to your ability to put on your defense. Obviously if you were aware of this "essential element" you could easily mount a defense. That is exactly why they leave it out. They know you are ignorant of the law and therefore use that ignorance to usurp that undelegated power to "punish".

The following case explains, in depth, the details surrounding Title 18 U.S.C. § 7(3) and the removal of the phrase "within the special maritime and territorial jurisdiction of the United States" from the criminal statutes, stating that:

> In the 1909 Act, which comprehensively codified all existing federal criminal law, **Congress for the first time <u>created a separate section</u> devoted solely to defining jurisdiction.** [That section differs only slightly from the present § 7(3), as stated in the full opinion (my note)]

Accordingly, the 1909 Act, like the 1790 Act, was **limited to lands within the exclusive jurisdiction of the United States** and, therefore, to lands within the territorial boundaries of the United States.

Senator Heyburn of Pennsylvania, the Senate manager of the bills that became the 1909 Act, put the matter most bluntly, stating that the proposed legislation does not enlarge the jurisdiction of the United States courts by a hairs breadth .... Senators will find that we have not attempted to enlarge the jurisdiction of the United States either technically or geographically. We have simply gathered up a large number of existing provisions in the various statutes ... **in order to avoid the repetition with each separate section of this geographical ju-**

> **risdiction** ... The committee ... [has] not enlarged the jurisdiction territorially or technically of the United States courts. 42 CONG. REC. 1186 (1908)(emphasis added). United States v. Gatlin, 216 F3d 207, 217-220 (CA2, 2000)

As we can see from the above court opinion, in 1909 Congress created § 7(3) of Title 18 U.S.C. (which concerns land acquired in accordance with Article I, § 8, clause 17 of the United States Constitution), to avoid repeating that geographical jurisdiction in each separate section related to the different Federal crimes. Like the 1909 Act, the current 1948 Act (Title 18 U.S.C.), codifies all existing federal criminal law (except drug crimes), and is limited to lands within the exclusive jurisdiction of the United States (Federal Government). The majority of felonious Federal criminal statutes do not contain the information that they must occur within the "special maritime and territorial jurisdiction of the United

States", an "essential element". Because of this, the courts hold that the indictment is sufficient if charged in the language of the statute. Fortunately the courts also hold that it is only where the statute is in general terms and does not set out expressly and with certainty all of the elements necessary to constitute the offense that the indictment must descend to particulars and charge every constituent ingredient of which the crime is composed. In other words, you need to file a "Bill of Particulars" surrounding this "essential element" of the crime as evidenced by the provisions that limit the statutes territorial reach. No one ever does this and you can expect to be denied by the courts for obvious reasons.

Since you are ignorant of the law you are obviously unaware of the statutory provisions that limit the territorial reach of these felonious federal crimes. Remember, we learned earlier that:

> It is a longstanding principle of American law that legislation of Congress, unless a contrary intent appears, is meant to apply

> only within the territorial jurisdiction of the United States. Morrison v. National Australia Bank LTD, 177 Led2d 535, 547 (2010)

Congress has clearly defined the territorial jurisdiction of the United States at Title 18 U.S.C. § 7. The only exceptions to this "essential element" requirement are, (1) where the power to "punish" is delegated (enumerated) in the Constitution, and (2) where a misdemeanor offense is charged in connection with the execution of a delegated power. As the old saying goes, "The law is the law." In Title 18 U.S.C., Congress has defined "Interstate commerce and foreign commerce"

> The term "foreign commerce", as used in this title, includes commerce with a foreign country. 18 U.S.C. § 10

This provision cannot be applied to us unless we have imported or exported from or into a Union State or territory of the United States into or from a foreign country. Confer 20 Op. Atty. Gen. 590 (May 8, 1893), "No Federal court has jurisdiction to try persons whether or not claiming to be American citizens for crimes committed in foreign countries. There are no common law offenses against the United States [Federal Government (my note)]." It should be noted that neither the high seas, within 12 nautical miles from the coast of any ONE OF the several 50 Union States, nor the additional 12 miles (the contiguous zone), is "Territory or other Property belonging to the United States" within the meaning of the property clause.[203]

Congress can provide for the felonious punishment of importation or exportation into or from the "Customs territory of the United States,"[204] from or into a foreign country, which power comes from Article I, §

---

[203] Article IV, § 3, cl. 2, U.S. Constitution

[204] Customs territory of the United States means the several States, the District of Columbia, and Puerto Rico." Title 21 C.F.R. § 1300.01, Definitions relating to controlled substances.

8, cl. 10,"[205] not from the power to regulate commerce with foreign nations under the commerce clause. In a similar vein, Congress has also defined "interstate commerce":

> The term "Interstate Commerce", as used in this title, includes commerce between one State, Territory, Possession, or the District of Columbia and another State, Territory, Possession, or the District of Columbia. Title 18 U.S.C. § 10

The Federal Rules of Criminal Procedure, are made explicitly applicable to the United States district courts:

---

[205] "To define and punish Piracies and Felonies committed on the high Seas, and Offenses against the Law of Nations." Article I, § 8, cl. 10

These rules govern the procedure in all criminal proceedings in the United States district courts. FRCrP, Rule 1(a) (1).

Under the Federal Rules of Criminal Procedure:

State includes the District of Columbia, and any commonwealth, territory, or possession of the United States. FRCrP, Rule 1(b) (9).

As we can plainly see, the criminal rules of procedure govern[206] every criminal proceeding in all United States district courts. These rules trump all laws in conflict with them:

---

[206] Govern. To direct and control the actions or conduct of, either by established laws or by arbitrary will; to direct and control, rule, or regulate, by authority. To be a rule, precedent, law or deciding principle for. Black's Law Dictionary, Sixth Edition, page 695.

Such rules shall not abridge, enlarge or modify any substantive right. **All laws in conflict with such rules shall be of no further force or effect after such rules have taken effect.** Title 28 U.S.C. § 2072(b), Rules of procedure and evidence; power to prescribe.

We learned earlier in this Manifesto that neither these rules nor the legislation of Congress automatically apply to the several Union States, nor to any ONE OF the several Union States.[207] We also learned that it is a cardinal rule of statutory construction that words or phrases omitted were <u>intentionally</u> omitted; and that, where these missing words are not in the rules or statutes, the courts have a <u>duty</u> not to read them into those rules and statutes. This is be-

---

[207] See Title 18 U.S.C. §§ 836, 891, *supra*; and Title 26 U.S.C. § 3121 (e), *supra*.

cause, again, the Constitution vests Congress (the Legislative branch), with the sole power to legislate.[208]

The courts possess no legislative power to construe meanings to definitions using words or phrases Congress has left out. If the definition of "State" included places not mentioned it would not be necessary to define the places it does because they would automatically be included. Therefore, neither the several Union States, nor any ONE OF the several Union States, can be construed into the definition of "State" in FRCrP, Rule 1(b)(9), pursuant to the term "State" in the definition of "interstate commerce" at 18 U.S.C. § 10, because they are not mentioned.

Even where the definition of "State", for certain crimes, includes the "several States", those definitions are in conflict with the rules, which we already know supersede all laws in conflict with them. The obvious reason the rules limit the territorial reach of the "interstate commerce" statute (18 U.S.C. § 10), as it relates to Title 18 U.S.C. interstate commerce crimes, is be-

---

[208] "All legislative Powers herein granted shall be vested in a Congress of the United States which shall consist of a Senate and House of Representatives." Article I, § 1, U.S. Constitution.

cause Congress has no inherent power to "punish" felonious crimes under the Commerce Clause because the power to "punish" is not enumerated (delegated) there. The <u>Federal Rules of Criminal Procedure</u>, equally apply to all misdemeanor cases:

> In General. These rules apply in petty offenses and other misdemeanor cases and on appeal to a district judge in a case tried by a magistrate judge, unless this rule provides otherwise. <u>FRCrP</u>, Rule 58(a)(1), Petty Offenses and Other Misdemeanors

For example, the following Title 18 U.S.C. misdemeanor offenses are limited by the definition of "State" in the Federal Rules of Criminal Procedure:

> As used in this section, the term "<u>State</u>" includes the <u>several</u>

States, Territories, and possessions of the United States, and the District of Columbia. 18 U.S.C. § 836, Transportation of fireworks into State prohibiting sale or use.

The term "State" includes any State, the District of Columbia, the Commonwealth of Puerto Rico, the Northern Mariana Islands, the Virgin Islands, American Samoa, and the Trust Territory of the Pacific Islands. 18 U.S.C. § 1033(b)(1), (f)(3)(4), Crimes by or affecting persons engaged in the business of insurance whose activities affect interstate commerce.

Whoever transports by mail or otherwise to or within the District of Columbia or any Possession of the United States or uses the mails or any instrumentality of interstate commerce for the purpose of sending or bringing into any State or Territory.... 18 U.S.C. § 1821, Transportation of dentures.

It seems plausible that the reason the Federal Rules of Criminal Procedure limit the aforementioned misdemeanor offenses related to interstate transportation and commerce is because the "United States district courts" are legislative courts. What other reason could possibly exist for doing so? If the "United States district courts" were Article III courts it would not be necessary to limit their subject-matter jurisdiction to these territorial places since, under the Constitution, Congress is authorized to provide for misdemeanor offenses as "necessary & proper" for carrying into execution their delegated power to regulate commerce among the several Union States.

The reality of the "United States district courts" as legislative courts and the magnitude of the consequences as a result are devastating to our freedom and inalienable rights secured under the U.S. Constitution. For example, under the racketeering statute, legislative courts do not have subject-matter jurisdiction over "foreign commerce" violations, even if we did commit the alleged criminal activity, unless that activity occurred into or from a territory of the Federal Government. The several Union States are not territories of the Federal Government. Only that property which is owned by Congress and under their exclusive or concurrent jurisdiction is considered the "United States" in a similar vein as their own territories.

Like "foreign commerce," the same is true for "interstate commerce" under the racketeering statute. The single difference being that the alleged criminal activity must occur between land under the exclusive or concurrent jurisdiction of the Federal Government and other land under the exclusive or concurrent jurisdiction of the Federal Government.

The language, "'State' means any State of the United States," as used in the Racketeering statute,[209] is simply describing lands under the exclusive or con-

---

[209] Title 18 U.S.C. § 1961(2)

current jurisdiction of the Federal Government. This is more apparent than we generally believe because the term "United States" has already been defined in a territorial sense to mean all places subject to the jurisdiction of the United States. These territorial places subject to the jurisdiction of the United States have also been defined. *Confer* Title 18 U.S.C. § 7(3).

It should be duly noted that the District of Columbia is not a Union State but, rather, a "Federal State." There appears to be a misunderstanding about this because the District of Columbia has their own Constitution (like each of the several Union States), and refers to itself as the State of New Columbia. We know the District of Columbia is not a "Union State" because the Constitution states that:

> New States may be admitted by the Congress into this Union; but no State shall be formed or erected within the Jurisdiction of any other State; nor any State be formed by the Junction of two or more States, or parts of States,

without the Consent of the Legislatures of the States concerned as well as of the Congress. <u>Article IV, § 3, cl. I</u>, U.S. Constitution

If the District of Columbia were a Union State then it would not have been necessary for Maryland and Virginia to cede jurisdiction (exclusive legislation) to the Federal Government over the 10 miles square for the "Seat of Government of the United States." What Congress has done, since they are authorized to legislate exclusively within the District of Columbia, is create not only the D.C. Code (laws applicable only to this area), but also a Constitution for this area. Likewise, the territory of Puerto Rico has its own Constitution and is also a "Federal State" under the law.

Consequently there is a distinct and definite difference between those who are born in places subject to the jurisdiction of the United States (land under the Federal Government's concurrent or exclusive jurisdiction), which are "<u>c</u>itizens of the United States," and <u>C</u>itizens of the United States (those born within the jurisdiction of a Union State). The former can<u>not</u> be President. They can be Representatives of the House of Congress and Senators. It should also be noted here that Washington D.C., Guam, the Virgin Islands, the Northern Mariana Islands, Puerto Rico, and American Samoa have no Representatives in Congress. Instead they have "Delegates", except for Puerto Rico which has a "Resident Commissioner". This is made clear by the U.S. Constitution which states that:

> No Person shall be a Representative who shall not have attained to the Age of twenty-five Years, and been seven Years a <u>C</u>itizen of the United States [Union States United], and who shall not, when elected, be an Inhabitant of that State in which he shall be chosen. <u>Article I, § 2, cl. 2</u>, U.S. Constitution

> No Person shall be a Senator who shall not have attained to the

Age of thirty Years, and been nine Years a Citizen of the United States [Union States United], and who shall not, when elected, be an Inhabitant of that State for which he shall be chosen. Article I, § 3, cl. 3, U.S. Constitution

No person except a natural born Citizen, or a Citizen of the United States [Union States United], at the time of the Adoption of this Constitution, shall be eligible to Office of President; neither shall any person be eligible to that Office who shall not have attained to the Age of thirty-five Years, and been fourteen Years a Resident within the United States [Union States United]. Article II, § 1, cl. 5, U.S. Constitution

The Citizens of each State shall be entitled to all Privileges and Immunities of Citizens in the several States. <u>Article IV, § 2, cl. 1</u>, U.S. Constitution

All persons born or naturalized in the United States, and <u>subject to the jurisdiction</u> thereof, are citizens of the United States [federal citizens] <u>and</u> of the State wherein they reside. No State shall make or enforce any law which shall abridge the privileges or immunities of citizens of the United States; nor shall any State deprive any person of life, liberty, or property, without due process of law; nor deny to any person within its jurisdiction the equal protection of the laws. <u>Fourteenth Amendment, § 1</u>, U.S. Constitution.

The Thirteenth Amendment, ratified in the year 1865, freed the black men & women who were, at that time, all slaves. The Fourteenth Amendment, was ratified three years later in the year 1868, in order to, as it states, provide the same privileges, immunities, and equal protection of the laws for the newly freed slaves, now "federal citizens" (citizens of the "United States" [federal government]), as the white "Citizens of the United States" [the several States united], which were at that time the "Posterity" future generations, *i.e.*, the descendants of "We the People". Of course, this distinction of who is or who is not the Posterity has been diluted by the mixing of the races, not just black & white but with all the races, because of intermingling with foreigners who obtain citizenship. Those born within the territorial jurisdiction of any ONE of the several Union States are now considered a "Citizen of the United States" regardless of their ethnicity. The Fourteenth Amendment also had the simultaneous effect of providing the same protections to "federal citizens" (citizens of the United States) born in the District of Columbia, Federal Territories, like Puerto Rico, and foreigners granted citizenship, whenever they are within any of the several Union States. It should be noted here that the "Citizens of the United States" possess inalienable rights. They do not need the protections the Fourteenth Amendment provides to "citizens of the United States" ("federal citizens"), as they are each already adequately protected by their own Union State Constitution.

The Supreme Court of the United States opined that, "The distinction between citizenship of the United States and citizenship of a state is clearly recognized and established." United States v. Wong Kim Ark, 169 US 649, 676-677 (1898). The privileges and immunities clause, as well as the due process clause, provided in the Fourteenth Amendment, make this very clear. If the "citizens of the United States" and the "Citizens of the United States" were one and the same it would not have been necessary for Congress to provide a privileges and immunities clause, and due process clause, for their federal citizens. This is because they would already be adequately covered under the Privileges and Immunities clause and Due Process clause at Article IV, § 2, cl. 1, U.S. Constitution, and the Fifth Amendment, respectively.

Likewise, the American Jurisprudence (1940 edition), contains explanatory definitions which have been removed from later editions.

Both the Fourteenth Amendment to the United States Constitution and 8 USCS § 1401(a), provide that **persons born in the United States, and subject to the jurisdiction thereof, are citizens of the United States.** 3A Am Jur 2d, § 1419, Doctrine of jus soli, page 662

A person is born subject to the jurisdiction of the United States, for purposes of acquiring citizenship at birth, **if his birth occurs in territory over which the United States is sovereign**, even though another country provides all governmental services within the territory and the territory is subsequently ceded to the other country. 3A Am Jur 2d, § 1420, Who is born in United States and subject to United States jurisdiction, page 662.

Jus Soli, Latin for "right of the soil," is defined as, "The principle that a person's nationality at birth is determined by the territory within which he was born." Collins English Dictionary, Complete and Unabridged. Note the term "United States," in the above provision, is used in its singular sense, that is, "...territory over which the United States is sovereign." Note, in particular, the pivotal word "sovereign," which controls the entire meaning of that passage. The Federal Government (United States) is only sovereign over land within the territorial boundaries of the Union States if ONE OF the 50 Union States relinquishes territorial (legislative) jurisdiction over that land through cession or consent to purchase, with acceptance.

I would like to mention that while federal citizens are not "natural born" for purposes of the Presidency, they can become Citizens by simply choosing to reside within the Union States. How long they have to reside within the Union States to obtain Citizenship may need to be determined by each Union State's particular laws. However, in order for citizens to be eligible as Representatives of the House, and Senators, they must reside within the Union States for seven and nine years, respectively. This brings us to consider drug crimes under Title 21 U.S.C. which states that:

> The term "State" means a State of the United States, the District of Columbia, and any commonwealth, territory, or possession of the United States. Title 21 U.S.C. § 801(26)

> The term "United States", when used in a geographic sense, means all places and waters, continental or insular, subject to the jurisdiction of the United States. Title 21 U.S.C. § 801(28)

So, under the Federal drug laws codified at 21 U.S.C. § 801 *et seq.*,[210] a "State" is any place subject

---

[210] Et seq. An abbreviation for et sequentes (masculine and feminine plural) or et sequential (neuter), "and the following." Thus a Continued on next page.

to the jurisdiction of the Federal Government. In the several Union States these places are limited by the Constitution to lands under the exclusive or concurrent jurisdiction of the Federal Government. It is these places where legislative courts have criminal jurisdiction (subject-matter jurisdiction over crimes). [211] Article III courts also have subject-matter jurisdiction over crimes that occur on lands within the exterior territorial boundaries of any Union State under the concurrent or exclusive legislative (territorial) jurisdiction of the Federal Government ("United States"). Even if the term "State of the United States" meant all of the several Union States, it would be in conflict with the Federal Rules of Criminal Procedure ("FRCrP"). As we have previously shown earlier in this Manifesto, the words "any person," as used in the drug laws codified in Title 21 U.S.C. § 801, *et seq.*, do not literal-

---

reference to "p. 1, et seq." means "page first and the following pages." Also abbreviated "et seq.," which is preferred by some authorities for a reference to more than one following page. Black's Law Dictionary, Sixth Edition, page 554.

[211] Even though Congress can provide for the prosecution of felonies where the power to "punish" is delegated in the Constitution, the legislative courts only have jurisdiction if the crime occurs over land owned by the Federal Government and under their exclusive or concurrent jurisdiction, regardless of where the power to "punish" is delegated in the Constitution.

ly mean any person in the world but, rather, is limited by the above mentioned provisions to persons within the territorial (legislative) jurisdiction of the "United States" (Federal Government). This limitation is set in stone and cannot be applied to you, even as a misdemeanor pursuant to the execution of the power to regulate interstate commerce, because the drug laws expose you to more than one year imprisonment. Remember, we learned earlier that whether an offense is a felony, or not, depends on the punishment which may be imposed, not on the punishment which is imposed.

We also learned that, under positive law (Title 28 U.S.C. § 2072(b)), the rules of procedure and evidence supersede all laws in conflict with them. Since the Federal Rules of Criminal Procedure govern procedure in all criminal proceedings in the "United States district courts"[212] and define "State" to include only the District of Columbia, and any commonwealth, territory, or possession of the United States,[213] no federal crime has been committed which the Federal

---

[212] Rule 1(a)(1)

[213] Rule 1(b)(9)

courts can take cognizance of if the alleged criminal "interstate commerce" crime, or drug crime, occurs outside of those places.

If the definition of "State" in the Federal Rules of Criminal Procedure included places not mentioned, like the several Union States for example, it would not have been necessary to define this term at all. It would also not have been necessary to enact a statutory provision informing us that the rules of procedure supersede all laws in conflict with them. Because the term "several States" has been used in other definitions of "State" (see, for example, 18 U.S.C. § 836, Paragraph 4), yet has not been used in the definition of "State" in the Federal Rules of Criminal Procedure, it should not be implied. See Wong Kim Bo, *supra* at 722:

> [W]here Congress has carefully employed a term in one place and excluded it in another, it should not be implied where excluded.

The same principle applies to the term "State of the United States," which term is also conspicuously absent from the definition of "State" in the Federal Rules of Criminal Procedure. The term "Include" is a word of limitation and defined as:

> (Lat. Inclaudere, to shut in, keep within.) To confine within, hold as in an enclosure, take in, attain, shut up, contain, enclose, comprise, comprehend, embrace, involve. Term may, according to context, express an enlargement and have the meaning of "and" or "in addition to", or merely specify a particular thing already included within general words theretofore [up to that time] used. "Including" within statute is interpreted as a word of enlargement or of illustrative application as well as a word

of limitation. <u>Black's L.aw Dictionary</u>, Sixth Edition, page 763.

When the term "includes" is meant to be used as a term of enlargement certain general words will come before it. For example, "The steak dinner <u>includes</u> a baked potato." The general words "steak dinner" is merely specifying a particular thing, the "baked potato", already included.

Another example is, "The 'United States of America', being composed of 50 Union States, <u>includes</u> ["and"] the District of Columbia, any commonwealth, territory, or possession of the United States." As utilized in that example, the term "includes" has the meaning of "and."

When the term "includes" is used as a word of limitation it will "contain" or "embrace" only certain meanings. For example, "Fruit, includes apples, oranges, and water melon." Is there any reason to believe the definition of "Fruit" given includes other fruit not mentioned? Is it not true that if the definition of "Fruit" given included unmentioned fruit, it would not be necessary to define the term "Fruit" to include the fruit it does, because the term "Fruit" would then be given it's natural, plain, ordinary and commonly understood meaning of every type of fruit imaginable? See Wong Kim Bo, *supra* at 722:

> In construing statutes, words are to be given their natural, plain, ordinary and commonly understood meaning unless it is clear that some other meaning was intended.

The term "Fruit" must be given its "known and ordinary signification, unless that sense be repelled by the context." Lessee of Levy et al. v. M'Cartee, 31 US 102, 6 Pet. 102, 110 (1832).

The term "context" is defined as "those parts of a writing which precede and follow a phrase or passage in question, and which may be looked at to explain the meaning of the phrase or passage". The Law Dictionary, Copyright (c)2002 Anderson Publishing Co.

In order to determine the meaning of the term "Fruit", as we have defined it above, we must look to the words which precede or follow it. Since no words precede it to help us determine the meaning of "Fruit" we must look to the words that follow it. We can therefore explain the term "Fruit" to mean apples, oranges, and water melon. As we can see, without that explanatory context, the term "Fruit" would be given its ordinary, usually plural, and commonly understood meaning of every type of fruit imaginable, *i.e.*, "The produce of a tree or plant which contains the seed or is used for food. The edible reproductive body of a seed or plant." Black's Law Dictionary, Sixth Edition, page 669.

The same is true for the term "State" as defined in the Federal Rules of Criminal Procedure. Because the words (context) that follow the term "State" do not include the "several States", we can explain its meaning to be limited to the "District of Columbia, any commonwealth, territory, or possession of the United States". Since we know the power to "punish" is not enumerated (delegated) under the "Commerce Clause" and Congress does not have territorial jurisdiction (exclusive legislation) over all of the several

Union States (if they did jurisdiction would not need to be ceded), and because we know the definition of "State" in the Federal Rules of Criminal Procedure does not include unmentioned places, our interpretation of this rule of criminal procedure is in perfect harmony with the doctrines of law and cardinal rule of statutory construction that words or phrases omitted were intended to be omitted. For example, the definition of "Northwest Territory" does not include other States not mentioned: "This area includes the present states of Ohio, Indiana, Illinois, Michigan, Wisconsin, and the eastern part of Minnesota." Black's Law Dictionary, Eighth Edition, page 1087.

Think of it this way, if the term "Wabadeedoobadee," includes apples, oranges, green peppers, 1969 Camaro super sport cars, turtles, and motorcycles, what else does it include? Answer: Nothing else. It only includes the items expressly mentioned defining that term.

Because Congress alone can legislate, [214] the courts cannot construe meanings to definitions using words or phrases that Congress has left out. This is why courts have a duty not to read missing words or phrases into congressional legislation which are not there. It is because in doing so they would be legislating, which they have no constitutional authority to do.

I just want to explain one more thing. Title 21 U.S.C. states that:

> Rules and regulations. The Attorney General may promulgate and enforce any rules, regulations, and procedures which he may deem necessary and appropriate for the efficient execution of his functions under this title. Title 28 U.S.C. § 871(b)

---

[214] Even though Congress can provide for the prosecution of felonies where the power to "punish" is delegated in the Constitution, legislative courts only have jurisdiction if the crime occurs over land owned by the Federal Government and under their exclusive or concurrent jurisdiction, regardless of where the power to "punish" is delegated in the Constitution.

The Code of Federal Regulations state that:

> Jurisdiction of the United States means the <u>customs territory</u> of the United States,[215] Virgin Islands, the Canal Zone, Guam, American Samoa, and the Trust Territories of the Pacific Islands. <u>Title 21 C.F.R. § 1300.01</u>, Definitions relating to controlled substances.
>
> <u>Customs territory</u> of the United States means the <u>several States</u>, the District of Columbia, and Puerto Rico. <u>Title 21 C.F.R. §</u>

---

[215] Customs. This term is usually applied to those <u>taxes</u> which are payable upon goods and merchandise <u>imported or exported</u>. The duties, toll, tribute, or tariff payable upon merchandise exported or imported. Federal agency responsible for assessing imported goods and collecting duties. <u>Black's Law Dictionary</u>, Sixth Edition, page 386.

<u>1300.01</u>, Definitions relating to controlled substances.

Do not be discouraged or confused by the fact that these <u>regulations</u> define the jurisdiction of the United States to mean the several States (Customs territory of the United States). These are regulations relating to commerce. They are not criminal statutes. They do <u>not</u>, and can<u>not</u>, expand the jurisdiction of the Federal Government to punish felonies. The word "jurisdiction" has been broadly expanded, by forced constructions, over the years to distort its true meaning and unconstitutionally expand the very limited powers delegated to the Federal Government. The regulation defining the jurisdiction of the United States (Federal Government) to include the "several States" is being used in the same sense as the word "authority", and is <u>not</u> expanding the territorial jurisdiction of the Federal Government to punish felonious crimes. See "Jurisdiction":

The right or power to interpret and apply the law. **Authority or control.** The territorial range over which an authority extends. Webster' New Basic Dictionary, Office Edition, page 392.

The limits imposed on Congress by the Constitution are set in stone. The only way to change those limitations is to amend the Constitution. Remember, we learned earlier that:

Congress can<u>not</u> by legislation, enlarge the Federal jurisdiction, nor can it be enlarged by the treaty-making power.

Special provision is made in the constitution for the <u>cession</u> of jurisdiction from States over <u>places</u> where the federal government shall establish forts or other military works. **And it is only in these places**, or in the territories of the United States, **where it can exercise a general jurisdiction**. United States v. Illinois Central R. Co., 154 US 225, 239-241 (1894) (quoting New Orleans v. United States, 35 US 662, 10 Pet 662, 736-737, 9 LEd 573 (1836))

Absent, (1) documentation showing ownership by the United States (Federal Government), over the exact geographical location(s) wherein the charging document alleges the criminal activity occurred, (2) evidentiary documentation showing a cession by the Legislature(s) of the particular Union State(s) surrendering exclusive or concurrent jurisdiction over the same exact geographical location(s); or evidentiary documentation showing purchase by consent of the Legislature of the particular Union State, and (3) documentation showing acceptance of jurisdiction by the United States (Federal Government), over the same geographical location(s), the "United States district courts" have no subject-matter jurisdiction over felony offenses where the power to "punish" is not enumerated (delegated) in the Constitution (assuming arguendo they are Article III courts).

Without the delegated (enumerated) power to "punish" or ownership and territorial (general) jurisdiction (concurrent or exclusive legislation) over the place (land) where the crime occurred (which can only be obtained through consent to purchase, or cession, and acceptance), no felony "offense against the laws of the United States" can be charged with which the "United States district courts" can take cognizance (assuming arguendo they are Article III courts). This is because that land (place) is not territory of the United States in the same vein as the District of Columbia or Puerto Rico. In other words, Congress does not have sovereignty and dominion (general/ territorial jurisdiction) over those places (land). The Supreme Court previously explained that:

> Where lands are acquired without such <u>consent</u>, the possession of

the United States, unless political jurisdiction be ceded to them in some other way, is simply that of an ordinary proprietor. [216] Fort Leavenworth R.R. Co. v. Lowe, 114 US 525, 531-533, 29 LEd 264 (1885)

As we can clearly see, if the several Union States were already territories belonging to the United States (Federal Government), jurisdiction would not need to be ceded,[217] and the property clause,[218] as well as Article III, would be superfluous. The Framers of the Constitution were not morons adding and ratifying completely useless and meaningless provisions to the Constitution.

The obvious reason Congress has defined the term "United States" in a territorial sense at 18 U.S.C.

---

[216] Proprietor. One who has the legal right or exclusive title to property, business, etc. In many instances it is synonymous with owner. Black's Law Dictionary, Sixth Edition, page 1,220

[217] Article I, § 8, cl.17, U.S. Constitution

[218] Article IV, § 3, cl. 2, U.S. Constitution

§ 5 is because the United States (Federal Government) owns land throughout the several 50 Union States where concurrent or exclusive legislative (territorial) jurisdiction has been relinquished to them via Article I, § 8, cl. 17. The full statutory definition of the "United States" being defined at 18 U.S.C. § 7, *i.e.*, territorial places "subject to the jurisdiction of the United States". In light of this territorial definition of the "United States," we can better understand the lawful constitutional application of the numerous felonious crimes codified in Title 18 U.S.C. as being limited to certain geographical places under the concurrent or exclusive legislative jurisdiction of the Federal Government.

Since the Constitution only delegates to the Federal Government the power to "punish" three crimes feloniously: counterfeiting, piracies & felonies committed on the high seas, and treason, we can logically deduce that other felonious federal crimes have no constitutional application within the Union States. Therefore the majority of felonious federal crimes are enacted pursuant to other enumerated powers where the power to "punish" is not delegated, for example, the "Exclusive Legislation Clause" (Article I, § 8, cl.

17) and the "Territory Clause" (Article IV, § 3, cl 2). Their constitutional application is limited to lands where the Federal Government exercises concurrent or exclusive legislative jurisdiction, such as federal enclaves and the territories.

As we learned earlier in this Manifesto, Congress has defined the jurisdiction of both the Article III and legislative federal and Union State courts:

> The district courts of the United States shall have original jurisdiction, exclusive of the courts of the States, of all offenses against the laws of the United States.
>
> Nothing in this title shall be held to take away or impair the jurisdiction of the courts of the several States under the laws thereof. Title 18 U.S.C. § 3231

It appears the "United States district courts," and Union State courts, are the "courts of the State" as distinguished from the constitutional Article III "district courts of the United States." The last paragraph is simply stating that nothing in Title 18 U.S.C. shall be held to take away or impair the jurisdiction of any Union State court regarding their own laws.

Remember, the term "district court of the United States", as defined in Title 28 U.S.C. § 451, includes the legislative "United States district court" for the Judicial District of Puerto Rico in that term, which definition is only applicable to Title 28 U.S.C. *Confer*, "As used in this title". It does not make the "United States district courts" applicable to the term "district courts of the United States", in Title 18 U.S.C. § 3231, which term, standing alone and without further qualification, includes only constitutional courts established under Article III.[219] The Ninth Circuit explained that:

---

[219] "The term 'District Court of the United States,' [in its historic and proper sense] ... has its historic significance. It describes the constitutional courts created under article 3 of the Constitution." Mookini v. United States, 303 US 201, 205 (1938)

The words 'district court of the United States' [in their historic, technical sense], commonly describe constitutional courts creat-
Continued on next page.

> Non-Article III courts [can] enforce federal criminal laws <u>in special geographic areas</u> where, pursuant to clause 17,[220] it functions as <u>a state government</u>. <u>United States v. Jenkins</u>, 734 F2d 1322, 1325-1326 (9th Cir. 1983) (citing <u>United States v. Palmore</u>, 411 US 389 (1973)

As we can clearly see, legislative (non-Article III) courts, operate like a "<u>state</u> government" in special geographic areas where jurisdiction has been relinquished under <u>Article I, § 8, cl. 17</u>. These "special geographic areas" are the "States" the <u>FRCrP</u>, are describing under Rule 1(b)(9). Any place (land) that is under the exclusive or concurrent jurisdiction of Congress is a "State" under the <u>FRCrP</u>. See, for example

---

ed under Article 3 of the Constitution." <u>International L. & W. U. v. Juneau Corp.</u>, 342 US 237, 241 (1952)

[220] <u>Article I, § 8, cl. 17</u>, U.S. Constitution

Federal Rules of Bankruptcy Procedure ("FRBP"), Rule 9006, "New subdivision (a)(6) defines ... the term 'state' ... to include the District of Columbia and any commonwealth or territory of the United States. Thus, ... 'state' includes the District of Columbia, Guam, American Samoa, the U.S. Virgin Islands, the Commonwealth of Puerto Rico, and the Commonwealth of the Northern Mariana Islands." Id. at History; Ancillary Laws and Directives; other provisions; Notes of Advisory Committee on 2009 amendments; Note to Subdivision (a)(6). See also Title 48 U.S.C. § 1801, "'Territory or possession' with respect to the United States includes the District of Columbia, the Commonwealth of Puerto Rico, the Virgin Islands, Guam and American Samoa." ID. at History; Ancillary Laws and Directives; Other provisions; Covenant to Establish Commonwealth of the Northern Mariana Islands in Political Union with the United States of America; Section 1005 (d). The same is true for Title 26 U.S.C. which states that:

> (a) When used in this title, where not otherwise distinctly expressed

or manifestly incompatible with the intent thereof-

(9) United States. The term "United States" when used in a geographical sense includes only the States and the District of Columbia.

(10) State. The term "State" shall be construed to include the District of Columbia, where such construction is necessary to carry out provisions of this title. Title 26 U.S.C. § 7701, Definitions.

The only place where the term "United States" means (not "includes" all territories, but "means" only specified lands and territories) either the "50 States" or the "several States" is 26 U.S.C. § 4612(a)(4)(A), and Title 26 U.S.C., Subtitle D, Miscellaneous Excise Taxes; History; Ancillary Laws and Directives; Other provisions; Imposition of annual fee on health insurance providers, (h)(2), respectively. The only place where the term "State" includes "any of the 50 States", is 26 U.S.C. § 6103(b)(5)(A). Even so, we know that the power to "punish" has not been delegated in aid of Congress' taxing power. [221] Notwithstanding the fact that legislative and constitutional courts have no jurisdiction over crimes that occur outside of places (lands) under the exclusive or concurrent jurisdiction of the Federal Government ("United States"), Article III courts only have subject-matter jurisdiction over felonious crimes that occur throughout the "several" or "50 [Union] States", if the crime is pursuant to a provision where the power to "punish" is delegated (enumerated) in the Constitution. We also know that all federal criminal laws where the definition of "State" is defined, or otherwise made applicable, that are in conflict with the definition of "State" in FRCrP, Rule 1(b)(9), which govern criminal proceedings in "United States district courts" pursuant to Rule 1(a)(1), are null and void pursuant to positive law codified at Title 28 U.S.C. § 2072(b).

---

[221] Article I, § 8, cl. 1, U.S. Constitution; and the Sixteenth Amendment

To reiterate, the fact that the definition of "State" in the Federal Rules of Criminal Procedure does not contain or embrace the words "several States" affirms the 50 Union States are not included in that definition. We can logically deduce that this omission was intentionally and purposefully done to reflect the evident fact that the power to "punish" is not enumerated under the "Commerce Clause" (which proves it is not delegated and consequently reserved to the Union States via the Tenth Amendment), therefore limiting Congress' power to provide for the punishment of felonious "interstate commerce" crimes within the territorial (legislative) jurisdiction of the several 50 Union States. As the Supreme Court explained:

> In expounding the Constitution of the United States, every word must have its due force, and appropriate meaning; for it is evident from the whole instrument, that no word [like the power to "punish" (my note)] was unnecessarily used, or needless-

ly added. The many discussions which have taken place upon the construction of the Constitution have proved the correctness of this proposition; and shown the high talent, the caution, and the foresight of the illustrious men who framed it. Every word [including the difference between "citizen" and "Citizen" (my note)] appears to have been weighed with the utmost deliberation, and its force and effect to have been fully understood. <u>Wright v. United States</u>, 302 US 583 588 (1938)(citing cases)

"To disregard such a deliberate choice of words and their natural meaning would be a departure from the first principle of constitutional interpretation." Id. Keeping that in mind we can plainly see that the power to punish is not delegated under the Sixteenth Amendment. This means that Congress cannot punish felonious "tax" crimes, 26 U.S.C. § 7201 *et seq.*, within the territorial (legislative) jurisdiction of any 1 of the 50 Union States, except where land has been purchased by the "United States" (Federal Government) with the consent of the particular Union State or where concurrent or exclusive legislative (territorial) jurisdiction has been subsequently relinquished through cession, and accepted. These are the places where Congress, via Article I, § 8, cl. 17, is authorized under the Constitution to punish felonies (or legislate exclusively) other than where the power to "punish" is enumerated (delegated). See for example Title 26 U.S.C. § 7201 which, like the drug crimes, contains the words "any person" and is a felony. As we showed earlier in this Manifesto, the words "<u>any person</u>" or "<u>every person</u>" do not literally mean everyone that the legislature is able to catch but, rather, only those who are subject to such legislation. Remember, Congress cannot "punish" felonies generally. Accordingly, absent a constitutional foundation supporting an extra-territorial application of the felonious tax crime, for example, a delegated (enumerated) power to "punish", such legislation is limited to Federal Territories or other property (lands) under the concurrent or exclusive legislative (territorial) jurisdiction of the "United States" (Federal Government).

Considering Congress' ability to establish legislative courts under Article I, § 8, cl. 17 respecting property throughout the several 50 Union States under their concurrent or exclusive legislative (territorial) jurisdiction, how do we determine the "United States district courts" status as legislative or Article III courts when they clearly are not continuations of the former constitutional "district courts of the United States" established under Article III? Especially when the current Judiciary Act does not reflect the status of the "United States district courts" as being "ordained & established" under Article III or clearly convey through a name change provision that they are the former Article III "district courts of the United States"? This is compounded by the fact that the term "United States district court" historically refers to territorial courts.

Even though Title 28 U.S.C. defines the term "district court of the United States" to embrace the "United States district courts" that term also embraces the "United States district court" for the Judicial District of Puerto Rico. The aforementioned may not, by itself, amount to proof of the "United States district courts" status as legislative courts. However, coupled with the limitations under the Federal Rules of Criminal Procedure pertaining to the term "State", as it relates to felonious and misdemeanor crimes, it certainly raises some red flags. We can be certain, in light of all the ambiguity surrounding the "United States district courts" status as either legislative courts or as continuations of the former Article III "district courts of the United States", and the complete absence of any congressional legislation providing some clarification on this issue, that the law on this point is vague for a reason.

SUBSTANTIAL EFFECTS TEST?

I would just like to say that under the Constitution there is no such thing as a substantial effects test. All you medical marijuana growers and those convicted of drug crimes will appreciate this section. As many of you are well aware, the Federal Government is now prosecuting drug and felon in possession of firearms crimes without any interstate nexus.[222] There is always an excuse and ruse to expand the jurisdiction of the United States (Federal Government) in order to prosecute crimes without any lawful authority under the Constitution (our Supreme Law) to do so. Because We the People have not been vigilant in guarding our freedom and other personal liberties, tyrants have crept in. They work continuously in an effort to advance their own personal interests under the guise that it is all in our best interests. I don't know about everyone else, but the very fact that we have limited the Federal Government's power under the Constitution says exactly what We the People believe

---

[222] Nexus. CONNECTION, LINK. Webster's Ninth New Collegiate Dictionary, 1991, page 797.

is best for Us. Unfortunately, those who's sworn oath and first duty is to uphold our Constitution are doing everything but upholding it.

Before I speak further about the substantial effects test, I want to discuss a few articles from "Rolling Stone" magazine. This section should be of equal interest to those Union States that have voted to legalize marijuana for medical use or decriminalize it. A March 1, 2012, article in "Rolling Stone" magazine entitled "Obama's War on Pot," by Tim Dickinson, illustrates the oppressive control on the States by the Federal Government that we are all currently facing. It states that, "Back when he was running for president in 2008, Barack Obama insisted that medical marijuana was an issue best left to state and local governments." In that article they quote the president (then a candidate) as saying that, "I'm not going to be using Justice Department resources to try to circumvent state laws on this issue." It goes on to further state that a multiagency crackdown has been quietly unleashed on growers who are in full compliance with state laws. This, all in total disregard for the estimated 730,000 nationwide patients who are seriously ill or dying and reliant on "state-sanctioned marijuana" prescribed by their doctors.

The article states that local officials in the City of Oakland, California, "Moved to raise millions in taxes by licensing high-tech indoor facilities for growing medical marijuana." However, after the Federal Government threatened that they would vigorously enforce the Controlled Substances Act (Federal Drug Laws) against individuals and organizations, "Even if such activities are permitted under state law," the article states that, "Oakland quickly scuttled its plans, even though the taxes provided by the indoor grows could have single-handedly wiped out the city's $31 million deficit." I guess Oakland will just have to stay in debt even though the Federal Government has no authority under the Constitution to do anything about it.

That same article states that the ATF warned gun sellers that, "It is unlawful to sell any firearm or ammunition to any person who is addicted to marijuana, regardless of whether his or her state has passed legislation authorizing marijuana use for medicinal purposes." In other words, if a doctor prescribes you medical marijuana, then you would be stripped of your Second Amendment right to own a gun.

Lastly the article states that these illegally enforced, oppressive, federal laws have also deprived San Francisco, California of $180,000 in annual tax revenue; That in San Diego alone 2,500 jobs were destroyed by the Federal Government; That in Colorado, top banks, "Including Chase, Wells Fargo and Bank of America—are refusing to do business with state-licensed dispensaries, for fear of federal prosecution for money laundering and other federal drug crimes." The Federal Government also shut down, "Harbor Health Center, one of the largest and most respected providers of medical cannabis in California. Its Oakland branch, serving 83,000 patients in conforming with state law, paid more than $1 million in City taxes." Unfortunately for California and those 83,000 patients, the I.R.S. stepped in and slapped a bogus $2.5 million bill for back taxes on the Health Center. They now face bankruptcy.

Another "Rolling Stone" article in their December 20, 2012—January 3, 2013 issue, entitled, "Obama's

Pot Problem," by Tim Dickinson, states the following in an editorial entitled, "Mr. President, End This War":

> As a Teenager, Barack Obama liked to get high in the back of a friend's VW bus. His hallmark: a smoking technique he called Total Absorption. He knows, as did George W. Bush and Bill Clinton before him, what we all know: that pot is essentially harmless. Yet the government continues to wage a costly war on marijuana, treating pot as if it were more dangerous than crack cocaine.
>
> More than 750,000 Americans were arrested last year—87 percent for simple possession. The costs of prohibition are staggering—nearly $8 <u>billion</u> a year wasted on police and prisons alone, with billions more squandered by not taxing pot like

tobacco or alcohol. Nearly 30 million Americans enjoyed pot at least once last year.

Maybe the Union States prefer being told what to do and kept in debt by a Federal Government with no lawful authority under the Constitution to do so? If that is true, then why did We the People not amend the Constitution to allow this tyrannical, oppressive, control to be exercised by the Federal Government lawfully? The Representatives in Congress are made up from the Union States. How is it then that the Union States are voting to legalize medical marijuana yet the Federal Government (made up of those Union State Representatives), continue to criminalize marijuana? And with no interstate-nexus to boot! As the March 1, 2012, "Rolling Stone" magazine article states, medical pot, "Is legal in 16 states **and the District of Columbia**." How's that for a nice swift kick in the teeth?

According to the Supreme Court, once articles of commerce become commingled with the property of the State, the power of regulation ends.[223] However, the Supreme Court has also explained about regulating articles of commerce solely within a Union State because of their substantial affect on interstate commerce. This is called the "substantial effects test." That term and Supreme Court case law relied on to support it have been contorted by the Federal Government, in the usual fashion, to reach items wholly within a Union State not intended for interstate transportation, like marijuana. It is well known that Congress cannot regulate every item wholly within the intrastate commerce of any Union State which has an economic effect on like items in interstate commerce. The Supreme Court explained that:

> It is well established by decisions of this court that the power to regulate commerce includes the

---

[223] "[P]ower of regulation continues until the final delivery of the imported articles." Wabash R. Co. v. Pearce, 192 US 179, 188 (1904)

power to regulate prices at which commodities in that commerce are dealt in and practices affecting such prices.

Home-grown wheat in this sense competes with wheat in commerce. Wickard v. Filburn, 317 US 111, 128 (1942)

In Wickard the farmer agreed to only grow a certain allotted amount of wheat. This limitation on the supply of wheat would increase its value. Farmer Filburn would then receive more money for his supply of wheat than he would have received on the open market. Farmer Filburn, however, decided to grow wheat in excess of the limitations agreed on. He claimed that the excess wheat was only for his personal use and not intended for interstate commerce. The Supreme Court found that because Filburn would not have to purchase or retain the wheat he needed, it economically affected the price on the other wheat being sold in interstate commerce. Because of this, Congress was allowed to regulate that wheat even though it was not intended for interstate commerce. We have to keep in mind that Congress was not regulating all wheat grown by other farmers but, rather, like Farmer Filburn, only those who contracted with the Federal Government to grow a certain amount of wheat. Since Congress has made marijuana illegal, they are not contracting with anyone to grow it, and therefore are not regulating its price. Homegrown marijuana then, not intended for interstate commerce, has no economic affect on marijuana traveling in interstate commerce. Congress does not have federal control to regulate whatever object they believe is a national matter. *Cf.* United States v. Lopez, *infra.*

It should be duly noted that the Controlled Substances Act ("C.S.A.") does not make it a crime to transport drugs through interstate commerce. Congress talks about their interest in federal control over intrastate and interstate trafficking in controlled substances, however, none of the penalties under the C.S.A. (21 U.S.C. § 801, *et seq.*), mention anything about transporting drugs through interstate commerce. Neither do they mention anything about such activity having a substantial effect on interstate commerce. Congress only makes it unlawful for anyone to possess with intent to distribute drugs. Interstate commerce is not even mentioned. In fact, the only "drug law" that even mentions "interstate commerce" is 28 U.S.C. § 863(a)(2), Drug paraphernalia, which states that it is unlawful for any person—"to use the mails or any other facility of interstate commerce to transport drug paraphernalia." It then defines "Drug paraphernalia" at (d), which does not include any drugs, only devices for using drugs.

Remember, Congress has zero power to prohibit drugs on a nationwide scale. See footnote 236, infra, "Congress understood that it could not establish nationwide prohibitions. Nor was there any statute that purported to regulate activities with 'substantial effects' on interstate commerce". They have nothing approaching a police power, they have no territorial jurisdiction, and they have no delegated power to "punish" drugs under the Constitution. Even if the Constitution delegated to Congress the enumerated power to "punish" under the Commerce Clause (which it obviously does not), Congress has not legislated this way by making it a crime to sell or transport drugs in or through interstate commerce under the drug laws. Nor have they made it a crime to substantially effect interstate commerce by growing, selling, or transporting drugs intrastate. Last time I checked we were at the very least entitled to be made aware that such conduct was unlawful. However, it cannot be unlawful if Congress has not made it against the law in the first place.

It is apparent that the reason the drug laws do not make it a crime to substantially effect or transport drugs in or through interstate commerce is because they have no such delegated power to "punish" felonies under the Commerce Clause. The Supreme Court recently reiterated that

> A criminal statute must clearly define the conduct it proscribes. If it does not give a person of ordinary intelligence fair notice of its scope, it denies due process. Bond v. United States, 2014 BL 151637, U.S., No. 12-158 (2014)(citing United States v. Batchelder, 442 US 114, 123 (1979))

Other cases relied on by the Federal Government to regulate items of commerce wholly within the Union States that substantially affect interstate commerce are based on the fact that the items in question are intended for interstate commerce.[224] The Supreme Court explained that:

> At the formation of the Union, the states delegated to the Federal Government authority to regulate commerce among the states. So long as the things done within the States by the United States are valid under that power, there can be no interference with the sovereignty of the State. **It is the nondelegated power** which under the Tenth Amendment

---

[224] United States v. Darby, 312 US 100, 114 (1941); Seven Cases v. United States, 239 US 510 (1916); Hamilton v. Kentucky Distilleries & Warehouse Co., 251 US 146, 156 (1919)

remains in the state or the people. United States v. Appalachain Electric Company, 311 US 377, 428 (1940)

We learned earlier in this Manifesto that the Supreme Court related the Police Power to violent crimes,[225] and stated that, "The Federal Government has nothing approaching a police power."[226] This is, again, because the Federal Government has no territorial jurisdiction except where it has been relinquished through cession or consent to purchase and because, "The police power of the States [territorial jurisdiction to "punish" felonies or enact other legislation within the several 50 Union States not consistent with, or in excess of, their delegated powers] was not surrendered when the people of the United States conferred upon Congress the general power to regulate commerce with foreign nations and between

---

[225] United States v. Morrison, *supra* at 618.

[226] United States v. Lopez, 514 US 549, 584-585 (1995)

the several States.[227] The Supreme Court has continuously explained:

> That the United States lacks the police power and that this was reserved to the states by the 10th Amendment is true. Hamilton v. Kentucky Distilleries & Warehouse Co., 251 US 146, 156 (1919)

Chief Justice Roberts, speaking for the Supreme Court, recently opined concerning the "police power" reserved to the several Union States as follows:

> In our federal system, the National Government possesses only limited powers; the States

---

[227] Patterson v. Kentucky, 97 US 501, 505 (1879)

and the people retain the remainder.

The Federal Government "is acknowledged by all to be one of <u>enumerated powers</u>." *Ibid*. That is, rather than granting general authority to perform all the conceivable functions of government, the Constitution lists, or enumerates, the Federal Government's powers. Congress may, for example, "coin Money", "establish Posts Offices", and "raise and support Armies". Art. I, § 8, cls. 5, 7, 12. **The enumeration of powers is also a <u>limitation of powers, because</u> "[t]he <u>enumeration presupposes something not enumerated</u>."** <u>Gibbons v. Ogden</u>, 22 US 1, 9 Wheat 1, 195, 6 LEd 23 (1824). The Constitution's express conferral of some powers makes clear that it does not grant others.

And the Federal Government "can exercise only the powers granted to it." McCulloch, *supra*, at 405, 4 Wheat 316, 4 LEd 579.

Today, the restrictions on government power foremost in many Americans' minds are likely to be affirmative prohibitions, such as contained in the Bill of Rights. These affirmative prohibitions come into play, however, only where the Government possesses authority to act in the first place. **If no <u>enumerated power</u> authorizes Congress to pass a certain law, that law may not be enacted**, even if it would not violate any of the express prohibitions in the Bill of Rights or elsewhere in the Constitution.

Indeed, the Constitution did not initially include a Bill of Rights at least partly because the Framers felt the enumeration of powers sufficed to restrain the Government. As Alexander Hamilton put it, "the Constitution is itself, in every rational sense, and to every useful purpose, A BILL OF RIGHTS." The Federalist No. 84, p. 515 (C. Rossiter ed. 1961). And when the Bill of Rights was ratified, it made express what the enumeration of powers necessarily implied: "The powers not delegated to The United States by the Constitution ... are reserved to the States respectively, or to the people." U.S. Const., Amdt. 10. The Federal Government has expanded dramatically over the past two centuries, but it still must show that a constitutional grant of power authorizes each of its actions. See, e.g., United States v. Comstock, 130 SCt 1949 (2010).

The same does not apply to the States, because the Constitution is not the source of their power. The Constitution may restrict state governments—as it does, for example, by forbidding them to deny any person the equal protection of the laws. But where such prohibitions do not apply, state governments do not need constitutional authorization to act. The States thus can and do perform many of the vital functions of modern government—punishing street crime, running public schools, and zoning property for development, to name but a few—even though the Constitution's text does not authorize any government to do so. Our cases refer to this general power of governing, possessed by the States but not by the Federal Government, as the "police power." See, e.g., United States v. Morrison, 529 US 598, 618-619 (2000).

"State sovereignty is not just an end in itself: Rather, federalism secures to citizens the liberties that derive from the diffusion of sovereign power." New York v. United States, 505 US 144, 181 (1992). Because the police power is controlled by 50 different States instead of one national sovereign, **the facets of governing that touch on citizens' daily lives are normally administered by smaller governments closer to the governed.** The Framers thus insured that **powers which "in the ordinary course of affairs, concern the lives, liberties, and properties of the people" were held by governments more local and more accountable** than a distant federal bureaucracy. The Federalist No. 45, at 293 (J. Madison). The independent power of the States also serves as a check on the power of the Federal Government: "By denying any one government complete jurisdiction over all the concerns of public life, federalism protects the liberty of the individual from arbitrary power." Bond v. United States, 131 SCt 2355 (2011). National Federation of Indep. Bus. v. Sebelius, 183 LEd2d 450, 465-466 (2012)

I would like to quickly reiterate that the obvious reason the 50 Union States remained separate sovereigns, each with their own separate and individual governments and laws, instead of combining into one individual sovereignty, growing larger with each new addition of territory, was to maintain liberty, and suppress any possibility of tyranny, by keeping the governments small and close to the people, so they could be more easily controlled and held accountable.

Moving on, it should be noted that the Supreme Court in <u>Comstock</u> decided that a sexually dangerous person could be civilly detained under the necessary and proper clause if the person had been convicted of a federal crime. The dissenting opinion argued that in doing so Congress was not acting in pursuance of the exercise of a delegated power. As we have learned in this Manifesto, a person is actually innocent of committing a sexually dangerous federal criminal felony within a Union State if the criminal activity has not occurred on land where concurrent or exclusive jurisdiction has been relinquished through consent to purchase or cession, with acceptance. The Supreme Court failed to mention this at all, explaining that:

> Of course, as Chief Justice Marshall stated, a federal statute, in addition to being authorized by Art. I, § 8, must also "not [be] prohibited" by the Constitution. But as we have already stated,

the present statute's validity under provisions of the Constitution <u>other than the Necessary and Proper Clause</u> is an issue that is <u>not</u> before us. Under the question presented, the relevant inquiry is simply "whether the means chosen are 'reasonably adapted' to the attainment of a legitimate end under the commerce clause power" <u>or under other powers</u> that the Constitution grants Congress the authority to implement. <u>United States v. Comstock</u>, 146 LEd2d 878, 890 (2010)

As we learned earlier, the necessary and proper clause "is not the delegation of a new and independent power, but simply provision for making effective the powers granted." <u>Kansas v. Colorado</u>, 206 US 46 (1907). The <u>Comstock</u> opinion is an artful stratagem with the sole purpose being to confuse the public at large as to what the law <u>really</u> is. It mentions that there is an "<u>implied</u> power to punish". This is blatant subterfuge by the Supreme Court and proof of their *mens rea* (criminal intent). We learned previously that the power to "punish" is a right inherent in sovereignty (dominion over the land), and that "it [is] a fundamental precept that the rights of sovereignty are not to be taken away by implication." Fort Leavenworth R. R. Co. v. Lowe, 114 US 525, 538-539 (1885)

The truth is that if the crime occurred on land under the exclusive or concurrent jurisdiction of the "United States" (Federal Government), then there is an implied power to "punish the felony" because they would then have sovereignty (dominion), over that land. However, the Supreme Court purposely avoided this issue, which is directly relevant to Federal jurisdiction, in order to sustain Comstock's felony conviction. The Supreme Court would also be without subject-matter jurisdiction to consider the merits, except and only to decide that the lower court erred in hearing the case. This avoidance of jurisdiction is in direct conflict with several Supreme Court decisions which state that:

> [E]ven if not raised by the parties, **we can<u>not</u> ignore the absence of federal jurisdiction**. <u>Lake Country Estates v. Tahoe Planning Agcy.</u>, 440 US 391, 398 (1979), and that;
>
> We <u>must</u> also notice the <u>possible</u> absence of jurisdiction because <u>we are obligated to do so</u> even when the issue is not raised by a party. <u>Izumi Seimitsu Kogyo v. U.S. Phillips</u>, 510 US 27, 33 (1993)

It appears that the Supreme Court has no problem whatsoever ignoring the absence of Federal jurisdiction. So much for their "obligation." Getting back to the "substantial effects" issue, the Supreme Court in 1995 attempted to set the record straight, explaining that:

The Constitution not only uses the word "commerce" in a narrower sense than our case law might suggest, it also does not support the proposition that Congress has authority over all activities that "substantially affect" interstate commerce. The Commerce Clause[228] does not state that Congress may "regulate matters that substantially affect commerce with foreign Nations, and among the several States, and with the Indian Tribes." In contrast, the Constitution itself temporarily prohibited amendments that would "affect"

---

[228] Even to speak of "the Commerce Clause" perhaps obscures the actual scope of that Clause. As an original matter, Congress did not have authority to regulate all commerce; Congress could only "regulate Commerce with foreign Nations, and among the several States, and with the Indian Tribes." US Const, Art I, § 8, cl 3. Although the precise line between interstate/foreign commerce and purely intrastate commerce was hard to draw, the Court attempted to adhere to such a line for the first 150 years of our Nation. See *infra*, at 593-599, 131 LEd2d, at 659-663. United States v. Lopez, 514 US 549, n. 2 (1995)

Congress' lack of authority to prohibit or restrict the slave trade [229] or to enact unproportioned direct taxation. Art V.[230]

Clearly, the Framers could have drafted a Constitution that contained a "substantially affects interstate commerce" Clause had that been their objective.

In addition to its powers under the Commerce Clause, Congress has the authority to enact such laws as are "necessary and proper" to carry into execution its power to regulate commerce among the several States. US Const, Art I, § 8, cl 18. But on this

---

[229] This changed with the ratification of the 13th Amendment.

[230] Article V, provided that no Amendment to the Constitution made "prior to the Year One Thousand eight hundred and eight shall in any Manner effect the first and fourth Clauses in the Ninth Section of the first Articles."

"No capitation, or other direct, Tax shall be laid, unless in Proportion to the Census or Enumeration herein before directed to be taken." Article I, § 9, cl. 4, U.S. Constitution

Court's understanding of congressional power under these two Clauses, many of Congress' other enumerated powers under Art I, § 8, are wholly superfluous. After all, if Congress may regulate all matters that substantially affect commerce, there is no need for the Constitution to specify that Congress may enact bankruptcy laws, cl 4, or coin money and fix the standard of weights and measures, cl 5, or punish counterfeiters of United States coin and securities, cl 6. Likewise, Congress would not need the separate authority to establish post offices and post roads, cl 7, or to grant patents and copyrights, cl 8, or to "punish Piracies and Felonies committed on the high Seas," cl 10. It might not even need the power to raise and support an Army and Navy, cls

12 and 13, for fewer people would engage in commercial shipping if they thought that a foreign power could expropriate their property with ease. Indeed, if Congress could regulate matters that substantially affect interstate commerce, there would have been no need to specify that Congress can regulate international trade and commerce with the Indians. As the Framers surely understood, these other branches of trade substantially affect interstate commerce.

Put simply, much if not all of Art I, § 8 (including portions of the Commerce Clause itself), would be surplusage if Congress had been given authority over matters that substantially affect interstate commerce. An interpretation of cl 3 that makes the rest of § 8 superfluous simply cannot be correct. Yet this Court's Commerce Clause jurisprudence has endorsed just such an interpretation: The power we have accorded Congress has swallowed Art I, § 8.[231]

Indeed, if a "substantial effects" test can be appended to the Commerce Clause, why not to every other power of the Federal Government? There is no reason for singling out the Commerce Clause for special treatment. Accordingly, Congress could regulate all matters that "substantially affect" the Army and Navy, bankruptcies, tax collection, ex-

---

[231] "There are other powers granted to Congress outside of Art I, § 8, that may become wholly superfluous as well due to our distortion of the Commerce Clause. For instance, Congress has plenary power over the District of Columbia and the territories. See US Const, Art I, § 8, cl 17, and Art IV, § 3, cl 2. The grant of comprehensive legislative power over certain areas of the Nation, when read in conjunction with the rest of the Constitution, further confirms that Congress was not ceded plenary power over the whole Nation." United States v. Lopez, 514 US 549, n. 3 (1995)

penditures, and so on. In that case, the Clauses of § 8 all mutually overlap, <u>something we can assume the Founding Fathers never intended</u>.

Our construction of the scope of congressional authority has the additional problem of coming close to turning the Tenth Amendment on its head. Our case law could be read to reserve to the United States all powers not expressly prohibited by the Constitution. Taken together, these fundamental textual problems should, at the very least, convince us that the "substantial effects" test should be reexamined.

The exchanges during the ratification campaign reveal the relatively limited reach of the Commerce Clause and of federal power generally. The Founding Fathers confirmed that most areas of life (even many matters that would have substantial effects on commerce) would remain outside the reach of the Federal Government. Such affairs would continue to be under the exclusive control of the States.

If the principle dissent's understanding of our early case law were correct, there might be some reason to doubt this view of the original understanding of the Constitution. According to that dissent, Chief Justice Marshall's opinion in Gibbons v. Ogden, 9 Wheat 1, 6 LEd 23 (1824), established that Congress may control all local activities that "significantly affect interstate commerce," post,[232] at 615, 131 LEd2d, at 673. And, "with the exception of one wrong turn subsequently corrected," this has been the "traditiona[l]" method of interpreting the Commerce Clause. Post, at 631, 131 LEd2d, at 683 (citing Gibbons and United States v. Darby, 312 US 100, 116-117, 85 LEd 609, 61 SCt 451, 132 ALR 1430 (1941))

In my view, the dissent is wrong about the holding and reasoning of Gibbons. Because this error leads the dissent to characterize the first 150 years of this Court's case law as a "wrong turn," I feel compelled to put the last 50 years in proper perspective.

---

[232] Post. After; as occurring in a report or a textbook, term is used to send the reader to a subsequent part of the book. Same as "*infra.*" Black's Law Dictionary. Sixth Edition, page 1,166.

In Gibbons, the Court examined whether a federal law that licensed ships to engage in the "coasting trade" pre-empted a New York law granting a 30-year monopoly to Robert Livingston and Robert Fulton to navigate the State's waterways by steamship. In concluding that it did, the Court noted that Congress could regulate "navigation" because "[a]ll America ... has uniformly understood, the word 'commerce,' to comprehend navigation. It was so understood, and must have been so understood, when the constitution was framed." 9 Wheat, at 190, 6 LEd 23. The Court also observed that federal power over commerce "among the several States" meant that Congress could regulate commerce conducted partly within a State. Because a portion of interstate commerce and foreign commerce would almost always take place within one or more States, federal power over interstate and foreign commerce necessarily would extend into the States. Id., at 195-196, 6 LEd 23.

At the same time, **the Court took great pains to make clear that Congress could <u>not</u> regulate commerce "which is completely internal, which is carried on between man and man in a State, or between different parts of the same State, and which <u>does not extend to or affect the other States</u>."** Id., at 194, 6 LEd 23. Moreover, while suggesting that the Constitution might not permit States to regulate interstate or foreign commerce, the Court observed that "[i]nspection laws, quarantine laws, health laws of every description, as well as laws regulating the internal commerce of a State" were but a small part "of that immense mass of legislation ... not surrendered to a general government." Id., at 203, 6 LEd 23. From an early moment, the Court rejected the notion that Congress can regulate everything that affects interstate commerce. That the internal commerce of the States and the numerous state inspection, quarantine, and health laws had substantial effects on interstate commerce cannot be doubted. Nevertheless, they were not "surrendered to the general government."

Of course, the principle dissent is not the first to misconstrue Gibbons. For instance, the Court has stated that Gibbons "described the federal commerce power with a breadth never yet exceeded."

Wickard v. Filburn, 317 US 111, 120, 87 LEd 122, 63 S Ct 82 (1942). See also Perez v. United States, 402 US 146, 151, 28 LEd2d 686, 91 SCt 1357 (1971) (claiming that with Darby and Wickard, "the broader view of the Commerce Clause announced by Chief Justice Marshall had been restored"). I believe that this misreading stems from two statements in Gibbons.

First, the Court made the uncontroversial claim that **federal power does not encompass "commerce" that "does not extend to or affect other States."**[233] 9 Wheat, at 194, 6 LEd 23 (emphasis added). From this statement, the principle dis-

---

[233] Obviously commerce does not extend to or affect other States when an item is not shipped into a Union State from another Union State.

sent infers that whenever an activity affects interstate commerce, it necessarily follows that Congress can regulate such activities. Of course, Chief Justice Marshall said no such thing and the inference the dissent makes cannot be drawn.

There is a much better interpretation of the "affect[s]" language: Because the Court had earlier noted that **the commerce power did not extend to wholly intrastate commerce**, the Court was acknowledging that although the line between intrastate and interstate/foreign commerce would be difficult to draw, federal authority could not be construed to cover purely intrastate commerce. **Commerce that did not affect another State could <u>never</u> be said to be commerce "among the several States."**

But even if one were to adopt the dissent's reading, the "affect[s]" language, at most, permits Congress to regulate only intrastate commerce that substantially affects interstate and foreign commerce. There is no reason to believe that Chief Justice Marshall was asserting that Congress could regulate all activities that affect interstate commerce. See *ibid.*

The second source of confusion stems from the Court's praise for the Constitution's division of power between the States and the Federal Government:

"The genius and character of the whole government seem to be, that its action is to be applied to all external concerns of the nation, and to those internal concerns which affect the States generally; **but not to those which are completely within a particular State, which do not affect other States**, and with which it is not necessary to interfere, for the purpose of executing some of the general powers of the government." Id., at 195, 6 LEd 23.

In this passage, the Court merely was making the well understood point that the Constitution commits matters of "national" concern to Congress and leaves "local" matters to the States. The Court was not saying that whatever Congress believes is a national matter becomes an object of federal control. The matters of national concern are enumerated in the Constitution: war, taxes, patents, and copyrights, uniform rules of naturalization and bankruptcy, types of commerce, and so on. See generally Art I, § 8. Gibbons' emphatic statements that Congress could not regulate many matters that affect commerce confirm that the Court did not read the Commerce Clause as granting Congress control over matters that "affect the States generally." [234] Gibbons simply cannot be construed as the principle dissent would have it.

---

[234] "None of the other Commerce Clause opinions during Chief Justice Marshall's tenure, which concerned the "dormant" Commerce Clause, even suggested that Congress had authority over all matters substantially affecting commerce. See Brown v. Maryland, 12 Wheat 419, 6 LEd 678 (1827); Wilson v. Black Bird Creek Marsh Co., 2 Pet 245, 7 LEd 412 (1829)." United States v. Lopez, 514 US 549, n. 5 (1995)

All Chief Justice Marshall meant by his "affects" analysis is that, commerce which is intended to be transported from one Union State to another, or other, Union State(s), i.e., "interstate commerce", affects other Union States and can therefore be regulated by Congress. Commerce not intended to be transported from one Union State to another, or other, Union State(s), does not affect other Union States and therefore cannot be regulated by Congress.

I am aware of no cases prior to the New Deal[235] that characterized the power flowing from the Commerce Clause as sweepingly as does our substantial effects test. **My review of the case law indicates that the substantial effects test is but an innovation of the 20th century**.

Even before Gibbons, Chief Justice Marshall, writing for the Court in Cohens v. Virginia, 6 Wheat 264, 5 LEd 257 (1821), noted that Congress had "no right to punish murder committed within any of the States," id., at 426, 5 LEd 257, **and that it was "clear that Congress could not punish felonies generally**," id., at 428, 5

---

[235] New Deal. The legislative and administrative program of social reform during the 1930's. The period of this program. A governmental program resembling the Roosevelt New Deal in objectives or techniques. Webster's Ninth New Collegiate Dictionary, (1991), page 796.

LEd 257. The Court's only, qualification was that Congress could enact such laws for places where it enjoyed plenary powers—for instance, over the District of Columbia. Id., at 426, 5 LEd 257. Thus, whatever effect ordinary murders, or robbery, or gun possession might have on interstate commerce (or any other subject of federal concern) was irrelevant to the question of congressional power. [236] United States v.

---

[236] "It is worth noting that Congress, in the first federal criminal Act, did not establish nationwide prohibitions against murder and the like. See Act of Apr. 30, 1790, ch 9, 1 Stat 112. To be sure, Congress outlawed murder, manslaughter, maiming, and larceny, but only when those acts were either committed on United States territory not part of a State or on the high seas. Ibid. See US Const, Art I, § 8, cl 10 (authorizing Congress to outlaw piracy and felonies on high seas); Art IV, § 3, cl 2 (plenary authority over United States territory and property). When Congress did enact nationwide criminal laws, it acted pursuant to direct grants of authority found in the Constitution. Compare Act of Apr. 30, 1790, *supra*, §§ 1 and 14 (prohibitions against treason and the counterfeiting of U.S. securities), with US Const, Art I, § 8, cl 6 (counterfeiting); Art III, § 3, cl 2 (treason). Notwithstanding any substantial effects that murder, kidnaping, or gun possession might have on interstate commerce, Congress understood that it could not establish nationwide prohibitions.

Continued on next page.

Lopez, 514 US 549, 588-597 (1995) (Justice Thomas, concurring)

Your writer believes that the purpose of the "substantial effects test," *i.e.*, to expand the jurisdiction of the Federal Government in violation of the Constitution, is proven by 219,000 federal inmates being held for federal crimes over which the Federal Government has zero jurisdiction or judicial authority under the

---

Likewise, there were no laws in the early Congresses that regulated manufacturing and agriculture. Nor was there any statute that purported to regulate activities with 'substantial effects' on interstate commerce." United States v. Lopez, 514 US 549, n. 6 (1995).

To be sure, congressional power pursuant to the Commerce Clause was alternatively described less narrowly or more narrowly during this 150-year period. Compare United States v. Coombs, 12 Pet 72, 78, 9 LEd 1004 (1838) (commerce power 'extends to such acts, done on land, which interfere with, obstruct, or prevent the due exercise of the power to regulate [interstate and international] commerce' such as stealing goods from a beached ship), with United States v. E .C. Knight Co., 156 US 1, 13, 39 LEd 325, 15 SCt 249 (1895) ('Contracts to buy, sell, or exchange goods to be transported among the several States, the transportation and its instrumentalities ... may be regulated, but this is because they form part of interstate trade or commerce'). During this period, however, this Court never held that Congress could regulate everything that substantially affects commerce." United States v. Lopez, 514 US 549, n. 7 (1995)

Constitution to prosecute. Even if Congress could constitutionally regulate activity under a "substantial effects test," this does not enlarge their jurisdiction to punish felonious crimes. We have already learned that federal jurisdiction, which is necessary to punish felonious crimes (except where the power to punish has been delegated by enumeration), cannot be expanded through legislation.[237] Again, the Supreme Court has explained that:

> **Congress can<u>not</u> by legislation, enlarge the Federal jurisdiction**, nor can it be enlarged by the treaty-making power. New Orleans v United States, 35 US 662, 10 Pet 662, 736-737, 9 LEd 573 (1836).

---

[237] Legislate. To enact laws or pass resolutions via legislation, in contrast to court-made law. Black's Law Dictionary, Sixth Edition, page 899.

Legislation. The act of giving or enacting laws; the power to make laws; the act of legislating; preparation and enactment of laws. Black's Law Dictionary, Sixth Edition, page 899.

The Supreme Court opined in 2005, ten years after the Lopez court, that the categorical prohibition, under the Controlled Substances Act, of the manufacture and possession of marijuana, did not—as applied to the intrastate manufacture and possession of marijuana for medical purposes pursuant to a state statute—exceed Congress' authority under the Federal Constitution's commerce clause (Art. I, § 8, cl. 3), as: (1) Congress had a rational bases for concluding that leaving home-consumed marijuana outside federal control would affect interstate price and market conditions, for (a) it was likely that the high demand for marijuana in the interstate market would draw homegrown marijuana into the market; (b) the diversion of homegrown marijuana would tend to frustrate the federal interests in entirely eliminating commercial transactions in the interstate market; and (c) production of marijuana meant for home consumption had a substantial effect on supply and demand in the national market for marijuana. See Gonzales v. Raich, 545 US 1 (2005). However, the Honorable Justice Thomas, in a dissenting opinion, stated as follows:

Respondents Diane Monson and Angel Raich use marijuana that has never been bought or sold, that has never crossed state lines, and that has had no demonstrable effect on the national market for marijuana. If Congress can regulate this under the Commerce Clause, then it can regulate virtually anything—and the Federal Government is no longer one of limited and enumerated powers.

Respondents' local cultivation and consumption is not "Commerce ... among the several States." U.S. Const., Art. I, § 8, cl. 3. By holding that Congress may regulate activity that is neither interstate nor commerce under the Interstate Commerce Clause, the Court abandons any attempt to enforce the Constitution's limits on federal power. The majority supports this conclusion by invoking, without explanation, the Necessary and Proper Clause. Regulating respondents' conduct, however, is not "necessary and proper for carrying into Execution" Congress' restrictions on the interstate drug trade. Art. I, § 8, cl. 18. Thus, neither the Commerce Clause nor the Necessary and Proper Clause grants Congress the power to regulate respondents conduct.

As I explained at length in United States v. Lopez, 514 US 549 (1995), the Commerce Clause empowers Congress to regulate the buying and selling of goods and services trafficked across state lines. Id., at 586-589 (concurring opinion). The Clause's text, structure, and history all indicate that, at the time of the founding, the term "commerce" consisted of selling, buying, and bartering, as well as transporting for these purposes." Id., at 585 (Thomas, J., concurring). Commerce, or trade, stood in contrast to productive activities like manufacturing and agriculture. Id., at 586-587 (Thomas, J. concurring). Throughout founding-era dictionaries, Madison's notes from the Constitutional Convention, The Federalist Papers, and the ratification debates, the term "commerce" is consistently used to mean trade or exchange—not all economic or gainful activity that has some attenuated connection to trade or exchange. Ibid. (Thomas, J. concurring); Barnett, The Original Meaning of the Commerce Clause, 68 U. Chi. L. Rev. 101, 112-125 (2001). The term "commerce" commonly meant trade or exchange (and shipping for these purposes) not simply to those involved in the drafting and ratification processes, but also to the general public. Barnett, New Evidence of the Original Meaning of the Commerce Clause, 55 Ark. L. Rev. 847, 857-862 (2003).

Even the majority does not argue that respondents' conduct is itself "Commerce among the several States," Art. I, § 8, cl. 3. Monson and Raich neither buy nor sell the marijuana that they consume. They cultivate their cannabis entirely in the State of California—it never crosses state lines, much less as part of a commercial transaction. Certainly no evidence from the founding suggests that "commerce" included the mere possession of a good or some purely personal activity that did not involve trade or exchange for value. In the early days of the Republic, it would have been unthinkable that Congress could prohibit the local cultivation, possession, and consumption of marijuana.

On this traditional understanding of "commerce," the Controlled Substances Act (CSA), 21 U.S.C. § 801 *et seq.*, regulates a great deal of marijuana trafficking that is interstate and commercial in character. The CSA does not, however, criminalize only the interstate buying and selling of marijuana. Instead, it bans the entire market—intrastate or interstate, noncommercial or commercial—for marijuana. Respondents are correct that the CSA exceeds Congress' commerce power as applied to their conduct, which is purely intrastate and noncommercial.

Finally, the majority's view—that because some of the CSA's applications are constitutional, they must all be constitutional—undermines its reliance on the substantial effects test. The intrastate conduct swept within a general regulatory scheme may or may not have a substantial effect on the relevant interstate market. "[O]ne always can draw the circle broadly enough to cover an activity that, when taken in isolation, would not have substantial effects on commerce." Id., at 600 (Thomas, J., concurring). The breadth of legislation that Congress enacts says nothing about whether the intrastate activity substantially affects interstate commerce, let alone whether it is necessary to the scheme. Because medical marijuana users in California and elsewhere are not placing substantial amounts of cannabis into the stream of interstate commerce, Congress may not regulate them under the substantial effects test, no matter how broadly it drafts the CSA.

The majority prevents States like California from devising drug policies that they have concluded provide much-needed respite to the seriously ill. It does so without any serious inquiry into the necessity for federal regulation or the propriety of "displac[ing] state regulation in areas of traditional state concern," id., at 583 (Kennedy, J., concurring.). The majority's rush to embrace federal power "is especially unfortunate given the importance of showing respect for the sovereign States that comprise our Federal Union." United States v.

<u>Oakland Cannabis Buyers' Co-operative</u>, 532 US 483, 502 (2001) (Stevens, J., concurring in judgment). Our federalist system, properly understood, allows California and a growing number of other States to decide for themselves how to safeguard the health and welfare of their citizens. I would affirm the judgment of the Court of Appeals. I respectfully dissent.

In a similar vein, the Federal Government is currently attempting to unconstitutionally expand their jurisdiction to punish felonies under their treaty-making power.[238] The purpose being, like the sub-

---

[238] The President " ... shall have Power, by and with the Advice and Consent of the Senate, to make Treaties, provided two-thirds of the Senators present concur." <u>Article II, § 2</u>, U.S. Constitution

"This Constitution, and the Laws of the United States which shall be made in Pursuance thereof; and all Treaties made, or which shall be made, under the Authority of the United Continued on next page.

stantial effects test, to obliterate the absolute necessity for jurisdiction to be relinquished through consent to purchase or cession, with acceptance, and for delegating, by enumeration, the power to "punish." As the Supreme Court explained:

> The source of national power in this country is the Constitution of the United States; and the government, as to our internal affairs, possesses no inherent sovereign power not derived from that instrument, and inconsistent with its letter and spirit.
>
> Indeed, a treaty which undertook to take away what the Constitution secured, or to enlarge Federal jurisdiction, would simply be void.

States, shall be the supreme Law of the Land." Article VI, cl. 2, U.S. Constitution

> It need hardly be said that a treaty cannot change the Constitution, or be held valid if it be in violation of that instrument. This results from the nature and fundamental principles of our government. <u>Downes v. Bidwell</u>, 182 US 244, 369-370 (1901)

In the year 2010 the Supreme Court granted certiorari review in a federal case[239] originating from the Union State of Pennsylvania to a women who is being prosecuted for using chemicals she purchased to inflict harm on her best friend whom she found out was having an affair with, and pregnant by, her husband. The Federal Government prosecuted her and she claimed they were violating the Tenth Amendment. She made this claim, without doubt, based on the fact that there was no interstate-nexus in her case. In other words, she did not travel through "interstate commerce" to commit her crime or cause the chemi-

---

[239] <u>Carol Anne Bond v. United States</u>, 131 SCt 2355 (2011)

cals to be transported through interstate commerce. The Third Circuit held that only a Union State could make a Tenth Amendment claim. Other Circuits held the same and still others held that a person could make a Tenth Amendment claim. Hence, a "Circuit split." The Supreme Court on certiorari review held that a person could make a Tenth Amendment claim. They also held that because incarceration causes a concrete injury redressable by invalidation of the conviction, the "case or controversy" clause under Article III is therefore satisfied.

On remand, the Third Circuit upheld her conviction, concluding that Congress did not exceed its constitutional powers when it passed the law as a means of effectuating the chemical-weapons **treaty** and that the law was not unconstitutionally applied to her. As of this writing, the Supreme Court has granted an unheard of certiorari review for the second time which is currently pending an outcome. Eleven Union States signed onto an *amicus curiae* brief arguing that the Federal Government was acting far beyond its enumerated powers in a way that is not necessary and proper to fulfilling the nation's treaty obligations. As we already know, the Federal Government cannot expand its criminal jurisdiction under the "treaty-making power."

The Supreme Court recently returned its second certiorari opinion in the Carol Anne Bond case. They did decide the case in Bond's favor. However, it was for the wrong reasons because they never addressed the jurisdictional issue. They again decided what they believe the reach the statute in question (18 U.S.C. § 229) was intended by Congress to have and not what the limits the constitution and supreme Law enacted by Congress actually have on its territorial reach. Instead they decided that the Federal Government overreached its authority when it decided to prosecute a purely local crime under the treaty-making power by claiming that, because Bond had put some chemicals on the mail-box handle, it gave them federal jurisdiction to prosecute her conduct criminally under the 1998 Chemical Weapons Convention Implementation Act treaty. In the official opinion the Supreme Court opined that:

> In our federal system, the National Government possesses

only limited powers; the States and the People retain the remainder. The States have broad authority to enact legislation for the public good—what we have often called a "police power". The Federal Government, by contrast, has no such authority and "can exercise only the powers granted to it", including the power to make "all Laws which shall be necessary and proper for carrying into Execution," the <u>enumerated</u> powers. For nearly two centuries it has been "clear" that, lacking a police power, "Congress can<u>not</u> punish felonies generally."

The Constitution confers upon Congress <u>not all</u> governmental powers, but <u>only discrete</u>, <u>enumerated ones</u>. And, of course, enumeration presupposes something not enumerated.

No great substantive and independent power can be implied as incidental to other powers, or used as a means of executing them. Bond v. United States, 2014 BL 151637, U.S., No. 12-158 (2014)

James Madison, the Father of the Constitution, stated in a document authored by him entitled the "Virginia Resolution of 1798":

That the General Assembly doth also express its deep regret, that a spirit has in sundry instances, been manifested by the federal government, to enlarge its powers by forced constructions of the constitutional charter which defines them; and that implications have appeared of a design to expound certain general phrases (which having been copied from the very limited grant of power, in the former articles of confederation were the less liable to be misconstrued) so as to destroy the meaning and effect, of the particular enumeration which necessarily explains and limits the general phrases; and so as to consolidate the states by degrees, into one sovereignty, the obvious tendency and inevitable consequence of which would be, to transform the present republican system of the United States, into an absolute, or at best a mixed monarchy.

As we now know, the Federal Government has succeeded in unconstitutionally enlarging its powers by forced construction of the constitutional power to regulate commerce among the Union States (interstate commerce), by exercising a power to "punish" not enumerated (and therefore not delegated) under that provision. What the Federal Government is doing is enforcing exclusive legislation even though they have no exclusive jurisdiction over the place where the felonious criminal activity is alleged to have occurred. We are now living in a mixed monarchy[240] and they are continuously working on making their power absolute (absolutism). That same year (1798), Thomas Jefferson, Founding Father, Creator and signer of the Declaration of Independence, and former President of the United States, stated that:

> [T]he friendless alien has indeed been selected as the safest subject of a first experiment; but the

---

[240] Mixed. Formed by admixture or commingling; partaking of the nature, character, or legal attributes of two or more distinct kinds of classes. Black's Law Dictionary, Sixth Edition, page 1,002.

Monarchy. A government in which supreme power is vested in a single person. Where a monarch is invested with absolute power, the monarchy is termed "despotic"; where the supreme power is virtually in the laws, though the majesty of government and the administration are vested in a single person, it is a "limited" or "constitutional" monarchy. Black's Law Dictionary , Sixth Edition, page 1,005.

citizen will soon follow, or rather, has already followed...

[T]hese and successive acts of the same character, unless arrested at the threshold, necessarily drive these States into revolution and blood and will furnish new calumnies against republican government, and new pretexts for those who wish it to be believed that man cannot be governed but by a rod of iron: that it would be a dangerous delusion were a confidence in the men of our choice to silence our fears for the safety of our rights: that confidence is everywhere the parent of despotism — free government is founded in jealousy, and not in confidence; it is jealousy and not confidence which prescribes limited constitutions, to bind down those whom we are obliged to trust with power: that our Constitution has accordingly fixed the limits to which, and no further, our confidence may go.

In questions of powers, then, let no more be heard of confidence in man, but bind him down from mischief by the chains of the Constitution.

That this commonwealth does therefore call on its co-States for an expression of their sentiments on the acts concerning aliens and for the punishment of certain crimes herein before specified, plainly declaring whether these acts are or are not authorized by the federal compact. And it doubts not that their sense will be so announced as to prove their attachment unaltered to limited government, whether general or particular. And that the rights and liberties of their co-States will be exposed to no dangers by remaining embarked in a common bottom with their own. That they will concur with this commonwealth in considering the said acts as so palpably against the Constitution as to amount to an undisguised declaration that the compact is not meant to be the measure of the powers of the General Government, but that it will proceed in the exercise over these States, of all powers whatsoever: that they will view this as seizing the rights of the States, and consolidating them in the hands of the General Government, with a power assumed to bind the States (not merely as the cases made federal, *casus foederis* but), in all cases whatsoever, by laws made, not with their consent, but by others against their consent: that this would be to surrender the form of government we have chosen, and live under one deriving its powers from its own will, and not from our authority; and that the co-States, recurring to their natural right in cases not made federal, will concur in declaring these acts void, and of no force, and will each take measures of its own for providing that neither these acts, nor any others of the General Government not plainly and intentionally authorized by the Constitution, shalt be exercised within their respective territories. <u>The Kentucky Resolutions of 1798</u>

Encroachment on our rights and the sovereignty and jurisdiction of the Union States was not done in leaps and bounds. It was done in incremental steps. The Federal Government advances a little, and we submit. They advance a little further, and we still submit. We must stop them immediately! We must choose liberty or suffer a fate far removed from freedom and our Constitution. The line has been drawn by "We the People" via the Constitution. That line is being crossed and a tyrannical government has become an entrenched usurpation. We are in deep trouble! They must be pushed back across the line to their lawful perimeter. You must say, "Enough!" As the Supreme Court explained:

> The Constitution itself <u>never</u> yields to treaty or enactment; **it neither changes with time nor does it in theory bend to the force of circumstances**. It may be amended according to its own permission; but while it stands it is 'a law for rulers and for people, equally in war and in peace, and covers with the shield of its protection all classes of men, at all times and under all circumstanc-

es.' It's principles cannot, therefore, be set aside in order to meet the supposed necessities of great crisis. 'No doctrine involving more pernicious consequences was ever invented by the wit of man than that any of its provisions can be suspended during any of the great exigencies of government.' <u>Downes v. Bidwell</u>, 182 US 244, 370 (1901)

The fact that the federal courts are condoning felonious criminal prosecutions by the Executive branch under the guise of regulating "interstate commerce", by asserting subject-matter jurisdiction under false pretentions, is prima facie evidence of the design against our freedom and the sovereignty of the Union States.

WHAT HAVE WE LEARNED?

In this Manifesto we learned that the U.S. Constitution is the Supreme Law of the Land in America and that Congress cannot punish felonies within the Union States except when the crime occurs on land under their exclusive or concurrent jurisdiction or where the power to "punish" is delegated in the Constitution. Congress can also provide for misdemeanor offenses within the Union States but only if it has some relation to the execution of a delegated power.

We also learned that the "United States district courts" are not the former "district courts of the United States" and their status as either legislative or Article III courts is surrounded by obscurity, ambiguity, and mystery. Their subject-matter jurisdiction over crimes is therefore drawn into question. Article III of the Constitution, of which the Union States are united under compact, commands that, "The judicial Power shall extend to <u>all</u> Cases, in Law and Equity[241] , arising un-

---

[241] law. The set of rules or principles dealing with a specific area of a legal system. The judicial and administrative pro-
Continued on next page.

der [it], the Laws of the United States [Federal Government], and Treaties made, or which shall be made, under their Authority."[242] That is <u>mandatory</u>![243] That is the Supreme Law! Even if we wanted to, we can<u>not</u> waive our right to be tried in a court with jurisdiction over the subject-matter, and instead be tried by a court with <u>zero</u> jurisdiction over the subject-matter to adjudicate the case. Period! Remember, we learned earlier in this Manifesto that:

> [C]ases are legion holding that a party may not waive a defect in subject-matter jurisdiction or invoke federal jurisdiction simply by

---

cess; legal action and proceedings. <u>Black's Law Dictionary</u>, Seventh Edition, page 889.

equity. Fairness; impartiality; evenhanded dealing. <u>Black's Law Dictionary</u>, Seventh Edition, page 560.

[242] <u>Article III, § 2, cl. 1</u>, U.S. Constitution

[243] Shall. As used in statutes, contracts, or the like, this word is generally imperative or mandatory. In common or ordinary parlance, and in its ordinary signification, the term "shall" is a word of command, and one of which has always or which must be given compulsory meaning; as is denoting obligation. The word in ordinary usage means "must" and is inconsistent with a concept of discretion. <u>Black's Law Dictionary</u>, Sixth Edition, page 1,375.

consent. Pennsylvania v. Union Gas Co., 491 US 1, 26 (1989) (citing cases)

In order to successfully usurp the sovereignty and jurisdiction of the Union States and prosecute felonious "interstate commerce" crimes in violation of the Constitution the U.S. Attorneys and federal courts conspire together. They always proceed under the pretense that the Constitution allows them to "punish" felonious crimes by "implication" as "necessary & proper" for carrying into execution their "Commerce Clause" power. They do this even though the law limits the alleged criminal activity to land under their concurrent or exclusive jurisdiction.[244] The fact that

---

[244] Title 40 U.S.C. § 3112, Federal Jurisdiction, "(c) Presumption. It is conclusively presumed that jurisdiction has not been accepted until the Government accepts jurisdiction over land as provided in this section."

Because the power to punish is not delegated under the Commerce Clause, the Federal Government cannot provide for the punishment of felonious interstate commerce crimes, unless jurisdiction over land (territorial/general jurisdiction) where the crime occurred has been obtained through consent to purchase or cession by the particular Union State. However, because Congress has defined "interstate commerce" in Title 18 U.S.C. § 10, the alleged criminal activity must occur between land under Continued on next page.

the courts routinely claim subject-matter jurisdiction under Title 18 U.S.C. § 3231 when the presumption is against jurisdiction is suspicious to say the least and definitely raises serious due process and separation of powers concerns. Especially when the U.S. Attorneys have not only failed to prove this essential element (territorial jurisdiction) but also, by its omission, have failed to charge an "offense against the laws of the United States". Since the burden of proof is on the prosecution it is obvious why the U.S. Attorneys routinely and purposefully omit this jurisdictional element from the indictments.

---

the concurrent or exclusive legislative (territorial) jurisdiction of the federal government and another like place in order to be guilty of an "interstate commerce" crime under that particular title of the United States Code.

Misdemeanor "interstate commerce" offenses must also occur in the same places and in the same manner. See <u>Federal Rules of Criminal Procedure</u>, Rule 1(a)(1), "These rules govern the procedure in all criminal proceedings in the United States district courts"; Rule 1(b)(9), Definitions, "The following definitions apply to these rules, 'State', includes the District of Columbia, and any commonwealth, territory, or possession of the United States"; Rule 58(a)(1), Petty Offenses and Other Misdemeanors, "In General. These rules apply in petty offenses and other misdemeanor cases"; and Title 28 U.S.C § 2072(b), Rules of procedure and evidence, "All laws in conflict with such rules shall be of no further force or effect after such rules have taken effect."

The "interstate commerce" and drug laws do not contain this jurisdictional element within the language of their statutes. Because of this the prosecution is able to charge the federal crime in the language of the statute without including this jurisdictional language in the indictment. This ruse provides the means for charging and prosecuting unknowing and unsuspecting victims with federal crimes they are not guilty of committing. In so doing they effectively violate their inalienable rights, usurp the sovereignty and jurisdiction of the Union States, and fundamentally alter our lawful Republican form of government, all with blatant and reckless disregard of their sworn oaths to uphold the Constitution.

Conspiring to fundamentally alter our constitutional (lawful) form of government is the same thing as attempting to overthrow it. Is this not levying War? Is this not treason? Yes, it is! These people have sold out their country for a weekly paycheck. The Federal Government steals your money utilizing the force of law (taxes), and then they pay these people to do it. They are the enemy (although many may not realize this because of their ignorance of the law-which is no excuse). The lower courts will continuously deny your petitions without remorse or opinion by simply stating they are frivolous or meritless, until finally leaving you to the mercy of the Supreme Court. There you will petition for a writ of habeas corpus.

Because the Supreme Court is sanctioning this unconstitutional system they will deny your writ of certiorari. However, the Supreme Court will hopefully grant your habeas corpus petition which, most likely, will be only after you have exhausted all of your procedural remedies. The important thing to remember, if you wish to attempt redress in the federal courts, is to follow procedure. Do not waiver from it. If your judicial district of incarceration is the same as your judicial district of conviction you can file a habeas corpus petition (28 U.SC. § 2241) with the Supreme Court without first applying to the "United States district court" in your judicial district of conviction. The Supreme Court explained that:

> [I]t is equally well settled that when a prisoner is held under sentence of any court of the United States in regard to a matter

wholly beyond or without the jurisdiction of that court, it is not only within the authority of the Supreme Court but it is its duty to inquire into the cause of commitment when the matter is properly brought to its attention, and if found to be as charged, a matter of which such court had no jurisdiction, to discharge the prisoner from confinement. Ex Parte Yarbrough, 110 US 651, 653 (1884)(citing cases)

Just keep in mind that the Federal Government and "United States district courts" will try to convince you that you are wrong, and that this Manifesto is a scam, by fatiguing you into accepting what they have done to you. We do not need them to admit the truth for us to be able to prove it. We can clearly see it with our own eyes. Your doubt is what they will prey upon, a doubt that exists because we grew up believing they had this power. They do not! Most people believe the

Federal Government has this power the same way they believe the Federal Government has jurisdiction to punish murder and other felonious crimes that occur in Federal Prisons. In expounding this belief, the Second Circuit opined that:

> The power of the federal government to acquire land within a state, either by purchase or condemnation, is "well established." In general, there are two ways that the United States can also obtain jurisdiction over such land within a state: consent and cession.
>
> Significantly, under either method, the state must agree to the transfer of jurisdiction for it to be valid. In addition, the federal government itself must accept jurisdiction. "[U]nless and until the United States has accepted jurisdiction over lands hereafter to be

acquired…, it shall be conclusively presumed that no such jurisdiction has been accepted."

The upshot of all this is that the United States does not have jurisdiction over all lands owned by the federal government within the states. [T]he Supreme Court and other courts have held in various cases that the federal government lacked jurisdiction over certain federal military installations, post offices, and hospitals, even though they were on federal land. "[A]lthough some may assume" that federal installations of these sorts "automatically come [] within Federal jurisdiction, that assumption is incorrect." "[T]he mere fact that the federal government owns or makes use of a parcel of land is not sufficient to establish federal jurisdiction over that land."

> Put simply, the mere fact that the assault took place in a federal prison on federal land ... does not mean that the federal government had jurisdiction over the location of the assault. And, contrary to what the district court told the jury, the Government could not satisfy the jurisdictional element of the offense simply "by proving that the alleged assault occurred in a federal prison on federal land." <u>United States v. Davis</u>, 726 F3d 357, 363-365 (CA2, 2013) (citations omitted)

The power to "punish" felonies under the commerce clause was <u>never</u> delegated. Just because it is happening on a grand scale is not proof that you are wrong or that they are right. If you rob a bank every week for 30 years and all the bank employees believe that you are allowed to do so, at what time does it actually become lawful and okay? Does anyone reasonably believe the bank robbers would ever admit they had no right to do so? Especially if the majority of bank employees believed they had this right?

This "system" has taken over and succeeds because we are ignorant of the law. It could not have succeeded otherwise. This is why we are not taught the Constitution's true meaning and what the Law really is. It is so they can forcefully impose their will upon us through arbitrary power. This is what they want for themselves, not for us! This is how they make their careers and money. The Constitution provides a method for peacefully resolving this problem by voting all of the Representatives in Congress, both the House and the Senate, out of office! Impeach the Supreme Court Justices for failing to serve during "good behavior." Replace these people with ones who will follow the Constitution. Educate your children and demand that the Constitution, and limitations on the Federal Government under it, be taught in school. Until that time, expect to be increasingly oppressed & tyrannized by a Federal Government without any lawful authority to "punish" felonies under the commerce clause, the treaty-making power, or the necessary and proper clause of the Constitution. The Supreme Court has explained that:

"The government, then, of the United States, can claim no powers which are not granted to it by the Constitution, and the powers actually granted must be such as are expressly given, or given by necessary implication."

"The very existence of the general government depends on that of the state governments. The state legislatures are to choose the Senators. Without a Senate there can be no Congress. The state legislatures are also to direct the manner of choosing the President. Unless, therefore, there are state legislatures to direct that manner, no President can be chosen. The same observation may be made as to the

House of Representatives. Thus it is evident that the very existence of the general government depends on that of the state legislatures." 4 Elliot's Debates, p. 78. See also The Federalist, No. 45, [The Alleged Danger From The Powers Of The Union To The State Governments Considered (Madison)]. The Federal features of our government are so clear and have been so often declared that no valuable discussion can proceed upon the opposite assumption. Newberry v. United States, 256 US 232, 249 (1921) (citing Martin v. Hunter, 1 Wheat 304, 326 (1816))

PRETRIAL REMEDY

Prior to indictment or after you are indicted or otherwise under arrest, you can file a writ of *habeas corpus* under 28 U.S.C. § 2241. The Supreme Court explained that when one is being prosecuted criminally, *habeas corpus* to inquire into the legality of detention was a new suit to enforce a civil right, and not a proceeding in the prosecution. See Ex parte Tom Tong, 108 US 556 (1883).

Although *habeas corpus* proceedings are characterized as "civil", the label is gross and inexact; essentially the proceeding is unique. See Harris v. Nelson, 394 US 286 (1969). Since *habeas corpus* is civil in nature we can utilize the Federal Rules of Civil Procedure ("FRCP") and the Federal Rules of Evidence ("FREv"). The application and procedure for implementing writs of *habeas corpus* are codified at Title 28 U.S.C. § 2241, 2242, 2243.

The Federal Rules of Civil Procedure state that:

These rules govern the procedure in all civil actions and proceedings in the United States district courts. FRCP, Rule 1. Scope and Purpose.

(a) Applicability to particular proceedings.

(4) Special Writs. These rules apply to proceedings for *habeas corpus*. FRCP, Rule 81, Applicability of the Rules in General; Removed Actions

Under FREv, 201, we can request that the court take mandatory judicial notice of certain adjudicative facts. For example, that the law requires the alleged criminal activity to occur within the "special maritime and territorial jurisdiction of the United States." That the indictment fails to charge an "offense against the laws of the United States". That the government has not entered into the record evidence documentation showing ownership, cession, and acceptance of jurisdiction by the "United States" (Federal Government) over the place where the criminal activity is alleged to have occurred. And testimony that you were not in any place within the concurrent or exclusive legislative (territorial) jurisdiction of the Federal Government. The Federal Rules of Evidence state that:

> The omission of any treatment of legislative facts results from fundamental differences between adjudicative facts and legislative facts. Adjudicative facts are simply the facts of the particular case. Legislative facts, on the other hand, are those which have relevance to legal reasoning and the law making process, whether in the formulation of a legal principle or ruling by a judge or court or in the enactment of a legislative body.

The usual method of establishing adjudicative facts is through the introduction of evidence, ordinarily consisting of testimony of witnesses. If particular facts are outside of reasonable controversy, this process is dispensed with as unnecessary. A high degree of indisputability is the essential prerequisite. FREv, 201, History; Ancillary Laws and Directives, Other provisions: Notes of Advisory Committee on Rules.

We can also cast a rebuttable presumption against federal jurisdiction under FREv, 301, in support of our request for mandatory judicial notice and introduce as supporting evidence the relevant statutory provisions and rules of procedure. Although FREv, 301 states that it applies in a "civil case", other provisions define that term to mean a "civil action" or proceeding which term the Federal Rules of Civil Procedure make applicable to habeas corpus proceedings:

Scope. These rules apply to proceedings in United States courts. The specific courts and proceedings, to which the rules apply, along with exceptions, are set out in Rule 1101 (a), (b). FREv, Rule 101(a)

Definitions. In these rules "civil case" means a civil action or proceeding. FREv, Rule 101 (b)(1).

To Courts and Judges. These rules apply to proceedings before: United States district courts;

To Cases and Proceedings. These rules apply in: civil cases and proceedings. FREv, Rule 1101 (a), (b).

AFTER ARRAIGNMENT

Within 14 days of your arraignment, you can file a motion for a "Bill of Particulars" requesting to be informed of the essential facts constituting the offense charged. FRCrP, Rule 7(c), (f). Essential facts constituting the offense charged would be you showing in the law that the offense alleged is required to occur on land under the concurrent or exclusive legislative (territorial) jurisdiction of the "United States" (Federal Government). Your motion for a "Bill of Particulars" will request documentation showing the alleged criminal activity occurred in these places, which are the "essential facts" establishing the offense charged.

AFTER JUDGMENT

You can file a motion to arrest judgment within 14 days after the court accepts a verdict or finding of guilty, or after a plea of guilty, if (1) the indictment or information does not charge an offense; or (2) the court does not have jurisdiction of the charged offense. FRCrP, 34. See also FRCrP, 12(b)(3)(B)

PROPER PROCEDURE IN 12 STEPS

For those who want to know the proper procedure in the courts, here it is: Be warned that the Federal courts will most likely deny for years your lack of jurisdiction, actual innocence,[245] and Tenth Amendment

---

[245] You are actually innocent of committing a felonious federal crime if they do not have territorial (legislative) jurisdiction over the place wherein the criminal activity is alleged to have occurred. This simply means that no matter how far outside the record the Federal Government goes, it is impossible for them to prove you committed a felony offense against the laws of the United States, unless the alleged criminal activity occurred over land under their concurrent or exclusive territorial (legislative) jurisdiction or pursuant to a provision in the Constitution where the power to "punish" has been delegated, by enumeration. Remember, their power under a grant of concurrent jurisdiction is limited by the terms of the cession.

"'Actual innocence' means factual innocence, not mere legal insufficiency. In other words, the Government is not limited to the existing record to rebut any showing that petitioner might make." Bousley v. United States, 523 US, 614, 623-624 (1998).

Selling drugs is illegal in many countries. Like Australia and China, for example. This does not make you guilty of an Australian or Chinese crime. The same proposition is true for federal crimes. Unless you commit the criminal activity within some place under their exclusive or concurrent jurisdiction, or pursuant to a provision of the Constitution where the power to "punish" is delegated by enumeration, you have not committed a felonious federal crime. The only exception is that they can prosecute misdemeanor crimes if it has some relation to the execution of a
Continued on next page.

claims before you finally get any relief. After all, it's tantamount to pleading with a robber not to steal from you. You must remain vigilant, relentless, and persevere to obtain relief. I personally think it would be faster and more beneficial to our freedom to tell others about this Manifesto until it receives media attention. I highly recommend internet sites like youtube.com, facebook, wikileaks.com, reuters.com, associated press (ap.org), blogging, news groups, and chat rooms.

For what it's worth, the structural procedure is carried out this way: Trial, Appeal, Certiorari to the Supreme Court, 2255 petition (28 U.S.C. § 2255) to your trial court, Appeal (requesting a "certificate of appealability"), Panel/En Banc re-hearing, Certiorari to the Supreme Court, *Habeas corpus* petition (28 U.S.C. § 2241) to the United States district court in the Judicial District of your incarceration if different from your trial court (if the same as your trial court then 2241 *Habeas corpus* petition to the Supreme

---

delegated power. Again, if they had an inherent power to punish felonies, there would be no need for jurisdiction to be ceded or to delegate, by enumeration, the power to "punish."

Court), Appeal to the Circuit in which you are incarcerated, *Habeas corpus* petition (2241) to the Supreme Court. It is essential to carefully follow all the rules of procedure and local rules while proceeding through the federal court system. Be sure to pay close attention to the time limits for all of your filings.

The following is the practical application of that procedure. If you have recently been indicted, your best bet is to go to trial. After all it is highly likely you are (f)actually innocent of committing a felonious federal crime and unlikely the "United States district court" has subject-matter jurisdiction. The Supreme Court explained that:

> In a criminal case we have said that a person convicted by a court without jurisdiction over the place of the crime could be released from restraint by *habeas corpus*. United States v. Williams, 341 US 58, 66-67 (1951) (citing Bowen v. Johnston, 306 US 19, 27 (1939))

First, immediately after you are indicted, or during pre-trial, you should demand that your attorney file a *habeas corpus* petition (28 U.S.C. § 2241) challenging, (1) That the complaint/information or indictment fails to charge an offense against the laws of the United States because no jurisdiction has been ceded or accepted over the place where the criminal activity is alleged to have occurred, (2) That your trial court is without subject-matter jurisdiction under 18 U.S.C. § 3231, and (3) That your criminal statute exceeds the power of Congress as applied to your conduct, because it violates your "due process" rights secured under the Fifth Amendment, and encroaches on the sovereignty and jurisdiction of the State in violation of the Tenth Amendment and the fundamental principles of federalism. If your attorney refuses, demand a newly appointed attorney and repeat. Refuse to waive your Sixth Amendment right to the effective assistance of counsel in presenting your defense.

If you must, file the *habeas corpus* petition (28 U.S.C. § 2241) yourself, or challenge the subject-matter jurisdiction of the court openly while in session.

Simply stand and ask to be heard. Speak respectfully regardless of whether permission to speak is granted. State on and for the record that the Government has failed to submit into the record evidence: (1) Any documentation showing ownership by the United States (Federal Government) over the place where the criminal activity is alleged in the complaint/indictment to have occurred, and (2) Any cessions and acceptance of jurisdiction as required under Article I, § 8, cl. 17, and 40 U.S.C. § 3112. You must make these objections on the record in open court. Also, immediately ask for a transcribed copy of the proceedings. If at any time the Judge or U.S. Attorney continues to interrupt you or cut you off, ask the judge if you are being denied the opportunity to be heard and whether you are being rushed to judgment. That should get their attention.

The court will, most likely, note your objections or make an erroneous finding of jurisdiction and allow your prosecution to continue. The important thing is to keep establishing these substantive objections to jurisdiction on the record for your appeal. You can also file an extra-ordinary writ of Mandamus, first to the circuit court and then to the Supreme Court, asking the court to review the lower court's alleged finding of subject-matter jurisdiction. Remember, the court cannot lawfully proceed with your prosecution without subject-matter jurisdiction because it violates your "due process" rights secured under the Fifth Amendment.

Second, should you make it all the way to trial and lose, immediately appeal to the United States Court of Appeals for your Circuit. Make sure to follow the Federal Rules of Appellate Procedure and the Local Rules for your Circuit. Continue to challenge legislative (territorial) jurisdiction over the place where the crime is alleged in the complaint/ indictment to have occurred and the subject-matter jurisdiction of the court to have adjudicated the case and rendered judgment of conviction. Also continue to challenge the constitutionality of your criminal statute as exceeding the power of Congress because it violates the Tenth Amendment.

Third, should you lose your appeal, you have 90 days to file for certiorari review. Make sure you follow the Supreme Court Rules to the letter. Expect to be denied.

Fourth, you have 1 year from the denial of your petition for certiorari review to file a section 2255 petition (28 U.S.C. § 2255). Remember, there is no time limit for filing actual innocence and lack of jurisdiction claims. If the court cannot resolve your claims on the merits based on the record and pleadings, an evidentiary hearing may be scheduled. The court will most likely deny your petition without even ordering the Government (U.S. Attorney) to respond and without making any findings of fact and conclusions of law on the merits of your wrongful detention claim. You may have to file an extraordinary petition for "Writ of Mandamus" just to force the district court to deal with your *habeas corpus* petition. Expect to also be denied a "certificate of appealability" ("C.O.A.")[246] and the right to proceed as a poor person ("in *forma pauperis*"), using boilerplate[247] language.

Fifth, immediately file a notice of appeal with your district court.

---

[246] Title 28 U.S.C. § 2253(c)

[247] boilerplate. Ready-made or all-purpose language that will fit in a variety of documents. Black's Law Dictionary, Seventh Edition, page 167.

You must remember to follow the rules of procedure at all times. These are essential if you want success. Become familiar with them. They include the <u>Rules Governing 2255 Proceedings</u>, <u>Federal Rules of Criminal Procedure</u>, <u>Federal Rules of Civil Procedure</u>, <u>Federal Rules of Evidence</u>, and the <u>Federal Rules of Appellate Procedure</u>. Be sure to also follow each court's <u>Local Rules</u>.

On appeal, you will have a limited number of days, depending on your Circuit's local rules, to request a C.O.A. before they treat the notice of appeal you filed in the district court as a C.O.A. Check your Local Rules. You can expect the court of appeals to take the full amount of time under their rules before they deny you.

Sixth, immediately file a request for reconsideration/rehearing (panel/en banc), depending on your local rules. Where the local rules are silent on an issue, proceed under the Federal Rules of Appellate Procedure (which rules trump the local rules). Normally requests for reconsideration/rehearing are denied within 30 days. I have witnessed up to six months. That is not the norm, however.

Seventh, apply for certiorari review in the Supreme Court. Again, expect to be denied.

Eighth, file a *"habeas corpus"* petition under 28 U.S.C. § 2241 with the United States district court in the Judicial District of your incarceration (if the same as your trial court then file a 2241 *Habeas corpus* with the Supreme Court). This is different than a 2255 petition. Unlike a 2255 petition, there is no time limit in which you must file this. You should claim that you are actually innocent of committing an offense against the laws of the United States, that you were never given a full evidentiary hearing and that no findings of fact and conclusions of law were made on the merits of your claim of wrongful detention. You should also claim that, (1) The indictment/information fails to charge an offense against the laws of the United States because no jurisdiction has been ceded or accepted over the place where the criminal activity is alleged to have occurred, (2) That your trial court was without subject-matter jurisdiction, and (3) That your criminal statute exceeds the power of Congress because it violates the Tenth Amendment. Remember, if the Federal Government utilizes your criminal statute to reach a prohibited end the statute is then unconstitutional as applied to your conduct, regardless of whether the statute is constitutionally valid as written.[248]

Ninth, when the Magistrate Judge denies your petition, you must file a motion making specific objections to his/her Report & Recommendation within 14 days.

Tenth, if the District Judge adopts the Magistrate's Report & Recommendation immediately file a notice of appeal.

Eleventh, the Circuit Court may select your case for summary action which stays the filing of any briefs. Make sure you timely object to dispositive[249] summary action that does not dispose of your issues on the merits, as mandated by the rules of procedure:

---

[248] Even though Congress has written a law (statute) to reach a constitutional end (although so vague it should be unconstitutionally void), because it has been used to reach a prohibited end (used in a way that violates the constitution), it is unconstitutional.

[249] dispositive. Being a deciding factor; (of a fact or factor) bringing about a final determination.

> In General. In an action tried on the facts without a jury … <u>the court must find the facts</u> specially <u>and state its conclusions of law</u> separately. <u>FRCP</u>, 52(a)(1)

Twelfth, file a *Habeas corpus* (2241) with the Supreme Court.

You will probably not receive relief before you file in the Supreme Court, because the Federal district and appellate courts are all engaged in a conspiracy to usurp the sovereignty and jurisdiction of the several 50 Union States. This completes the procedural remedy.

A HELPFULL HINT

The habeas corpus petition under Title 28 U.S.C. § 2241 can only be used before conviction or where a 2255 petition is inadequate or ineffective. Inmates may also utilize a 2241 habeas corpus petition to challenge the manner in which their sentence is served or executed as well as due process violations relating to the loss of good conduct time. The filing fee is $5. On appeal, the circuit court will inform you that you must pay the $455 filing fee or file for in *forma pauperis* status. The $455 fee does not apply to these types of *habeas corpus* petitions under 2241 because they are not "civil actions" subject to the filing fee requirements under the Prison Litigation Reform Act ("P.L.R.A."). Even though the fees do not apply, the court's procedures require that you apply for in *forma pauperis* status. You must also request a waiver of the filing fee. You can utilize the following case law to help with the fee waiver (which allows you to file for free). The landmark case in which all others seem to be based is out of the Third Circuit and states:

> [W]hen the PLRA is read as a whole, it is apparent that Congress did not intend for the statute[250] to apply to habeas proceedings. For the foregoing reasons, we conclude that **the filing fee requirements of the PLRA** set forth in 28 U.S.C. § 1915(b) **do <u>not</u> apply to *habeas corpus* petitions <u>or to appeals</u> from the denial of such petitions**. Santana v. United States, 98 F3d 752, 756 (3d Cir. 1996)

Likewise, numerous other circuits have held the same. The Seventh Circuit, citing the First, Second, Third, Fourth, Fifth, Sixth, Ninth, Eleventh, and DC Circuits, stated that:

---

[250] Title 28 U.S.C. § 1915

We therefore hold today ... that **the PLRA does not apply to any requests for collateral relief under 28 U.S.C. § 2241**, 2254, 2255. Walker v. O'Brian, 216 F3d 626, 628-629 (7th Cir. 1999)

In another case, the United States Court of Appeals for the Fifth Circuit stated that:

> [W]e see no reason to distinguish a section 2241 proceeding from other types of habeas proceedings. Accordingly, agreeing with the Tenth and District of Columbia Circuits, we hold that because the nature of a section 2241 proceeding is the same as those under sections 2254 and 2255, section 2241 proceedings are not "civil actions" for the purposes of

section 1915. **The PLRA thus does not apply to section 2241 proceedings**. Davis v. Fechtel, 150 F3d 486, 490 (5th Cir. 1998)

Section 802(a) of the PLRA, which applies to "... civil actions with respect to prison conditions," explicitly excludes *habeas corpus* proceedings from its scope:

> Definitions. As used in this section—the term "civil action with respect to prison conditions" means any civil proceeding arising under Federal law with respect to the conditions of confinement or the effects of actions by government officials on the lives of persons confined in prison, but **does not include *habeas corpus* proceedings challenging the fact or duration

of confinement in prison. Title 18 U.S.C. § 3626(g)(2)

The provision of the PLRA regarding in *forma pauperis* status (which is the provision that applies to "civil actions"), is located at Title 28 U.S.C. § 1915. The Tenth Circuit, like the other Circuits, stated that:

> [W]e hold only that 2241 proceedings, and appeals of those proceedings, are not "civil actions" for purposes of 28 U.S.C. §§ 1915(a)(2) and (b). McIntosh v. United States Parole Comm'n, 115 F3d 809, 812 (10th Cir. 1997)

Even though the in *forma pauperis* provision of the PLRA codified at Title 28 U.S.C. § 1915, does not apply to *habeas corpus* proceedings under 2241 challenging the fact of our conviction or the correct implementation of our sentence, it is important to read and carefully follow the Local Rules. For example, the Third Circuit's Local Rules of Appellate Procedure state that:

> Failure to file any of the documents specified in Rule 24.1 will result in dismissal of the appeal by the clerk under L.A.R. 3.3 and L.A.R. Misc. 107.1. <u>3d Cir. L.A.R.</u>, 24.2
>
> (a) In civil cases which 28 U.S.C. § 1915 (b) applies; prisoners seeking to proceed on appeal in *forma pauperis* must file the following documents in the court of appeals:
>
> (1) an affidavit of poverty that includes the amount in the prisoner's prison account;

(2) a certified copy of the prison account statement(s) (or institutional equivalent) for the 6 month period immediately preceding the filing of the notice of appeal; and

(3) a signed form authorizing prison officials to assess and deduct the filing fees in accordance with 28 U.S.C. § 1915(b).

(b) After the filing of the document required in subsection (a) in civil cases in which 28 U.S.C. § 1915(b) applies, the clerk will issue an order directing the warden of the prison to assess and deduct the filing fees in accordance with 28 U.S.C. § 1915(b).

(c) In cases filed in which 28 U.S.C. § 1915(b) does not apply, prisoners seeking to proceed on appeal in *forma pauperis* must file an affidavit of poverty in the form prescribed by the Federal

Rules of Appellate Procedure accompanied by a certified statement of the prison account statement(s) (or institutional equivalent) for a 6 month period preceding the filing of the notice of appeal or petition for extraordinary writ. **No assessment order will be entered** <u>unless</u> the court determines that the case is subject to the requirements of § 1915(b) and directs that assessments be made. <u>3d Cir. L.A.R.</u>, 24.1, Documents Required with Application

(a) If a proceeding is docketed without prepayment of the applicable docketing fee, the appellant must pay the fee within 14 days after docketing. If the appellant fails to do so, the clerk is authorized to dismiss the appeal.

(b) If an action has been dismissed by the district court pursuant to 28 U.S.C. § 1915 as frivolous or malicious, or if the district court certifies pursuant to § 1915(a) and FRAP 24(a) that an appeal is not taken in good faith, the applicant may either pay the applicable docketing fee or file a motion to proceed in *forma pauperis* within 14 days after docketing the appeal. If the appellant fails to either pay the applicable docketing fee or file the motion to proceed in *forma pauperis* and any required supporting documents, the clerk is authorized to dismiss the appeal 30 days after docketing of the appeal. 3d Cir. L.A.R., 3.3, Payment of Fees

(a) The clerk is authorized to dismiss the appeal if the appellant does not pay the docketing fee within 14 days after the case is opened in the court of appeals, as prescribed by 3d Cir. L.A.R.

(b) The appellant's failure to comply with 3rd Cir. L.A.R. 11.1 regarding transcription fees shall be grounds for dismissal of the appeal. <u>3d Cir. L.A.R. Misc.</u>, 107.1, Dismissal of Appeal for Failure to Pay Certain Fees

As we can see from the aforementioned Local Rules, we are required to submit certain documentation even though neither the PLRA provision under Title 28 U.S.C. § 1915, nor the filing fee to appeal (currently $455), apply to us in *habeas corpus* proceedings. You must remember to always follow the rules or they will use them to deny your review.

I am currently preparing to file a *habeas corpus* petition with the Supreme Court within the next 2 to 5 months (watch their docket). Their rules state that, "This writ is rarely granted." Sup.Ct. R., 20.4(a). I figure that if they do grant it, they will not address the merits. If the Supreme Court denies me, that will be all the proof we need to show that they refuse to uphold the Constitution and that there is no remedy under the law available to us. Such a decision would surely be used to discourage you from even trying to obtain relief. This is what the lower federal courts are trying to do. This is how tyranny and oppression work. Once you're indicted you don't stand a chance. All this play toward the Constitution being the Supreme Law is just a ruse. Lip service to the public. They are not following it. In truth and in fact many of the people I am incarcerated with were not even indicted by a Grand Jury but, rather, by their prosecuting United States Attorney or some other court employee. An outright violation of their right secured under the Fifth Amendment to the U.S. Constitution. The federal courts grant very few petitions for relief and only do so in order to maintain the deception and give people hope. It is, however, a false hope. As you read in this

Manifesto, when confronted with the truth and Supreme Law under our Constitution they will not follow it.

The answer is a simple one. A little war strategy is being used against you. The old "divide and conquer" technique. They do not care about one person knowing the truth. Alone you cannot do anything about it because their agencies will not listen to you. You must tell your family, friends, everyone you know about this Manifesto. Concentrate on groups like the Sovereign Citizen movement, the Tea Party, the Hell's Angels motorcycle club, the National Organization for the Reform of Marijuana Laws (N.O.R.M.L."), "Tax Protestor" organizations and a group called "Anonymous." These are the groups that can obtain the media attention necessary. Only then will we see change. Only then will this vigilante justice system of tyranny and oppression end. Only then can we utilize the Constitution to truly "Beat the Feds in Court".

It should be noted that you can file an extraordinary writ of mandamus without paying the usual $455 filing fee under the PLRA, if it is pursuant to a *habeas corpus* petition. The application of the PLRA to mandamus petitions depends on the nature of the relief sought—only if the prisoner's mandamus claim is analogous to the typical suits brought under 42 USC § 1983, complaining about prison conditions or civil rights does the PLRA apply. See Andrews v. King, 398 F3d 1113, 1123 (CA9, 2004) (citing In re Nagy, 89 F3d 115, 117 (CA2, 1996)). Keep in mind that the courts will most likely deny your application for a writ of mandamus until after your *habeas corpus* petition has sat on the lower court's docket for more than 1 year.

SUE THEM

It may prove very beneficial to bring a lawsuit in State Court against your District Judge, the U.S. Attorney, the Magistrate Judge who issued the search warrant, or arrest warrant, and any F.B.I., D.E.A., or I.R.S. agents involved in your case. To be sure, they will attempt to have it removed to Federal Court. However, you can attempt to challenge that the Federal Courts are not constitutional courts established under Article III, and therefore are not authorized to extend the judicial power of the United States to your controversy. It is highly likely the Defendant's will cite Heck v. Humphrey, 512 US 477 (1994), which states that if you are incarcerated, or otherwise in custody under supervised release, *etc.*, then you cannot bring a civil suit against the government employees for acts done by them if the consequence of winning that lawsuit would render your conviction invalid (therefore entitling you to be released from incarceration), because there are other vehicles that you must pursue and use to challenge your underlying conviction (such as 28 U.S.C. § 2241, 2255, *etc.*). Notably, the Heck case cited above is only applicable after conviction.

The Supreme Court authority for suing judges and D.O.J. employees is <u>Bivens v. Six Unknown Fed. Narcotics Agents</u>, 409 US 388, 395 (1971). With regard to suing judges, the Supreme Court explained that:

> [T]he necessary inquiry in determining whether a defendant judge is immune from suit is whether at the time he took the challenged action he had jurisdiction over the subject-matter.
>
> [H]e will be subject to liability only when he has acted in the "clear absence of all jurisdiction." <u>Stump v. Sparkman</u>, 435 US 349, 356-357 (1978)

In an earlier case the Supreme Court explained that:

[W]ith reference to judges of limited and inferior authority it had been held that they were protected only when they acted within their jurisdiction.

A distinction must be here observed between excess of jurisdiction and the clear absence of all jurisdiction over the subject-matter. Where there is clearly no jurisdiction over the subject-matter, any authority exercised is a usurped authority, and for the exercise of such authority, when the want of jurisdiction is known to the judge, no excuse is permissible. Bradley v. Fisher, 80 US 335, 351-352 (1872)

This is exactly why the judges should assure themselves that they have jurisdiction over the subject-matter. Instead of assuring themselves that the criminal activity alleged occurred over land under the concurrent or exclusive legislative (territorial) jurisdiction of the Federal Government (United States), or pursuant to a provision in the Constitution where the power to "punish" is delegated, which is an essential element of any "offense against the laws of the United States" over which they have subject-matter jurisdiction, the judges act as if they are totally unaware of this mandatory requirement and simply state they have jurisdiction under 18 U.S.C. § 3231. This action by the judges has the analogous effect of making you guilty, thereby forcing you to endure prosecution, until you are able to prove your innocence. After all, without the "essential element" of jurisdiction over the place of the alleged criminal activity it is not possible for you to have committed an "offense against the laws of the United States" which deprives the courts of subject-matter jurisdiction to hear the prosecution.

We also know that Title 18 U.S.C. is written to occur within the territorial jurisdiction of the "United States" which is defined at 18 U.S.C. §§ 5, 7. This effectively limits Title 18 U.S.C. crimes to places under the concurrent or exclusive legislative (territorial) jurisdiction of the Federal Government unless the statute clearly indicates that it is meant to apply outside the "United States," that is, extra-territorially. A constitutional foundation must also exist to support an extra-territorial application of the statute. For example, the enumerated power to "punish".

SOMETHING TO CONSIDER

These people who pervert the Constitution (Our lawful form of government) make their money by taxing you for holding people illegally until they die of old age, if possible. What good is the law if the ones entrusted to uphold and enforce it are above it, or can act outside of it, at will, to our detriment?

I am certain the Federal Government, and perhaps others, will attempt to discredit this Manifesto as a fraud because I am currently incarcerated. They may not even care that this Manifesto has been written, being certain you will not believe it because their system has been in place and actively running for so long. People did not believe Christopher Columbus either when he told them the earth was round (which was later proven by Magellan) when they all believed it was flat. Neither did people believe Galileo when he told them that the Earth revolved around the Sun when they all believed the Sun revolved around the Earth. There is not a greater nuisance than the one who claims he can prove wrong something which was never doubted, like Christopher Columbus, Magellan, and Galileo.

You may come across those who adamantly support this unconstitutional system. Indeed, many inmates say to me, "What's the difference if I serve time in State or Federal prison?" To that I reply, one has the right to prosecute you under the law and the other does not. If the one that does not have any authority under the law to prosecute you, and makes their money by finding you guilty, and incarcerating you, for a crime you are not guilty of committing under their laws, at what time do you think they are going to care about your rights? Their sworn oaths to uphold the law? The laws they are bound by? They do not care. No right = tyranny. Tyranny = oppression. They are nothing more than a Racketeering Influenced Corrupt Organization (R.I.C.O.).

Perhaps these inmates would better understand their status as victims if their judge were to suddenly resentence them to life in prison? Many Citizens and people (tourists, foreigners, *etc.*), believe they are not susceptible. They should contemplate this: If the Federal Government is exercising powers not delegated to them by prosecuting crimes for which no authority exists for them to do, and We the People are unwilling to stop them, or do anything about it, what is to stop them from coming after whomever they choose? From coming after you? From making up any excuse to prosecute you for a federal crime you could not possibly be guilty of committing and then taking your money and property? From trampling upon, and ignoring, your rights secured under the very Constitution that supposes to limit their power? Ponder how they then demand that We the People pay them, through taxes, for doing so. The day the Federal Government realizes the People know and don't care, and will not do anything about it, you will see a level of tyranny and oppression never dreamed imaginable. That is what you will leave your Posterity, especially if the government is able to ban guns. [Please read, "THREE FELONIES A DAY," How the Feds Target the Innocent, by Harvey A. Silverglate]

Edward Snowden is a former N.S.A. subcontractor that told on members of the Federal Government who were breaking the law. What is his reward? Being forced to claim asylum in another country under threat to be prosecuted and incarcerated for life by the Federal Government, the very same government he told on. Can you say tyranny? Can you say oppression?

You do not need to take my word as true nor the word of those who will adamantly oppose this Manifesto as true. The evidence contained herein speaks for itself and can be readily verified through reliable sources such as University Law Libraries, the Internet, and the National Archives, to name a few. You have reviewed the evidence presented in this Manifesto with your own eyes. <u>Verify the information</u> then decide what you believe is true <u>based on your findings</u>. The Federal Government actively prosecutes authors of valid legal material. This is done in order to discourage others from believing the truth and, instead, summing the work up as a scam. The first thought that comes to mind is that it must be a scam or the Federal Government would not be prosecuting these authors. Perhaps they will try to prosecute me in the same manner in an attempt to convince others that this Manifesto I have authored is a scam. Nothing stops them ... **except lack-of jurisdiction**!

Ask yourself, if the Federal Government really can exercise an undelegated and implied power to "punish" under the commerce clause, then why do the Federal Rules of Criminal Procedure limit their territorial reach to prosecute felonious "interstate commerce" crimes and misdemeanor offenses as if the courts are legislative courts?[251] Perhaps the skeptics could **show us where in the law** it proves I am wrong? If they could do that then they will have accomplished something even the federal judges and U.S. Attorneys, which hold Masters and Doctorates of Law, have not been willing or able to do. The only answer they have been able to muster so far is that the Supreme Court told them they could exercise this power. I have news for you, judge made law (precedent) does not trump the Constitution if their opinions are in conflict with that instrument. However, the Su-

---

[251] Article I court. Legislative court. A type of federal legislative court that is not bound by the requirements of or protected under U.S. Const. art. III, § 2, and that performs functions similar to those of an administrative agency, such as issuing advisory opinions. U.S. Const. art. I, § 8. Black's Law Dictionary, Fourth Pocket Edition, page 47.

Territorial court. A U.S. court established in a U.S. territory (such as the Virgin Islands) and serving as both a federal and state court. The Constitution authorizes Congress to create such courts. U.S. Const. art. IV, § 3, cl.2. Black's L Dictionary, Eighth Edition, page 384.

preme Court told them no such thing. Even if the Supreme Court did, <u>they cannot legislate for Congress</u> who alone holds that power and, more importantly, has <u>not</u> legislated that way. Neither has the Constitution been amended, delegating, by enumeration, the power to define and "punish" felonies committed in interstate commerce.

Further, why do we keep utilizing Federal Reserve notes, which are a fiat currency, and paying interest on them? They are not real money, like silver & gold, they are debt instruments. Although, according to the U.S. Government Manual, the Federal Reserve is an agency of our government, its "stocks" (or coupons) are owned by private unknown individuals. When they print $100 million in Federal Reserve notes, it costs pennies on the dollar to do so. However, the American People are charged the full face value ($100 million) plus .02¢ for every dollar. That is $2 million in interest. You cannot pay debt with debt. I have listened to people tell me how we could instantly pay off our $17 trillion national debt if we wanted to. If that is true, why did we borrow a $1 trillion T.A.R.P. fund from China? We just felt like paying $600 million dollars a day in interest? Don't you think We the People could use all that money?

Another thing I hear is that, "Gold is just useless hunks of metal. What the people value is what is important." How We the People got tricked into accepting a private independent company's paper instead of gold is beyond me. One reason gold is valued is because it is a <u>specie</u> [252] of money. That means it cannot be counterfeited because it is a product of nature and not man-made and counterfeitable like paper. If gold is really useless then maybe someone would like to explain why the Federal Reserve Bank in New York, which is 1 of 10 throughout the country, admittedly has more gold 80 feet below the street surface than all the gold in Fort Knox! Again, the Federal Reserve Bank in New York is just 1 of 10 Federal Reserve Banks throughout America. If gold is so worthless maybe someone could explain why the Federal Reserve is hoarding it by the tons? If you bury $100 in Gold and $100 in Federal Reserve

---

[252] Specie. Coin of the precious metals, of a certain weight and fineness, and bearing the stamp of the government, denoting its value as currency. Metallic money; e.g. gold and silver coins. <u>Black's Law Dictionary</u>, Sixth Edition, page 1,398.

notes and dig it up after 100 years, the purchasing power of the gold will still be equivalent to what it was 100 years ago, because its value fluctuated with the economy. The purchasing power of the Federal Reserve notes will not be anywhere near what it was 100 years ago, because its value (or strength) as a debt instrument continues to weaken as the amount of debt rises. As more and more Federal Reserve notes are printed to cover their weakening value and purchasing power a rise in prices directly results, thus requiring more Federal reserve notes to purchase the same amount of merchandise. This is commonly referred to as inflation. Eventually, as this cycle continues, the value of the Federal Reserve note will weaken to a point where economic collapse results. It is your life. It is your choice. When one of us loses our liberties and rights, we all lose them together. You must choose for yourself. Freedom or Oppression through Tyranny. As Justice Brandeis so wisely urged:

> In a government of laws, existence of the government will be

imperiled if it fails to observe the law scrupulously. Our Government is the potent, the omnipresent teacher. For good or for ill, it teaches the whole people by its example. Crime is contagious. If the Government becomes a lawbreaker, it breeds contempt for law; it invites every man to become a law unto himself; it invites anarchy. To declare that in the administration of the criminal law the end justifies the means—to declare that the Government may commit crimes in order to secure the conviction of a private criminal— would bring terrible retribution. Against that pernicious doctrine this Court should resolutely set its face. Olmstead v. United States, 277 US 438, 485 (1928) (dissenting opinion)

Freedom is the Cornerstone of America's foundation. The colonial revolutionaries sacrificed life and limb for the sake of freedom. No one said it more eloquently than Patrick Henry when he stated against taking the easier course and not asserting one's rights in exchange for ease and comfort:

> Why stand here we idle? What is it that gentlemen wish? What would they have? Is life so dear, or peace so sweet, as to be purchased at the price of chains and slavery? Forbid it, Almighty God! I know not what course others may take, but as for me: Give me liberty, or give me death! Patrick Henry, Liberty or Death, Richmond, Va., (Mar. 23, 1775), reprinted in Gregory R. Suriano, Great American Speeches 4 (1993).

Now more than ever, the freedom of the individual upon which this government was anchored as its reason to be is revered. The world has joined in recognizing it as the moving force of nations. Without freedom of the individuals within a community, the people who live in that soil have no claim for nationhood. Where there is no freedom of the individuals there is no nation of any kind.

In the words of Samuel Adams (September 27, 1722 – October 2, 1803), American revolutionary, organizer of the Boston Tea Party, and governor of Massachusetts from 1793 to 1797:

> If ye love wealth greater than liberty, the tranquility of servitude greater than the animating contest for freedom, go home from us in peace. We seek not your counsel, nor your arms. Crouch down and lick the hand that feeds you; May your chains set lightly upon you, and may posterity forget that ye were our countrymen.

God bless and good luck.

-Edward Harvey

If you have any questions that were not answered in this Manifesto, please send $2.00 and a self addressed stamped envelope <u>per question</u> to:

Beat Feds Book
4520 Howe Rd.
Wayne, Michigan 48184

Answers may take up to 8 weeks, so be patient.

To order a copy of this book send a certified check or post-office money order for $57.67 ($47.67 plus a $10.00 non-refundable shipping and handling fee) to:

Beat Feds Book
4520 Howe Rd.
Wayne, Michigan 48184

Delivery may take up to 8 weeks, so be patient. It is recommended that inmates have their order sent to a family member, as we are unable to forward your order if rejected by the institution.

APPENDIX

RON PAUL FAREWELL SPEECH

Farewell to Congress

This may well be the last time I speak on the House Floor. At the end of the year I'll leave Congress after 23 years in office over a 36 year period. My goals in 1976 were the same as they are today: promote peace and prosperity by a strict adherence to the principles of individual liberty.

It was my opinion, that the course the U.S. embarked on in the latter part of the 20th Century would bring us a major financial crisis and engulf us in a foreign policy that would overextend us and undermine our national security.

To achieve the goals I sought, government would have had to shrink in size and scope, reduce spending, change the monetary system, and reject the unsustainable costs of policing the world and expanding the American Empire.

The problems seemed to be overwhelming and impossible to solve, yet from my view point, just following the constraints placed on the federal government by the Constitution would have been a good place to start.

How Much Did I Accomplish?

In many ways, according to conventional wisdom, my off-and-on career in Congress, from 1976 to 2012, accomplished very little. No named legislation, no named federal buildings or highways—thank goodness. In spite of my efforts, the government has grown exponentially, taxes remain excessive, and the prolific increase of incomprehensible regulations continues. Wars are constant and pursued without Congressional declaration, deficits rise to the sky, poverty is rampant and dependency on the Federal Government is now worse than any time in our history.

All this with minimal concerns for the deficits and unfunded liabilities that common sense tells us cannot go on much longer. A grand, but never mentioned, bipartisan agreement allows for the well-kept secret that keeps the spending going. One side doesn't give up one penny on military spending, the other side doesn't give up one penny on welfare spending, while both sides support the bailouts and subsidies for the banking and corporate elite. And the spending continues as the economy weakens and the downward spiral continues. As the government continues fiddling around, our liberties and our wealth burn in the flames of a foreign policy that makes us less safe.

The major stumbling block to real change in Washington is the total resistance to admitting that the country is broke. This has made compromising, just to agree to increase spending, inevitable since neither side has any intention of cutting spending.

The country and the Congress will remain divisive since there's no "loot left to divvy up."

Without this recognition the spenders in Washington will continue the march toward a fiscal cliff much bigger than the one anticipated this coming January.

I have thought a lot about why those of us who believe in liberty, as a solution, have done so poorly in convincing others of its benefits. If liberty is what we claim it is—the principle that protects all personal, social and economic decisions necessary for maximum prosperity and the best chance for peace—it should be an easy sell. Yet, history has shown that the masses have been quite receptive to the promises of authoritarians which are rarely if ever fulfilled.

Authoritarianism vs. Liberty

If authoritarianism leads to poverty and war and less freedom for all individuals and is controlled by rich special interests, the people should be begging for liberty. There certainly was a strong enough sentiment for more freedom at the time of our founding that motivated those who were willing to fight in the revolution against the powerful British government.

During my time in Congress the appetite for liberty has been quite weak; the understanding of its significance negligible. Yet the good news is that compared to 1976 when I first came to Congress, the desire for more freedom and less government in 2012 is much greater and growing, especially in grassroots America. Tens of thousands of teenagers and college age students are, with great enthusiasm, welcoming the message of liberty.

I have a few thoughts as to why the people of a country like ours, once the freest and most prosperous, allowed the conditions to deteriorate to the degree that they have.

Freedom, private property, and enforceable voluntary contracts, generate wealth. In our early history we were very much aware of this. But in the early part of the 20th century our politicians promoted the notion that the tax and monetary systems had to change if we were to involve ourselves in excessive domestic and military spending. That is why Congress gave us the Federal Reserve and the income tax. The majority of Americans and many government officials agreed that sacrificing some liberty was necessary to carry out what some claimed to be "progressive" ideas. Pure democracy became acceptable.

They failed to recognized that what they were doing was exactly opposite of what the colonists were seeking when they broke away from the British.

Some complain that my arguments makes no sense, since great wealth and the standard of living improved for many Americans over the last 100 years, even with these new policies.

But the damage to the market economy, and the currency, has been insidious and steady. It took a long time to consume our wealth, destroy the currency and undermine productivity and get our financial obligations to a point of no return. Confidence sometimes lasts longer than deserved. Most of our wealth today depends on debt.

The wealth that we enjoyed and seemed to be endless, allowed concern for the principle of a free society to be neglected. As long as most people believed the material abundance would last forever, worrying about protecting a competitive productive economy and individual liberty seemed unnecessary.

The Age of Redistribution

This neglect ushered in an age of redistribution of wealth by government kowtowing to any and all special interests, except for those who just wanted to be left alone. That is why today money in politics far surpasses money currently going into research and development and productive entrepreneurial efforts.

The material benefits became more important than the understanding and promoting the principles of liberty and a free market. It is good that material abundance is a result of liberty but if materialism is all that we care about, problems are guaranteed.

The crisis arrived because the illusion that wealth and prosperity would last forever has ended. Since it was based on debt and a pretense that debt can be papered over by an out-of-control fiat monetary system, it was doomed to fail. We have ended up with a system that doesn't produce enough even to finance the debt and no fundamental understanding of why a free society is crucial to reversing these trends.

If this is not recognized, the recovery will linger for a long time. Bigger government, more spending, more debt, more poverty for the middle class, and a more intense scramble by the elite special interests will continue.

We Need an Intellectual Awakening

Without an intellectual awakening, the turning point will be driven by economic law. A dollar crisis will bring the current out-of-control system to its knees.

If it's not accepted that big government, fiat money, ignoring liberty, central economic planning, welfarism, and warfarism caused our crisis we can expect a continuous and dangerous march toward corporatism and even fascism with even more loss of our ties. Prosperity for a large middle class though will become an abstract dream.

This continuous move is no different than what we have seen in how our financial crisis of 2008 was handled. Congress first directed, with bipartisan support, bailouts for the wealthy. Then it was the Federal Reserve with its endless quantitative easing. If at first it doesn't succeed try again; QE1, QE2, and QE3 and with no results we try QE indefinitely—that is until it too fails. There's a cost to all of this and let me assure you delaying the payment is no longer an option. The rules of the market will extract its pound of flesh and it won't be pretty.

The current crisis elicits a lot of pessimism. And the pessimism adds to less confidence in the future. The two feed on themselves, making our situation worse.

If the underlying cause of the crisis is not understood we cannot solve our problems. The issues of warfare, welfare, deficits, inflationism, corporatism, bailouts and authoritarianism cannot be ignored. By only expanding these policies we cannot expect good results.

Everyone claims support for freedom. But too often it's for one's own freedom and not for others. Too many believe that there must be limits on freedom. They argue that freedom must be directed and managed to achieve fairness and equality thus making it acceptable to curtail, through force, certain liberties.

Some decide what and whose freedoms are to be limited. These are the politicians whose goal in life is power. Their success depends on gaining support from special interests.

No More 'isms'

The great news is the answer is not to be found in more "isms." The answers are to be found in more liberty which cost so much less. Under these circumstances spending goes down, wealth production goes up, and the quality of life improves.

Just this recognition—especially if we move in this direction—increases optimism which in itself is beneficial. The follow through with sound policies are required which must be understood and supported by the people.

But there is good evidence that the generation coming of age at the present time is supportive of moving in the direction of more liberty and self-reliance. The more this change in direction and the solutions become known, the quicker will be the return of optimism.

Our job, for those of us who believe that a different system than the one that we have had for the last 100 years, has driven us to this unsustainable crisis, is to be more convincing that there is a wonderful, uncomplicated, and moral system that provides the answers. We had a taste of it in our early history. We need not give up on the notion of advancing this cause.

It worked, but we allowed our leaders to concentrate on the material abundance that freedom generates, while ignoring freedom itself. Now we have neither, but the door is open, out of necessity, for an answer. The answer available is based on the Constitution, individual liberty and prohibiting the use of government force to provide privileges and benefits to all special interests.

After over 100 years we face a society quite different from the one that was intended by the Founders. In many ways their efforts to protect future generations with the Constitution from this danger has failed. Skeptics, at the time the Constitution was written in 1787, warned us of today's possible outcome. The insidious nature of the erosion of our liberties and the reassurance our great abundance gave us, allowed the process to evolve into the dangerous period in which we now live.

Dependency on Government Largesse

Today we face a dependency on government largesse for almost every need. Our liberties are restricted and government operates outside the rule of law, protecting and rewarding those who buy or coerce government into satisfying their demands. Here are a few examples:

Undeclared wars are commonplace.

Welfare for the rich and poor is considered an entitlement.

The economy is over regulated, overtaxed and grossly distorted by a deeply flawed monetary system.

Debt is growing exponentially.

The Patriot Act and FISA legislation passed without much debate have resulted in a steady erosion of our 4th Amendment rights.

Tragically our government engages in preemptive war, otherwise known as aggression, with no complaints from the American people.

The drone warfare we are pursuing worldwide is destined to end badly for us as the hatred builds for innocent lives lost and the international laws flaunted. Once we are financially weakened and militarily challenged, there will be a lot of resentment thrown our way.

It's now the law of the land that the military can arrest American citizens, hold them indefinitely, without charges or a trial.

Rampant hostility toward free trade is supported by a large number in Washington.

Supporters of sanctions, currency manipulation and WTO trade retaliation, call the true free traders "isolationists."

Sanctions are used to punish countries that don't follow our orders.

Bailouts and guarantees for all kinds of misbehavior are routine.

Central economic planning through monetary policy, regulations and legislative mandates has been an acceptable policy.

Questions

Excessive government has created such a mess it prompts many questions:

Why are sick people who use medical marijuana put in prison?

Why does the federal government restrict the drinking of raw milk?

Why can't Americans manufacture rope and other products from hemp?

Why are Americans not allowed to use gold and silver as legal tender as mandated by the Constitution?

Why is Germany concerned enough to consider repatriating their gold held by the FED for her in New York? Is it that the trust in the U.S. and dollar supremacy is beginning to wane?

Why do our political leaders believe it's unnecessary to thoroughly audit our own gold?

Why can't Americans decide which type of light bulbs they can buy?

Why is the TSA permitted to abuse the rights of any American traveling by air?

Why should there be mandatory sentences—even up to life for crimes without victims—as our drug laws require?

Why have we allowed the federal government to regulate commodes in our homes?

Why is it political suicide for anyone to criticize AIPAC ?

Why haven't we given up on the drug war since it's an obvious failure and violates the people's rights? Has nobody noticed that the authorities can't even keep drugs out of the prisons? How can making our entire society a prison solve the problem?

Why do we sacrifice so much by getting needlessly involved in border disputes and civil strife around the world and ignore the root cause of the most deadly border in the world-the one between Mexico and the US?

Why does Congress willingly give up its prerogatives to the Executive Branch?

Why does changing the party in power never change policy? Could it be that the views of both parties are essentially the same?

Why did the big banks, the large corporations, and foreign banks and foreign central banks get bailed out in 2008 and the middle class lost their jobs and their homes?

Why do so many in the government and the federal officials believe that creating money out of thin air creates wealth?

Why do so many accept the deeply flawed principle that government bureaucrats and politicians can protect us from ourselves without totally destroying the principle of liberty?

Why can't people understand that war always destroys wealth and liberty?

Why is there so little concern for the Executive Order that gives the President authority to establish a "kill list," including American citizens, of those targeted for assassination?

Why is patriotism thought to be blind loyalty to the government and the politicians who run it, rather than loyalty to the principles of liberty and support for the people? Real patriotism is a willingness to challenge the government when it's wrong.

Why is it claimed that if people won't or can't take care of their own needs, that people in government can do it for them?

Why did we ever give the government a safe haven for initiating violence against the people?

Why do some members defend free markets, but not civil liberties?

Why do some members defend civil liberties but not free markets? Aren't they the same?

Why don't more defend both economic liberty and personal liberty?

Why are there not more individuals who seek to intellectually influence others to bring about positive changes than those who seek power to force others to obey their commands?

Why does the use of religion to support a social gospel and preemptive wars, both of which requires authoritarians to use violence, or the threat of violence, go unchallenged? Aggression and forced redistribution of wealth has nothing to do with the teachings of the world's great religions.

Why do we allow the government and the Federal Reserve to disseminate false information dealing with both economic and foreign policy?

Why is democracy held in such high esteem when it's the enemy of the minority and makes all rights relative to the dictates of the majority?

Why should anyone be surprised that Congress has no credibility, since there's such a disconnect between what politicians say and what they do?

Is there any explanation for all the deception, the unhappiness, the fear of the future, the loss of confidence in our leaders, the distrust, the anger and frustration? Yes there is, and there's a way to reverse these attitudes. The negative perceptions are logical and a consequence of bad policies bringing about our problems. Identification of the problems and recognizing the cause allow the proper changes to come easy.

Trust Yourself, Not the Government

Too many people have for too long placed too much confidence and trust in government and not enough in themselves. Fortunately, many are now becoming aware of the seriousness of the gross mistakes of the past several decades. The blame is shared by both political parties. Many Americans now are demanding to hear the plain truth of things and want the demagoguing to stop. Without this first step, solutions are impossible.

Seeking the truth and finding the answers in liberty and self-reliance promotes the optimism necessary for restoring prosperity. The task is not that difficult if politics doesn't get in the way.

We have allowed ourselves to get into such a mess for various reasons.

Politicians deceive themselves as to how wealth is produced. Excessive confidence is placed in the judgment of politicians and bureaucrats. This replaces the confidence in a free society. Too many in high places of authority became convinced that only they, armed with arbitrary government power, can bring about fairness, while facilitating wealth production. This always proves to be a utopian dream and destroys wealth and liberty. It impoverishes the people and rewards the special interests who end up controlling both political parties.

It's no surprise then that much of what goes on in Washington is driven by aggressive partisanship and power seeking, with philosophic differences being minor.

Economic Ignorance

Economic ignorance is commonplace. Keynesianism continues to thrive, although today it is facing healthy and enthusiastic rebuttals. Believers in military Keynesianism and domestic Keynesianism continue to desperately promote their failed policies, as the economy languishes in a deep slumber.

Supporters of all government edicts use humanitarian arguments to justify them.

Humanitarian arguments are always used to justify government mandates related to the economy, monetary policy, foreign policy, and personal liberty. This is on purpose to make it more difficult to challenge. But, initiating violence for humanitarian reasons is still violence. Good intentions are no excuse and are just as harmful as when people use force with bad intentions. The results are always negative.

The immoral use of force is the source of man's political problems. Sadly, many religious groups, secular organizations, and psychopathic authoritarians endorse government initiated force to change the world. Even when the desired goals are well-intentioned—or especially when well-intentioned—the results are dismal. The good results sought never materialize. The new problems created require even more government force as a solution. The net result is institutionalizing government initiated violence and morally justifying it on humanitarian grounds.

This is the same fundamental reason our government uses force for invading other countries at will, central economic planning at home, and the regulation of personal liberty and habits of our citizens.

It is rather strange, that unless one has a criminal mind and no respect for other people and their property, no one claims it's permissible to go into one's neighbor's house and tell them how to behave, what they can eat, smoke and drink or how to spend their money.

Yet, rarely is it asked why it is morally acceptable that a stranger with a badge and a gun can do the same thing in the name of law and order. Any resistance is met with brute force, fines, taxes, arrests, and even imprisonment. This is done more frequently every day without a proper search warrant.

No Government Monopoly over Initiating Violence

Restraining aggressive behavior is one thing, but legalizing a government monopoly for initiating aggression can only lead to exhausting liberty associated with chaos, anger and the breakdown of civil society. Permitting such authority and expecting saintly behavior from the bureaucrats and the politicians is a pipe dream. We now have a standing army of armed bureaucrats in the TSA, CIA, FBI, Fish and Wildlife, FEMA, IRS, Corp of Engineers, *etc.* numbering over 100,000. <u>Citizens are guilty until proven innocent in the unconstitutional administrative courts</u>.

Government in a free society should have no authority to meddle in social activities or the economic transactions of individuals. Nor should government meddle in the affairs of other nations. All things peaceful, even when controversial, should be permitted.

We must reject the notion of prior restraint in economic activity just as we do in the area of free speech and religious liberty. But even in these areas government is starting to use a backdoor approach of political correctness to regulate speech-a dangerous trend. Since 9/11 monitoring speech on the Internet is now a problem since warrants are no longer required.

The Proliferation of Federal Crimes

<u>The Constitution established four federal crimes</u>. Today the experts can't even agree on how many federal crimes are now on the books—they number into the thousands. No one person can comprehend the enormity of the legal system—especially the tax code. Due to the ill-advised drug war and the endless

federal expansion of the criminal code we have over 6 million people under correctional suspension, more than the Soviets ever had, and more than any other nation today, including China. I don't understand the complacency of the Congress and the willingness to continue their obsession with passing more Federal laws. Mandatory sentencing laws associated with drug laws have compounded our prison problems.

The federal register is now 75,000 pages long and the tax code has 72,000 pages, and expands every year. <u>When will the people start shouting, "enough is enough," and demand Congress cease and desist</u>?

Achieving Liberty

Liberty can only be achieved when government is denied the aggressive use of force. If one seeks liberty, a precise type of government is needed. To achieve it, more than lip service is required.

Two choices are available.

A government designed to protect liberty—a natural right—as its sole objective. The people are expected to care for themselves and reject the use of any force for interfering with another person's liberty. Government is given a strictly limited authority to enforce contracts, property ownership, settle disputes, and defend against foreign aggression.

A government that pretends to protect liberty but is granted power to arbitrarily use force over the people and foreign nations. Though the grant of power many times is meant to be small and limited, it inevitably metastasizes into an omnipotent political cancer. This is the problem for which the world has suffered throughout the ages. Though meant to be limited it nevertheless is a 100% sacrifice of a principle that would-be-tyrants find irresistible. It is used vigorously—though incrementally and insidiously. Granting power to government officials always proves the adage that: "power corrupts."

Once government gets a limited concession for the use of force to mold people's habits and plan the economy, it causes a steady move toward tyrannical government. Only a revolutionary spirit can reverse the process and deny to the government this arbitrary use of aggression. There's no in-between. Sacrificing a little liberty for imaginary safety always ends badly.

Today's mess is a result of Americans accepting option #2, even though the Founders attempted to give us Option #1.

The results are not good. As our liberties have been eroded our wealth has been consumed. The wealth we see today is based on debt and a foolish willingness on the part of foreigners to take our dollars for goods and services. They then loan them back to us to perpetuate our debt system. It's amazing that it has worked for this long but the impasse in Washington, in solving our problems, indicate that many are starting to understand the seriousness of the world - wide debt crisis and the dangers we face. The longer this process continues the harsher the outcome will be.

The Financial Crisis Is a Moral Crisis

Many are now acknowledging that a financial crisis looms but few understand it's, in reality, a moral crisis. It's the moral crisis that has allowed our liberties to be undermined and permits the exponential growth of illegal government power. Without a clear understanding of the nature of the crisis it will be difficult to prevent a steady march toward tyranny and the poverty that will accompany it.

Ultimately, the people have to decide which form of government they want; option #1 or option #2. There is no other choice. Claiming there is a choice of a "little" tyranny is like describing pregnancy as a "touch of pregnancy." It is a myth to believe that a mixture of free markets and government central economic planning is a worthy compromise. What we see today is a result of that type of thinking. And the results speak for themselves.

A Culture of Violence

America now suffers from a culture of violence. It's easy to reject the initiation of violence against one's neighbor but it's ironic that the people arbitrarily and freely anoint government officials with monopoly power to initiate violence against the American people—practically at will.

Because it's the government that initiates force, most people accept it as being legitimate. Those who exert the force have no sense of guilt. It is believed by too many that governments are morally justified in initiating force supposedly to "do good." They incorrectly believe that this authority has come from the "consent of the people." The minority, or victims of government violence, never consented to suffer the abuse of government mandates, even when dictated by the majority. Victims of TSA excesses never consented to this abuse.

This attitude has given us a policy of initiating war to "do good," as well. It is claimed that war, to prevent war for noble purposes, is justified. This is similar to what we were once told that: "destroying a village to save a village" was justified. It was said by a US Secretary of State that the loss of 500,000 Iraqis, mostly children, in the 1990s, as a result of American bombs and sanctions, was "worth it" to achieve the "good" we brought to the Iraqi people. And look at the mess that Iraq is in today.

Government use of force to mold social and economic behavior at home and abroad has justified individuals using force on their own terms. The fact that violence by government is seen as morally justified, is the reason why violence will increase when the big financial crisis hits and becomes a political crisis as well.

First, we recognize that individuals shouldn't initiate violence, then we give the authority to government. Eventually, the immoral use of government violence, when things go badly, will be used to justify an individual's "right" to do the same thing. Neither the government nor individuals have the moral right to initiate violence against another yet we are moving toward the day when both will claim this authority. If this cycle is not reversed society will break down.

When needs are pressing, conditions deteriorate and rights become relative to the demands and the whims of the majority. It's then not a great leap for individuals to take it upon themselves to use violence to get what they claim is theirs. As the economy deteriorates and the wealth discrepancies increase—as are already occurring— violence increases as those in need take it in their own hands to get what they believe is theirs. They will not wait for a government rescue program.

When government officials wield power over others to bail out the special interests, even with disastrous results to the average citizen, they feel no guilt for the harm they do. Those who take us into undeclared wars with many casualties resulting, never lose sleep over the death and destruction their bad decisions caused. They are convinced that what they do is morally justified, and the fact that many suffer just can't be helped.

When the street criminals do the same thing, they too have no remorse, believing they are only taking what is rightfully theirs. All moral standards become relative. Whether it's bailouts, privileges, government subsidies or benefits for some from inflating a currency, it's all part of a process justified by a philosophy of forced redistribution of wealth. Violence, or a threat of such, is the instrument required and unfortunately is of little concern of most members of Congress.

Some argue it's only a matter of "fairness" that those in need are cared for. There are two problems with this. First, the principle is used to provide a greater amount of benefits to the rich than the poor. Second, no one seems to be concerned about whether or not it's fair to those who end up paying for the benefits. The costs are usually placed on the backs of the middle class and are hidden from the public eye. Too many people believe government handouts are free, like printing money out of thin air, and there is no cost. That deception is coming to an end. The bills are coming due and that's what the economic slowdown is all about.

Sadly, we have become accustomed to living with the illegitimate use of force by government. It is the tool for telling the people how to live, what to eat and drink, what to read and how to spend their money.

To develop a truly free society, the issue of initiating force must be understood and rejected. Granting to government even a small amount of force is a dangerous concession.

Limiting Government Excesses vs. a Virtuous Moral People

Our Constitution, which was intended to limit government power and abuse, has failed. The Founders warned that a free society depends on a virtuous and moral people. The current crisis reflects that their concerns were justified.

Most politicians and pundits are aware of the problems we face but spend all their time in trying to reform government. The sad part is that the suggested reforms almost always lead to less freedom and the importance of a virtuous and moral people is either ignored, or not understood. The new reforms serve only to further undermine liberty. The compounding effect has given us this steady erosion of liberty and the massive expansion of debt. The real question is: if it is liberty we seek, should most of the emphasis be placed on government reform or trying to understand what "a virtuous and moral people" means and how to promote it. The Constitution has not prevented the people from demanding handouts for both rich and poor in their efforts to reform the government, while ignoring the principles of a free society. <u>All branches of our government today are controlled by individuals who use their power to undermine liberty and enhance the welfare/warfare state-and frequently their own wealth and power</u>.

If the people are unhappy with the government performance it must be recognized that government is merely a reflection of an immoral society that rejected a moral government of constitutional limitations of power and love of freedom.

If this is the problem all the tinkering with thousands of pages of new laws and regulations will do nothing to solve the problem.

It is self-evident that our freedoms have been severely limited and the apparent prosperity we still have, is nothing more than leftover wealth from a previous time. This fictitious wealth based on debt and benefits from a false trust in our currency and credit, will play havoc with our society when the bills come due. This means that the full consequence of our lost liberties is yet to be felt.

But that illusion is now ending. Reversing a downward spiral depends on accepting a new approach.

Expect the rapidly expanding home schooling movement to play a significant role in the revolutionary reforms needed to build a free society with Constitutional protections. We cannot expect a Federal government controlled school system to provide the intellectual ammunition to combat the dangerous growth of government that threatens our liberties.

The Internet will provide the alternative to the government/media complex that controls the news and most political propaganda. This is why it's essential that the Internet remains free of government regulation.

Many of our religious institutions and secular organizations support greater dependency on the state by supporting war, welfare and corporatism and ignore the need for a virtuous people.

I never believed that the world or our country could be made more free by politicians, if the people had no desire for freedom.

Under the current circumstances the most we can hope to achieve in the political process is to use it as a podium to reach the people to alert them of the nature of the crisis and the importance of their need to assume responsibility for themselves, if it is liberty that they truly seek. Without this, a constitutionally protected free society is impossible.

If this is true, our individual goal in life ought to be for us to seek virtue and excellence and recognize that self-esteem and happiness only comes from using one's natural ability, in the most productive manner possible, according to one's own talents.

Productivity and creativity are the true source of personal satisfaction. Freedom, and not dependency, provides the environment needed to achieve these goals. Government cannot do this for us; it only gets in the way. When the government gets involved, the goal becomes a bailout or a subsidy and these cannot provide a sense of personal achievement.

Achieving legislative power and political influence should not be our goal. Most of the change, if it is to come, will not come from the politicians, but rather from individuals, family, friends, intellectual leaders and our religious institutions. The solution can only come from rejecting the use of coercion, compulsion, government commands, and aggressive force, to mold social and economic behavior. Without accepting these restraints, inevitably the consensus will be to allow the government to mandate economic equality and obedience to the politicians who gain power and promote an environment that smothers the freedoms of everyone. It is then that the responsible individuals who seek excellence and self-esteem by being self-reliant and productive, become the true victims.

Conclusion

What are the greatest dangers that the American people face today and impede the goal of a free society? There are five.

1. The continuous attack on our civil liberties which threatens the rule of law and our ability to resist the onrush of tyranny.

2. Violent anti-Americanism that has engulfed the world. Because the phenomenon of "blow-back" is not understood or denied, our foreign policy is destined to keep us involved in many wars that we have no business being in. National bankruptcy and a greater threat to our national security will result.

3. The ease in which we go to war, without a declaration by Congress, but accepting international authority

from the UN or NATO even for preemptive wars, otherwise known as aggression.

4. A financial political crisis as a consequence of excessive debt, unfunded liabilities, spending, bailouts, and gross discrepancy in wealth distribution going from the middle class to the rich. The danger of central economic planning, by the Federal Reserve, must be understood.

5. World government taking over local and US sovereignty by getting involved in the issues of war, welfare, trade, banking, a world currency, taxes, property ownership, and private ownership of guns.

Happily, there is an answer for these very dangerous trends.

What a wonderful world it would be if everyone accepted the simple moral premise of rejecting all acts of aggression. The retort to such a suggestion is always: it's too simplistic, too idealistic, impractical, naïve, utopian, dangerous, and unrealistic to strive for such an ideal.

The answer to that is that for thousands of years the acceptance of government force, to rule over the people, at the sacrifice of liberty, was considered moral and the only available option for achieving peace and prosperity.

What could be more utopian than that myth—considering the results especially looking at the state sponsored killing, by nearly every government during the 20th Century, estimated to be in the hundreds of millions. It's time to reconsider this grant of authority to the state.

No good has ever come from granting monopoly power to the state to use aggression against the people to arbitrarily mold human behavior. Such power, when left unchecked, becomes the seed of an ugly tyranny. This method of governance has been adequately tested, and the results are in: reality dictates we try liberty.

The idealism of non-aggression and rejecting all offensive use of force should be tried. The idealism of government sanctioned violence has been abused throughout history and is the primary source of poverty and war. The theory of a society being based on individual freedom has been around for a long time. It's time to take a bold step and actually permit it by advancing this cause, rather than taking a step backwards as some would like us to do.

Today the principle of *habeas corpus*, established when King John signed the Magna Carta in 1215, is under attack. There's every reason to believe that a renewed effort with the use of the Internet that we can instead advance the cause of liberty by spreading an uncensored message that will serve to rein in government authority and challenge the obsession with war and welfare.

What I'm talking about is a system of government guided by the moral principles of peace and tolerance.

The Founders were convinced that a free society could not exist without a moral people. Just writing rules won't work if the people choose to ignore them. Today the rule of law written in the Constitution has little meaning for most Americans, especially those who work in Washington DC.

Benjamin Franklin claimed "only a virtuous people are capable of freedom." John Adams concurred: "Our Constitution was made for a moral and religious people. It is wholly inadequate to the government of any other."

A moral people must reject all violence in an effort to mold people's beliefs or habits.

A society that boos or ridicules the Golden Rule is not a moral society. All great religions endorse the Golden Rule. The same moral standards that individuals are required to follow should apply to all government officials. They cannot be exempt.

The ultimate solution is not in the hands of the government.

The solution falls on each and every individual, with guidance from family, friends and community.

The #1 responsibility for each of us is to change ourselves with hope that others will follow. This is of greater importance than working on changing the government; that is secondary to promoting a virtuous society. If we can achieve this, then the government will change.

It doesn't mean that political action or holding office has no value. At times it does nudge policy in the right direction. But what is true is that when seeking office is done for personal aggrandizement, money or power, it becomes useless if not harmful. When political action is taken for the right reasons it's easy to understand why compromise should be avoided. It also becomes clear why progress is best achieved by working with coalitions, which bring people together, without anyone sacrificing his principles.

Political action, to be truly beneficial, must be directed toward changing the hearts and minds of the people, recognizing that it's the virtue and morality of the people that allow liberty to flourish.

The Constitution or more laws per se, have no value if the people's attitudes aren't changed.

To achieve liberty and peace, two powerful human emotions have to be overcome. Number one is "envy" which leads to hate and class warfare. Number two is "intolerance" which leads to bigoted and judgmental policies. These emotions must be replaced with a much better understanding of love, compassion, tolerance and free market economics. Freedom, when understood, brings people together. When tried, freedom is popular.

The problem we have faced over the years has been that economic interventionists are swayed by envy, whereas social interventionists are swayed by intolerance of habits and lifestyles. The misunderstanding that tolerance is an endorsement of certain activities, motivates many to legislate moral standards which should only be set by individuals making their own choices. Both sides use force to deal with these misplaced emotions. Both are authoritarians. Neither endorses voluntarism. Both views ought to be rejected.

I have come to one firm conviction after these many years of trying to figure out "the plain truth of things." The best chance for achieving peace and prosperity, for the maximum number of people worldwide, is to pursue the cause of LIBERTY.

If you find this to be a worthwhile message, spread it throughout the land.

—For an excellent understanding of how simplistic the law really is and should be, and how it has been contorted by socialism, please read, "THE LAW", by Frederick Bastiat.

INSPIRATIONAL QUOTES

"When the people fear their government, there is tyranny; when the government fears the people, there is liberty." –Thomas Jefferson

"I prefer dangerous freedom over peaceful slavery." –Thomas Jefferson

"A small body of determined spirits fired by an unquenchable faith in their mission can alter the course of history." –Mahatma Gandhi

"The ultimate measure of a man is not where he stands in moments of comfort and convenience, but where he stands at times of challenge and controversy." –Martin Luther King, Jr.

"Unthinking respect for authority is the greatest enemy of truth." –Albert Einstein

"Rightful liberty is unobstructed action according to our will within limits drawn around us by the equal rights of others. I do not add 'within the limits of the law' because the law is often but the tyrant's will, and always so when it violates the rights of the individual."
–Thomas Jefferson

"You obey an evil system most effectively by obeying its orders and decrees. An evil system never deserves such allegiance. Allegiance to it means partaking of the evil. A good person will resist an evil system with his or her whole soul." –Mahatma Gandhi

"Freedom is never voluntarily given by the oppressor; it must be demanded by the oppressed." –Martin Luther King, Jr.

"It does not require a majority to prevail, but rather an irate, tireless minority keen to set brush fires in people's minds." –Samuel Adams

"Knowing is not enough; we must apply. Willing is not enough; we must do." –Bruce Lee

"Where justice is denied, where poverty is enforced, where ignorance prevails, and where any one class is made to feel that society is an organized conspiracy to oppress, rob and degrade them, neither persons nor property will be safe." –Federick Douglas

"Make yourselves sheep and the wolves will eat you." –Benjamin Franklin

"You will not fight for the right when you can easily win without bloodshed, if you will not fight when your victory will be sure and not so costly, you may come to the moment when you will have to fight with all the odds against you and only a precarious chance for survival. There may be a worse case. You may have to fight when there is no chance of victory, because it is better to perish than to live as slaves." –Winston Churchill

"Education is the best security for maintaining liberties, and, a nation of well-informed men who have been taught to know and prize the rights which God has given them cannot be enslaved. It is in the region of ignorance that tyranny reigns." –Benjamin Franklin, Autobiography

"It will be of little avail to the people that the laws are made by men of their own choice, if the laws be so voluminous that they cannot be read, or so incoherent that they cannot be understood; if they be repealed or revised before they are promulgated, or undergo such incessant changes that no man who knows what the law is today can guess what it will be tomorrow." –James Madison, Federalist no. 62, February 27, 1788

"The problem isn't what we don't know, the problem is what we believe to be so and isn't so." –Will Rodgers

"They that can give up essential liberty to obtain a little temporary safety deserve neither liberty nor safety." –Benjamin Franklin

"Once a government is committed to the principle of silencing the voice of opposition, it has only one way to go, and that is down the path of increasingly repressive measures, until it becomes a source of terror to all its citizens and creates a country where everyone lives in fear." –Harry S. Truman

"The people are the masters of both Congress and the courts, not to overthrow the Constitution, but to overthrow the men who would pervert it!" –Abraham Lincoln

"Dissent is the highest form of patriotism." – Thomas Jefferson

"As government expands, liberty contracts." – Ronald Reagan

"Who controls the food supply controls the people; who controls the energy can control whole continents; who controls money can control the world." –Henry Kissenger

"There are more instances of the abridgment of the freedom of the people by gradual and silent encroachments of those in power than by violent and sudden usurpation."   –James Madison (1751-1836)

"We are fast approaching the stage of the ultimate inversion: the stage where the government is free to do anything it pleases, while the citizens may act only by permission; which is the stage of rule by brute force." –Ayn Rand, The Nature of Government

OTHER INFORMATIVE DEFINITIONS

The following definitions are taken from the Sixth Edition of Black's Law Dictionary.

Collusion. An agreement between two or more persons to defraud a person of his rights by the forms of law, or to obtain an object forbidden by law. It implies the existence of fraud of some kind, the employment of fraudulent means, or of lawful means for the accomplishment of an unlawful purpose. page, 264.

Color of law. The appearance or semblance, without the substance, of legal right. Misuse of power ... made possible only because wrongdoer is clothed with authority. page 265.

Color of office. Pretense of official right to do act made by one who has no such right. An act under color of office is an act of an officer who claims authority to do the act by reason of his office when the office does not confer on him any such authority. page, 266.

De Facto. In fact, in deed, actually. This phrase is used to characterize an officer, a government, a past action, or a state of affairs which must be accepted for all practical purposes, but is illegal or illegitimate. In this sense it is the contrary of de jure, which means rightful, legitimate, just, or constitutional. Thus an officer, king, or government de facto is one who is in actual possession of the office or supreme power, but by usurpation, or without lawful title. page, 416.

De facto judge. A judge who functions under color of authority but whose authority is defective in some procedural form. page, 416.

De Jure. Descriptive of a condition in which there has been total compliance with all requirements of law. Of right; legitimate; lawful; by right and just title. page, 425.

U.S. NATIONAL ARCHIVES & RECORDS ADMINISTRATION

www.archives.gov   July 3, 2014

Magna Carta Translation

[Preamble] Edward by the grace of God King of England, lord of Ireland and duke of Aquitaine sends greetings to all to whom the present letters come. We have inspected the great charter of the lord Henry, late King of England, our father, concerning the liberties of England in these words:

Henry by the grace of God King of England, lord of Ireland, duke of Normandy and Aquitaine and count of Anjou sends greetings to his archbishops, bishops, abbots, priors, earls, barons, sheriffs, reeves, ministers and all his bailiffs and faithful men inspecting the present charter. Know that we, at the prompting of God and for the health of our soul and the souls of our ancestors and successors, for the glory of holy Church and the improvement of our realm, freely and out of our good will have given and granted to the archbishops, bishops, abbots, priors, earls, barons and all of our realm these liberties written below to hold in our realm of England in perpetuity.

[1] In the first place we grant to God and confirm by this our present charter for ourselves and our heirs in perpetuity that the English Church is to be free and to have all its rights fully and its liberties entirely. We furthermore grant and give to all the freemen of our realm for ourselves and our heirs in perpetuity the liberties written below to have and to hold to them and their heirs from us and our heirs in perpetuity.

[2] If any of our earls or barons, or anyone else holding from us in chief by military service should die, and should his heir be of full age and owe relief, the heir is to have his inheritance for the ancient relief, namely the heir or heirs of an earl for a whole county £100, the heir or heirs of a baron for a whole barony 100 marks, the heir or heirs of a knight for a whole knight's fee 100 shillings at most, and he who owes less will give less, according to the ancient custom of (knights') fees.

[3] If, however, the heir of such a person is under age, his lord is not to have custody of him and his land until he has taken homage from the heir, and after such an heir has been in custody, when he comes of age, namely at twenty-one years old, he is to have his inheritance without relief and without fine, saving that if, whilst under age, he is made a knight, his land will nonetheless remain in the custody of his lords until the aforesaid term.

[4] The keeper of the land of such an heir who is under age is only to take reasonable receipts from the heir's land and reasonable customs and reasonable services, and this without destruction or waste of men or things. And if we assign custody of any such land to a sheriff or to anyone else who should answer to us for the issues, and such a person should commit destruction or waste, we will take recompense from him and the land will be assigned to two law-worthy and discreet men of that fee who will answer to us or to the person to whom we assign such land for the land's issues. And if we give or sell to anyone custody of any such land and that person commits destruction or waste, he is to lose custody and the land is to be

assigned to two law-worthy and discreet men of that fee who similarly will answer to us as is aforesaid.

[5] The keeper, for as long as he has the custody of the land of such (an heir), is to maintain the houses, parks, fishponds, ponds, mills and other things pertaining to that land from the issues of the same land, and he will restore to the heir, when the heir comes to full age, all his land stocked with ploughs and all other things in at least the same condition as when he received it. All these things are to be observed in the custodies of archbishoprics, bishoprics, abbeys, priories, churches and vacant offices which pertain to us, save that such custodies ought not to be sold.

[6] Heirs are to be married without disparagement.

[7] A widow, after the death of her husband, is immediately and without any difficulty to have her marriage portion and her inheritance, nor is she to pay anything for her dower or her marriage portion or for her inheritance which her husband and she held on the day of her husband's death, and she shall remain in the chief dwelling place of her husband for forty days after her

husband's death, within which time dower will be assigned her if it has not already been assigned, unless that house is a castle, and if it is a castle which she leaves, then a suitable house will immediately be provided for her in which she may properly dwell until her dower is assigned to her in accordance with what is aforesaid, and in the meantime she is to have her reasonable necessities (estoverium) from the common property. As dower she will be assigned the third part of all the lands of her husband which were his during his lifetime, save when she was dowered with less at the church door. No widow shall be distrained to marry for so long as she wishes to live without a husband, provided that she gives surety that she will not marry without our assent if she holds of us, or without the assent of her lord, if she holds of another.

[8] Neither we nor our bailiffs will seize any land or rent for any debt, as long as the existing chattels of the debtor suffice for the payment of the debt and as long as the debtor is ready to pay the debt, nor will the debtor's guarantors be distrained for so long as the principal debtor is able to pay the debt; and should the principal debtor default in his payment of

the debt, not having the means to repay it, or should he refuse to pay it despite being able to do so, the guarantors will answer for the debt and, if they wish, they are to have the lands and rents of the debtor until they are repaid the debt that previously they paid on behalf of the debtor, unless the principal debtor can show that he is quit in respect to these guarantors.

[9] The city of London is to have all its ancient liberties and customs. Moreover we wish and grant that all other cities and boroughs and vills and the barons of the Cinque Ports and all ports are to have all their liberties and free customs.

[10] No-one is to be distrained to do more service for a knight's fee or for any other free tenement than is due from it.

[11] Common pleas are not to follow our court but are to be held in a certain fixed place.

[12] Recognisances of novel disseisin and of mort d'ancestor are not to be taken save in their particular counties and in the following way. We or, should we

be outside the realm, our chief justiciar, will send our justices once a year to each county, so that, together with the knights of the counties, that may take the aforesaid assizes in the counties; and those assizes which cannot be completed in that visitation of the county by our aforesaid justices assigned to take the said assizes are to be completed elsewhere by the justices in their visitation; and those which cannot be completed by them on account of the difficulty of various articles (of law) are to be referred to our justices of the Bench and completed there.

[13] Assizes of darrein presentment are always to be taken before our justices of the Bench and are to be completed there.

[14] A freeman is not to be amerced for a small offence save in accordance with the manner of the offence, and for a major offence according to its magnitude, saving his sufficiency (salvo contenemento suo), and a merchant likewise, saving his merchandise, and any villain other than one of our own is to be amerced in the same way, saving his necessity (salvo waynagio) should he fall into our mercy, and none of

the aforesaid amercements is to be imposed save by the oath of honest and law-worthy men of the neighbourhood. Earls and barons are not to be amerced save by their peers and only in accordance with the manner of their offence.

[15] No town or free man is to be distrained to make bridges or bank works save for those that ought to do so of old and by right.

[16] No bank works of any sort are to be kept up save for those that were in defense in the time of King H(enry II) our grandfather and in the same places and on the same terms as was customary in his time.

[17] No sheriff, constable, coroner or any other of our bailiffs is to hold pleas of our crown.

[18] If anyone holding a lay fee from us should die, and our sheriff or bailiff shows our letters patent containing our summons for a debt that the dead man owed us, our sheriff or bailiff is permitted to attach and enroll all the goods and chattels of the dead man found in lay fee, to the value of the said debt, by view

of law-worthy men, so that nothing is to be removed thence until the debt that remains is paid to us, and the remainder is to be released to the executors to discharge the will of the dead man, and if nothing is owed to us from such a person, all the chattels are to pass to the (use of) the dead man, saving to the dead man's wife and children their reasonable portion.

[19] No constable or his bailiff is to take corn or other chattels from anyone who not themselves of a vill where a castle is built, unless the constable or his bailiff immediately offers money in payment of obtains a respite by the wish of the seller. If the person whose corn or chattels are taken is of such a vill, then the constable or his bailiff is to pay the purchase price within forty days.

[20] No constable is to distrain any knight to give money for castle guard if the knight is willing to do such guard in person or by proxy of any other honest man, should the knight be prevented from doing so by just cause. And if we take or send such a knight into the army, he is to be quit of (castle) guard in accordance with the length of time the we have him in the

army for the fee for which he has done service in the army.

[21] No sheriff or bailiff of ours or of anyone else is to take anyone's horses or carts to make carriage, unless he renders the payment customarily due, namely for a two-horse cart ten pence per day, and for a three-horse cart fourteen pence per day. No demesne cart belonging to any churchman or knight or any other lady (sic) is to be taken by our bailiffs, nor will we or our bailiffs or anyone else take someone else's timber for a castle or any other of our business save by the will of he to whom the timber belongs.

[22] We shall not hold the lands of those convicted of felony save for a year and a day, whereafter such land is to be restored to the lords of the fees.

[23] All fish weirs (kidelli) on the Thames and the Medway and throughout England are to be entirely dismantled, save on the sea coast.

[24] The writ called 'praecipe' is not to be issued to anyone in respect to any free tenement in such a way that a free man might lose his court.

[25] There is to be a single measure for wine throughout our realm, and a single measure for ale, and a single measure for Corn, that is to say the London quarter, and a single breadth for dyed cloth, russets, and haberjects, that is to say two yards within the lists. And it shall be the same for weights as for measures.

[26] Henceforth there is to be nothing given for a writ of inquest from the person seeking an inquest of life or member, but such a writ is to be given freely and is not to be denied.

[27] If any persons hold from us at fee farm or in socage or burgage, and hold land from another by knight service, we are not, by virtue of such a fee farm or socage or burgage, to have custody of the heir or their land which pertains to another's fee, nor are we to have custody of such a fee farm or socage or burgage unless this fee farm owes knight service. We are

not to have the custody of an heir or of any land which is held from another by knight service on the pretext of some small serjeanty held from us by service of rendering us knives or arrows or suchlike things.

[28] No bailiff is henceforth to put any man on his open law or on oath simply by virtue of his spoken word, without reliable witnesses being produced for the same.

[29] No freeman is to be taken or imprisoned or disseised of his free tenement or of his liberties or free customs, or outlawed or exiled or in any way ruined, nor will we go against such a man or send against him save by lawful judgement of his peers or by the law of the land. To no-one will we sell or deny of delay right or justice.

[30] All merchants, unless they have been previously and publicly forbidden, are to have safe and secure conduct in leaving and coming to England and in staying and going through England both by land and by water to buy and to sell, without any evil exactions, according to the ancient and right customs, save in

time of war, and if they should be from a land at war against us and be found in our land at the beginning of the war, they are to be attached without damage to their bodies or goods until it is established by us or our chief justiciar in what way the merchants of our land are treated who at such a time are found in the land that is at war with us, and if our merchants are safe there, the other merchants are to be safe in our land.

[31] If anyone dies holding of any escheat such as the honour of Wallingford, Boulogne, Nottingham, Lancaster or of other escheats which are in our hands and which are baronies, his heir is not to give any other relief or render any other service to us that would not have been rendered to the baron if the barony were still held by a baron, and we shall hold such things in the same way as the baron held them, nor, on account of such a barony or escheat, are we to have the escheat or custody of any of our men unless the man who held the barony or the escheat held elsewhere from us in chief.

[32] No free man is henceforth to give or sell any more of his land to anyone, unless the residue of his land is sufficient to render due service to the lord of the fee as pertains to that fee.

[33] All patrons of abbeys which have charters of the kings of England over advowson or ancient tenure or possession are to have the custody of such abbeys when they fall vacant just as they ought to have and as is declared above.

[34] No-one is to be taken or imprisoned on the appeal of woman for the death of anyone save for the death of that woman's husband.

[35] No county court is to be held save from month to month, and where the greater term used to be held, so will it be in future, nor will any sheriff or his bailiff make his tourn through the hundred save for twice a year and only in the place that is due and customary, namely once after Easter and again after Michaelmas, and the view of frankpledge is to be taken at the Michaelmas term without exception, in such a way that every man is to have his liberties which he had or

used to have in the time of King H(enry II) my grandfather or which he has acquired since. The view of frankpledge is to be taken so that our peace be held and so that the tithing is to be held entire as it used to be, and so that the sheriff does not seek exceptions but remains content with that which the sheriff used to have in taking the view in the time of King H(enry) our grandfather.

[36] Nor is it permitted to anyone to give his land to a religious house in such a way that he receives it back from such a house to hold, nor is it permitted to any religious house to accept the land of anyone in such way that the land is restored to the person from whom it was received to hold. If anyone henceforth gives his land in such a way to any religious house and is convicted of the same, the gift is to be entirely quashed and such land is to revert to the lord of that fee.

[37] Scutage furthermore is to be taken as it used to be in the time of King H(enry) our grandfather, and all liberties and free customs shall be preserved to archbishops, bishops, abbots, priors, Templars, Hospitallers, earls, barons and all others, both eccle-

siastical and secular persons, just as they formerly had.

All these aforesaid customs and liberties which we have granted to be held in our realm in so far as pertains to us are to be observed by all of our realm, both clergy and laity, in so far as pertains to them in respect to their own men. For this gift and grant of these liberties and of others contained in our charter over the liberties of the forest, the archbishops, bishops, abbots, priors, earls, barons, knights, fee holders and all of our realm have given us a fifteenth part of all their movable goods. Moreover we grant to them for us and our heirs that neither we nor our heirs will seek anything by which the liberties contained in this charter might be infringed or damaged, and should anything be obtained from anyone against this it is to count for nothing and to be held as nothing. With these witnesses: the lord S(tephen) archbishop of Canterbury, E(ustace) bishop of London, J(ocelin) bishop of Bath, P(eter) bishop of Winchester, H(ugh) bishop of Lincoln, R(ichard) bishop of Salisbury, W. bishop of Rochester, W(illiam) bishop of Worcester, J(ohn) bishop of Ely, H(ugh) bishop of Hereford,

R(anulf) bishop of Chichester, W(illiam) bishop of Exeter, the abbot of (Bury) St Edmunds, the abbot of St Albans, the abbot of Battle, the abbot of St Augustine's Canterbury, the abbot of Evesham, the abbot of Westminster, the abbot of Peterborough, the abbot of Reading, the abbot of Abingdon, the abbot of Malmesbury, the abbot of Winchcombe, the abbot of Hyde (Winchester), the abbot of Chertsey, the abbot of Sherborne, the abbot of Cerne, the abbot of Abbotsbury, the abbot of Milton (Abbas), the abbot of Selby, the abbot of Cirencester, H(ubert) de Burgh the justiciar, H. earl of Chester and Lincoln, W(illiam) earl of Salisbury, W(illiam) earl Warenne, G. de Clare earl of Gloucester and Hertford, W(illiam) de Ferrers earl of Derby, W(illiam) de Mandeville earl of Essex, H(ugh) Bigod earl of Norfolk, W(illiam) earl Aumale, H(umphrey) earl of Hereford, J(ohn) constable of Chester, R(obert) de Ros, R(obert) fitz Walter, R(obert) de Vieuxpont, W(illiam) Brewer, R(ichard) de Montfiquet, P(eter) fitz Herbert, W(illiam) de Aubigné, G. Gresley, F. de Braose, J(ohn) of Monmouth, J(ohn) fitz Alan, H(ugh) de Mortemer, W(illiam) de Beauchamp, W(illiam) de St John, P(eter) de Maulay, Brian de Lisle, Th(omas) of Moulton, R(ichard) de Argentan,

G(eoffrey) de Neville, W(illiam) Mauduit, J(ohn) de Baalon and others. Given at Westminster on the eleventh day of February in the ninth year of our reign.

We, holding these aforesaid gifts and grants to be right and welcome, conceed and confirm them for ourselves and our heirs and by the terms of the present (letters) renew them, wishing and granting for ourselves and our heirs that the aforesaid charter is to be firmly and inviably observed in all and each of its articles in perpetuity, including any articles contained in the same charter which by chance have not to date been observed. In testimony of which we have had made these our letters patent. Witnessed by Edward our son, at Westminster on the twelfth day of October in the twenty-fifth year of our reign. (Chancery warranty by John of) Stowe.

Translation by Professor Nicholas Vincent, Copyright Sotheby's Inc. 2007

U.S. National Archives & Records Administration
8601 Adelphi Road, College Park, MD, 20740-6001, •
1-86-NARA-NARA • 1-866-272-6272

www.ourdocuments.gov   July 3, 2014

Transcript of Declaration of Independence (1776)

IN CONGRESS, July 4, 1776.

www.ourdocuments.gov   July 3, 2013

The unanimous Declaration of the thirteen united States of America,

When in the Course of human events, it becomes necessary for one people to dissolve the political bands which have connected them with another, and to assume among the powers of the earth, the separate and equal station to which the Laws of Nature and of Nature's God entitle them, a decent respect to the opinions of mankind requires that they should declare the causes which impel them to the separation.

We hold these truths to be self-evident, that all men are created equal, that they are endowed by their Creator with certain unalienable Rights, that among these are Life, Liberty and the pursuit of Happiness.-- That to secure these rights, Governments are instituted among Men, deriving their just powers from the consent of the governed, --That whenever any Form of Government becomes destructive of these ends, it is the Right of the People to alter or to abolish it, and to institute new Government, laying its foundation on such principles and organizing its powers in such form, as to them shall seem most likely to effect their Safety and Happiness. Prudence, indeed, will dictate that Governments long established should not be changed for light and transient causes; and accordingly all experience hath shewn, that mankind are more disposed to suffer, while evils are sufferable, than to right themselves by abolishing the forms to which they are accustomed. But when a long train of abuses and usurpations, pursuing invariably the same Object evinces a design to reduce them under absolute Despotism, it is their right, it is their duty, to throw off such Government, and to provide new Guards for their future security.--Such has been the patient sufferance of these Colonies; and such is now the necessity which constrains them to alter their former Systems of Government. The history of the present King of Great Britain is a history of repeated injuries and usurpations, all having in direct object the establishment of an absolute Tyranny over these States. To prove this, let Facts be submitted to a candid world.

He has refused his Assent to Laws, the most wholesome and necessary for the public good.

He has forbidden his Governors to pass Laws of immediate and pressing importance, unless suspended in their operation till his Assent should be obtained; and when so suspended, he has utterly neglected to attend to them.

He has refused to pass other Laws for the accommodation of large districts of people, unless those people would relinquish the right of Representation in the Legislature, a right inestimable to them and formidable to tyrants only.

He has called together legislative bodies at places unusual, uncomfortable, and distant from the depository of their public Records, for the sole purpose of fatiguing them into compliance with his measures.

He has dissolved Representative Houses repeatedly, for opposing with manly firmness his invasions on the rights of the people.

He has refused for a long time, after such dissolutions, to cause others to be elected; whereby the Legislative powers, incapable of Annihilation, have returned to the People at large for their exercise; the State remaining in the mean time exposed to all the dangers of invasion from without, and convulsions within.

He has endeavoured to prevent the population of these States; for that purpose obstructing the Laws for Naturalization of Foreigners; refusing to pass others to encourage their migrations hither, and raising the conditions of new Appropriations of Lands.

He has obstructed the Administration of Justice, by refusing his Assent to Laws for establishing Judiciary powers.

He has made Judges dependent on his Will alone, for

the tenure of their offices, and the amount and payment of their salaries.

He has erected a multitude of New Offices, and sent hither swarms of Officers to harrass our people, and eat out their substance.

He has kept among us, in times of peace, Standing Armies without the Consent of our legislatures.

He has affected to render the Military independent of and superior to the Civil power.

He has combined with others to subject us to a jurisdiction foreign to our constitution, and unacknowledged by our laws; giving his Assent to their Acts of pretended Legislation:

For Quartering large bodies of armed troops among us:

For protecting them, by a mock Trial, from punishment for any Murders which they should commit on the Inhabitants of these States:

For cutting off our Trade with all parts of the world:

For imposing Taxes on us without our Consent:

For depriving us in many cases, of the benefits of Trial by Jury:

For transporting us beyond Seas to be tried for pretended offences

For abolishing the free System of English Laws in a neighbouring Province, establishing therein an Arbitrary government, and enlarging its Boundaries so as to render it at once an example and fit instrument for introducing the same absolute rule into these Colonies:

For taking away our Charters, abolishing our most valuable Laws, and altering fundamentally the Forms of our Governments:

For suspending our own Legislatures, and declaring themselves invested with power to legislate for us in all cases whatsoever.

He has abdicated Government here, by declaring us out of his Protection and waging War against us.

He has plundered our seas, ravaged our Coasts, burnt our towns, and destroyed the lives of our people.

He is at this time transporting large Armies of foreign Mercenaries to compleat the works of death, desolation and tyranny, already begun with circumstances of Cruelty & perfidy scarcely paralleled in the most barbarous ages, and totally unworthy the Head of a civilized nation.

He has constrained our fellow Citizens taken Captive on the high Seas to bear Arms against their Country, to become the executioners of their friends and Brethren, or to fall themselves by their Hands.

He has excited domestic insurrections amongst us, and has endeavoured to bring on the inhabitants of our frontiers, the merciless Indian Savages, whose known rule of warfare, is an undistinguished destruction of all ages, sexes and conditions.

In every stage of these Oppressions We have Petitioned for Redress in the most humble terms: Our repeated Petitions have been answered only by repeated injury. A Prince whose character is thus marked by every act which may define a Tyrant, is unfit to be the ruler of a free people.

Nor have We been wanting in attentions to our Brittish brethren. We have warned them from time to time of attempts by their legislature to extend an unwarrantable jurisdiction over us. We have reminded them of the circumstances of our emigration and settlement here. We have appealed to their native justice and magnanimity, and we have conjured them by the ties of our common kindred to disavow these usurpations, which, would inevitably interrupt our connections and correspondence. They too have been deaf to the voice of justice and of consanguinity. We must, therefore, acquiesce in the necessity, which denounces our Separation, and hold them, as we hold the rest of mankind, Enemies in War, in Peace Friends.

We, therefore, the Representatives of the united States of America, in General Congress, Assembled, appealing to the Supreme Judge of the world for the rectitude of our intentions, do, in the Name, and by Authority of the good People of these Colonies, solemnly publish and declare, That these United Colonies are, and of Right ought to be Free and Independent States; that they are Absolved from all Allegiance to the British Crown, and that all political connection between them and the State of Great Britain, is and ought to be totally dissolved; and that as Free and Independent States, they have full Power to levy War, conclude Peace, contract Alliances, establish Commerce, and to do all other Acts and Things which Independent States may of right do. And for the support of this Declaration, with a firm reliance on the protection of divine Providence, we mutually pledge to each other our Lives, our Fortunes and our sacred

Honor.

The 56 signatures on the Declaration appear in the positions indicated:

Column 1
Georgia:
  Button Gwinnett
  Lyman Hall
  George Walton

Column 2
North Carolina:
  William Hooper
  Joseph Hewes
  John Penn
South Carolina:
  Edward Rutledge
  Thomas Heyward, Jr.
  Thomas Lynch, Jr.

Arthur Middleton

Column 3
Massachusetts:
John Hancock
Maryland:
Samuel Chase
William Paca
Thomas Stone
Charles Carroll of Carrollton
Virginia:
George Wythe
Richard Henry Lee
Thomas Jefferson
Benjamin Harrison
Thomas Nelson, Jr.
Francis Lightfoot Lee
Carter Braxton

Column 4
Pennsylvania:
Robert Morris
Benjamin Rush
Benjamin Franklin

John Morton
George Clymer
James Smith
George Taylor
James Wilson
George Ross

Delaware:
Caesar Rodney
George Read
Thomas McKean

Column 5
New York:
William Floyd
Philip Livingston
Francis Lewis
Lewis Morris

New Jersey:
Richard Stockton
John Witherspoon
Francis Hopkinson
John Hart
Abraham Clark

Column 6

New Hampshire:
- Josiah Bartlett
- William Whipple

Massachusetts:
- Samuel Adams
- John Adams
- Robert Treat Paine
- Elbridge Gerry

Rhode Island:
- Stephen Hopkins
- William Ellery

Connecticut:
- Roger Sherman
- Samuel Huntington
- William Williams
- Oliver Wolcott

New Hampshire:
- Matthew Thornton

U.S. National Archives & Records Administration
700 Pennsylvania Avenue NW, Washington, DC

20408 • 1-86-NARA-NARA • 1-866-272-6272

www.archives.gov

Transcript of Articles of Confederation (1777)

To all to whom these Presents shall come, we, the undersigned Delegates of the States affixed to our Names send greeting. Whereas the Delegates of the United States of America in Congress assembled did on the fifteenth day of November in the year of our Lord One Thousand Seven Hundred and Seventy seven, and in the Second Year of the Independence of America agree to certain articles of Confederation and perpetual Union between the States of New Hampshire, Massachusetts-bay, Rhode Island and Providence Plantations, Connecticut, New York, New Jersey, Pennsylvania, Delaware, Maryland, Virginia, North Carolina, South Carolina, and Georgia in the Words following, viz. "Articles of Confederation and perpetual Union between the States of New Hampshire, Massachusetts-bay, Rhode Island and Providence Plantations, Connecticut, New York, New Jersey, Pennsylvania, Delaware, Maryland, Virginia, North Carolina, South Carolina, and Georgia.

Article I. The Stile of this confederacy shall be, "The United States of America."

Article II. Each state retains its sovereignty, freedom and independence, and every Power, Jurisdiction and right, which is not by this confederation expressly delegated to the United States, in Congress assembled.

Article III. The said states hereby severally enter into a firm league of friendship with each other, for their common defence, the security of their Liberties, and their mutual and general welfare, binding themselves to assist each other, against all force offered to, or attacks made upon them, or any of them, on account of religion, sovereignty, trade, or any other pretence whatever.

Article IV. The better to secure and perpetuate mutual friendship and intercourse among the people of the different states in this union, the free inhabitants of each of these states, paupers, vagabonds and fugitives from Justice excepted, shall be entitled to all privileges and immunities of free citizens in the several states; and the people of each state shall have free ingress and regress to and from any other state, and shall enjoy therein all the privileges of trade and commerce, subject to the same duties, impositions and restrictions as the inhabitants thereof respectively, provided that such restrictions shall not extend so far as to prevent the removal of property imported into any state, to any other State of which the Owner is an inhabitant; provided also that no imposition, duties or restriction shall be laid by any state, on the property of the united states, or either of them.

If any Person guilty of, or charged with, treason, felony, or other high misdemeanor in any state, shall flee from Justice, and be found in any of the united states, he shall upon demand of the Governor or executive power of the state from which he fled, be delivered up, and removed to the state having jurisdiction of his offence.

Full faith and credit shall be given in each of these states to the records, acts and judicial proceedings of the courts and magistrates of every other state.

Article V. For the more convenient management of the general interests of the united states, delegates shall be annually appointed in such manner as the legislature of each state shall direct, to meet in Congress on the first Monday in November, in every year, with a power reserved to each state to recall its delegates, or any of them, at any time within the year, and to send others in their stead, for the remainder of the Year.

No State shall be represented in Congress by less than two, nor by more than seven Members; and no person shall be capable of being delegate for more than three years, in any term of six years; nor shall any person, being a delegate, be capable of holding any office under the united states, for which he, or another for his benefit receives any salary, fees or emolument of any kind.

Each State shall maintain its own delegates in a meeting of the states, and while they act as members of the committee of the states.

In determining questions in the united states, in Congress assembled, each state shall have one vote.

Freedom of speech and debate in Congress shall not be impeached or questioned in any Court, or place out of Congress, and the members of congress shall be protected in their persons from arrests and imprisonments, during the time of their going to and from, and attendance on congress, except for treason, felony, or breach of the peace.

Article VI. No State, without the Consent of the united States, in congress assembled, shall send any embassy to, or receive any embassy from, or enter into any conference, agreement, alliance, or treaty, with any King prince or state; nor shall any person holding any office of profit or trust under the united states, or any of them, accept of any present, emolument, office, or title of any kind whatever, from any king, prince, or foreign state; nor shall the united states, in congress assembled, or any of them, grant any title of nobility.

No two or more states shall enter into any treaty, confederation, or alliance whatever between them, without the consent of the united states, in congress assembled, specifying accurately the purposes for which the same is to be entered into, and how long it shall continue.

No State shall lay any imposts or duties, which may interfere with any stipulations in treaties, entered into by the united States in congress assembled, with any king, prince, or State, in pursuance of any treaties already proposed by congress, to the courts of France and Spain.

No vessels of war shall be kept up in time of peace, by any state, except such number only, as shall be deemed necessary by the united states, in congress assembled, for the defence of such state, or its trade; nor shall any body of forces be kept up, by any state, in time of peace, except such number only as, in the judgment of the united states, in congress assembled, shall be deemed requisite to garrison the forts necessary for the defence of such state; but every state shall always keep up a well regulated and disciplined militia, sufficiently armed and accounted, and shall provide and constantly have ready for use, in public stores, a due number of field pieces and tents, and a proper quantity of arms, ammunition, and camp equipage.

No State shall engage in any war without the consent of the united States in congress assembled, unless such State be actually invaded by enemies, or shall have received certain advice of a resolution being formed by some nation of Indians to invade such State, and the danger is so imminent as not to admit of a delay till the united states in congress assembled, can be consulted: nor shall any state grant commissions to any ships or vessels of war, nor letters of marque or reprisal, except it be after a declaration of war by the united states in congress assembled, and then only against the kingdom or State, and the subjects thereof, against which war has been so declared, and under such regulations as shall be established by the united states in congress assembled, unless such state be infested by pirates, in which case vessels of war may be fitted out for that occasion, and kept so long as the danger shall continue, or until the united states in congress assembled shall determine otherwise.

Article VII. When land forces are raised by any state, for the common defence, all officers of or under the rank of colonel, shall be appointed by the legislature of each state respectively by whom such forces shall be raised, or in such manner as such state shall direct, and all vacancies shall be filled up by the state which first made appointment.

Article VIII. All charges of war, and all other expenses that shall be incurred for the common defence or general welfare, and allowed by the united states in congress assembled, shall be defrayed out of a common treasury, which shall be supplied by the several states, in proportion to the value of all land within each state, granted to or surveyed for any Person, as such land and the buildings and improvements thereon shall be estimated, according to such mode as the united states, in congress assembled, shall, from time to time, direct and appoint. The taxes for paying that proportion shall be laid and levied by the authority and direction of the legislatures of the several states within the time agreed upon by the united states in congress assembled.

Article IX. The united states, in congress assembled, shall have the sole and exclusive right and power of determining on peace and war, except in the cases mentioned in the sixth article - of sending and receiving ambassadors - entering into treaties and alliances, provided that no treaty of commerce shall be made, whereby the legislative power of the respective states shall be restrained from imposing such imposts and duties on foreigners, as their own people are subjected to, or from prohibiting the exportation or importation of any species of goods or commodities whatsoever - of establishing rules for deciding, in all cases, what captures on land or water shall be legal, and in what manner prizes taken by land or naval forces in the service of the united Sates, shall be divided or appropriated - of granting letters of marque and reprisal in times of peace - appointing courts for the trial of piracies and felonies committed on the high seas; and establishing courts; for receiving and determining finally appeals in all cases of captures; provided that no member of congress shall be appointed a judge of any of the said courts.

The united states, in congress assembled, shall also be the last resort on appeal, in all disputes and differences now subsisting, or that hereafter may arise between two or more states concerning boundary, jurisdiction, or any other cause whatever; which authority shall always be exercised in the manner following. Whenever the legislative or executive authority, or lawful agent of any state in controversy with another, shall present a petition to congress, stating the matter in question, and praying for a hearing, notice thereof shall be given, by order of congress, to the legislative or executive authority of the other state in controversy, and a day assigned for the appearance of the parties by their lawful agents, who shall then be directed to appoint, by joint consent, commissioners or judges to constitute a court for hearing and determining the matter in question: but if they cannot agree, congress shall name three persons out of each of the united states, and from the list of such persons each party shall alternately strike out one, the petitioners beginning, until the number shall be reduced to thirteen; and from that number not less than seven, nor more than nine names, as congress shall direct, shall, in the presence of congress, be drawn out by lot, and the persons whose names shall be so drawn, or any five of them, shall be commissioners or judges, to hear and finally determine the controversy, so always as a major part of the judges, who shall hear the cause, shall agree in the determination: and if either party shall neglect to attend at the day appointed, without showing reasons which congress shall judge sufficient, or being present, shall refuse to strike, the congress shall proceed to nominate three persons out of each State, and the secretary of congress shall strike in behalf of such party absent or refusing; and the judgment and sentence of the court, to be appointed in the manner before prescribed, shall be final and conclusive; and if any of the parties shall refuse to submit to the authority of such court, or to appear or defend their claim or cause, the court shall nevertheless proceed to pronounce sentence, or judgment, which shall in like manner be final and decisive; the judgment or sentence and other proceedings being in either case transmitted to congress, and lodged among the acts of congress, for the security of the parties concerned: provided that every commissioner, before he sits in judgment, shall take an oath to be administered by one of the judges of the supreme or superior court of the State where the cause shall be tried, "well and truly to hear and determine the matter in question, according to the best of his judgment, without favour, affection, or hope of reward: "provided, also, that no State shall be deprived of territory for the benefit of the united states.

All controversies concerning the private right of soil claimed under different grants of two or more states, whose jurisdictions as they may respect such lands, and the states which passed such grants are adjusted, the said grants or either of them being at the same time claimed to have originated antecedent to such settlement of jurisdiction, shall, on the petition of either party to the congress of the united states, be finally determined, as near as may be, in the same manner as is before prescribed for deciding disputes respecting territorial jurisdiction between different states.

The united states, in congress assembled, shall also have the sole and exclusive right and power of regulating the alloy and value of coin struck by their own authority, or by that of the respective states - fixing the standard of weights and measures throughout the united states - regulating the trade and managing all affairs with the Indians, not members of any of the states; provided that the legislative right of any state, within its own limits, be not infringed or violated - establishing and regulating post-offices from one state to another, throughout all the united states, and exacting such postage on the papers passing through the same, as may be requisite to defray the expenses of the said office - appointing all officers of the land forces in the service of the united States, excepting regimental officers - appointing all the officers of the naval forces, and commissioning all officers whatever in the service of the united states; making rules for the government and regulation of the said land and naval forces, and directing their operations.

The united States, in congress assembled, shall have authority to appoint a committee, to sit in the recess of congress, to be denominated, "A Committee of the States," and to consist of one delegate from each State; and to appoint such other committees and civil officers as may be necessary for managing the general affairs of the united states under their direction - to appoint one of their number to preside; provided that no person be allowed to serve in the office of president more than one year in any term of three years; to ascertain the necessary sums of money to be raised for the service of the united states, and to appropriate and apply the same for defraying the public expenses; to borrow money or emit bills on the credit of the united states, transmitting every half year to the respective states an account of the sums of money so borrowed or emitted, - to build and equip a navy - to agree upon the number of land forces, and to make requisitions from each state for its quota, in proportion to the number of white inhabitants in such state, which requisition shall be binding; and thereupon the legislature of each state shall appoint the regimental officers, raise the men, and clothe, arm, and equip them, in a soldier-like manner, at the expense of the united states; and the officers and men so clothed, armed, and equipped, shall march to the place appointed, and within the time agreed on by the united states, in congress assembled; but if the united states, in congress assembled, shall, on consideration of circumstances, judge proper that any state should not raise men, or should raise a smaller number than its quota, and that any other state should raise a greater number of men than the quota thereof, such extra number shall be raised, officered, clothed, armed, and equipped in the same manner as the quota of such state, unless the legislature of such state shall judge that such extra number cannot be safely spared out of the same, in which case they shall raise, officer, clothe, arm, and equip, as many of such extra number as they judge can be safely spared. And the officers and men so clothed, armed, and equipped, shall march to the place appointed, and within the time agreed on by the united states in congress assembled.

The united states, in congress assembled, shall never engage in a war, nor grant letters of marque and reprisal in time of peace, nor enter into any treaties or alliances, nor coin money, nor regulate the value thereof nor ascertain the sums and expenses necessary for the defence and welfare of the united states, or any of them, nor emit bills, nor borrow money on the credit of the united states, nor appropriate money, nor agree upon the number of vessels of war to be built or purchased, or the number of land or sea forces to be raised, nor appoint a commander in chief of the army or navy, unless nine states assent to the same, nor shall a question on any other point, except for adjourning from day to day, be determined, unless by the votes of a majority of the united states in congress assembled.

The congress of the united states shall have power to adjourn to any time within the year, and to any place within the united states, so that no period of adjournment be for a longer duration than the space of six Months, and shall publish the Journal of their proceedings monthly, except such parts thereof relating to treaties, alliances, or military operations, as in their judgment require secrecy; and the yeas and nays of the delegates of each State, on any question, shall be entered on the Journal, when it is desired by any delegate; and the delegates of a State, or any of them, at his or their request, shall be furnished with a transcript of the said Journal, except such parts as are above excepted, to lay before the legislatures of the several states.

Article X. The committee of the states, or any nine of them, shall be authorized to execute, in the recess of congress, such of the powers of congress as the united states, in congress assembled, by the consent of nine states, shall, from time to time, think expedient to vest them with; provided that no power be delegated to the said committee, for the exercise of which, by the articles of confederation, the voice of nine states, in the congress of the united states assembled, is requisite.

Article XI. Canada acceding to this confederation, and joining in the measures of the united states, shall be admitted into, and entitled to all the advantages of this union: but no other colony shall be admitted into the same, unless such admission be agreed to by nine states.

Article XII. All bills of credit emitted, monies borrowed, and debts contracted by or under the authority of congress, before the assembling of the united states, in pursuance of the present confederation, shall be deemed and considered as a charge against the united States, for payment and satisfaction whereof the said united states and the public faith are hereby solemnly pledged.

Article XIII. Every State shall abide by the determinations of the united states, in congress assembled, on all questions which by this confederation are submitted to them. And the Articles of this confederation shall be inviolably observed by every state, and the union shall be perpetual; nor shall any alteration at any time hereafter be made in any of them, unless such alteration be agreed to in a congress of the united states, and be afterwards con-firmed by the legislatures of every state.

And Whereas it hath pleased the Great Governor of the World to incline the hearts of the legislatures we respectively represent in congress, to approve of, and to authorize us to ratify the said articles of confederation and perpetual union, Know Ye, that we, the undersigned delegates, by virtue of the power and authority to us given for that purpose, do, by these presents, in the name and in behalf of our respective constituents, fully and entirely ratify and confirm each and every of the said articles of confederation and perpetual union, and all and singular the matters and things therein contained. And we do further solemnly plight and engage the faith of our respective constituents, that they shall abide by the determinations of the united states in congress assembled, on all questions, which by the said confederation are submitted to them. And that the articles thereof shall be inviolably observed by the states we respectively represent, and that the union shall be perpetual. In Witness whereof, we have hereunto set our hands, in Congress. Done at Philadelphia, in the State of Pennsylvania, the ninth Day of July, in the Year of our Lord one Thousand seven Hundred and Seventy eight, and in the third year of the Independence of America.

U.S. National Archives & Records Administration 700 Pennsylvania Avenue NW, Washington, DC 20408 * 1-86-NARA-NARA * 1-866-272-6272

THE U.S. NATIONAL ARCHIVES & RECORDS ADMINISTRATION

www.archives.gov

The Constitution of the United States: A Transcription

Items that are hyperlinked have since been amended or superseded.

We the People of the United States, in Order to form a more perfect Union, establish Justice, insure domestic Tranquility, provide for the common defence, promote the general Welfare, and secure the Blessings of Liberty to ourselves and our Posterity, do ordain and establish this Constitution for the United States of America.

Article. I.

Section. 1.

All legislative Powers herein granted shall be vested in a Congress of the United States, which shall consist of a Senate and House of Representatives.

Section. 2.

The House of Representatives shall be composed of Members chosen every second Year by the People of the several States, and the Electors in each State shall have the Qualifications requisite for Electors of the most numerous Branch of the State Legislature.

No Person shall be a Representative who shall not have attained to the Age of twenty five Years, and been seven Years a Citizen of the United States, and who shall not, when elected, be an Inhabitant of that State in which he shall be chosen.

<u>Representatives and direct Taxes shall be apportioned among the several States which may be included within this Union, according to their respective Numbers, which shall be determined by adding to the whole Number of free Persons, including those bound to Service for a Term of Years, and excluding Indians not taxed, three fifths of all other Persons</u>. The actual Enumeration shall be made within three Years after the first Meeting of the Congress of the United States, and within every subsequent Term of ten Years, in such Manner as they shall by Law direct. The Number of Representatives shall not exceed one for every thirty Thousand, but each State shall have at Least one Representative; and until such enumeration shall be made, the State of New Hampshire shall be entitled to chuse three, Massachusetts eight, Rhode-Island and Providence Plantations one, Connecticut five, New-York six, New Jersey four, Pennsylvania eight, Delaware one, Maryland six, Virginia ten, North Carolina five, South Carolina five, and Georgia three.

When vacancies happen in the Representation from any State, the Executive Authority thereof shall issue Writs of Election to fill such Vacancies.

The House of Representatives shall chuse their Speaker and other Officers; and shall have the sole Power of Impeachment.

Section. 3.

The Senate of the United States shall be composed of two Senators from each State, <u>chosen by the Legislature</u> thereof for six Years; and each Senator shall have one Vote.

Immediately after they shall be assembled in Consequence of the first Election, they shall be divided as equally as may be into three Classes. The Seats of the Senators of the first Class shall be vacated at the Expiration of the second Year, of the second Class at the Expiration of the fourth Year, and of the third Class at the Expiration of the sixth Year, so that one third may be chosen every second Year; <u>and if Vacancies happen by Resignation, or otherwise, during the Recess of the Legislature of any State, the Executive thereof may make temporary Appointments until the next Meeting of the Legislature, which shall then fill such Vacancies.</u>

No Person shall be a Senator who shall not have attained to the Age of thirty Years, and been nine Years a Citizen of the United States, and who shall not, when elected, be an Inhabitant of that State for which he shall be chosen.

The Vice President of the United States shall be President of the Senate, but shall have no Vote, unless they be equally divided.

The Senate shall chose their other Officers, and also a President pro tempore, in the Absence of the Vice President, or when he shall exercise the Office of President of the United States.

The Senate shall have the sole Power to try all Impeachments. When sitting for that Purpose, they shall be on Oath or Affirmation. When the President of the United States is tried, the Chief Justice shall preside: And no Person shall be convicted without the Concurrence of two thirds of the Members present.

Judgment in Cases of Impeachment shall not extend further than to removal from Office, and disqualification to hold and enjoy any Office of honor, Trust or Profit under the United States: but the Party convicted shall nevertheless be liable and subject to Indictment, Trial, Judgment and Punishment, according to Law.

Section. 4.

The Times, Places and Manner of holding Elections for Senators and Representatives, shall be prescribed in each State by the Legislature thereof; but the Congress may at any time by Law make or alter such Regulations, except as to the Places of choosing Senators.

The Congress shall assemble at least once in every Year, and such Meeting shall <u>be on the first Monday in December</u>, unless they shall by Law appoint a different Day.

Section. 5.

Each House shall be the Judge of the Elections, Returns and Qualifications of its own Members, and a Majority of each shall constitute a Quorum to do Business; but a smaller Number may adjourn from day to day, and may be authorized to compel the Attendance of absent Members, in such Manner, and under such Penalties as each House may provide.

Each House may determine the Rules of its Proceedings, punish its Members for disorderly Behaviour, and, with the Concurrence of two thirds, expel a Member.

Each House shall keep a Journal of its Proceedings, and from time to time publish the same, excepting such Parts as may in their Judgment require Secrecy; and the Yeas and Nays of the Members of either House on any question shall, at the Desire of one fifth of those Present, be entered on the Journal.

Neither House, during the Session of Congress, shall, without the Consent of the other, adjourn for more than three days, nor to any other Place than that in which the two Houses shall be sitting.

Section. 6.

The Senators and Representatives shall receive a Compensation for their Services, to be ascertained by Law, and paid out of the Treasury of the United States. They shall in all Cases, except Treason, Felony and Breach of the Peace, be privileged from Arrest during their Attendance at the Session of their respective Houses, and in going to and returning from the same; and for any Speech or Debate in either House, they shall not be questioned in any other Place.

No Senator or Representative shall, during the Time for which he was elected, be appointed to any civil Office under the Authority of the United States, which shall have been created, or the Emoluments whereof shall have been encreased during such time; and no Person holding any Office under the United States, shall be a Member of either House during his Continuance in Office.

Section. 7.

All Bills for raising Revenue shall originate in the House of Representatives; but the Senate may propose or concur with Amendments as on other Bills.

Every Bill which shall have passed the House of Representatives and the Senate, shall, before it become a Law, be presented to the President of the United States: If he approve he shall sign it, but if not he shall return it, with his Objections to that House in which it shall have originated, who shall enter the Objections at large on their Journal, and proceed to reconsider it. If after such Reconsideration two thirds of that House shall agree to pass the Bill, it shall be sent, together with the Objections, to the other House, by which it shall likewise be reconsidered, and if approved by two thirds of that House, it shall become a Law. But in all such Cases the Votes of both Houses shall be determined by yeas and Nays, and the Names of the Persons voting for and against the Bill shall be entered on the Journal of each House respectively. If any Bill shall not be returned by the President within ten Days (Sundays excepted) after it shall have been presented to him, the Same shall be a Law, in like Manner as if he had signed it, unless the Congress by their Adjournment prevent its Return, in which Case it shall not be a Law.

Every Order, Resolution, or Vote to which the Concurrence of the Senate and House of Representatives may be necessary (except on a question of Adjournment) shall be presented to the President of the United States; and before the Same shall take Effect, shall be approved by him, or being disapproved by him, shall be repassed by two thirds of the Senate and House of Representatives, according to the Rules and Limitations prescribed in the Case of a Bill.

Section. 8.

The Congress shall have Power To lay and collect Taxes, Duties, Imposts and Excises, to pay the Debts and provide for the common Defence and general Welfare of the United States; but all Duties, Imposts and Excises shall be uniform throughout the United States;

To borrow Money on the credit of the United States;

To regulate Commerce with foreign Nations, and among the several States, and with the Indian Tribes;

To establish an uniform Rule of Naturalization, and uniform Laws on the subject of Bankruptcies throughout the United States;

To coin Money, regulate the Value thereof, and of foreign Coin, and fix the Standard of Weights and Measures;

To provide for the Punishment of counterfeiting the Securities and current Coin of the United States;

To establish Post Offices and post Roads;

To promote the Progress of Science and useful Arts, by securing for limited Times to Authors and Inventors the exclusive Right to their respective Writings and Discoveries;

To constitute Tribunals inferior to the supreme Court;

To define and punish Piracies and Felonies committed on the high

Seas, and Offences against the Law of Nations;

To declare War, grant Letters of Marque and Reprisal, and make Rules concerning Captures on Land and Water;

To raise and support Armies, but no Appropriation of Money to that Use shall be for a longer Term than two Years;

To provide and maintain a Navy;

To make Rules for the Government and Regulation of the land and naval Forces;

To provide for calling forth the Militia to execute the Laws of the Union, suppress Insurrections and repel Invasions;

To provide for organizing, arming, and disciplining, the Militia, and for governing such Part of them as may be employed in the Service of the United States, reserving to the States respectively, the Appointment of the Officers, and the Authority of training the Militia according to the discipline prescribed by Congress;

To exercise exclusive Legislation in all Cases whatsoever, over such District (not exceeding ten Miles square) as may, by Cession of particular States, and the Acceptance of Congress, become the Seat of the Government of the United States, and to exercise like Authority over all Places purchased by the Consent of the Legislature of the State in which the Same shall be, for the Erection of Forts, Magazines, Arsenals, dock-Yards, and other needful Buildings;--And

To make all Laws which shall be necessary and proper for carrying into Execution the foregoing Powers, and all other Powers vested by this Constitution in the Government of the United States, or in any Department or Officer thereof.

Section. 9.

The Migration or Importation of such Persons as any of the States now existing shall think proper to admit, shall not be prohibited by the Congress prior to the Year one thousand eight hundred and eight, but a Tax or duty may be imposed on such Importation, not exceeding ten dollars for each Person.

The Privilege of the Writ of *Habeas Corpus* shall not be suspended, unless when in Cases of Rebellion or Invasion the public Safety may require it.

No Bill of Attainder or ex post facto Law shall be passed.

No Capitation, or other direct, Tax shall be laid, <u>unless in Proportion to the Census or enumeration herein before directed to be taken</u>.

No Tax or Duty shall be laid on Articles exported from any State.

No Preference shall be given by any Regulation of Commerce or Revenue to the Ports of one State over those of another; nor shall Vessels bound to, or from, one State, be obliged to enter, clear, or pay Duties in another.

No Money shall be drawn from the Treasury, but in Consequence of Appropriations made by Law; and a regular Statement and Account of the Receipts and Expenditures of all public Money shall be published from time to time.

No Title of Nobility shall be granted by the United States: And no Person holding any Office of Profit or Trust under them, shall, without the Consent of the Congress, accept of any present, Emolument, Office, or Title, of any kind whatever, from any King, Prince, or foreign State.

Section. 10.

No State shall enter into any Treaty, Alliance, or Confederation; grant Letters of Marque and Reprisal; coin Money; emit Bills of Credit; make any Thing but gold and silver Coin a Tender in Payment of Debts; pass any Bill of Attainder, ex post facto Law, or Law impairing the Obligation of Contracts, or grant any Title of Nobility.

No State shall, without the Consent of the Congress, lay any Imposts or Duties on Imports or Exports, except what may be absolutely necessary for executing it's inspection Laws: and the net Produce of all Duties and Imposts, laid by any State on Imports or Exports, shall be for the Use of the Treasury of the United States; and all such Laws shall be subject to the Revision and Control of the Congress.

No State shall, without the Consent of Congress, lay any Duty of Tonnage, keep Troops, or Ships of War in time of Peace, enter into any Agreement or Compact with another State, or with a foreign Power, or engage in War, unless actually invaded, or in such imminent Danger as will not admit of delay.

Article. II.

Section. 1.

The executive Power shall be vested in a President of the United States of America. He shall hold his Office during the Term of four Years, and, together with the Vice President, chosen for the same Term, be elected, as follows:

Each State shall appoint, in such Manner as the Legislature thereof may direct, a Number of Electors, equal to the whole Number of Senators and Representatives to which the State may be entitled in the Congress: but no Senator or Representative, or Person holding an Office of Trust or Profit under the United States, shall be appointed an Elector.

<u>The Electors shall meet in their respective States, and vote by Ballot for two Persons, of whom one at least shall not be an Inhabitant of the same State with themselves. And they shall make a List of all the Persons voted for, and of the Number of Votes for each; which List they shall sign and certify, and transmit sealed to the Seat of the Govern-</u>

ment of the United States, directed to the President of the Senate. The President of the Senate shall, in the Presence of the Senate and House of Representatives, open all the Certificates, and the Votes shall then be counted. The Person having the greatest Number of Votes shall be the President, if such Number be a Majority of the whole Number of Electors appointed; and if there be more than one who have such Majority, and have an equal Number of Votes, then the House of Representatives shall immediately chuse by Ballot one of them for President; and if no Person have a Majority, then from the five highest on the List the said House shall in like Manner chuse the President. But in chusing the President, the Votes shall be taken by States, the Representation from each State having one Vote; A quorum for this purpose shall consist of a Member or Members from two thirds of the States, and a Majority of all the States shall be necessary to a Choice. In every Case, after the Choice of the President, the Person having the greatest Number of Votes of the Electors shall be the Vice President. But if there should remain two or more who have equal Votes, the Senate shall chuse from them by Ballot the Vice President.

The Congress may determine the Time of chusing the Electors, and the Day on which they shall give their Votes; which Day shall be the same throughout the United States.

No Person except a natural born Citizen, or a Citizen of the United States, at the time of the Adoption of this Constitution, shall be eligible to the Office of President; neither shall any Person be eligible to that Office who shall not have attained to the Age of thirty five Years, and been fourteen Years a Resident within the United States.

In Case of the Removal of the President from Office, or of his Death, Resignation, or Inability to discharge the Powers and Duties of the said Office, the Same shall devolve on the Vice President, and the Congress may by Law provide for the Case of Removal, Death, Resignation or Inability, both of the President and Vice President, declaring what Officer shall then act as President, and such Officer shall act accordingly, until the Disability be removed, or a President shall be elected.

The President shall, at stated Times, receive for his Services, a Compensation, which shall neither be increased nor diminished during the Period for which he shall have been elected, and he shall not receive within that Period any other Emolument from the United States, or any of them.

Before he enter on the Execution of his Office, he shall take the following Oath or Affirmation:--"I do solemnly swear (or affirm) that I will faithfully execute the Office of President of the United States, and will to the best of my Ability, preserve, protect and defend the Constitution of the United States."

Section. 2.

The President shall be Commander in Chief of the Army and Navy of the United States, and of the Militia of the several States, when called into the actual Service of the United States; he may require the Opinion, in writing, of the principal Officer in each of the executive Departments, upon any Subject relating to the Duties of their respective Offices, and he shall have Power to grant Reprieves and Pardons for Offences against the United States, except in Cases of Impeachment.

He shall have Power, by and with the Advice and Consent of the Senate, to make Treaties, provided two thirds of the Senators present concur; and he shall nominate, and by and with the Advice and Consent of the Senate, shall appoint Ambassadors, other public Ministers and Consuls, Judges of the supreme Court, and all other Officers of the United States, whose Appointments are not herein otherwise provided for, and which shall be established by Law: but the Congress may by Law vest the Appointment of such inferior Officers, as they think proper, in the President alone, in the Courts of Law, or in the Heads of Departments.

The President shall have Power to fill up all Vacancies that may happen during the Recess of the Senate, by granting Commissions which shall expire at the End of their next Session.

Section. 3.

He shall from time to time give to the Congress Information of the State of the Union, and recommend to their Consideration such Measures as he shall judge necessary and expedient; he may, on extraordinary Occasions, convene both Houses, or either of them, and in Case of Disagreement between them, with Respect to the Time of Adjournment, he may adjourn them to such Time as he shall think proper; he shall receive Ambassadors and other public Ministers; he shall take Care that the Laws be faithfully executed, and shall Commission all the Officers of the United States.

Section. 4.

The President, Vice President and all civil Officers of the United States, shall be removed from Office on Impeachment for, and Conviction of, Treason, Bribery, or other high Crimes and Misdemeanors.

Article III.

Section. 1.

The judicial Power of the United States shall be vested in one supreme Court, and in such inferior Courts as the Congress may from time to time ordain and establish. The Judges, both of the supreme and inferior Courts, shall hold their Offices during good Behaviour, and shall, at stated Times, receive for their Services a Compensation, which shall not be diminished during their Continuance in Office.

Section. 2.

The judicial Power shall extend to all Cases, in Law and Equity, arising under this Constitution, the Laws of the United States, and Treaties made, or which shall be made, under their Authority;--to all Cases affecting Ambassadors, other public Ministers and Consuls;--to all Cases of admiralty and maritime Jurisdiction;--to Controversies to which the United States shall be a Party;--to Controversies between two or more States;--<u>between a State and Citizens of another State</u>,--between Citizens of different States,--between Citizens of the same State claiming Lands under Grants of different States, and between a State, or the Citizens thereof, and foreign States, Citizens or Subjects.

In all Cases affecting Ambassadors, other public Ministers and Consuls, and those in which a State shall be Party, the supreme Court shall have original Jurisdiction. In all the other Cases before mentioned, the supreme Court shall have appellate Jurisdiction, both as to Law and Fact, with such Exceptions, and under such Regulations as the Congress shall make.

The Trial of all Crimes, except in Cases of Impeachment, shall be by Jury; and such Trial shall be held in the State where the said Crimes shall have been committed; but when not committed within any State, the Trial shall be at such Place or Places as the Congress may by Law have directed.

Section. 3.

Treason against the United States, shall consist only in levying War against them, or in adhering to their Enemies, giving them Aid and Comfort. No Person shall be convicted of Treason unless on the Testimony of two Witnesses to the same overt Act, or on Confession in open Court.

The Congress shall have Power to declare the Punishment of Treason, but no Attainder of Treason shall work Corruption of Blood, or Forfeiture except during the Life of the Person attainted.

Article. IV.

Section. 1.

Full Faith and Credit shall be given in each State to the public Acts, Records, and judicial Proceedings of every other State. And the Congress may by general Laws prescribe the Manner in which such Acts, Records and Proceedings shall be proved, and the Effect thereof.

Section. 2.

The Citizens of each State shall be entitled to all Privileges and Immunities of Citizens in the several States.

A Person charged in any State with Treason, Felony, or other Crime, who shall flee from Justice, and be found in another State, shall on Demand of the executive Authority of the State from which he fled, be delivered up, to be removed to the State having Jurisdiction of the Crime.

<u>No Person held to Service or Labour in one State, under the Laws thereof, escaping into another, shall, in Consequence of any Law or Regulation therein, be discharged from such Service or Labour, but shall be delivered up on Claim of the Party to whom such Service or Labour may be due.</u>

Section. 3.

New States may be admitted by the Congress into this Union; but no new State shall be formed or erected within the Jurisdiction of any other State; nor any State be formed by the Junction of two or more States, or Parts of States, without the Consent of the Legislatures of the States concerned as well as of the Congress.

The Congress shall have Power to dispose of and make all needful Rules and Regulations respecting the Territory or other Property belonging to the United States; and nothing in this Constitution shall be so construed as to Prejudice any Claims of the United States, or of any particular State.

Section. 4.

The United States shall guarantee to every State in this Union a Republican Form of Government, and shall protect each of them against Invasion; and on Application of the Legislature, or of the Executive (when the Legislature cannot be convened), against domestic Violence.

Article. V.

The Congress, whenever two thirds of both Houses shall deem it necessary, shall propose Amendments to this Constitution, or, on the Application of the Legislatures of two thirds of the several States, shall call a Convention for proposing Amendments, which, in either Case, shall be valid to all Intents and Purposes, as Part of this Constitution, when ratified by the Legislatures of three fourths of the several States, or by Conventions in three fourths thereof, as the one or the other Mode of Ratification may be proposed by the Congress; Provided that no Amendment which may be made prior to the Year One thousand eight hundred and eight shall in any Manner affect the first and fourth Clauses in the Ninth Section of the first Article; and that no State, without its Consent, shall be deprived of its equal Suffrage in the Senate.

Article. VI.

All Debts contracted and Engagements entered into, before the Adoption of this Constitution, shall be as valid against the United States under this Constitution, as under the Confederation.

This Constitution, and the Laws of the United States which shall be made in Pursuance thereof; and all Treaties made, or which shall be made, under the Authority of the United States, shall be the supreme Law of the Land; and the Judges in every State shall be bound thereby, any Thing in the Constitution or Laws of any State to the Contrary notwithstanding.

The Senators and Representatives before mentioned, and the Members of the several State Legislatures, and all executive and judicial Officers, both of the United States and of the several States, shall be bound by Oath or Affirmation, to support this Constitution; but no religious Test shall ever be required as a Qualification to any Office or public Trust under the United States.

Article. VII.

The Ratification of the Conventions of nine States, shall be sufficient for the Establishment of this Constitution between the States so ratifying the Same.

The Word, "the," being interlined between the seventh and eighth Lines of the first Page, the Word "Thirty" being partly written on an Erazure in the fifteenth Line of the first Page, The Words "is tried" being interlined between the thirty second and thirty third Lines of the first Page and the Word "the" being interlined between the forty third and forty fourth Lines of the second Page.

Attest William Jackson Secretary

done in Convention by the Unanimous Consent of the States present the Seventeenth Day of September in the Year of our Lord one thousand seven hundred and Eighty seven and of the Independance of the United States of America the Twelfth In witness whereof We have hereunto subscribed our Names,

G°.Washington
Presidt and deputy from Virginia

Delaware
Geo:Read.Gunning.Bedford.jun

John.Dickinson
Richard.Bassett
Jaco: Broom

Maryland
James.McHenry
Dan.of.St.Thos.Jenifer
Danl. Carroll

Virginia
John.Blair
James Madison Jr.

North.Carolina
Wm.Blount
Richd.Dobbs.Spaight
Hu Williamson

South.Carolina
J.Rutledge
Charles.Cotesworth.Pinckney
Charles.Pinckney
Pierce Butler

Georgia
William.Few
Abr Baldwin

New.Hampshire
John.Langdon
Nicholas Gilman

Massachusetts
Nathaniel.Gorham
Rufus King

Connecticut
Wm.Saml.Johnson

Roger Sherman

New.York
Alexander Hamilton

New.Jersey
Wil.Livingston
David.Brearley
Wm.Paterson
Jona: Dayton

Pennsylvania
B.Franklin
Thomas.Mifflin
Robt.Morris
Geo.Clymer
Thos.FitzSimons
Jared.Ingersoll
James.Wilson
Gouv Morris

U.S. National Archives & Records Administration

Amendments to the Constitution of the United States of America

The first ten amendments to the Constitution—the Bill of Rights—were ratified effective December 15, 1791.

Amendment I

Congress shall make no law respecting an establishment of religion, or prohibiting the free exercise thereof; or abridging the freedom of speech, or of the press; or the right of the people peaceably to assemble, and to petition the Government for a redress of grievances.

Amendment II

A well regulated Militia, being necessary to the security of a free State, the right of the people to keep and bear Arms, shall not be infringed.

Amendment III

No Soldier shall, in time of peace be quartered in any house, without the consent of the Owner, nor in time of war, but in a manner to be prescribed by law.

Amendment IV

The right of the people to be secure in their persons, houses, papers, and effects, against unreasonable searches and seizures, shall not be violated, and no Warrants shall issue, but upon probable cause, supported by Oath or affirmation, and particularly describing the place to be searched, and the persons or things to be seized.

Amendment V

No person shall be held to answer for a capital, or otherwise infamous crime, unless on a presentment or indictment of, a Grand Jury, except in cases arising in the land or naval forces, or in the Militia, when in actual service in time of War or public danger; nor shall any person be subject for the same offense to be twice put in jeopardy of life or limb; nor shall be compelled in any criminal case to be a witness against himself, nor be deprived of life, liberty, or property, without due process of law; nor shall private property be taken for public use, without just compensation.

Amendment VI

In all criminal prosecutions, the accused shall enjoy the right to a speedy and public trial, by an impartial jury of the State and district wherein the crime shall have been committed, which district shall have been previously ascertained by law, and to be informed of the nature and cause of the accusation; to be confronted with the witnesses against him; to have compulsory process for obtaining witnesses in his favor, and to have the Assistance of counsel for his defence.

Amendment VII

In Suits at common law, where the value in controversy shall exceed twenty dollars, the right of trial by jury shall be preserved, and no fact tried by a jury, shall be otherwise re-examined in any Court of the United States, than according to the rules of the common law.

Amendment VIII

Excessive bail shall not be required, nor excessive fines imposed, nor cruel and unusual punishments inflicted.

Amendment IX

The enumeration in the Constitution, of certain rights, shall not be construed to deny or disparage others retained by the people.

Amendment X

The powers not delegated to the United States by the Constitution, nor prohibited by it to the States, are reserved to the States respectively, or to the people.

Amendment XI

Ratified February 7, 1795

The Judicial power of the United States shall not be construed to extend to any suit in law or equity, commenced or prosecuted against one of the United States by Citizens of another State, or by Citizens or Subjects of any Foreign State.

Amendment XII

Ratified June 15, 1804

The Electors shall meet in their respective states, and vote by ballot for President and Vice-President, one of whom, at least, shall not be an inhabitant of the same state with themselves; they shall name in their ballots the person voted for as President, and in distinct ballots the person voted for as Vice-President, and They shall make distinct lists of all persons voted for as President, and of all persons voted for as Vice-President and of the number of votes for each, which lists they shall sign and certify, and transmit sealed to the seat of the government of the United States, directed to the President of the Senate; -- the President of the Senate shall, in the presence of the Senate and House of Representatives, open all the certificates and the votes shall then be counted; --The person having the greatest number of votes for President, shall be the President, if such number be a majority of the whole number of Electors appointed; and if no person have such majority, then from the persons having the highest numbers not exceeding three on the list of those voted for as president, the House of Representatives shall choose immediately, by ballot, the President. But in choosing the President, the votes shall be taken by states, the representation from each state having one vote; a quorum for this purpose shall consist of a member or members from two-thirds of the states and a majority of all the states shall be necessary to a choice. [And if the House of Representatives shall not choose a President whenever the right of choice shall devolve upon them, before the fourth day of March next following, then the Vice-President shall act as President, as in the case of the death or other constitutional disability of the President.][253] The person having the greatest number of votes as Vice-President, shall be the Vice-President, if such number be a majority of the whole number of Electors appointed, and if no person have a majority, then from the two highest numbers on the list, the Senate shall choose the Vice-President; a quorum for the purpose shall consist of two-thirds of the whole number of Senators, and a majority of the whole number shall be necessary to a choice. But no person constitutionally ineligible to the office of President shall be eligible to that of Vice-President of the United States.

Amendment XIII
Ratified December 6, 1865

Section 1. Neither slavery nor involuntary servitude, except as a punishment for crime whereof the party shall have been duly convicted, shall exist within the United States, or any place subject to their jurisdiction.

Section 2. Congress shall have power to enforce this article by appropriate legislation.

---

[253] Superseded by Section 3 of the Twentieth Amendment.

Amendment XIV

Ratified July 9, 1868

Section 1. All persons born or naturalized in the United States, and subject to the jurisdiction thereof, are citizens of the United States and of the State wherein they reside. No State shall make or enforce any law which shall abridge the privileges or immunities of citizens of the United States; nor shall any State deprive any person of life, liberty, or property, without due process of law; nor deny to any person within its jurisdiction the equal protection of the laws.

Section 2. Representatives shall be apportioned among the several States according to their respective numbers, counting the whole number of persons in each State, excluding Indians not taxed. But when the right to vote at any election for the choice of electors for President and Vice-President of the United States, Representatives in Congress, the Executive and Judicial officers of a State, or the members of the Legislature thereof, is denied to any of the male inhabitants of such State, being twenty-one years of age,[254] and citizens of the United States, or in any way abridged, except for participation in rebellion, or other crime, the basis of representation therein shall be reduced in the proportion which the number of such male citizens shall bear to the whole number of male citizens twenty-one years of age in such State.

Section 3. No person shall be a Senator or Representative in Congress, or elector of President and Vice-President, or hold any office, civil or military, under the United States, or under

---

[254] Changed by Section 1 of the Twenty-Sixth Amendment.

any State, who, having previously taken an oath, as a member of Congress, or as an officer of the United States, or as a member of any State legislature, or as an executive or judicial officer of any State to support the Constitution of the United States, shall have engaged in insurrection or rebellion against the same, or given aid or comfort to the enemies thereof. But Congress may by a veto of two-thirds of each House, remove such disability.

Section 4. The validity of the public debt of the United States, authorized by law, including debts incurred for payment of pensions and bounties for services in suppressing insurrection or rebellion, shall not be questioned. But neither the United States nor any State shall assume or pay any debt or obligation incurred in aid of insurrection or rebellion against the United States, or any claim for the loss or emancipation of any slave; but all such debts, obligations and claims shall be held illegal and void.

Section 5. The Congress shall have power to enforce, by appropriate legislation, the provisions of this article.

Amendment XV
Ratified February 3, 1870

Section 1. The Right of citizens of the United States to vote shall not be denied or abridged by the United States or by any State on account of race, color, or previous condition of servitude.

Section 2. The Congress shall have power to enforce this article by appropriate legislation.

Amendment XVI

Ratified February 3, 1913

The Congress shall have power to lay and collect taxes on incomes, from whatever source derived, without apportionment among the several States, and without regard to any census or enumeration.

Amendment XVII

Ratified April 8, 1913

The Senate of the United States shall be composed of two Senators from each State, elected by the people thereof, for six years; and each Senator shall have one vote. The electors in each State shall have the qualifications requisite for electors of the most numerous branch of the State legislatures.

When vacancies happen in the representation of any State in the Senate, the executive authority of such State shall issue writs of election to fill such vacancies: *Provided*, That the legislature of any State may empower the executive thereof to make temporary appointments until the people fill the vacancies by election as the legislature may direct.

This amendment shall not be so construed as to affect the election or term of any Senator chosen before it becomes valid as part of the Constitution.

Amendment XVIII
Ratified January 16, 1919

Section 1. After one year from the ratification of this article the manufacture, sale, or transportation of intoxicating liquors within, the importation thereof into, or the exportation thereof from the United States and all territory subject to the jurisdiction thereof for beverage purposes is hereby prohibited.

Section 2. The Congress and the several States shall have concurrent power to enforce this article by appropriate legislation.

Section 3. This article shall be inoperative unless it shall have been ratified as an amendment to the Constitution by the legislatures of the several States, as provided in the Constitution, within seven years from the date of the submission hereof to the States by the Congress.][255]

Amendment XIX
Ratified August 18, 1920

The right of citizens of the United States to vote shall not be denied or abridged by the United States of by any State on account of sex.

Congress shall have power to enforce this article by appropriate legislation.

---

[255] Repealed by the Twenty-First Amendment.

Amendment XX
Ratified January 23, 1933

Section 1. The terms of the President and Vice President shall end at noon on the 20th day of January, and the terms of Senators and Representatives at noon on the 3d day of January, of the years in which such terms would have ended if this article had not been ratified; and the terms of their successors shall then begin.

Section 2. The Congress shall assemble at least once in every year, and such meeting shall begin at noon of the 3d day of January, unless they shall by law appoint a different day.

Section 3. If, at the time fixed for the beginning of the term of the President, the President elect shall have died, the Vice President elect shall become President. If a President shall not have been chosen before the time fixed for the beginning of his term, or if the President elect shall have failed to qualify, then the Vice President elect shall act as President until a President shall have qualified; and the Congress may by law provide for the case wherein neither a President elect nor a Vice President elect shall have qualified, declaring who shall then act as President, or the manner in which one who is to act shall be selected, and such person shall act accordingly until a President or Vice President shall have qualified.

Section 4. The Congress may by law provide for the case of the death of any of their persons from whom the House of Representatives may choose a President whenever the right of choice shall have devolved upon them, and for the case of the death of any of the persons from whom the Senate may choose a Vice President whenever the right of choice shall have devolved upon them.

Section 5. Sections 1 and 2 shall take effect on the 15th day of October following the ratification of this article.

Section 6. This article shall be inoperative unless it shall have been ratified as an amendment to the Constitution by the legislatures of three-fourths of the several States within seven years from the date of its submission.

Amendment XXI

Ratified December 5, 1933

Section 1. The eighteenth article of amendment to the Constitution of the United States is hereby repealed.

Section 2. The transportation or importation into any State, Territory, or possession of the United States for delivery or use therein of intoxicating liquors, in violation of the laws thereof, is hereby prohibited.

Section 3. The article shall be inoperative unless it shall have been ratified as an amendment to the Constitution by conventions in the several States, as provided in the Constitution, within seven years from the date of the submission hereof to the States by the Congress.

Amendment XXII

Ratified February 27, 1951

Section 1. No person shall be elected to the office of the President more than twice, and no person who has held the office of President, or acted as President, for more than two years of a term to which some other person was elected President shall be elected to the office of the President more than once. But this Article shall not apply to any person holding the office of President, when this Article was proposed by the Congress, and shall not prevent any person who may be holding the office of President, or acting as President, during the term within which this Article becomes operative from holding the office of President or acting as President during the remainder of such term.

Section 2. This article shall be inoperative unless it shall have been ratified as an amendment to the Constitution by the legislatures of three-fourths of the several States within seven years from the date of its submission to the States by the Congress.

Amendment XXIII

Ratified March 29, 1961

Section 1. The district constituting the seat of Government of the United States shall appoint in such manner as the Congress may direct:

A number of electors of President and Vice President equal to the whole number of Senators and Representatives in Congress to which the District would be entitled if it were a State, but in no event more than the least populous State; they shall be in addition to those appointed by the States, but they shall be considered, for the purposes of the election of President and Vice President, to be electors appointed by a State; and they shall meet in the District and perform such duties as provided by the twelfth article of amendment.

Section 2. The Congress shall have power to enforce this article by appropriate legislation.

Amendment XXV
Ratified February 10, 1967

Section 1. In case of the removal of the President from office or of his death or resignation, the Vice President shall become President.

Section 2. Whenever there is a vacancy in the office of the Vice President, the President shall nominate a Vice President who shall take office upon confirmation by a majority vote of both Houses of Congress.

Section 3. Whenever the President transmits to the President pro tempore of the Senate and the Speaker of the House of Representatives his written declaration to the contrary, such powers and duties shall be discharged by the Vice President as Acting President.

Section 4. Whenever the Vice President and a majority of either the principal officers of the executive departments or of such other body as Congress may by law provide, transmit to the President pro tempore of the Senate and the Speaker of the House of Representatives their written declaration that the President is unable to discharge the powers and duties of his office, the Vice President shall immediately assume the powers and duties of the office as Acting President.

Thereafter, when the President transmits to the President pro tempore of the Senate and the Speaker of the House of Representatives his written declaration that no inability exists, he shall resume the powers and duties of his office unless the Vice President and a majority of either the principal officers of the executive department or of such other body as Congress may by law provide, transmit within four days to the President pro tempore of the Senate and the Speaker of the House of Representatives their written declaration that the President is unable to discharge the powers and duties of his office. Thereupon Congress shall decide the issue, assembling within forty-eight hours for that purpose if not in session. If the Congress, within twenty-one days after receipt of the latter written declaration, or, if Congress is not in session, within twenty-one days after Congress is required to assemble, determines by two-thirds vote of both Houses that the President is unable to discharge the powers and duties of his office, the Vice President shall continue to discharge the same as Acting President; otherwise, the President shall resume the powers and duties of his office.

Amendment XXVI

Ratified July 1, 1971

Section 1. The right of citizens of the United States, who are eighteen years of age or older, to vote shall not be denied or abridged by the United States or by any State on account of age.

Section 2. The Congress shall have power to enforce this article by appropriate legislation.

Amendment XXVII

Ratified May 7, 1992

No law varying the compensation for the services of the Senators and Representatives shall take effect, until an election of Representatives shall have intervened.

The following resolutions were proposed to the Kentucky Legislature, and this version was adopted on November 10, 1798, as a protest against the Alien and Sedition Acts passed by Congress. They were authored by Thomas Jefferson, but he did not make public the fact until years later. This represents one of the clearest expressions of his views on how the Constitution was supposed to be interpreted.

The Kentucky Resolutions of 1798

1. *Resolved*, That the several States composing, the United States of America, are not united on the principle of unlimited submission to their general government; but that, by a compact under the style and title of a Constitution for the United States, and of amendments thereto, they constituted a general government for special purposes — delegated to that government certain definite powers, reserving, each State to itself, the residuary mass of right to their own self-government; and that whensoever the general government assumes undelegated powers, its acts are unauthoritative, void, and of no force: that to this compact each State acceded as a State, and is an integral part, its co-States forming, as to itself, the other party: that the government created by this compact was not made the exclusive or final judge of the extent of the powers delegated to itself; since

that would have made its discretion, and not the Constitution, the measure of its powers; but that, as in all other cases of compact among powers having no common judge, each party has an equal right to judge for itself, as well of infractions as of the mode and measure of redress.

2. *Resolved*, That the Constitution of the United States, having delegated to Congress a power to punish treason, counterfeiting the securities and current coin of the United States, piracies, and felonies committed on the high seas, and offenses against the law of nations, and no other crimes, whatsoever; and it being true as a general principle, and one of the amendments to the Constitution having also declared, that "the powers not delegated to the United States by the Constitution, not prohibited by it to the States, are reserved to the States respectively, or to the people," therefore the act of Congress, passed on the 14th day of July, 1798, and intituled "An Act in addition to the act intituled An Act for the punishment of certain crimes against the United States," as also the act passed by them on the — day of June, 1798, intituled "An Act to punish frauds committed on the bank of the United States," (and all their other acts which assume to create, define, or punish crimes, other than those so enumerated in the Constitution,) are altogether void, and of no force; and that the power to create, define, and punish such other crimes is reserved, and, of right, appertains solely and exclusively to the respective States, each within its own territory.

3. *Resolved*, That it is true as a general principle, and is also expressly declared by one of the amendments to the Constitutions, that "the powers not delegated to the United States by the Constitution, our prohibited by it to the States, are reserved to the States respectively, or to the people"; and that no power over the freedom of religion, freedom of speech, or freedom of the press being delegated to the United States by the Constitution, nor prohibited by it to the States, all lawful powers respecting the same did of right remain, and were reserved to the States or the people: that thus was manifested their determination to retain to themselves the right of judging how far the licentiousness of speech and of the press may be abridged without lessening their useful freedom, and how far those abuses which cannot be separated from their use should be tolerated, rather than the use be destroyed. And thus also they guarded against all abridgment by the United States of the freedom of religious opinions and exercises, and retained to themselves the right of protecting the same, as this State, by a law passed on the general demand of its citizens, had already protected them from all human restraint or interference. And that in addition to this general principle and express declaration, another and more special provision has been made by one of the amendments to the Constitution, which expressly declares, that "Congress shall make no law respecting an establishment of religion, or prohibiting the free exercise thereof, or abridging the freedom of speech or of the press": thereby guarding in the same sentence, and under the same words, the freedom of religion, of speech, and of the press: insomuch, that whatever violated either, throws down the sanctuary which covers the others, arid that libels, falsehood,

and defamation, equally with heresy and false religion, are withheld from the cognizance of federal tribunals. That, therefore, the act of Congress of the United States, passed on the 14th day of July, 1798, intituled "An Act in addition to the act intituled An Act for the punishment of certain crimes against the United States," which does abridge the freedom of the press, is not law, but is altogether void, and of no force.

4. *Resolved*, That alien friends are under the jurisdiction and protection of the laws of the State wherein they are: that no power over them has been delegated to the United States, nor prohibited to the individual States, distinct from their power over citizens. And it being true as a general principle, and one of the amendments to the Constitution having also declared, that "the powers not delegated to the United States by the Constitution, nor prohibited by it to the States, are reserved to the States respectively, or to the people," the act of the Congress of the United States, passed on the — day of July, 1798, intituled "An Act concerning aliens," which assumes powers over alien friends, not delegated by the Constitution, is not law, but is altogether void, and of no force.

5. *Resolved*. That in addition to the general principle, as well as the express declaration, that powers not delegated are reserved, another and more special provision, inserted in the Constitution from abundant caution, has declared that "the migration or importation of such persons as any of the States now existing shall think proper to admit, shall not be prohibited by the Congress

prior to the year 1808" that this commonwealth does admit the migration of alien friends, described as the subject of the said act concerning aliens: that a provision against prohibiting their migration, is a provision against all acts equivalent thereto, or it would be nugatory: that to remove them when migrated, is equivalent to a prohibition of their migration, and is, therefore, contrary to the said provision of the Constitution, and void.

6. *Resolved*, That the imprisonment of a person under the protection of the laws of this commonwealth, on his failure to obey the simple order of the President to depart out of the United States, as is undertaken by said act intituled "An Act concerning aliens" is contrary to the Constitution, one amendment to which has provided that "no person shalt be deprived of liberty without due progress of law"; and that another having provided that "in all criminal prosecutions the accused shall enjoy the right to public trial by an impartial jury, to be informed of the nature and cause of the accusation, to be confronted with the witnesses against him, to have compulsory process for obtaining witnesses in his favor, and to have the assistance of counsel for his defense;" the same act, undertaking to authorize the President to remove a person out of the United States, who is under the protection of the law, on his own suspicion, without accusation, without jury, without public trial, without confrontation of the witnesses against him, without heating witnesses in his favor, without defense, without counsel, is contrary to the provision also of the Constitution, is therefore not law, but utterly void, and of no force: that transferring the power of judging any person, who is under the protection of the laws from the courts, to the Presi-

dent of the United States, as is undertaken by the same act concerning aliens, is against the article of the Constitution which provides that "the judicial power of the United States shall be vested in courts, the judges of which shall hold their offices during good behavior"; and that the said act is void for that reason also. And it is further to be noted, that this transfer of judiciary power is to that magistrate of the general government who already possesses all the Executive, and a negative on all Legislative powers.

7. *Resolved*, That the construction applied by the General Government (as is evidenced by sundry of their proceedings) to those parts of the Constitution of the United States which delegate to Congress a power "to lay and collect taxes, duties, imports, and excises, to pay the debts, and provide for the common defense and general welfare of the United States," and "to make all laws which shall be necessary and proper for carrying into execution, the powers vested by the Constitution in the government of the United States, or in any department or officer thereof," goes to the destruction of all limits prescribed to their powers by the Constitution: that words meant by the instrument to be subsidiary only to the execution of limited powers, ought not to be so construed as themselves to give unlimited powers, nor a part to be so taken as to destroy the whole residue of that instrument: that the proceedings of the General Government under color of these articles, will be a fit and necessary subject of revisal and correction, at a time of greater tranquillity, while those specified in the preceding resolutions call for immediate redress.

8th. *Resolved*, That a committee of conference and correspondence be appointed, who shall have in charge to communicate the preceding resolutions to the Legislatures of the several States: to assure them that this commonwealth continues in the same esteem of their friendship and union which it has manifested from that moment at which a common danger first suggested a common union: that it considers union, for specified national purposes, and particularly to those specified in their late federal compact, to be friendly, to the peace, happiness and prosperity of all the States: that faithful to that compact, according to the plain intent and meaning in which it was understood and acceded to by the several parties, it is sincerely anxious for its preservation: that it does also believe, that to take from the States all the powers of self-government and transfer them to a general and consolidated government, without regard to the special delegations and reservations solemnly agreed to in that compact, is not for the peace, happiness or prosperity of these States; and that therefore this commonwealth is determined, as it doubts not its co-States are, to submit to undelegated, and consequently unlimited powers in no man, or body of men on earth: that in cases of an abuse of the delegated powers, the members of the general government, being chosen by the people, a change by the people would be the constitutional remedy; but, where powers are assumed which have not been delegated, a nullification of the act is the rightful remedy: that every State has a natural right in cases not within the compact, (*casus non fœderis*) to nullify of their own authority all assumptions of power by others within their limits: that without this right, they would be under the dominion, absolute and unlimited, of whosoever might exercise this right of judgment for them: that nevertheless, this commonwealth, from motives of regard and respect for its co States, has wished to communicate with them on the subject: that with them alone it is proper to communicate, they alone being parties to the compact, and solely authorized to judge in the last resort of the powers exercised under it, Congress being not a party, but merely the creature of the compact, and subject as to its assumptions of power to the final judgment of those by whom, and for whose use itself and its powers were all created and modified: that if the acts before specified should stand, these conclusions would flow from them; that the general government may place any act they think proper on the list of crimes and punish it themselves whether enumerated or not enumerated by the constitution as cognizable by them: that they may transfer its cognizance to the President, or any other person, who may himself be the accuser, counsel, judge and jury, whose suspicions may be the evidence, his order the sentence, his officer the executioner, and his breast the sole record of the transaction: that a very numerous and valuable description of the inhabitants of these States being, by this precedent, reduced, as outlaws, to the absolute dominion of one man, and the barrier of the Constitution thus swept away from us all, no ramparts now remains against the passions and the powers of a majority in Congress to protect from a like exportation, or other more grievous punishment, the minority of the same body, the legislatures, judges, governors and counsellors of the States, nor their other peaceable inhabitants, who may venture to reclaim the constitutional rights and liberties of the States and people, or who for other causes, good or bad, may be obnoxious to the views, or marked by the suspicions of the President, or be thought dangerous to his or their election, or other interests, public or personal; that the friendless alien has indeed been selected as the safest subject of a first experiment; but the citizen will soon follow, or rather, has already followed, for already has a sedition act marked him as its prey: that these and successive acts of the same character, unless arrested at the threshold, necessarily drive these States into revolution and blood and will furnish new calumnies against republican government, and new pretexts for those who wish it to be believed that man cannot be governed but by a rod of iron: that it would be a dangerous delusion were a confidence in the men of our choice to silence our fears for the safety of our rights: that confidence is everywhere the parent of despotism — free government is founded in jealousy, and not in confidence; it is jealousy and not confidence which prescribes limited constitutions, to bind down those whom we are obliged to trust with power: that our Constitution has accordingly fixed the limits to which, and no further, our confidence may go; and let the honest advocate of confidence read the Alien and Sedition acts, and say if the Constitution has not been wise in fixing limits to the government it created, and whether we should be wise in destroying those limits, Let him say what the government is, if it be not a tyranny, which the men of our choice have conferred on our President, and the President of our choice has assented to, and accepted over the friendly stranger to whom the mild spirit of our country and its law have pledged hospitality and protection: that the men of our choice have more respected the bare suspicion of the President, than the solid right of innocence, the claims of justification, the sacred force of truth, and the forms and substance of law and justice. In questions of powers, then, let no more be heard of confidence in man, but bind him down from mischief by the chains of the Constitution. That this commonwealth does therefore call on its co-States for an expression of their sentiments on the acts concerning aliens and for the punishment of certain crimes herein before specified, plainly declaring whether these acts are or are not authorized by the federal compact. And it doubts not that their sense will be so announced as to prove their attachment unaltered to limited government, weather general or particular. And that the rights and liberties of their co-States will be exposed to no dangers by remaining embarked in a common bottom with their own. That they will concur with this commonwealth in considering the said acts as so palpably against the Constitution as to amount to an undisguised declaration that that compact is not meant to be the measure of the powers of the General Government, but that it will proceed in the exercise over these States, of all powers whatsoever: that they will view this as seizing the rights of the States, and consolidating them in the hands of the General Government, with a power assumed to bind the States (not merely as the cases made federal, casus fœderis but), in all cases whatsoever, by laws made, not with their consent, but by others against their consent: that this would be to surrender the form of government we have chosen, and live under one deriving its powers from its own will, and not from our authority; and that the co-States, recurring to their natural right in cases not made federal, will concur in declaring these acts void, and of no force, and will each take measures of its own for providing that neither these acts, nor any others of the General Government not plainly and intentionally authorized by the Constitution, shalt be exercised within their respective territories.

9th. *Resolved*, That the said committee be authorized to communicate by writing or personal conference, at any times or places whatever, with any person or persons who may be appointed by any one or more co-States to correspond or *confer* with them; and that they lay their proceedings before the next session of Assembly.

The Kentucky Resolutions of 1798-99

The Kentucky and Virginia Resolutions of 1798-99 were a series of resolutions passed by the legislatures of these states protesting the Alien and Sedition Acts. The Kentucky Resolutions were drafted by Thomas Jefferson and the Virginia Resolutions by James Madison. They are a democratic protest against what Jefferson, Madison and other Republicans considered to be a dangerous usurpation of power by the federal government. The Kentucky Resolution of 1799 was the most radical of the resolutions and asserted that states had the power to nullify the laws of the federal government.

As you read, think about how the Kentucky Resolutions reflected Democratic-Republican ideology and why it makes sense that Democratic-Republicans like Jefferson and Madison would have opposed the Alien and Sedition Acts.

The representatives of the good people of this commonwealth [of Kentucky], in General Assembly convened, have maturely considered the answers of sundry states in the Union, to [the ongoing debate and discussion of]... certain unconstitutional laws of Congress, commonly called the Alien and Sedition Laws, would be faithless, indeed, to themselves and to those they represent, were they silently to acquiesce in the principles and doctrines attempted to be maintained.... Our opinions of these alarming measures of the general government, together with our reasons for those opinions, were detailed with decency, and with temper and submitted to the discussion and judgment of our fellow-citizens throughout the Union.... Faithful to the true principles of the federal Union, unconscious of any designs to disturb the harmony of that Union, arid anxious only to escape the fangs of despotism, the good people of this commonwealth are regardless of censure or calumniation. Lest, however, the silence of this commonwealth should be construed into an acquiescence in the doctrines and principles advanced... therefore,

Resolved, That this commonwealth considers the federal Union, upon the terms and for the purposes specified in... [the Constitution], conducive to the liberty and happiness of the several states: That it does now unequivocally declare its attachment to the Union, and to that compact... and will be among the last to seek its dissolution: That if those who administer the general government be permitted to transgress the limits fixed by that compact [the Constitution], by a total disregard to the special delegations of power therein contained, an annihilation of the state governments... will be the inevitable consequence: [That the construction of the Constitution argued for by many] state legislatures, that the general government is the exclusive judge of the extant of the powers delegated to it, stop not short of despotism -since the discretion of those who administer the government, and not the Constitution, would be the measure of their powers: That the several states who formed that Instrument [the Constitution] being sovereign and independent, have the unquestionable right to judge of the infraction; and, That a nullification of those sovereignties, of all unauthorized acts done under the color of that instrument is the rightful remedy: That this commonwealth does, under the most deliberate reconsideration, declare, that the said Alien and Sedition Laws are, in their opinion, palpable violations of the said Constitution.... although this commonwealth, as a party to the federal compact, will bow to the laws of the Union, yet, it does at the same time declare, that it will not now, or ever hereafter, cease to oppose in a constitutional manner, every attempt at what quarter soever offered, to violate that compact.... This commonwealth does now enter against [the Alien and Sedition Acts] in solemn PROTEST.

The following resolution was adopted by the Virginia Senate on December 24, 1798, as a protest against the Alien and Sedition Acts passed by Congress. It was authored by James Madison, in collaboration with Thomas Jefferson, who authored a set of resolutions for Kentucky.

Virginia Resolution of 1798

RESOLVED, That the General Assembly of Virginia, doth unequivocably express a firm resolution to maintain and defend the Constitution of the United States, and the Constitution of this State, against every aggression either foreign or domestic, and that they will support the government of the United States in all measures warranted by the former.

That this assembly most solemnly declares a warm attachment to the Union of the States, to maintain which it pledges all its powers; and that for this end, it is their duty to watch over and oppose every infraction of those principles which constitute the only basis of that Union, because a faithful observance of them, can alone secure it's existence and the public happiness.

That this Assembly doth explicitly and peremptorily declare, that it views the powers of the federal government, as resulting from the compact, to which the states are parties; as limited by the plain sense and intention of the instrument constituting the compact; as no further valid that they are authorized by the grants enumerated in that compact; and that in case of a deliberate, palpable, and dangerous exercise of other powers, not granted by the said compact, the states who are parties thereto, have the right, and are in duty bound, to interpose for arresting the progress of the evil, and for maintaining within their respective limits, the authorities, rights and liberties appertaining to them.

That the General Assembly doth also express its deep regret, that a spirit has in sundry instances, been manifested by the federal government, to enlarge its powers by forced constructions of the constitutional charter which defines them; and that implications have appeared of a design to expound certain general phrases (which having been copied from the very limited grant of power, in the former articles of confederation were the less liable to be misconstrued) so as to destroy the meaning and effect, of the particular enumeration which necessarily explains and limits the general phrases; and so as to consolidate the states by degrees, into one sovereignty, the obvious tendency and inevitable consequence of which would be, to transform the present republican system of the United States, into an absolute, or at best a mixed monarchy.

That the General Assembly doth particularly protest against the palpable and alarming infractions of the Constitution, in the two late cases of the Alien and Sedition Acts" passed at the last session of Congress; the first of which exercises a power no where delegated to the federal government, and which by uniting legislative and judicial powers to those of executive, subverts the general principles of free government; as well as the particular organization, and positive provisions of the federal constitution; and the other of which acts, exercises in like manner, a power not delegated by the constitution, but on the contrary, expressly and positively forbidden by one of the amendments thereto; a power, which more than any other, ought to produce universal alarm, because it is levelled against that right of freely examining public characters and measures, and of free communication among the people thereon, which has ever been justly deemed, the only effectual guardian of every other right.

That this state having by its Convention, which ratified the federal Constitution, expressly declared, that among other essential rights, "the Liberty of Conscience and of the Press cannot be cancelled, abridged, restrained, or modified by any authority of the United States," and from its extreme anxiety to guard these rights from every possible attack of sophistry or ambition, having with other states, recommended an amendment for that purpose, which amendment was, in due time, annexed to the Constitution; it would mark a reproachable inconsistency, and criminal degeneracy, if an indifference were now shewn, to the most palpable violation of one of the Rights, thus declared and secured; and to the establishment of a precedent which may be fatal to the other.

That the good people of this commonwealth, having ever felt, and continuing to feel, the most sincere affection for their brethren of the other states; the truest anxiety for establishing and perpetuating the union of all; and the most scrupulous fidelity to that constitution, which is the pledge of mutual friendship, and the instrument of mutual happiness; the General Assembly doth solemnly appeal to the like dispositions of the other states, in confidence that they will concur with this commonwealth in declaring, as it does hereby declare, that the acts aforesaid, are unconstitutional; and that the necessary and proper measures will be taken by each, for co-operating with this state, in maintaining the Authorities, Rights, and Liberties, referred to the States respectively, or to the people.

That the Governor be desired, to transmit a copy of the foregoing Resolutions to the executive authority of each of the other states, with a request that the same may be communicated to the Legislature thereof; and that a copy be furnished to each of the Senators and Representatives representing this state in the Congress of the United States.

Agreed to by the Senate, December 24, 1798.

Also see the Kentucky Resolutions of 1798, authored by Thomas Jefferson, for the same purpose, and a follow-up Kentucky Resolution of 1799 adopted by the Kentucky Legislature a year later in 1799.

The Judiciary Act of 1789

September 24, 1789.
1 Stat. 73.

CHAP. XX.–An Act to establish the Judicial Courts of the United States.

SECTION 1. Be it enacted by the Senate and House of Representatives of the United States of America in Congress assembled, That the supreme court of the United States shall consist of a chief justice and five associate justices, any four of whom shall be a quorum, and shall hold annually at the seat of government two sessions, the one commencing the first Monday of February, and the other the first Monday of August. That the associate justices shall have precedence according to the date of their commissions, or when the commissions of two or more of them bear date on the same day, according to their respective ages.

SEC . 2. And be it further enacted, That the United States shall be, and they hereby are divided into thirteen districts, to be limited and called as follows, to wit: one to consist of that part of the State of Massachusetts which lies easterly of the State of New Hampshire, and to be called Maine District; one to consist of the State of New Hampshire, and to be called New Hampshire District; one to consist of the remaining part of the State of Massachusetts, and to be called Massachusetts district; one to consist of the State of Connecticut, and to be called Connecticut District; one to consist of the State of New York, and to be called New York District; one to consist of the State of New Jersey, and to be called New Jersey District; one to consist of the State of Pennsylvania, and to be called Pennsylvania District; one to consist of the State of Delaware, and to be called Delaware District; one to consist of the State of Maryland, and to be called Maryland District; one to consist of the State of Virginia, except that part called the District of Kentucky, and to be called Virginia

District; one to consist of the remaining part of the State of Virginia, and to be called Kentucky District; one to consist of the State of South Carolina, and to be called South Carolina District; and one to consist of the State of Georgia, and to be called Georgia District.

SEC . 3. And be it further enacted, That there be a court called a District Court, in each of the afore mentioned districts, to consist of one judge, who shall reside in the district for which he is appointed, and shall be called a District Judge, and shall hold annually four sessions, the first of which to commence as follows, to wit: in the districts of New York and of New Jersey on the first, in the district of Pennsylvania on the second, in the district of Connecticut on the third, and in the district of Delaware on the fourth, Tuesdays of November next; in the districts of Massachusetts, of Maine, and of Maryland, on the first, in the district of Georgia on the second, and in the districts of New Hampshire, of Virginia, and of Kentucky, on the third Tuesdays of December next; and the other three sessions progressively in the respective districts on the like Tuesdays of every third calendar month afterwards, and in the district of South Carolina, on the third Monday in March and September, the first Monday in July, and the second Monday in December of each and every year, commencing in December next; and that the District Judge shall have power to hold special courts at his discretion. That the stated District Court shall be held at the places following, to wit: in the district of Maine, at Portland and Pownalsborough alternately, beginning at the first; in the district of New Hampshire, at Exeter and Portsmouth alternately, beginning at the first; in the district of Massachusetts, at Boston and Salem alternately, beginning at the first; in the district of Connecticut, alternately at Hartford and New Haven, beginning at the first; in the district of New York, at New York; in the district of New Jersey, alternately at New Brunswick and Burlington, beginning at the first; in the district of Pennsylvania, at Philadelphia and York Town alternately, beginning at the first; in the district of Delaware, alternately at Newcastle and Dover, beginning at the first; in the district of Maryland, alternately at Baltimore and Easton, beginning at the first; in the district of Virginia, alternately at Richmond and Williamsburgh, beginning at the first; in the district of Kentucky, at Harrodsburgh; in the district of South Carolina, at Charleston; and in the district of Georgia, alternately at Savannah and Augusta, beginning at the first; and that the special courts shall be held at the same place in each district as the stated courts, or in districts that have two, at either of them, in the discretion of the judge, or at such other place in the district, as the nature of the business and his discretion shall direct. And that in the districts that have but one place for holding the District Court, the records thereof shall be kept at that place; and in districts that have two, at that place in each district which the judge shall appoint.

SEC. 4. And be it further enacted, That the before mentioned districts, except those of Maine and Kentucky, shall be divided into three circuits, and be called the eastern, the middle, and the southern circuit. That the eastern circuit shall consist of the districts of New Hampshire, Massachusetts, Connecticut and New York; that the middle circuit shall consist of the districts of New Jersey, Pennsylvania, Delaware, Maryland and Virginia; and that the southern circuit shall consist of the districts of South Carolina and Georgia, and that there shall be held annually in each district of said circuits, two courts, which shall be called Circuit Courts, and shall consist of any two justices of the Supreme Court, and the district judge of such districts, any two of whom shall constitute a quorum: Provided, That no district judge shall give a vote in any case of appeal or error from his own decision; but may assign the reasons of such his decision.

SEC. 5. And be it further enacted, That the first session of the said circuit court in the several districts shall commence at the times following, to wit: in New Jersey on the second, in New York on the fourth, in Pennsylvania on the eleventh, in Connecticut on the twenty-second, and in Delaware on the twenty-seventh, days of April next; in Massachusetts on the third, in Maryland on the seventh, in South Carolina on the twelfth, in New Hampshire on the twentieth, in Virginia on the twenty-second, and in Georgia on the twenty-eighth, days of May next, and the subsequent sessions in the respective districts on the like days of every sixth calendar month afterwards, except in South Carolina, where the session of the said court shall commence on the first, and in Georgia where it shall commence on the seventeenth day of October, and except when any of those days shall happen on a Sunday, and then the session shall commence on the next day following. And the sessions of the said circuit court shall be held in the district of New Hampshire, at Portsmouth and Exeter alternately, beginning at the first; in the district of Massachusetts, at Boston; in the district of Connecticut, alternately at Hartford and New Haven, beginning at the last; in the district of New York, alternately at New York and Albany, beginning at the first; in the district of New Jersey, at Trenton; in the district of Pennsylvania, alternately at Philadelphia and Yorktown, beginning at the first; in the district of Delaware, alternately at New Castle and Dover, beginning at the first; in the district of Maryland, alternately at Annapolis and Easton, beginning at the first; in the district of Virginia, alternately at Charlottesville and Williamsburgh, beginning at the first; in the district of South Carolina, alternately at Columbia and Charleston, beginning at the first; and in the district of Georgia, alternately at Savannah and Augusta, beginning at the first. And the circuit courts shall have power to hold special sessions for the trial of criminal causes at any other time at their discretion, or at the discretion of the Supreme Court.

SEC . 6. And be it further enacted, That the Supreme Court may, by any one or more of its justices being present, be adjourned from day to day until a quorum be convened; and that a circuit court may also be adjourned from day to day by any one of its judges, or if none are present, by the marshal of the district until a quorum be convened; and that a district court, in case of the inability of the judge to attend at the commencement of a session, may by virtue of a written order from the said judge, directed to the marshal of the district, be adjourned by the said marshal to such day, antecedent to the next stated session of the said court, as in the said order shall be appointed; and in case of the death of the said judge, and his vacancy not being supplied, all process, pleadings and proceedings of what nature soever, pending before the said court, shall be continued of course until the next stated session after the appointment and acceptance of the office by his successor.

SEC . 7. And be it [further] enacted, That the Supreme Court, and the district courts shall have power to appoint clerks for their respective courts, and that the clerk for each district court shall be clerk also of the circuit court in such district, and each of the said clerks shall, before he enters upon the execution of his office, take the following oath or affirmation, to wit: "I, A. B., being appointed clerk of, do solemnly swear, or affirm, that I will truly and faithfully enter and record all the orders, decrees, judgments and proceedings of the said court, and that I will faithfully and impartially discharge and perform all the duties of my said office, according to the best of my abilities and understanding. So help me God." Which words, so help me God, shall be omitted in all cases where an affirmation is admitted instead of an oath. And the said clerks shall also severally give bond, with sufficient sureties, (to be approved of by the Supreme and district courts respectively) to the United States, in the sum of two thousand dollars, faithfully to discharge the duties of his office, and seasonably to record the decrees, judgments and determinations of the court of which he is clerk.

SEC . 8. And be it further enacted, That the justices of the Supreme Court, and the district judges, before they proceed to execute the duties of their respective offices, shall take the following oath or affirmation, to wit: "I, A. B., do solemnly swear or affirm, that I will administer justice without respect to persons, and do equal right to the poor and to the rich, and that I will faithfully and impartially discharge and perform all the duties incumbent on me as, according to the best of my abilities and understanding, agreeably to the constitution, and laws of the United States. So help me God."

SEC . 9. And be it further enacted, That the district courts shall have, exclusively of the courts of the several States, cognizance of all crimes and offences that shall be cognizable under the authority of the United States, committed within their respective districts, or upon the high seas; where no other punishment than whipping, not exceeding thirty stripes, a fine not exceeding one hundred dollars, or a term of imprisonment not exceeding six months, is to be inflicted; and shall also have exclusive original cognizance of all civil causes of admiralty and maritime jurisdiction, including all seizures under laws of impost, navigation or trade of the United States, where the seizures are made, on waters which are navigable from the sea by vessels of ten or more tons burthen, within their respective districts as well as upon the high seas; saving to suitors, in all cases, the right of a common law remedy, where the common law is competent to give it; and shall also have exclusive original cognizance of all seizures on land, or other waters than as aforesaid, made, and of all suits for penalties and forfeitures incurred, under the laws of the United States. And shall also have cognizance, concurrent with the courts of the several States, or the circuit courts, as the case may be, of all causes where an alien sues for a tort only in violation of the law of nations or a treaty of the United States. And shall also have cognizance, concurrent as last mentioned, of all suits at common law where the United States sue, and the matter in dispute amounts, exclusive of costs, to the sum or value of one hundred dollars. And shall also have jurisdiction exclusively of the courts of the several States, of all suits against consuls or vice-consuls, except for offences above the description aforesaid. And the trial of issues in fact, in the district courts, in all causes except civil causes of admiralty and maritime jurisdiction, shall be by jury.

SEC . 10. And be it further enacted, That the district court in Kentucky district shall, besides the jurisdiction aforesaid, have jurisdiction of all other causes, except of appeals and writs of error, hereinafter made cognizable in a circuit court, and shall proceed therein in the same manner as a circuit court, and writs of error and appeals shall lie from decisions therein to the Supreme Court in the same causes, as from a circuit court to the Supreme Court, and under the same regulations. And the district court in Maine district shall, besides the jurisdiction herein before granted, have jurisdiction of all causes, except of appeals and writs of error herein after made cognizable in a circuit court, and shall proceed therein in the same manner as a circuit court: And writs of error shall lie from decisions therein to the circuit court in the district of Massachusetts in the same manner as from other district courts to their respective circuit courts.

SEC . 11. And be it further enacted, That the circuit courts shall have original cognizance, concurrent with the courts of the several States, of all suits of a civil nature at common law or in equity, where the matter in dispute exceeds, exclusive of costs, the sum or value of five hundred dollars, and the United States are plaintiffs, or petitioners; or an alien is a party, or the suit is between a citizen of the State where the suit is brought, and a citizen of another State. And shall have exclusive cognizance of all crimes and offences cognizable under the authority of the United States, except where this act otherwise provides, or the laws of the United States shall otherwise direct, and concurrent jurisdiction with the district courts of the crimes and offences cognizable therein. But no person shall be arrested in one district for trial in another, in any civil action before a circuit or district court. And no civil suit shall be brought before either of said courts against an inhabitant of the United States, by any original process in any other district than that whereof he is an inhabitant, or in which he shall be found at the time of serving the writ, nor shall any district or circuit court have cognizance of any suit to recover the contents of any promissory note or other chose in action in favour of an assignee, unless a suit might have been prosecuted in such court to recover the said contents if no assignment had been made, except in cases of foreign bills of exchange. And the circuit courts shall also have appellate jurisdiction from the district courts under the regulations and restrictions herein after provided.

SEC . 12. And be it further enacted, That if a suit be commenced in any state court against an alien, or by a citizen of the state in which the suit is brought against a citizen of another state, and the matter in dispute exceeds the aforesaid sum or value of five hundred dollars, exclusive of costs, to be made to appear to the satisfaction of the court; and the defendant shall, at the time of entering his appearance in such state court, file a petition for the removal of the cause for trial into the next circuit court, to be held in the district where the suit is pending, or if in the district of Maine to the district court next to be holden therein, or if in Kentucky district to the district court next to be holden therein, and offer good and sufficient surety for his entering in such court, on the first day of its session, copies of said process against him, and also for his there appearing and entering special bail in the cause, if special bail was originally requisite therein, it shall then be the duty of the state court to accept the surety, and proceed no further in the cause, and any bail that may have been originally taken shall be discharged, and the said copies being entered as aforesaid, in such court of the United States, the cause shall there proceed in the same manner as if it had been brought there by original process. And any attachment of the goods or estate of the defendant by the original process, shall hold the goods or estate so attached, to answer the final judgment in the same manner as by the laws of such state they would have been holden to answer final judgment, had it been rendered by the court in which the suit commenced. And if in any action commenced in a state court, the title of land be concerned, and the parties are citizens of the same state, and the matter in dispute exceeds the sum or value of five hundred dollars, exclusive of costs, the sum or value being made to appear to the satisfaction of the court, either party, before the trial, shall state to the court and make affidavit if they require it, that he claims and shall rely upon a right or title to the land, under a grant from a state other than that in which the suit is pending, and produce the original grant or an exemplification of it, except where the loss of public records shall put it out of his power, and shall move that the adverse party inform the court, whether he claims a right or title to the land under a grant from the state in which the suit is pending; the said adverse [party] shall give such information, or otherwise not be allowed to plead such grant, or give it in evidence upon the trial, and if he informs that he does claim under such grant, the party claiming under the grant first mentioned may then, on motion, remove the cause for trial to the next circuit court to be holden in such district, or if in the district of Maine, to the court next to be holden therein; or if in Kentucky district, to the district court next to be holden therein; but if he is the defendant, shall do it under the same regulations as in the before-mentioned case of the removal of a cause into such court by an alien; and neither party removing the cause, shall be allowed to plead or give evidence of any other title than that by him stated as aforesaid, as the ground of his claim; and the trial of issues in fact in the circuit courts shall, in all suits, except those of equity, and of admiralty, and maritime jurisdiction, be by jury.

SEC. 13. And be it further enacted, That the Supreme Court shall have exclusive jurisdiction of all controversies of a civil nature, where a state is a party, except between a state and its citizens; and except also between a state and citizens of other states, or aliens, in which latter case it shall have original but not exclusive jurisdiction. And shall have exclusively all such jurisdiction of suits or proceedings against ambassadors, or other public ministers, or their domestics, or domestic servants, as a court of law can have or exercise consistently with the law of nations; and original, but not exclusive jurisdiction of all suits brought by ambassadors, or other public ministers, or in which a consul, or vice consul, shall be a party. And the trial of issues in fact in the Supreme Court, in all actions at law against citizens of the United States, shall be by jury. The Supreme Court shall also have appellate jurisdiction from the circuit courts and courts of the several states, in the cases herein after specially provided for; and shall have power to issue writs of prohibition to the district courts, when proceeding as courts of admiralty and maritime jurisdiction, and writs of mandamus, in cases warranted by the principles and usages of law, to any courts appointed, or persons holding office, under the authority of the United States.

SEC. 14. And be it further enacted, That all the before-mentioned courts of the United States, shall have power to issue writs of scire facias, habeas corpus, and all other writs not specially provided for by statute, which may be necessary for the exercise of their respective jurisdictions, and agreeable to the principles and usages of law. And that either of the justices of the supreme court, as well as judges of the district courts, shall have power to grant writs of habeas corpus for the purpose of an inquiry into the cause of commitment.——Provided, That writs of habeas corpus shall in no case extend to prisoners in gaol, unless where they are in custody, under or by colour of the authority of the United States, or are committed for trial before some court of the same, or are necessary to be brought into court to testify.

SEC . 15. And be it further enacted, That all the said courts of the United States, shall have power in the trial of actions at law, on motion and due notice thereof being given, to require the parties to produce books or writings in their possession or power, which contain evidence pertinent to the issue, in cases and under circumstances where they might be compelled to produce the same by the ordinary rules of proceeding in chancery; and if a plaintiff shall fail to comply with such order, to produce books or writings, it shall be lawful for the courts respectively, on motion, to give the like judgment for the defendant as in cases of nonsuit; and if a defendant shall fail to comply with such order, to produce books or writings, it shall be lawful for the courts respectively on motion as aforesaid, to give judgment against him or her by default.

SEC . 16. And be it further enacted, That suits in equity shall not be sustained in either of the courts of the United States, in any case where plain, adequate and complete remedy may be had at law.

SEC . 17. And be it further enacted, That all the said courts of the United States shall have power to grant new trials, in cases where there has been a trial by jury for reasons for which new trials have usually been granted in the courts of law; and shall have power to impose and administer all necessary oaths or affirmations, and to punish by fine or imprisonment, at the discretion of said courts, all contempts of authority in any cause or hearing before the same; and to make and establish all necessary rules for the orderly conducting business in the said courts, provided such rules are not repugnant to the laws of the United States.

SEC. 18. And be it further enacted, That when in a circuit court, judgment upon a verdict in a civil action shall be entered, execution may on motion of either party, at the discretion of the court, and on such conditions for the security of the adverse party as they may judge proper, be stayed forty-two days from the time of entering judgment, to give time to file in the clerk's office of said court, a petition for a new trial. And if such petition be there filed within said term of forty-two days, with a certificate thereon from either of the judges of such court, that he allows the same to be filed, which certificate he may make or refuse at his discretion, execution shall of course be further stayed to the next session of said court. And if a new trial be granted, the former judgment shall be thereby rendered void.

SEC. 19. And be it further enacted, That it shall be the duty of circuit courts, in causes in equity and of admiralty and maritime jurisdiction, to cause the facts on which they found their sentence or decree, fully to appear upon the record either from the pleadings and decree itself, or a state of the case agreed by the parties, or their counsel, or if they disagree by a stating of the case by the court.

SEC. 20. And be it further enacted, That where in a circuit court, a plaintiff in an action, originally brought there, or a petitioner in equity, other than the United States, recovers less than the sum or value of five hundred dollars, or a libellant, upon his own appeal, less than the sum or value of three hundred dollars, he shall not be allowed, but at the discretion of the court, may be adjudged to pay costs.

SEC. 21. And be it further enacted, That from final decrees in a district court in causes of admiralty and maritime jurisdiction, where the matter in dispute exceeds the sum or value of three hundred dollars, exclusive of costs, an appeal shall be allowed to the next circuit court, to be held in such district. Provided nevertheless, That all such appeals from final decrees as aforesaid, from the district court of Maine, shall be made to the circuit court, next to be holden after each appeal in the district of Massachusetts.

SEC . 22. And be it further enacted, That final decrees and judgments in civil actions in a district court, where the matter in dispute exceeds the sum or value of fifty dollars, exclusive of costs, may be reexamined, and reversed or affirmed in a circuit court, holden in the same district, upon a writ of error, whereto shall be annexed and returned therewith at the day and place therein mentioned, an authenticated transcript of the record, an assignment of errors, and prayer for reversal, with a citation to the adverse party, signed by the judge of such district court, or a justice of the Supreme Court, the adverse party having at least twenty days' notice. And upon a like process, may final judgments and decrees in civil actions, and suits in equity in a circuit court, brought there by original process, or removed there from courts of the several States, or removed there by appeal from a district court where the matter in dispute exceeds the sum or value of two thousand dollars, exclusive of costs, be reexamined and reversed or affirmed in the Supreme Court, the citation being in such case signed by a judge of such circuit court, or justice of the Supreme Court, and the adverse party having at least thirty days' notice. But there shall be no reversal in either court on such writ of error for error in ruling any plea in abatement, other than a plea to the jurisdiction of the court, or such plea to a petition or bill in equity, as is in the nature of a demurrer, or for any error in fact. And writs of error shall not be brought but within five years after rendering or passing the judgment or decree complained of, or in case the person entitled to such writ of error be an infant, feme covert, non compos mentis, or imprisoned, then within five years as aforesaid, exclusive of the time of such disability. And every justice or judge signing a citation on any writ of error as aforesaid, shall take good and sufficient security, that the plaintiff in error shall prosecute his writ to effect, and answer all damages and costs if he fail to make his plea good.

SEC. 23. And be it further enacted, That a writ of error as aforesaid shall be a supersedeas and stay execution in cases only where the writ of error is served, by a copy thereof being lodged for the adverse party in the clerk's office where the record remains, within ten days, Sundays exclusive, after rendering the judgment or passing the decree complained of. Until the expiration of which term of ten days, executions shall not issue in any case where a writ of error may be a supersedeas; and whereupon such writ of error the Supreme or a circuit court shall affirm a judgment or decree, they shall adjudge or decree to the respondent in error just damages for his delay, and single or double costs at their discretion.

SEC. 24. And be it further enacted, That when a judgment or decree shall be reversed in a circuit court, such court shall proceed to render such judgment or pass such decree as the district court should have rendered or passed; and the Supreme Court shall do the same on reversals therein, except where the reversal is in favour of the plaintiff, or petitioner in the original suit, and the damages to be assessed, or matter to be decreed, are uncertain, in which case they shall remand the cause for a final decision. And the Supreme Court shall not issue execution in causes that are removed before them by writs of error, but shall send a special mandate to the circuit court to award execution thereupon.

SEC. 25. And be it further enacted, That a final judgment or decree in any suit, in the highest court of law or equity of a State in which a decision in the suit could be had, where is drawn in question the validity of a treaty or statute of, or an authority exercised under the United States, and the decision is against their validity; or where is drawn in question the validity of a statute of, or an authority exercised under any State, on the ground of their being repugnant to the constitution, treaties or laws of the United

States, and the decision is in favour of such their validity, or where is drawn in question the construction of any clause of the constitution, or of a treaty, or statute of, or commission held under the United States, and the decision is against the title, right, privilege or exemption specially set up or claimed by either party, under such clause of the said Constitution, treaty, statute or commission, may be re-examined and reversed or affirmed in the Supreme Court of the United States upon a writ of error, the citation being signed by the chief justice, or judge or chancellor of the court rendering or passing the judgment or decree complained of, or by a justice of the Supreme Court of the United States, in the same manner and under the same regulations, and the writ shall have the same effect, as if the judgment or decree complained of had been rendered or passed in a circuit court, and the proceeding upon the reversal shall also be the same, except that the Supreme Court, instead of remanding the cause for a final decision as before provided, may at their discretion, if the cause shall have been once remanded before, proceed to a final decision of the same, and award execution. But no other error shall be assigned or regarded as a ground of reversal in any such case as aforesaid, than such as appears on the face of the record, and immediately respects the before mentioned questions of validity or construction of the said constitution, treaties, statutes, commissions, or authorities in dispute.

SEC. 26. And be it further enacted, That in all causes brought before either of the courts of the United States to recover the forfeiture annexed to any articles of agreement, covenant, bond, or other speciality, where the forfeiture, breach or non-performance shall appear, by the default or confession of the defendant, or upon demurrer, the court before whom the action is, shall render judgment therein for the plaintiff to recover so much as is due according to equity. And when the sum for which judgment should be rendered is uncertain, the same shall, if either of the parties request it, be assessed by a jury.

SEC. 27. And be it further enacted, That a marshal shall be appointed in and for each district for the term of four years, but shall be removable from office at pleasure, whose duty it shall be to attend the district and circuit courts when sitting therein, and also the Supreme Court in the District in which that court shall sit. And to execute throughout the district, all lawful precepts directed to him, and issued under the authority of the United States, and he shall have power to command all necessary assistance in the execution of his duty, and to appoint as there shall be occasion, one or more deputies, who shall be removable from office by the judge of the district court, or the circuit court sitting within the district, at the pleasure of either; and before he enters on the duties of his office, he shall become bound for the faithful performance of the same, by himself and by his deputies before the judge of the district court to the United States, jointly and severally, with two good and sufficient sureties, inhabitants and freeholders of such district, to be approved by the district judge, in the sum of twenty thousand dollars, and shall take before said judge, as shall also his deputies, before they enter on the duties of their appointment, the following oath of office: "I, A. B., do solemnly swear or affirm, that I will faithfully execute all lawful precepts directed to the marshal of the district of under the authority of the United States, and true returns make, and in all things well and truly, and without malice or partiality, perform the duties of the office of marshal (or marshal's deputy, as the case may be) of the district of , during my continuance in said office, and take only my lawful fees. So help me God."

SEC . 28. And be it further enacted, That in all causes wherein the marshal or his deputy shall be a party, the writs and precepts therein shall be directed to such disinterested person as the court, or any justice or judge thereof may appoint, and the person so appointed, is hereby authorized to execute and return the same. And in case of the death of any marshal, his deputy or deputies shall continue in office, unless otherwise specially removed; and shall execute the same in the name of the deceased, until another marshal shall be appointed and sworn: And the defaults or misfeasance's in office of such deputy or deputies in the mean time, as well as before, shall be adjudged a breach of the condition of the bond given, as before directed, by the marshal who appointed them; and the executor or administrator of the deceased marshal shall have like remedy for the defaults and misfeasance's in office of such deputy or deputies during such interval, as they would be entitled to if the marshal had continued in life and in the exercise of his said office, until his successor was appointed, and sworn or affirmed: And every marshal or his deputy when removed from office, or when the term for which the marshal is appointed shall expire, shall have power notwithstanding to execute all such precepts as may be in their hands respectively at the time of such removal or expiration of office; and the marshal shall be held answerable for the delivery to his successor of all prisoners which may be in his custody at the time of his removal, or when the term for which he is appointed shall expire, and for that purpose may retain such prisoners in his custody until his successor shall be appointed and qualified as the law directs.

SEC . 29. And be it further enacted, That in cases punishable with death, the trial shall be had in the county where the offence was committed, or where that cannot be done without great inconvenience, twelve petit jurors at least shall be summoned from thence. And jurors in all cases to serve in the courts of the United States shall be designated by lot or otherwise in each State respectively according to the mode of forming juries therein now practised, so far as the laws of the same shall render such designation practicable by the courts or marshals of the United States; and the jurors shall have the same qualifications as are requisite for jurors by the laws of the State of which they are citizens, to serve in the highest courts of law of such State, and shall be returned as there shall be occasion for them, from such parts of the district from time to time as the court shall direct, so as shall be most favourable to an impartial trial, and so as not to incur an unnecessary expense, or unduly to burthen the citizens of any part of the district with such services. And writs of venire facias when directed by the court shall issue from the clerk's office, and shall be served and returned by the marshal in his proper person, or by his deputy, or in case the marshal or his deputy is not an indifferent person, or is interested in the event of the cause, by such fit person as the court shall specially appoint for that purpose, to whom they shall administer an oath or affirmation that he will truly and impartially serve and return such writ. And when from challenges or otherwise there shall not be a jury to determine any civil or criminal cause, the marshal or his deputy shall, by order of the court where such defect of jurors shall happen, return jurymen de talibus circumstantibus sufficient to complete the pannel; and when the marshal or his deputy are disqualified as aforesaid, jurors may be returned by such disinterested person as the court shall appoint.

SEC . 30. And be it further enacted, That the mode of proof by oral testimony and examination of witnesses in open court shall be the same in all the courts of the United States, as well in the trial of causes in equity and of admiralty and maritime jurisdiction, as of actions at common law. And when the testimony of any person shall be necessary in any civil cause depending in any district in any court of the United States, who shall live at a greater distance from the place of trial than one hundred miles, or is bound on a voyage to sea, or is about to go out of the United States, or out of such district, and to a greater distance from the place of trial than as aforesaid, before the time of trial, or is ancient or very infirm, the deposition of such person may be taken de bene esse before any justice or judge of any of the courts of the United States, or before any chancellor, justice or judge of a supreme or superior court, mayor or chief magistrate of a city, or judge of a county court or court of common pleas of any of the United States, not being of counsel or attorney to either of the parties, or interested in the event of the cause, provided that a notification from the magistrate before whom the deposition is to be taken to the adverse party, to be present at the taking of the same, and to put interrogatories, if he think fit, be first made out and served on the adverse party or his attorney as either may be nearest, if either is within one hundred miles of the place of such caption, allowing time for their attendance after notified, not less than at the rate of one day, Sundays exclusive, for every twenty miles travel. And in causes of admiralty and maritime jurisdiction, or other cases of seizure when a libel shall be filed, in which an adverse party is not named, and depositions of persons circumstanced as aforesaid shall be taken before a claim be put in, the like notification as aforesaid shall be given to the person having the agency or possession of the property libelled at the time of the capture or seizure of the same, if known to the libellant. And every person deposing as aforesaid shall be carefully examined and cautioned, and sworn or affirmed to testify the whole truth, and shall subscribe the testimony by him or her given after the same shall be reduced to writing, which shall be done only by the magistrate taking the deposition, or by the deponent in his presence. And the depositions so taken shall be retained by such magistrate until he deliver the same with his own hand into the court for which they are taken, or shall , together with a certificate of the reasons as aforesaid of their being taken, and of the notice if any given to the adverse party, be by him the said magistrate sealed up and directed to such court, and remain under his seal until opened in court. And any person may be compelled to appear and depose as aforesaid in the same manner as to appear and testify in court. And in the trial of any cause of admiralty or maritime jurisdiction in a district court, the decree in which may be appealed from, if either party shall suggest to and satisfy the court that probably it will not be in his power to produce the witnesses there testifying before the circuit court should an appeal be had, and shall move that their testimony be taken down in writing, it shall be so done by the clerk of the court. And if an appeal be had, such testimony may be used on the trial of the same, if it shall appear to the satisfaction of the court which shall try the appeal, that the witnesses are then dead or gone out of the United States, or to a greater distance than as aforesaid from the place where the court is sitting, or that by reason of age, sickness, bodily infirmity or imprisonment, they are unable to travel and appear at court, but not otherwise. And unless the same shall be made to appear on the trial of any cause, with respect to witnesses whose depositions may have been taken therein, such depositions shall not be admitted or used in the cause. Provided, That nothing herein shall be construed to prevent any court of the United States from granting a dedimus potestatem to take depositions according to common usage, when it may be necessary to prevent a failure or delay of justice, which power they shall severally possess, nor to extend to depositions taken in perpetuam rei memoriam, which if they relate to matters that may be cognizable in any court of the United States, a circuit court on application thereto made as a court of equity, may, according to the usages in chancery direct to be taken.

SEC . 31. And be it [further] enacted, That where any suit shall be depending in any court of the United States, and either of the parties shall die before final judgment, the executor or administrator of such deceased party who was plaintiff, petitioner, or defendant, in case the cause of action doth by law survive, shall have full power to prosecute or defend any such suit or action until final judgment; and the defendant or defendants are hereby obliged to answer thereto accordingly; and the court before whom such cause may be depending, is hereby empowered and directed to hear and determine the same, and to render judgment for or against the executor or administrator, as the case may require. And if such executor or administrator having been duly served with a scire facias from the office of the clerk of the court where such suit is depending, twenty days beforehand, shall neglect or refuse to become a party to the suit, the court may render judgment against the estate of the deceased party, in the same manner as if the executor or administrator had voluntarily made himself a party to the suit. And the executor or administrator who shall become a party as aforesaid, shall, upon motion to the court where the suit is depending, be entitled to a continuance of the same until the next term of the said court. And if there be two or more plaintiffs or defendants, and one or more of them shall die, if the cause of action shall survive to the surviving plaintiff or plaintiffs, or against the surviving defendant or defendants, the writ or action shall not be thereby abated; but such death being suggested upon the record, the action shall proceed at the suit of the surviving plaintiff or plaintiffs against the surviving defendant or defendants.

SEC . 32. And be it further enacted, That no summons, writ, declaration, return, process, judgment, or other proceedings in civil causes in any of the courts of the United States, shall be abated, arrested, quashed or reversed, for any defect or want of form, but the said courts respectively shall proceed and give judgment according as the right of the cause and matter in law shall appear unto them, without regarding any imperfections, defects, or want of form in such writ, declaration, or other pleading, return, process, judgment, or course of proceeding whatsoever, except those only in cases of demurrer, which the party demurring shall specially sit down and express together with his demurrer as the cause thereof. And the said courts respectively shall and may, by virtue of this act, from time to time, amend all and every such imperfections, defects and wants of form, other than those only which the party demurring shall express as aforesaid, and may at any time permit either of the parties to amend any defect in the process or pleadings, upon such conditions as the said courts respectively shall in their discretion, and by their rules prescribe.

SEC . 33. And be it further enacted, That for any crime or offence against the United States, the offender may, by any justice or judge of the United States, or by any justice of the peace, or other magistrate of any of the United States where he may be found agreeably to the usual mode of process against offenders in such state, and at the expense of the United States, be arrested, and imprisoned or bailed, as the case may be, for trial before such court of the United States as by this act has cognizance of the offence. And copies of the process shall be returned as speedily as may be into the clerk's office of such court, together with the recognizances of the witnesses for their appearance to testify in the case; which recognizances the magistrate before whom the examination shall be, may require on pain of imprisonment. And if such commitment of the offender, or the witnesses shall be in a district other than that in which the offence is to be tried, it shall be the duty of the judge of that district where the delinquent is imprisoned, seasonably to issue, and of the marshal of the same district to execute, a warrant for the removal of the offender, and the witnesses, or either of them, as the case may be, to the district in which the trial is to be had. And upon all arrests in criminal cases, bail shall be admitted, except where the punishment may be death, in which cases it shall not be admitted but by the supreme or a circuit court, or by a justice of the supreme court, or a judge of a district court, who shall exercise their discretion therein, regarding the nature and circumstances of the offence, and of the evidence, and the usages of law. And if a person committed by a justice of the supreme or a judge of a district court for an offence not punishable with death, shall afterwards procure bail, and there be no judge of the United States in the district to take the same, it may be taken by any judge of the supreme or superior court of law of such state.

SEC . 34. And be it further enacted, That the laws of the several states, except where the constitution, treaties or statutes of the United States shall otherwise require or provide, shall be regarded as rules of decision in trials at common law in the courts of the United States in cases where they apply.

SEC . 35. And be it further enacted, That in all courts of the United States, the parties may plead and manage their own causes personally or by assistance of such counsel or attorneys at law as by the rules of the said courts respectively shall be permitted to manage and conduct causes therein. And there shall be appointed in each district a meet person learned in the law to act as attorney for the United States.

Approved, September 24, 1789

The Judiciary Act of 1801

February 13, 1801.
2 Stat. 89.

CHAP. IV.—An Act to provide for the more convenient organization of the Courts of the United States.

SECTION 1. Be it enacted by the Senate and House of Representatives of the United States of America in Congress assembled, That from and after the next session of the Supreme Court of the United States, the said court shall be holden by the justices thereof, or any four of them, at the city of Washington, and shall have two sessions in each and every year thereafter, to commence on the first Monday of June and December respectively; and that if four of the said justices shall not attend within ten days after the times hereby appointed for the commencement of the said sessions respectively, the said court shall be continued over till the next stated session thereof: Provided always, that any one or more of the said justices, attending as aforesaid, shall have power to make all necessary orders touching any suit, action, appeal, writ of error, process, pleadings, or proceeding, returned to the said court or depending therein, preparatory to the hearing, trial or decision of such action, suit, appeal, writ of error, process, pleadings or proceedings.

SEC. 2. And be it further enacted, That the said court shall have power, and is hereby authorized, to issue writs of prohibition, mandamus, scire facias, habeas corpus, certiorari, procedendo, and all other writs not specially provided for by statute, which may be necessary for the exercise of its jurisdiction, and agreeable to the principles and usages of law.

SEC. 3. And be it further enacted, That from and after the next vacancy that shall happen in the said court, it shall consist of five justices only; that is to say, of one chief justice, and four associate justices.

SEC. 4. And be it further enacted, That for the better establishment of the circuit courts of the United States, the said states shall be, and hereby are divided into districts, in manner following; that is to say, one to consist of that part of the state of Massachusetts, which is called the district of Maine, and to be called the district of Maine; one to consist of the state of New Hampshire, and to be called the district of New Hampshire; one to consist of the remaining part of the state of Massachusetts, and to be called the district of Massachusetts; one to consist of the state of Rhode Island and Providence Plantations, and to be called the district of Rhode Island; one to consist of the state of Connecticut, and to be called the district of Connecticut; one to consist of the state of Vermont, and to be called the district of Vermont; one to consist of that part of the state of New York which lies north of the counties of Dutchess and Ulster, and to be called the district of Albany; one to consist of the remaining part of the state of New York, and to be called the district of New York; one to consist of the state of New Jersey, and to be called the district of Jersey; one to consist of that part of the state of Pennsylvania which lies east of the river Susquehanna, and the northeast branch thereof, to the line betwixt Northumberland and Luzerne counties; thence westwardly along said line, betwixt Northumberland and Luzerne, and betwixt Luzerne and Lycoming counties, until the same strikes the line of the state of New York, and to be called the Eastern district of Pennsylvania; one to consist of the remaining part of the state of Pennsylvania, and to be called the Western district of Pennsylvania; one to consist of the state of Delaware, and to be called the district of Delaware; one to consist of the state of Maryland, and to be called the district of Maryland; one to consist of that part of the state of Virginia, which lies to the eastward of a line to be drawn from the river Potomac at Harper's ferry, along the Blue Ridge, with the line which divides the counties on the east side thereof from those on the west side thereof, to the North Carolina line, to be called the Eastern district of Virginia; one to consist of the remaining part of the said state of Virginia, to be called the Western district of Virginia; one to consist of the state of North Carolina, and to be called the district of North Carolina; one to consist of the state of South Carolina, and to be called the district of South Carolina; one to consist of the state of Georgia, and to be called the district of Georgia; one to consist of that part of the state of Tennessee which lies on the east side of Cumberland mountain, and to be called the district of East Tennessee; one to consist of the remaining part of said state, and to be called the district of West Tennessee; one to consist of the state of Kentucky, and to be called the district of Kentucky; and one to consist of the territory of the United States northwest of the Ohio, and the Indiana territory, and to be called the district of Ohio.

SEC. 5. And be it further enacted, That where any two adjoining districts of the United States shall be divided from each other, in whole or in part, by any river, bay, water, water-course or mountain, the whole width of such river, bay, water, water-course or mountain, as the case may be, shall be taken and deemed, to all intents and purposes, to be within both of the districts so to be divided thereby.

SEC. 6. And be it further enacted, That the said districts shall be classed into six circuits in manner following; that is to say: The first circuit shall consist of the districts of Maine, New Hampshire, Massachusetts, and Rhode Island; the second, of the districts of Connecticut, Vermont, Albany and New York; the third, of the districts of Jersey, the Eastern and Western districts of Pennsylvania, and Delaware; the fourth, of the districts of Maryland, and the Eastern and Western districts of Virginia; the fifth, of the districts of North Carolina, South Carolina, and Georgia; and the sixth, of the districts of East Tennessee, West Tennessee, Kentucky, and Ohio.

SEC. 7. And be it further enacted, That there shall be in each of the aforesaid circuits, except the sixth circuit, three judges of the United States, to be called circuit judges, one of whom shall be commissioned as chief judge; and that there shall be a circuit court of the United States, in and for each of the aforesaid circuits, to be composed of the circuit judges within the five first circuits respectively, and in the sixth circuit, by a circuit judge, and the judges of the district courts of Kentucky and Tennessee; the duty of all of whom it shall be to attend, but any two of whom shall form a quorum; and that each and every of the said circuit courts shall hold two sessions annually, at the times and places following, in and for each district contained within their several circuits respectively; that is to say, the circuit court of the first circuit, at Providence on the eighth day of May, and at Newport on the first day of November, in and for the district of Rhode Island; at Boston, in and for the district of Massachusetts, on the twenty-second day of May and fifteenth day of October; at Portsmouth on the eighth day of June, and at Exeter on the twenty-ninth day of September, in and for the district of New Hampshire; in and for the district of Maine, at Portland on the fifteenth day of June, and at Wiscasset on the twenty-second day of September. The circuit court of the second circuit, at New Haven on the fifteenth day of April, and at Hartford, on the twenty-fifth day of September, in and for the district of Connecticut; at Windsor on the fifth day of May, and at Rutland on the fifteenth day of October, in and for the district of Vermont; at the city of Albany, in and for the district of Albany, on the twentieth day of May and twenty-fifth day of October; at the city of New York, in and for the district of New York, on the fifth day of June and the tenth day of November. The circuit court of the third circuit, at Trenton, in and for the district of Jersey, on the second days of May and October; at the city of Philadelphia, in and for the Eastern district of Pennsylvania, on the eleventh day of May and eleventh day of October; at Bedford, in and for the Western district of Pennsylvania, on the twenty-fifth day of June and twenty-fifth day of November; and at Dover, in and for the district of Delaware, on the third day of June and twenty-seventh day of October. The circuit court of the fourth circuit, at Baltimore, in and for the district of Maryland, on the twentieth day of March and fifth day of November; at Lexington in Rockbridge county, in and for the Western district of Virginia, on the fifth day of April and twentieth day of November; and at the city of Richmond, in and for the Eastern district of Virginia, on the twenty-fifth day of April, and fifth day of December. The circuit court of the fifth circuit, at Raleigh, in and for the district of North Carolina, on the first day of June and the first day of November; at Charleston on the sixth day of May, and at Columbia on the thirtieth day of November, in and for the district of South Carolina; at Savannah on the tenth day of April, and at Augusta on the fifteenth day of December, in and for the district of Georgia; and the circuit court of the sixth circuit, at Knoxville, in and for the district of East Tennessee, on the twenty-fifth day of March and twenty-fifth day of September; at Nashville, in and for the district of West Tennessee, on the twentieth day of April and twentieth day of October; and at Bairdstown, in and for the district of Kentucky, on the fifteenth day of May and fifteenth day of November; and at Cincinnati in and for the district of Ohio, on the tenth day of June and on the tenth day of December; and so on the several days and at the several places aforesaid, in each and every year afterwards:

Provided always, that when any of the said days shall happen on Sunday, then the said court hereby directed to be holden on such day, shall be holden on the next day thereafter; and provided also, that there shall be appointed, in the sixth circuit, a judge of the United States, to be called a circuit judge, who together with the district judges of Tennessee and Kentucky, shall hold the circuit courts, hereby directed to be holden, within the said circuit; and that whenever the office of district judge, in the districts of Kentucky and Tennessee respectively, shall become vacant, such vacancies shall respectively be supplied by the appointment of two additional circuit judges, in the said circuit, who, together with the circuit judge first aforesaid, shall compose the circuit court of the said circuit.

SEC. 8. Provided always, and be it further enacted, That the said circuit courts hereby established shall have power, and hereby are authorized, to hold special sessions, for the trial of criminal causes, at any other time or times than is hereby directed, at their discretion.

SEC. 9. And provided also, and be it further enacted, That if in the opinion of any judge of any of the said circuit courts, it shall be dangerous to hold the next stated session of such court, for any district within the circuit to which such judge shall belong, at the place by law appointed for holding the same; it shall be lawful for such judge to issue his order, under his hand and seal, to the marshal of such court, directing him to adjourn the said session, to such other place within the same district as the said judge shall deem convenient; which said marshal shall, thereupon, adjourn the said court pursuant to such order, by making, in one or more public papers, printed within the said district, publication of such order and adjournment, from the time when he shall receive such order to the time appointed by law for commencing such stated session: and that the court so to be held, according to, and by virtue of such adjournment, shall have the same powers and authorities, and shall proceed in the same manner, as if the same had been held at the place appointed by law for that purpose.

SEC. 10. And be it further enacted, That the circuit courts shall have, and hereby are invested with, all the powers heretofore granted by law to the circuit courts of the United States, unless where otherwise provided by this act.

SEC. 11. And be it further enacted, That the said circuit courts respectively shall have cognizance of all crimes and offences cognizable under the authority of the United States, and committed within their respective districts, or upon the high seas; and also of all cases in law or equity, arising under the constitution and laws of the United States, and treaties made, or which shall be made, under their authority; and also of all actions, or suits of a civil nature, at common law, or in equity, where the United States shall be plaintiffs or complainants; and also of all seizures on land or water, and all penalties and forfeitures, made, arising or accruing under the laws of the United States; which cognizance of all penalties and forfeitures, shall be exclusively of the state courts, in the said circuit courts, where the offence, by which the penalty or forfeiture is incurred, shall have been committed within fifty miles of the place of holding the said courts; and also of all actions, or suits, matters or things cognizable by the judicial authority of the United States, under and by virtue of the constitution thereof, where the matter in dispute shall amount to four hundred dollars, and where original jurisdiction is not given by the constitution of the United States to the supreme court thereof, or exclusive jurisdiction by law to the district courts of the United States: Provided always, that in all cases where the title, or bounds of land shall come into question, the jurisdiction of the said circuit courts shall not be restrained, by reason of the value of the land in dispute.

SEC. 12. And be it further enacted, That the said circuit courts respectively shall have cognizance concurrently with the district courts, of all cases which shall arise, within their respective circuits, under the act to establish an uniform system of bankruptcy throughout the United States; and that each circuit judge, within his respective circuit, shall and may perform all and singular the duties enjoined by the said act, upon a judge of a district court: and that the proceedings under a commission of bankruptcy, which shall issue from a circuit judge, shall in all respects be conformable to the proceedings under a commission of bankruptcy, which shall issue from a district judge, mutatis mutandis.

SEC. 13. And be it further enacted, That where any action or suit shall be, or shall have been commenced, in any state court within the United States, against an alien, or by a citizen or citizens of the state in which such suit or action shall be, or shall have been commenced against a citizen or citizens of another state, and the matter in dispute, except in cases where the title or bounds of land shall be in question, shall exceed the sum or value of four hundred dollars, exclusive of costs, and the defendant or defendants in such suit or action shall be personally served with the original process therein, or shall appear thereto; or where, in any suit or action, so commenced or to be commenced, final judgment, for a sum exceeding four hundred dollars, exclusive of costs, shall have been rendered in such state court, against such defendant or defendants, without return of personal service on him, her, or them, of the original process in such suit or action, and without an appearance thereto, by him, her, or them, and a writ of error, or writ of review, shall be brought by such defendant or defendants, in such state court, to reverse the said judgment; or where any suit or action shall have been, or shall be commenced in any such court, against any person or persons, in any case arising under the constitution or laws of the United States, or treaties made or to be made under their authority; then, and in any of the said cases, it shall be lawful for the defendant or defendants, in such suit or action, at the time of entering his, her, or their appearance thereto, and for the plaintiff, or plaintiffs in such writ of error, or writ of review, at the time when such writ shall be returnable, to file in such court a petition for the removal of such suit, action, writ of error, or writ of review, to the next circuit court of the United States, hereby directed to be holden in and for the district within which such state court shall be holden, and to offer to such state court good and sufficient surety for entering, in such circuit court, on the first day of its next ensuing session, true copies of the process and proceedings, in such action, suit, writ of error, or writ of review, and also for his, her, or their appearance in the said circuit court, at the period aforesaid, and then and there entering special bail, in the said suit, or action, if special bail was originally demandable, and demanded therein; whereupon it shall be the duty of the said state court to accept the said security, and to stay all further proceedings in such suit, action, writ of error, or writ of review, and to discharge any bail that may have been given therein; and that the said copies being filed as aforesaid in such circuit court, and special bail, in manner aforesaid, being given therein, such suit, action, writ of error, or writ of review, shall be therein proceeded on, tried, heard and determined, in the same manner as if there originally commenced or brought:

Provided always, that any attachment of the goods or estate of the defendant, by the original process in such suit or action, shall hold the goods or estate so attached, to answer the final judgment in the said circuit court, in the same manner as by the laws of the state they would have been holden, to answer the final judgment, had it been rendered by the court in which the suit or action was commenced.

SEC. 14. And be it further enacted, That when any suit or action, commenced, or to be commenced, in any state court within the United States, between citizens of the same state, the title or bounds of land shall come into question, it shall be lawful for either party, before trial, to state to the said court, and make affidavit if thereby required, that he, she, or they, doth or do claim under, and at the hearing or trial shall rely upon a right or title to the lands in dispute, under a grant, or grants, from a state other than that wherein such suit or action is, or shall be pending; and to produce to the said court the original grant, or grants, so claimed under, or exemplifications thereof, except in cases where the loss of public records shall put it out of his, her or their power so to do; and to move that the adverse party do inform the said court, forthwith, whether he, she, or they, doth or do claim the land in dispute, under a grant or grants from the state wherein such suit or action is, or shall be pending; whereupon the said adverse party shall give such information, or otherwise not be allowed to plead, or give in evidence, in the cause any such grant; and that if it shall appear from such information, that the said adverse party doth claim the said lands, under any such grant, or grants, then it shall be lawful for the party moving for such information, if plaintiff or complainant in the said suit or action, to remove the same, by motion, to the next circuit court of the United States, hereby directed to be holden in and for the district within which such state court shall be holden; and if defendant in the said suit or action, then to remove the same, as aforesaid, in the same manner, and under the like regulations, terms, and conditions, as are provided in and by the preceding section of this act, in the cases of actions thereby directed to be removed; and that the said circuit courts respectively, into which such suit or action shall be removed, pursuant to the provisions in this section contained, shall proceed in, try, hear and determine the same, in like manner as if therein brought by original process:

Provided always, that neither party, so removing any suit or action, shall be allowed, on the trial or hearing thereof, to plead, give evidence of, or rely on, any other title than that by him, her, or them, so stated as aforesaid, as the ground of his, her, or their claim.

SEC. 15. And be it further enacted, That any one judge of any of the said circuit courts shall be, and hereby is, authorized and empowered, to hold the same from day to day, not exceeding five days, to impannel and charge the grand jury, to order process on any indictment or presentment found in the said court; to direct subpoenas for witnesses to attend the same, and the requisite process on the non-attendance of witnesses or jurors; to receive any presentment or indictment from the grand jury; to take recognizance for the attendance of any witness, or for the appearance of any person, presented or indicted; to award and issue process, and order commitment for contempts; to commit any person presented or indicted, for want of security or otherwise; to order publication of testimony; to issue commissions for the examination of witnesses, where allowable by law; to grant rules and orders of survey; to take order, where necessary, relative to jurors, to serve at the next stated session of the said court; to direct the examination of witnesses de bene esse, where allowed by law; to make rules of reference by consent of parties; and to grant continuances on the motion of either party, upon such terms and conditions, as shall be agreeable to practice and the usages of law; and that if some other judge of the said court shall not attend the same within five days after the commencement thereof, inclusive, then the said court shall, by virtue of this act, be continued over to the next stated session thereof; in which case, all writs, process, and recognizances, returned and returnable to the said court, and all actions, suits, process, pleadings, and other proceedings of what nature or kind soever, depending before the said court, shall, by virtue of this act, be continued to the next stated session of the same.

SEC. 16. And be it further enacted, That no person shall be arrested in one of the said districts, for trial in another, before any of the said circuit courts in any civil action; and that no civil action or suit shall be brought before any of the said courts, by any original process, against an inhabitant of the United States, in any other district than that whereof he is an inhabitant, or in which he shall be found at the time of serving the writ; nor shall any district or circuit court have cognizance of any suit to recover the contents of any promissory note, or other chose in action, in favour of an assignee, unless a suit might have been prosecuted in such court to recover the said contents, if no assignment had been made, except in cases of foreign bills of exchange.

SEC. 17. And be it further enacted, That the trials of all issues of fact, before any of the circuit courts hereby established, except in cases of equity, and admiralty and maritime jurisdiction, shall be by jury.

SEC. 18. And be it further enacted, That any judge of any of the said circuit courts shall be, and hereby is authorized and empowered, in all cases cognizable by the circuit court, whereof he shall be a judge, to grant writs of ne-exeat, and writs of injunction to stay waste, or to stay proceedings at law, on any judgment rendered by such circuit court, upon the like terms and conditions as such writs may be now granted, by the justices of the Supreme Court of the United States.

SEC. 19. And be it further enacted, That if in the opinion of any circuit judge, of the circuit within which such district may be situated, the life or lives of any person or persons, confined in the prison of such district, under or by virtue of any law of the United States, shall be in imminent danger, arising from the place of such confinement, it shall, in such case, be lawful for such judge, and he is hereby authorized and empowered, to direct the marshal of such district to remove, or cause to be removed, the person or persons so confined, to the next adjacent prison, there to be confined, until he, she, or they, may safely be removed back, to the place of his, her, or their first confinement; and that the said removals shall be at the expense of the United States.

SEC. 20. And be it further enacted, That all actions, suits, process, pleadings, and other proceedings of what nature or kind soever, depending or existing in any of the present circuit courts of the United States, or in any of the present district courts of the United States, acting as circuit courts, shall be, and hereby are, continued over to the circuit courts established by this act, in manner following, that is to say: all such as shall, on the fifteenth day of June next, be depending and undetermined, or shall then have been commenced and made returnable before the district court of Maine, acting as a circuit court, to the next circuit court hereby directed to be holden within and for the district of Maine; all such as shall be depending and undetermined before the circuit court for the district of New Hampshire, to the next circuit court hereby directed to be holden, within and for the district of New Hampshire; all such as shall be depending and undetermined before the circuit court for the district of Massachusetts, to the next circuit court hereby directed to be holden, within and for the district of Massachusetts; all such as shall be depending and undetermined before the circuit court of the district of Rhode Island, to the next circuit court hereby directed to be holden, within and for the district of Rhode Island; all such as shall be depending or undetermined before the circuit court for the district of Connecticut, to the next circuit court hereby directed to be holden, within and for the district of Connecticut; all such as shall be depending and undetermined before the circuit court for the district of Vermont, to the next circuit court hereby directed to be holden, within and for the district of Vermont; all such as shall be depending and undetermined before the circuit court for the district of New York, to the next circuit court hereby directed to be holden, within and for the district of New York; all such as shall be depending and undetermined before the circuit court for the district of New Jersey, to the next circuit court hereby directed to be holden, within and for the district of Jersey; all such as shall be depending and undetermined before the circuit court for the district of Pennsylvania, to the next circuit court hereby directed to be holden, within and for the eastern district of Pennsylvania; all such as shall be depending and undetermined before the circuit court for the district of Delaware, to the next circuit court hereby directed to be holden, within and for the district of Delaware; all such as shall be depending and undetermined before the circuit court for the district of Maryland, to the next circuit court hereby directed to be holden, within and for the district of Maryland; all such as shall be depending and undetermined before the circuit court for the district of Virginia, to the next circuit court hereby directed to be holden, within and for the eastern district of Virginia; all such as shall be depending and undetermined before the circuit court for the district of North Carolinia, to the next circuit court hereby directed to be holden, within and for the district of North Carolina; all such as shall be depending and undetermined before the circuit court for the district of South Carolina, to the next circuit court hereby directed to be holden, within and for the district of South Carolina; all such as shall be depending and undetermined before the circuit court for the district of Georgia, to the next circuit court hereby directed to be holden, within and for the district of Georgia; all such as shall be depending and undetermined before the district court of Tennessee, acting as a circuit court, to the next circuit court hereby directed to be holden, within and for the district of East Tennessee; all such as shall be depending and undetermined before the district court of Kentucky, acting as a circuit court, to the next circuit court hereby directed to be holden, within and for the district of Kentucky; and shall there be equally regular and effectual, and shall be proceeded in, in the same manner as they could have been, if this act had not been made.

SEC. 21. And be it further enacted, That for the better dispatch of the business of district courts of the United States, in the districts of Jersey, Maryland, Virginia, and North Carolina, additional district courts shall be established therein, in manner following, that is to say: The said district of Jersey shall be divided into two districts; one to consist of that part thereof, which is called East New Jersey, and to be called the district of East Jersey; a district court, in and for which, shall be holden at New Brunswick, by the district judge of the district of Jersey, on the fourth Tuesday in May, and on the fourth Tuesday in November, in each and every year; and one other, to consist of the remaining part of the said district of Jersey, and to be called the district of West Jersey, a district court, in and for which, shall be holden at Burlington, by the district judge last aforesaid, on the fourth Tuesday in February, and on the fourth Tuesday in August, in each and every year. And a new district shall be established, in the districts of Maryland and Virginia, to consist of the territory of Columbia, of all that part of the district of Maryland, which lies west and southwest of the river Patuxent, and of the western branch thereof, and south of the line which divides the county of Montgomery in the last mentioned district, from the county of Frederick, and of a line to be drawn from the termination of the last mentioned line, a northeast course to the western branch of the Patuxent; and of all that part of the district of Virginia, which lies north of the river Rappahannock, and east of the line which divides the counties of Fauquier and Loudon, in the last mentioned district from the counties of Fairfax, Prince William, and Stafford; which new district shall be called the district of Potomac, and a district court in and for the same, shall be holden at Alexandria, by the district judge of the district of Maryland, on the first Tuesday in April, and the first Tuesday in October, in each and every year. And there shall be a new district established in the district of Virginia, to be called the district of Norfolk, and to consist of all that part of the said district of Virginia, which is contained within the counties of Isle of Wight, Nansemond, Norfolk, Princess Anne, James City, New Kent, Warwick, York, Elizabeth City, Gloucester, Matthews, Middlesex, Accomac, and Northampton; a district court, in and for which district of Norfolk, shall be holden at Norfolk, by the district judge of the district of Virginia, on the first Tuesday in February, on the first Tuesday in May, on the first Tuesday in August, and on the first Tuesday in November, in each and every year. And the district of North Carolina shall be divided into three districts; one to consist of all that part thereof, which by the laws of the state of North Carolina, now forms the districts of Edenton and Halifax; which district shall be called the district of Albemarle, and a district court, in and for the same, shall be holden at Edenton, by the district judge of the district of North Carolina, on the third Tuesday in April, on the third Tuesday in August, and on the third Tuesday in December, in each and every year; one other to be called the district of Pamptico, and to consist of all that part of the district of North Carolina aforesaid, which by the laws of the said state now forms the district of Newbern and Hillsborough, together with all that part of the district of Wilmington, which lies to the northward and eastward of the river called New River, and for which district of Pamptico, a district court shall be holden at Newbern, by the district judge last aforesaid, on the first Tuesday in April, on the first Tuesday in August, and on the first Tuesday in December, in each and every year. And one other to consist of the remaining part of the said district of North Carolina, and to be called the district of Cape Fear, in and for which a district court shall be holden at Wilmington, by the district judge last aforesaid, on the last Tuesday in March, on the last Tuesday in July, and on the last Tuesday in November, in each and every year; which said courts, hereby directed to be holden, shall severally and respectively have and exercise, within their several and respective districts, the same powers, authority, and jurisdiction, in all cases and respects whatsoever, which are vested by law in the district courts of the United States.

SEC. 22. And be it further enacted, That there shall be clerks for each of the said courts to be appointed by the judge thereof, which clerks shall reside and keep the records of the said courts, at the places of holding the courts, whereto they respectively shall belong, and shall perform the same duties, and be entitled to and receive the same emoluments and fees, which are established by law, for the clerks of the district courts of the United States respectively; and that the marshals and attornies of the United States, for the districts, which are hereby divided, or within the limits of which new districts are hereby erected, shall continue to be marshals and attornies for the courts hereby appointed to be holden within the limits of their present districts respectively, and shall have, exercise, and perform, within the jurisdictions of those courts respectively, all the powers and duties, and receive all the fees and emoluments, appointed and established by law, for the marshals and attornies of the United States.

SEC. 23. And be it further enacted, That the stated sessions of the district court of the district of Maryland shall hereafter be holden at Baltimore only.

SEC. 24. And be it further enacted, That the district courts of the United States, in and for the districts of Tennessee and Kentucky, shall be, and hereby are, abolished; and that all and singular the powers, authority and jurisdiction of the said courts respectively shall be and hereby are vested in, and shall be exercised by the circuit courts, by this act directed to be holden in and for the districts of East Tennessee, West Tennessee and Kentucky, respectively, within the limits of their respective jurisdictions; and that the circuit judges to be appointed for the sixth circuit aforesaid, severally, shall be invested with, possess and exercise, all and singular the powers, now vested by law in the district judges of the United States.

SEC. 25. And be it further enacted, That in case of the inability of the district judge of either of the districts of the United States, to perform the duties of his office, and satisfactory evidence thereof being shown to the circuit court, in and for such district, it shall be the duty of such circuit court, from time to time, as occasion may require, to direct one of the judges of said circuit court, to perform the duties of such district judge, within and for said district, for and during the period the inability of the district judge shall continue. And it shall be the duty of the circuit judge, to whom the duties of the district judge shall be assigned in manner aforesaid, and he is hereby authorized to perform the duties of said district judge, during the continuance of his disability.

SEC. 26. And be it further enacted, That the several circuit courts hereby established shall have power to appoint clerks for their respective courts; that is to say, one for each district within which such court is or shall be directed by law to be holden; which clerks respectively shall take the same oath or affirmation, and give the like bonds, as are by law required to be taken and given by the clerk of the supreme court of the United States; and shall be entitled to demand and receive, for their services respectively, the same fees, to be recovered in the same manner, as have heretofore been allowed by law, for the like services, to the clerks of the circuit and district courts of the United States.

SEC. 27. And be it further enacted, That the circuit courts of the United States, heretofore established, shall cease and be abolished; and that the records and office papers of every kind, belonging to those courts respectively, shall be safely kept by the clerks thereof, who shall continue in all respects to act as heretofore in the business of the said courts, until it shall otherwise be ordered by the courts hereby established.

SEC. 28. And be it further enacted, That the supreme, circuit and district courts of the United States, shall be, and hereby are, constituted courts of record.

SEC. 29. And be it further enacted, That all writs and processes whatsoever, issuing from any of the circuit courts, hereby established, shall, after the first day of April next, bear test of the presiding judge of such court; before which time they shall bear test of the chief justice of the United States; all which said writs and processes shall be signed by the clerks of the courts respectively, from which the same shall issue, and shall be made returnable to the next stated or special session of such court, and all writs and processes which have issued, or which may issue before the first day of April next, returnable to the circuit courts heretofore established, or to any district court acting as a circuit court, shall be returned to the circuit courts hereby established, and shall be there proceeded in, in the same manner as they could, had they been originally returnable to the circuit courts hereby established.

SEC. 30. And be it further enacted, That every justice of the supreme court of the United States, and every judge of any circuit or district court shall be, and hereby is authorized and empowered, to grant writs of habeas corpus, for the purpose of inquiring into the cause of commitment, and thereupon to discharge from confinement, on bail or otherwise: Provided always, that no writ of habeas corpus, to be granted under this act, shall extend to any prisoner or prisoners in gaol, unless such prisoner or prisoners be in custody, under or by colour of the authority of the United States, or be committed for trial before some court of the same; or be necessary to be brought into court to give testimony.

SEC. 31. And be it further enacted, That the several courts of the United States shall be, and hereby are authorized and empowered to grant new trials and rehearings, on motion and cause shown, and to make and establish all necessary rules and regulations, for returning writs, filing pleas, and other proceedings; and for regulating the practice and enforcing the orderly conduct of business, in the said courts respectively: Provided always, that the said rules and regulations be not repugnant to the laws of the United States; and that all the courts of the United States, and each of the justices and judges thereof, shall be, and hereby are, authorized and empowered to administer all necessary oaths and affirmations, and to bind to the peace or good behaviour, with surety where necessary, in all cases, arising under the authority of the United States.

SEC. 32. And be it further enacted, That every person who shall be appointed a judge of any circuit court, hereby established, shall, before he shall begin to exercise the duties of his said office, take the following oath or affirmation; that is to say: "I, A. B. do solemnly swear" (or affirm) "that I will administer justice without respect to persons; and will do equal right to all persons; and will, in all things, faithfully and impartially discharge and perform, all the duties incumbent on me as a judge of according to the best of my abilities and understanding, and to the constitution and laws of the United States."

SEC. 33. And be it further enacted, That from all final judgments or decrees, in any of the district courts of the United States, an appeal, where the matter in dispute, exclusive of costs, shall exceed the sum or value of fifty dollars, shall be allowed to the circuit court next to be holden, in the district where such final judgment or judgments, decree or decrees, may be rendered; and the circuit court or courts are hereby authorized and required to receive, hear and determine such appeal; and that from all final judgments or decrees in any circuit court, in any cases of equity, of admiralty and maritime jurisdiction, and of prize or no prize, an appeal, where the matter in dispute, exclusive of costs, shall exceed the sum or value of two thousand dollars, shall be allowed to the supreme court of the United States; and that upon such appeal, a transcript of the libel, bill, answer, depositions, and all other proceedings of what kind soever in the cause, shall be transmitted to the said supreme court; and that no new evidence shall be received in the said court, on the hearing of such appeal; and that such appeals shall be subject to the same rules, regulations and restrictions, as are prescribed by law in case of writs of error; and that the said supreme court shall be, and hereby is authorized and required, to receive, hear and determine such appeals.

SEC. 34. And be it further enacted, That all final judgments in civil actions at common law, in any of the circuit courts hereby established, whether brought by original process in such court, or removed thereto from any state court, and all final judgments in any of the district courts of the United States may, where the matter in dispute, exclusive of costs, shall exceed the sum or value of two thousand dollars, be reexamined and reversed or affirmed, in the supreme court of the United States, by writ of error: whereto shall be annexed, and returned therewith at the day and place therein mentioned, an authenticated transcript of the record and assignment of errors, and prayer for reversal, and also a citation to the adverse party, signed by a judge of such circuit court, or by the district judge as the case may be; which citation shall be served on the adverse party personally, or by leaving a true copy thereof at his or their usual place or places of residence, at least thirty days before the time mentioned in such writ of error, for the return thereof.

SEC. 35. And be it further enacted, That the stipulation, bond or security, taken upon any writ of error or appeal to be brought or allowed as aforesaid, shall be returned by the judge taking the same, to the clerk or register of the court where the judgment or decree complained of was rendered, to be by him annexed to the transcript of the record, hereby directed to be sent up to the supreme court of the United States.

SEC. 36. And be it further enacted, That there shall be appointed, in and for each of the districts established by this act, a marshal, whose duty it shall be to attend the circuit courts of the United States hereby established, when sitting within such district, and who shall have and exercise, within such district, the same powers, perform the same duties, be subject to the same penalties, give the same bond with sureties, take the same oath, be entitled to and receive the same compensation and emoluments, and in all respects be subject to the same regulations, as are now prescribed by law, in respect to the marshals of the United States heretofore appointed: Provided always, that the several marshals of the United States, now in office, shall, during the periods for which they were respectively appointed, unless sooner removed by the President of the United States, be and continue marshals for the several districts hereby established, within which they respectively reside; and shall perform the duties, exercise the powers, and receive the emoluments, hereby directed to be performed, exercised and received, by marshals therein.

SEC. 37. And be it further enacted, That there shall be appointed for each of the districts hereby established, a person learned in the law, to act as attorney for the United States within such district, and in the circuit and district courts which may be holden therein; which attorney shall take an oath or affirmation for the faithful performance of the duties of his office, and shall prosecute, in such district, all delinquents for crimes and offences cognizable under the authority of the United States, and all civil actions or suits in which the United States shall be concerned, except actions or suits in the supreme court of the United States; and shall be entitled to, and receive, for their services respectively, such compensations, emoluments and fees, as by law are or shall be allowed, to the district attornies of the United States: Provided always, that the district attornies of the United States now in office shall, severally and respectively, be attornies for those districts hereby established, within which they reside, until removed by the President of the United States; and shall perform the duties, exercise the powers, and receive the emoluments, hereby directed to be performed, exercised and received, by the attorney of the United States therein.

SEC. 38. And be it further enacted, That jurors and witnesses attending any of the courts, hereby established, shall be entitled to and receive the same compensations respectively, as heretofore have been allowed by law to jurors and witnesses, attending the circuit and district courts of the United States.

SEC. 39. And be it further enacted, That the records of the several circuit courts, hereby established, shall hereafter be kept at the respective places at which the said courts are hereby directed to be holden: Provided always, that in the district wherein there are more than one place directed by this act for holding said circuit courts, the records of the circuit court in such district shall hereafter be kept in either of such places, as the said court in such district shall direct.

SEC. 40. And be it further enacted, That the privilege from arrest of every person going to, attending at, or returning from, any court of the United States, shall be computed and continue, from the time of his or her departure from his or her habitation, until his or her return thereto: Provided, that such time shall not exceed one day, Sundays excluded, for every twenty miles of the distance, which such person must necessarily travel in so going and returning, over and above the time of attendance.

SEC. 41. And be it further enacted, That each of the circuit judges of the United States, to be appointed by virtue of this act, shall be allowed as a compensation for his services, an annual salary of two thousand dollars, to be paid quarter-yearly at the treasury of the United States; except the judges of the sixth circuit, who shall be allowed the sum of fifteen hundred dollars each, to be paid in like manner; and that the salaries of the district judges of Kentucky and Tennessee shall be, and hereby are, severally augmented to the like sum of fifteen hundred dollars, annually, to be paid in like manner.

APPROVED, February 13, 1801.

The Judiciary Act of 1802

April 29, 1802.
2 Stat. 156.

CHAP. XXXI.—An Act to amend the Judicial System of the United States.

Be it enacted by the Senate and House of Representatives of the United States of America in Congress assembled, That from and after the passing of this act, the Supreme Court of the United States shall be holden by the justices thereof, or any four of them, at the city of Washington, and shall have one session in each and every year, to commence on the first Monday of February annually, and that if four of the said justices shall not attend within ten days after the time hereby appointed for the commencement of the said session, the business of the said court shall be continued over till the next stated session thereof. Provided always, that any one or more of the said justices attending as aforesaid shall have power to make all necessary orders touching any suit, action, writ of error, process, pleadings or proceedings returned to the said court or depending therein, preparatory to the hearing, trial or decision of such action, suit, appeal, writ of error, process, pleadings or proceedings. And so much of the act, entitled "An act to establish the judicial courts of the United States," passed the twenty-fourth day of September, seventeen hundred and eighty-nine, as provides for the holding a session of the supreme court of the United States on the first Monday of August, annually, is hereby repealed.

SEC. 2. And be it further enacted, That it shall be the duty of the associate justice resident in the fourth circuit formed by this act, to attend at the city of Washington on the first Monday of August next, and on the first Monday of August each and every year thereafter, who shall have power to make all necessary orders touching any suit, action, appeal, writ of error, process, pleadings or proceedings, returned to the said court or depending therein, preparatory to the hearing, trial or decision of such action, suit, appeal, writ of error, process, pleadings or proceedings: and that all writs and process may be returnable to the said court on the said first Monday in August, in the same manner as to the session of the said court, herein before directed to be holden on the first Monday in February, and may also bear teste on the said first Monday in August, as though a session of the said court was holden on that day, and it shall be the duty of the clerk of the supreme court to attend the said justice on the said first Monday of August, in each and every year, who shall make due entry of all such matters and things as shall or may be ordered as aforesaid by the said justice, and at each and every such August session, all actions, pleas, and other proceedings relative to any cause, civil or criminal, shall be continued over to the ensuing February session.

SEC. 3. And be it further enacted, That all actions, suits, process, pleadings and other proceedings, of what nature or kind soever, civil or criminal, which were continued from the supreme court of the United States, which was begun and holden on the first Monday of December last, to the next court to have been holden on the first Monday of June, under the act which passed on the thirteenth day of February, one thousand eight hundred and one, intitled, "An act to provide for the more convenient organization of the courts of the United States," and all writs, process and proceedings, as aforesaid, which are or may be made returnable to the same June session, shall be continued, returned to, and have day, in the session to be holden by this act, on the first Monday of August next; and such proceedings shall be had thereon, as is herein before provided.

SEC. 4. And be it further enacted, That the districts of the United States (excepting the districts of Maine, Kentucky, and Tennessee) shall be formed into six circuits, in manner following:

The districts of New Hampshire, Massachusetts and Rhode Island, shall constitute the first circuit;

The districts of Connecticut, New York and Vermont, shall constitute the second circuit;

The districts of New Jersey and Pennsylvania shall constitute the third circuit;

The districts of Maryland and Delaware shall constitute the fourth circuit;

The districts of Virginia and North Carolina shall constitute the fifth circuit; and

The districts of South Carolina and Georgia shall constitute the sixth circuit.

And there shall be holden annually in each district of the said circuits, two courts, which shall be called circuit courts. In the first circuit, the said circuit court shall consist of the justice of the supreme court residing within the said circuit, and the district judge of the district where such court shall be holden: and the sessions of the said court, in the district of New Hampshire, shall commence on the nineteenth day of May, and the second day of November, annually; in the district of Massachusetts, on the first day of June, and the twentieth day of October, annually; in the district of Rhode Island, on the fifteenth day of June, and the fifteenth day of November, annually.

In the second circuit, the said circuit court shall consist of the senior associate justice of the supreme court residing within the fifth circuit, and the district judge of the district, where such court shall be holden:

and the sessions of the said court in the district of Connecticut, shall commence on the thirteenth day of April, and the seventeenth day of September, annually; in the district of New York, on the first day of April, and the first day of September, annually; in the district of Vermont, on the first day of May, and the third day of October, annually.

In the third circuit, the said circuit court shall consist of the justice of the supreme court residing within the said circuit; and the district judge of the district where such court shall be holden: and the sessions of the said court, in the district of New Jersey, shall commence on the first day of April, and the first day of October, annually; in the district of Pennsylvania, on the eleventh day of April, and the eleventh day of October, annually.

In the fourth circuit, the said circuit court shall consist of the justice of the supreme court residing within the said circuit, and the district judge of the district where such court shall be holden: and the sessions of the said court, in the district of Delaware, shall commence on the third day of June, and the twenty-seventh day of October, annually; in the district of Maryland, on the first day of May, and the seventh day of November, annually; to be holden hereafter at the city of Baltimore only.

In the fifth circuit, the circuit court shall consist of the present chief justice of the supreme court, and the district judge of the district where such court shall be holden: and the sessions of the said court, in the district of Virginia, shall commence on the twenty-second day of May, and the twenty-second day of November, annually; in the district of North Carolina, on the fifteenth day of June, and the twenty-ninth day of December, annually.

In the sixth circuit, the said circuit court shall consist of the junior associate justice of the supreme court, in the fifth circuit, and the district judge of the district where such court shall be holden: and the sessions of the said court, in the district of South Carolina, shall commence at Charleston on the twentieth day of May, and at Columbia on the thirtieth day of November, annually; in the district of Georgia, on the sixth day of May at Savannah, and on the fourteenth day of December hereafter at Louisville, annually: Provided, that when only one of the judges hereby directed to hold the circuit courts, shall attend, such circuit court may be held by the judge so attending; and that when any of the said days shall happen on a Sunday, then the said court hereby directed to be holden on such day, shall be holden on the next day thereafter; and the circuit courts constituted by this act, shall be held at the same place or places in each district of every circuit, as by law they were respectively required to be held previous to the thirteenth day of February, one thousand eight hundred and one, excepting as is herein before directed. And none of the said courts shall be holden until after the first day of July next, and the clerk of each district court shall be also clerk of the circuit court in such district, except as is herein after excepted.

SEC. 5. And be it further enacted, That on every appointment which shall be hereafter made of a chief justice or associate justice, the said chief justice and associate justices shall allot themselves among the aforesaid circuits as they shall think fit, and shall enter such allotment on record. And in case no such allotment shall be made by them at their session next succeeding such appointment, and also, after the appointment of any judge, as aforesaid, and before any allotment shall have been made, it shall and may be lawful for the President of the United States to make such allotment as he shall deem proper, which allotment made in either case, shall be binding until another allotment shall be made; and the circuit courts constituted by this act, shall have all the power, authority and jurisdiction within the several districts of their respective circuits that before the thirteenth day of February, one thousand eight hundred and one, belonged to the circuit courts of the United States, and in all cases which, by appeal or writ of error, are or shall be removed from a district to a circuit court, judgment shall be rendered in conformity to the opinion of the judge of the supreme court presiding in such circuit court.

SEC. 6. And be it further enacted, That whenever any question shall occur before a circuit court, upon which the opinions of the judges shall be opposed, the point upon which the disagreement shall happen, shall, during the same term, upon the request of either party, or their counsel, be stated under the direction of the judges, and certified under the seal of the court, to the supreme court, at their next session to be held thereafter; and shall, by the said court, be finally decided. And the decision of the supreme court, and their order in the premises, shall be remitted to the circuit court, and be there entered of record, and shall have effect according to the nature of the said judgment and order: Provided, that nothing herein contained shall prevent the cause from proceeding, if, in the opinion of the court, farther proceedings can be had without prejudice to the merits: and provided also, that imprisonment shall not be allowed, nor punishment in any case be inflicted, where the judges of the said court are divided in opinion upon the question touching the said imprisonment or punishment.

SEC. 7. And be it further enacted, That the district of North Carolina shall be divided into three districts, one to consist of all that part thereof which, by the laws of the state of North Carolina, now forms the districts of Edenton and Halifax, which district shall be called the district of Albemarle, and a district court in and for the same shall be holden at Edenton by the district judge of North Carolina, on the third Tuesday in April, on the third Tuesday in August, and on the third Tuesday in December, in each and every year; one other to be called the district of Pamptico, and to consist of all that part of North Carolina which by the laws of the said state now forms the districts of Newbern and Hillsborough, together with all that part of the district of Wilmington which lies to the northward and eastward of New river; for which district of Pamptico, a district court shall be holden at Newbern by the district judge last aforesaid on the second Tuesday in April, on the second Tuesday in August, and on the second Tuesday in December in each and every year; and one other to consist of the remaining part of the said district of North Carolina, and to be called the district of Cape Fear, in and for which a district court shall be holden at Wilmington by the district judge last aforesaid, on the first Tuesday in April, on the first Tuesday in August, and on the first Tuesday in December, in each and every year; which said district courts hereby directed to be holden shall respectively have and exercise within their several districts, the same powers, authority and jurisdiction, which are vested by law in the district courts of the United States.

SEC. 8. And be it further enacted, That the circuit court and district courts for the district of North Carolina shall appoint clerks for the said courts respectively, which clerks shall reside and keep the records of the said courts at the places of holding the courts whereto they shall respectively belong, and shall perform the same duties and be entitled to and receive the same emoluments and fees, respectively, which are by law established for the clerks of the circuit and district courts of the United States respectively.

SEC. 9. And be it further enacted, That all actions, causes, pleas, process and other proceedings relative to any cause, civil or criminal, which shall be returnable to, or depending in the several circuit or district courts of the United States on the first day of July next, shall be and are hereby declared to be respectively transferred, returned and continued to the several circuit and district courts constituted by this act, at the times herein before and herein after appointed for the holding of each of the said courts, and shall be heard, tried and determined therein in the same manner and with the same effect, as if no change had been made in the said courts. And it shall be the duty of the clerk of each and every court hereby constituted, to receive and to take into his safe keeping the writs, process, pleas, proceedings and papers of all those causes and actions which by this act shall be transferred, returned or continued to such court, and also all the records and office papers of every kind respectively belonging to the courts abolished by the repeal of the act, intituled "An act to provide for the more convenient organization of the courts of the United States," and from which the said causes shall have been transferred as aforesaid.

SEC. 10. And be it further enacted, That all suits, process, pleadings and other proceedings, of what nature or kind soever, depending in the circuit court in the district of Ohio, and which shall have been, or may hereafter be commenced within the territory of the United States northwest of the river Ohio, in the said court, shall, from and after the first day of July next, be continued over, returned, and made cognizable, in the superior court of the said territory next thereafter to be holden, and all actions, suits, process, pleadings, and other proceedings as aforesaid depending in the circuit court of the said district, and which shall have been or may hereafter be commenced within the Indiana territory in said court, shall, from and after the first day of July next, be continued over, returned and made cognizable in the superior court of the said Indiana territory, next thereafter to be holden.

SEC. 11. And be it further enacted, That in all cases in which proceedings shall, on the said first day of July next, be pending under a commission of bankruptcy issued in pursuance of the aforesaid act, intituled "An act to provide for the more convenient organization of the courts of the United States," the cognizance of the same shall be, and hereby is transferred to, and vested in, the district judge of the district within which such commission shall have issued, who is hereby empowered to proceed therein in the same manner and to the same effect, as if such commission of bankruptcy had been issued by his order.

SEC. 12. And be it further enacted, That from and after the first day of July next, the district judges of Kentucky and Tennessee shall be and hereby are severally entitled to a salary of fifteen hundred dollars, annually, to be paid quarter-yearly at the treasury of the United States.

SEC. 13. And be it further enacted, That the marshals and attornies of the United States, for the districts which were not divided, or within the limits of which, new districts were not erected, by the act intituled "An act to provide for the more convenient organization of the courts of the United States," passed the thirteenth day of February, one thousand eight hundred and one, shall continue to be marshals and attornies for such districts respectively, unless removed by the President of the United States, and in all other districts which were divided or within the limits of which new districts were erected by the last recited act, the President of the United States be and hereby is empowered from and after the first day of July next to discontinue all such supernumerary marshals and district attornies of the United States in such districts respectively as he shall deem expedient, so that there shall be but one marshal and district attorney to each district; and every marshal and district attorney who shall be continued in office, or appointed by the President of the United States in such districts, shall have and exercise the same powers, perform the same duties, give the same bond with sureties, take the same oath, be subject to the same penalties and regulations as are, or may be prescribed by law, in respect to the marshals and district attornies of the United States. And every marshal and district attorney who shall be so discontinued as aforesaid shall be holden to deliver over all papers, matters and things in relation to their respective offices, to such marshals and district attornies respectively who shall be so continued or appointed as aforesaid in such district, in the same manner as is required by law in cases of resignation or removal from office.

SEC. 14. And be it further enacted, That there shall be appointed by the President of the United States, from time to time, as many general commissioners of bankruptcy, in each district of the United States, as he may deem necessary: and upon petition to the judge of a district court for a commission of bankruptcy he shall proceed as is provided in and by an act, intituled "An act to establish an uniform system of bankruptcy throughout the United States," and appoint, not exceeding three of the said general commissioners as commissioners of the particular bankrupt petitioned against; and the said commissioners, together with the clerk, shall each be allowed as a full compensation for their services, when sitting and acting under their commissions, at the rate of six dollars per day for every day which they may be employed in the same business, to be apportioned among the several causes on which they may act on the same day, and to be paid out of the respective bankrupt's estates: Provided, that the commissioners, who may have been, or may be appointed in any district before notice shall be given of the appointment of commissioners for such district by the President in pursuance of this act, and who shall not then have completed their business, shall be authorized to proceed and finish the same, upon the terms of their original appointment.

SEC. 15. And be it further enacted, That the stated session of the district court, for the district of Virginia, heretofore directed to be holden in the city of Williamsburg shall be holden in the town of Norfolk from and after the first day of July next, and the stated sessions of the district court for the district of Maryland, shall hereafter be holden in the city of Baltimore only, and in the district of Georgia, the stated sessions of the district court shall be held in the city of Savannah only.

SEC. 16. And be it further enacted, That for the better establishment of the courts of the United States within the state of Tennessee, the said state shall be divided in two districts, one to consist of that part of said state, which lies on the east side of Cumberland mountain, and to be called the district of East Tennessee, the other to consist of the remaining part of said state, and to be called the district of West Tennessee.

SEC. 17. And be it further enacted, That the district judge of the United States, who shall hereafter perform the duties of district judge, within the state of Tennessee, shall annually hold four sessions, two at Knoxville, on the fourth Monday of April, and the fourth Monday of October, in and for the district of East Tennessee, and two at Nashville, on the fourth Monday of May, and the fourth Monday of November, in and for the district of West Tennessee.

SEC. 18. And be it further enacted, That there shall be a clerk for each of the said districts of East and West Tennessee, to be appointed by the judge thereof, who shall reside and keep the records of the said courts, at the places of holding the courts, whereto they respectively shall belong, and shall perform the same duties, and be entitled to, and receive the same emoluments and fees, which are established by law for the clerks of the district courts of the United States, respectively.

SEC. 19. And be it further enacted, That there shall be appointed, in and for each of the districts of East and West Tennessee, a marshal, whose duty it shall be to attend the district courts hereby established, and who shall have and exercise within such district, the same powers, perform the same duties, be subject to the same penalties, give the same bond with sureties, take the same oath, be entitled to the same allowance, as a full compensation for all extra services, as hath heretofore been allowed to the marshal of the district of Tennessee, by a law, passed the twenty-eighth day of February, one thousand seven hundred and ninety-nine, and shall receive the same compensation and emoluments, and in all respects be subject to the same regulations as are now prescribed by law, in respect to the marshals of the United States, heretofore appointed: Provided, that the marshals of the districts of East and West Tennessee, now in office, shall, during the periods for which they have been appointed, unless sooner removed by the President of the United States, be and continue marshals for the several districts hereby established, within which they respectively reside.

SEC. 20. And be it further enacted, That there shall be appointed for each of the districts of East and West Tennessee, a person learned in the law, to act as attorney for the United States within such district; which attorney shall take an oath or affirmation for the faithful performance of the duties of his office, and shall prosecute in such district, all delinquencies, for crimes and offences, cognizable under the authority of the United States, and all civil actions or suits, in which the United States shall be concerned; and shall be entitled to the same allowance, as a full compensation for all extra services, as hath heretofore been allowed to attornies of the district of Tennessee, by a law passed the twenty-eighth day of February, one thousand seven hundred and ninety-nine, and shall receive such compensation, emoluments and fees, as by law are or shall be allowed to the district attornies of the United States, respectively: Provided, that the district attornies of East and West Tennessee, now in office, shall severally and respectively be attornies for those districts within which they reside, until removed by the President of the United States.

SEC. 21. And be it further enacted, That all actions, suits, process, pleadings and proceedings, of what nature or kind soever, which shall be depending or existing in the sixth circuit of the United States within the circuit courts of the districts of East and West Tennessee, shall be and hereby are continued over to the district courts established by this act in manner following, that is to say: All such as shall on the first day of July next, be depending and undetermined, or shall then have been commenced, and made returnable before the circuit court of East Tennessee, to the next district court hereby directed to be holden, within and for the district of East Tennessee; all such as shall be depending and undetermined, or shall have been commenced and made returnable before the circuit court of West Tennessee, to the next district court, hereby directed to be holden, within and for the district of West Tennessee, and all the said suits shall then be equally regular and effectual, and shall be proceeded in, in the same manner as they could have been if the law, authorizing the establishment of the sixth circuit of the United States, had not been repealed.

SEC. 22. And be it further enacted, That the next session of the district court for the district of Maine, shall be holden on the last Tuesday in May next; and that the session of the said court heretofore holden on the third Tuesday of June annually, shall thereafter be holden, annually, on the last Tuesday in May.

SEC. 23. And be it further enacted, That all writs and process which shall have been issued, and all recognizances returnable, and all suits and other proceedings which have been continued to the said district court on the third Tuesday in June next, shall be returned and held continued to the said last Tuesday of May next.

SEC. 24. And be it further enacted, That the chief judge of the district of Columbia shall hold a district court of the United States, in and for the said district, on the first Tuesday of April, and on the first Tuesday of October in every year; which court shall have and exercise, within the said district, the same powers and jurisdiction which are by law vested in the district courts of the United States.

SEC. 25. And be it further enacted, That in all suits in equity, it shall be in the discretion of the court, upon the request of either party, to order the testimony of the witnesses therein to be taken by depositions; which depositions shall be taken in conformity to the regulations prescribed by law for the courts of the highest original jurisdiction in equity, in cases of a similar nature, in that state in which the court of the United States may be holden: Provided however, that nothing herein contained shall extend to the circuit courts which may be holden in those states, in which testimony in chancery is not taken by deposition.

SEC. 26. And be it further enacted, That there shall be a clerk for the district court of Norfolk, to be appointed by the judge thereof, which clerk shall reside and keep the records of the said court at Norfolk aforesaid, and shall perform the same duties, and be entitled to, and receive the same fees and emoluments which are established by law for the clerks of the district courts of the United States.

SEC. 27. And be it further enacted, That from and after the first day of July next, there shall be holden, annually, in the district of Vermont, two stated sessions of the district court, which shall commence on the tenth day of October, at Rutland, and on the seventh day of May, at Windsor, in each year; and when either of the said days shall happen on a Sunday, the said court, hereby directed to be holden on such day, shall be holden on the day next thereafter.

SEC. 28. And be it further enacted, That the act, intituled "An act altering the time of holding the district court in Vermont," and so much of the second section of the act, intituled "An act giving effect to the laws of the United States within the state of Vermont," as provides for the holding four sessions, annually, of the said district court, in said district, from and after the first day of July next, be and hereby are repealed.

SEC. 29. And be it further enacted, That the clerk of the said district court shall not issue a process to summon, or cause to be returned, to any session of the said district court, a grand jury, unless by special order of the district judge, and at the request of the district attorney; nor shall he cause to be summoned or returned, a petit jury to such sessions of the said district court, in which there shall appear to be no issue proper for the trial by jury, unless by special order of the judge as aforesaid. And it shall be the duty of the circuit court in the district of Vermont, at their stated sessions, to give in charge to the grand juries, all crimes, offences and misdemeanors, as are cognizable, as well in the said district court, as the said circuit court, and such bills of indictment as shall be found in the circuit court, and cognizable in the said district court, shall, at the discretion of the said circuit court, be transmitted by the clerk of the said court, pursuant to the order of the said circuit court, with all matters and things relating thereto, to the district court next thereafter to be holden, in said district, and the same proceedings shall be had thereon in said district court, as though said bill of indictment had originated and been found in the said district court. And all recognizances of witnesses, taken by any magistrate in said district, for their appearance to testify in any case cognizable in either of the said courts, shall be to the circuit court next thereafter to be holden in said district.

SEC. 30. And be it further enacted, That from and after the passing of this act, no special juries shall be returned by the clerks of any of the said circuit courts; but that in all cases in which it was the duty of the said clerks to return special juries before the passing of this act, it shall be the duty of the marshal for the district where such circuit court may be held, to return special juries, in the same manner and form, as, by the laws of the respective states, the said clerks were required to return the same.

APPROVED, April 29, 1802.

The Jurisdiction and Removal Act of 1875

March 3, 1875.
18 Stat. 470.

CHAP. 137. – An act to determine the jurisdiction of circuit courts of the United States, and to regulate the removal of causes from State courts, and for other purposes.

Be it enacted by the Senate and House of Representatives of the United States of America in Congress assembled, That the circuit courts of the United States shall have original cognizance, concurrent with the courts of the several States, of all suits of a civil nature at common law or in equity, where the matter in dispute exceeds, exclusive of costs, the sum or value of five hundred dollars, and arising under the Constitution or laws of the United States, or treaties made, or which shall be made, under their authority, or in which the United States are plaintiffs or petitioners, or in which there shall be a controversy between citizens of different States or a controversy between citizens of the same State claiming lands under grants of different States, or a controversy between citizens of a State and foreign states, citizens, or subjects; and shall have exclusive cognizance of all crimes and offenses cognizable under the authority of the United States, except as otherwise provided by law, and concurrent jurisdiction with the district courts of the crimes and offenses cognizable therein. But no person shall be arrested in one district for trial in another in any civil action before a circuit or district court. And no civil suit shall be brought before either of said courts against any person by any original process or proceeding in any other district than that whereof he is an inhabitant, or in which he shall be found at the time of serving such process or commencing such proceeding, except as hereinafter provided; nor shall any circuit or district court have cognizance of any suit founded on contract in favor of an assignee, unless a suit might have been prosecuted in such court to recover thereon if no assignment had been made, except in cases of promissory notes negotiable by the law merchant and bills of exchange. And the circuit courts shall also have appellate jurisdiction from the district courts under the regulations and restrictions prescribed by law.

SEC. 2. That any suit of a civil nature, at law or in equity, now pending or hereafter brought in any State court where the matter in dispute exceeds, exclusive of costs, the sum or value of five hundred dollars, and arising under the Constitution or laws of the United States, or treaties made, or which shall be made, under their authority, or in which the United States shall be plaintiff or petitioner, or in which there shall be a controversy between citizens of different States, or a controversy between citizens of the same State claiming lands under grants of different States, or a controversy between citizens of a State and foreign States, citizens, or subjects, either party may remove said suit into the circuit court of the United States for the proper district. And when in any suit mentioned in this section there shall be a controversy which is wholly between citizens of different States, and which be fully determined as between them, then either one or more of the plaintiffs or defendants actually interested in such controversy may remove said suit to the circuit court of the United States for the proper district.

SEC. 3. That whenever either party, or any one or more of the plaintiffs or defendants entitled to remove any suit mentioned in the next preceding section shall desire to remove such suit from a State court to the circuit court of the United States, he or they may make and file a petition in such suit in such State court before or at the term at which said cause could be first tried and before the trial thereof for the removal of such suit into the circuit court to be held in the district where such suit is pending, and shall make and file therewith a bond, with good and sufficient surety, for his or their entering in such circuit court, on the first day of its then next session, a copy of the record in such suit, and for paying of all costs that may be awarded by the said circuit court, if said court shall hold that such suit was wrongfully or improperly removed thereto, and also for there appearing and entering special bail in such suit, if special bail was originally requisite therein, it shall then be the duty of the State court to accept said petition and bond, and proceed no further in such suit, and any bail that may have been originally taken shall be discharged; and the said copy being entered as aforesaid in the said circuit court of the United States, the cause shall then proceed in the same manner as if it had been originally commenced in the said circuit court; and if in any action commenced in a State court the title of land be concerned, and the parties are citizens of the same State, and the matter in dispute exceed the sum or value of five hundred dollars, exclusive of costs, the sum or value being made to appear, one or more of the plaintiffs or defendants, before the trial, may state to the court, and make affidavit, if the court require it, that he or they claim and shall rely upon a right or title to the land under a grant from a State, and produce the original grant, or an exemplification of it, except where the loss of public records shall put it out of his or their power, and shall move that any one or more of the adverse party inform the court whether he or they claim a right or title to the land under a grant from some other State, the party or parties so required shall give such information, or otherwise not be allowed to plead such grant, or give it in evidence upon the trial; and if he or they inform that he or they do claim under such grant, any one or more of the party moving for such information may then, on petition and bond as hereinbefore mentioned in this act, remove the cause for trial to the circuit court of the United States next to be holden in such district; and any one of either party removing the cause shall not be allowed to plead or give evidence of any other title than that by him or them stated as aforesaid as the ground of his or their claim, and the trial of issues of fact in the circuit courts shall, in all suits except those of equity and of admiralty and maritime jurisdiction, be by jury.

SEC. 4. That when any suit shall be removed from a State court to a circuit court of the United States, any attachment or sequestration of the goods or estate of the defendant had in such suit in the State court shall hold the goods or estate so attached or sequestered to answer the final judgment or decree in the same manner as by law they would have been held to answer final judgment or decree had it been rendered by the court in which such suit was commenced; and all bonds, undertakings, or security given by either party in suit prior to its removal shall remain valid and effectual, nothwithstanding said removal; and all injunctions, orders, and other proceedings had in such suit prior to its removal shall remain in full force and effect until dissolved or modified by the court to which such suit shall be removed.

SEC. 5. That if, in any suit commenced in a circuit court or removed from a State court to a circuit court of the United States, it shall appear to the satisfaction of said circuit court, at any time after such suit has been brought or removed thereto, that suit does not really and substantially involve a dispute or controversy properly within the jurisdiction of said circuit court, or that the parties to said suit have been improperly or collusively made or joined, either as plaintiffs or defendants, for the purpose of creating a case cognizable or removable under this act, the said circuit court shall proceed no further therein, but shall dismiss the suit or remand it to the court from which it was removed as justice may require, and shall make such order as to costs as shall be just; but the order of said circuit court dismissing or remanding said cause to the State court shall be reviewable by the Supreme Court on writ of error or appeal, as the case may be.

SEC. 6. That the circuit court of the United States shall, in all suits removed under the provisions of this act, proceed therein as if the suit had been originally commenced in said circuit court, and the same proceedings had been taken in such suit in said circuit court as shall have been had therein in said State court prior to its removal.

SEC. 7. That in all causes removable under this act, if the term of the circuit court to which the same is removable, then next to be holden, shall commence within twenty days after filing the petition and bond in the State court for its removal, then he or they who apply to remove the same shall have twenty days from such application to file said copy of record in said circuit court, and enter appearance therein; and if done within said twenty days, such filing and appearance shall be taken to satisfy the said bond in that behalf; that if the clerk of the State court in which any such cause shall be pending, shall refuse to any one or more of the parties or persons applying to remove the same, a copy of the record therein, after tender of legal fees for such copy, said clerk so offending shall be deemed guilty of a misdemeanor, and, on conviction thereof in the circuit court of the United States to which said action, or proceeding was removed, shall be punished by imprisonment not more than one year, or by fine not exceeding one thousand dollars, or both in the discretion of the court.

And the circuit court to which any cause, shall be removable under this act shall have power to issue a writ of certiorari to said State court commanding such State court to make return of the record in any such cause removed as aforesaid, or in which any one or more of the plaintiffs or defendants have complied with the provisions of this act for the removal of the same, and enforce said writ according to law; and if it shall be impossible for the parties or persons removing any cause under this act, or complying with the provision for the removal thereof, to obtain such copy, for the reason that the clerk of said State court refuses to furnish a copy, on payment of legal fees, or for any other reason, the circuit court shall make an order requiring the prosecutor in any such action or proceeding to enforce forfeiture or recover penalty as aforesaid, to file a copy of the paper or proceeding by which the same was commenced, within such time as the court may determine; and in default thereof the court shall dismiss the said action or proceeding; but if said order shall be complied with, then said circuit-court shall require the other party to plead, and said action, or proceeding shall proceed to final judgment; and the said circuit court may make an order requiring the parties thereto to plead de novo; and the bond given, conditioned as aforesaid, shall be discharged so far as it requires copy of the record to be filed as aforesaid.

SEC. 8. That when in any suit, commenced in any circuit court of the United States, to enforce any legal or equitable lien upon, or claim to, or to remove any incumbrance or lien or cloud upon the title to real or personal property within the district where such suit is brought, one or more of the defendants therein shall not be an inhabitant of, or found within, the said district, or shall not voluntarily appear thereto, it shall be lawful for the court to make an order directing such absent defendant or defendants to appear, plead, answer, or demur, by a day certain to be designated, which order shall be served on such absent defendant or defendants, if practicable, wherever found, and also upon the person or persons in possession or charge of said property, if any there be; or where such personal service upon such absent defendant or defendants is not practicable, such order shall be published in such manner as the court may direct, not less than once a week for six consecutive weeks; and in case such absent defendant shall not appear, plead, answer, or demur within the time so limited, or within some further time, to be allowed by the court, in its discretion, and upon proof of the service or publication of said order, and of the performance of the directions contained in the same, it shall be lawful for the court to entertain jurisdiction, and proceed to the hearing and adjudication of such suit in the same manner as if such absent defendant had been served with process within the said district; but said adjudication shall, as regards said absent defendant or defendants without appearance, affect only the property which shall have been the subject of the suit and under the jurisdiction of the court therein, within such district. And when a part of the said real or personal property against which such proceeding shall be taken shall be within another district, but within the same State, said suit may be brought in either district in said State; Provided, however, That any defendant or defendants not actually personally notified as above provided may, at any time within one year after final judgment in any suit mentioned in this section, enter his appearance in said suit in said circuit court, and thereupon the said court shall make an order setting aside the judgment therein, and permitting said defendant or defendants to plead therein on payment by him or them of such costs as the court shall deem just; and thereupon said suit shall be proceeded with to final judgment according to law.

SEC. 9. That whenever either party to a final judgment or decree which has been or shall be rendered in any circuit court has died or shall die before the time allowed for taking an appeal or bringing a writ of error has expired, it shall not be necessary to revive the suit by any formal proceedings aforesaid. The representative of such deceased party may file in the office of the clerk of such circuit court a duly certified copy of his appointment and thereupon may enter an appeal or bring writ of error as the party he represents might have done. If the party in whose favor such judgment or decree is rendered has died before appeal taken or writ of error brought, notice to his representatives shall be given from the Supreme court, as provided in case of the death of a party after appeal taken or writ of error brought.

SEC. 10. That all acts and parts of acts in conflict with the provisions of this act are hereby repealed.

Approved, March 3. 1875.

Establishment of the U.S. Circuit Courts of Appeals, 1891

March 3, 1891.
26 Stat. 826.

CHAP. 517. — An Act to establish circuits courts of appeals and to define and regulate in certain cases the jurisdiction of the courts of the United States, and for other purposes.

Be it enacted by the Senate and House of Representatives of the United States of America in Congress assembled, That there shall be appointed by the President of the United States, by and with the advice and consent of the Senate, in each circuit an additional circuit judge, who shall have the same qualifications, and shall have the same power and jurisdiction therein that the circuit judges of the United States, within their respective circuits, now have under existing laws, and who shall be entitled to the same compensation as the circuit judges of the United States in their respective circuits now have.

SEC. 2. That there is hereby created in each circuit a circuit court of appeals, which shall consist of three judges, of whom two shall constitute a quorum, and which shall be a court of record with appellate jurisdiction, as is hereafter limited and established. Such court shall prescribe the form and style of its seal and the form of writs and other process and procedure as may be conformable to the exercise of its jurisdiction as shall be conferred by law. It shall have the appointment of the marshal of the court with the same duties and powers under the regulations of the court as are now provided for the marshal of the Supreme Court of the United States, so far as the same may be applicable. The court shall also appoint a clerk, who shall perform and exercise the same duties and powers in regard to all matters within its jurisdiction as are now exercised and performed by the clerk of the Supreme Court of the United States, so far as the same may be applicable. The salary of the marshal of the court shall be twenty-five hundred dollars a year, and the salary of the clerk of the court shall be three thousand dollars a year, to be paid in equal proportions quarterly. The costs and fees in the Supreme Court now provided for by law shall be costs and fees in the circuit courts of appeals; and the same shall be expended, accounted for, and paid for, and paid over to the Treasury Department of the United States in the same manner as is provided in respect of the costs and fees in the Supreme Court.

The court shall have power to establish all rules and regulations for the conduct of the business of the court within its jurisdiction as conferred by law.

SEC. 3. That the Chief-Justice and the associate justices of the Supreme Court assigned to each circuit, and the circuit judges within each circuit, and the several district judges within each circuit, shall be competent to sit as judges of the circuit court of appeals within their respective circuits in the manner hereinafter provided. In case the Chief-Justice or an associate justice of the Supreme Court should attend at any session of the circuit court of appeals he shall preside, and the circuit judges in attendance upon the court in the absence of the Chief-Justice or associate justice of the Supreme Court shall preside in the order of the seniority of their respective commissions.
In case the full court at any time shall not be made up by the attendance of the Chief-Justice or an associate justice of the Supreme Court and circuit judges, one or more district judges within the circuit shall be competent to sit in the court according to such order or provision among the district judges as either by general or particular assignment shall be designated by the court: Provided, That no justice or judge before whom a cause or question may have been tried or heard in a district court, or existing circuits court, shall sit on the trial or hearing of such cause or question in the circuit court of appeals. A term shall be held an-

nually by the circuit court of appeals in the several judicial circuits at the following places: In first the circuit, in the city of Boston; in the second circuit, in the city of New York; in the third circuit, in the city of Philadelphia; in the fourth circuit, in the city of Richmond; in the fifth circuit, in the city of New Orleans; in the sixth circuit, in the city of Cincinnati; in the seventh circuit, in the city of Chicago; in the eighth circuit, in the city of St. Louis; in the ninth circuit, in the city of San Francisco; and in such other places in each of the above circuits as said court may from time to time designate. The first terms of said courts shall be held on the second Monday in January, eighteen hundred and ninety-one, and thereafter at such times as may be fixed by said courts.

SEC. 4. That no appeal, whether by writ of error or otherwise, shall hereafter be taken or allowed from any district court to the existing circuit courts, and no appellate jurisdiction shall hereafter be exercised or allowed by said existing circuit courts, but all appeals by writ of error otherwise, from said district courts shall only be subject to review in the Supreme Court of the United States or in the circuit court of appeals hereby established, as is hereinafter provided, and the review, by appeal, by writ of error, or otherwise, from the existing circuit courts shall be had only in the Supreme Court of the United States or in the circuit courts of appeals hereby established according to the provisions of this act regulating the same.

SEC. 5. That appeals or writs of error may be taken from the district courts or from the existing circuit courts direct to the Supreme Court in the following cases:

In any case in which the jurisdiction of the court is in issue; in such cases the question of jurisdiction alone shall be certified to the Supreme Court from the court below for decision.

From the final sentences and decrees in prize causes.

In cases of conviction of a capital or otherwise infamous crime.

In any case that involves the construction or application of the Constitution of the United States.

In any case in which the constitutionality of any law of the United States, or the validity or construction of any treaty made under its authority is drawn in question.

In any case in which the constitution or law of a State is claimed to be in contravention of the Constitution of the United States.

Nothing in this act shall affect the jurisdiction of the Supreme Court in cases appealed from the highest court of a State, nor the construction of the statute providing for review of such cases.

SEC. 6. That the circuit courts of appeals established by this act shall exercise appellate jurisdiction to review by appeal or by writ of error final decision in the district court and the existing circuit courts in all cases other than those provided for in the preceding section of this act, unless otherwise provided by law, and the judgments or decrees of the circuit courts of appeals shall be final in all cases in which the jurisdiction is dependent entirely upon the opposite parties to the suit or controversy, being aliens and citizens of the United States citizens or citizens of different States; also in all cases arising under the patent laws, under the revenue laws, and under criminal laws as in admiralty cases, excepting that in every such subject within its appellate jurisdiction the circuit court of appeals at any time may certify to the Supreme Court of the United States any questions or propositions of law concerning which it desires the instruction of that court for its proper decision. And thereupon the Supreme Court may either give its instruction on the questions and propositions certified to it, which shall be binding upon the circuit courts of appeals in such case, or it may require that the whole record and cause may be sent up to it for its consideration, and thereupon shall decide the whole matter in controversy in the same manner as if it had been brought there for review by writ of error or appeal.

And excepting also that in any such case as is hereinbefore made final in the circuit court of appeals it shall be competent for the Supreme Court to require, by certiorari or otherwise, any such case to be certified to the Supreme Court for its review and determination with the same power and authority in the case as if it had been carried by appeal or writ of error to the Supreme Court.

In all cases not hereinbefore, in this section, made final there shall be of right an appeal or writ of error or review of the case by the Supreme Court of the United States where the matter in controversy shall exceed one thousand dollars besides costs. But no such appeal shall be taken or writ of error sued out unless within one year after the entry of the order, judgment, or decree sought to be reviewed.

SEC. 7. That where, upon a hearing in equity in a district court, or in an existing circuit court, an injunction shall be granted or continued by an interlocutory order or decree, in a cause in which an appeal from a final decree may be taken under the provisions of this act to the circuit court of appeals, an appeal may be taken from such interlocutory order or decree granting or continuing such injunction to the circuit court of appeals: Provided, That the appeal must be taken within thirty days from the entry of such order or decree, and it shall take precedence in the appellate court; and the proceedings in other respects in the court below shall not be stayed unless otherwise ordered by that court during the pendency of such appeal.

SEC. 8. That any justice or judge, who, in pursuance of the provisions of this act, shall attend the circuit court of appeals held at any place other than where he resides shall, upon his written certificate, be paid by the marshal of the district in which the court shall be held his reasonable expenses for travel and attendance, not to exceed ten dollars per day, and such payments shall be allowed the marshal in the settlement of his accounts with the United States.

SEC. 9. That the marshals of the several districts in which said circuit court of appeals may be held shall, under the direction of the Attorney-General of the United States, and with his approval, provide such rooms in the public buildings of the United States as may be necessary, and pay all incidental expenses of said court, including criers, bailiffs, and messengers: Provided, however, That in case proper rooms can not be provided in such buildings, then the said marshals, with the approval of the Attorney-General of the United States, may, from time to time, lease such rooms as may be necessary for such courts. That the marshals, criers, clerks, bailiffs, and messengers shall be allowed the same compensation for their respective services as are allowed for similar services in the existing circuit courts.

SEC. 10. That whenever on appeal or writ of error or otherwise a case coming directly from the district court or existing circuit court shall be reviewed and determined in the Supreme Court the cause shall be remanded to the proper district or circuit court for further proceedings to be taken in pursuance of such determination. And whenever on appeal or writ of error or otherwise a case coming from a circuit court of appeals shall be reviewed and determined in the Supreme Court the cause shall be remanded by the Supreme Court to the proper district or circuit court for further proceedings in pursuance of such determination. Whenever on appeal or writ or error or otherwise a case coming from a district or circuit court shall be reviewed and determined in the circuit court of appeals in a case in which the decision in the circuit court of appeals is final such cause shall be remanded to the said district or circuit court for further proceedings to be there taken in pursuance of such determination.

SEC. 11. That no appeal or writ of error by which any order, judgment, or decree may be reviewed in the circuit courts of appeals under the provisions of this act shall be taken or sued out except within six months after the entry of the order, judgment, or decree sought to be reviewed: Provided however, That in all cases in which a lesser time is now by law limited for appeals or writs of error such limits of time shall apply to appeals or writs of error in such cases taken to or sued out from the circuit courts of appeals. And all provisions of law now in force regulating the methods and system of review, through appeals or writs of error, shall regulate the methods and system of appeals and writs of error provided for in this act in respect of the circuit courts of appeals, including all provisions for bonds or other securities to be required and taken on such appeals and writs of error, and any judge of the circuit courts of appeals, in respect of cases to be brought to that court, shall have the same powers and duties as to the allowance of appeals or writs of error, and the conditions of such allowance, as now by law belong to the justices or judges in respect of the existing courts of the United States respectively.

SEC. 12. That the circuit court of appeals shall have the powers specified in section seven hundred and sixteen of the Revised Statutes of the United States.

SEC. 13. Appeals and writs of error may be taken and prosecuted from the decisions of the United States court in the Indian Territory to the Supreme Court of the United States, or to the circuit court of appeals in the eighth circuit, in the same manner and under the same regulations as from the circuit or district courts of the United States, under this act.

SEC. 14. That section six hundred and ninety-one of the Revised Statutes of the United States and section three of an act entitled "An act to facilitate the disposition of cases in the Supreme Court, and for other purposes," approved February sixteenth, eighteen hundred and seventy-five, be, and the same are hereby repealed. And all acts and parts of acts relating to appeals or writs of error inconsistent with the provisions for review by appeals or writs of error in the preceding sections five and six of this act are hereby repealed.

SEC. 15. That the circuit court of appeal in cases in which the judgments of the circuit courts of appeal are made final by this act shall have the same appellate jurisdiction, by writ of error or appeal, to review the judgments, orders, and decrees of the supreme courts of the several Territories as by this act they may have to review judgments, orders, and decrees of the district court and circuit courts; and for that purpose the several Territories shall, by orders of the Supreme court, to be made from time to time, be assigned to particular circuits.

APPROVED, March 3, 1891.

OPINION OF HON. WILLIAM. H. H. MILLER, OF INDIANA

OPINION OF HON. WILLIAM. H. H. MILLER, OF INDIANA
APPOINTED MARCH 5, 1889
DEPARTMENT OF JUSTICE
19 Op. Atty Gen. 283; 1889 U.S. AG LEXIS 57
CASE OF MAJOR W. F. SMITH
April 13, 1889

Opinion

Opinion by: The SECRETARY OF WAR

Under the act of February 14, 1889, chapter 166, S. was appointed from civil life to the position of major of engineers in the Army, and thereupon was placed on the retired list of the Army as of that grade: *Advised,* that he must take the oath required by section 1756, Revised Statutes, and that this act would be in law a legal acceptance of the office and, as such, a sufficient formal acceptance.

The provisions of sections 1259, 1763, 1764, and 1765, Revised Statutes, do not require the annulment of the appointment held by S. as agent in charge of river and harbor work at Wilmington, Del., and that he be relieved from that work.

A retired officer of the Army is not ineligible to hold an appointment to a civil office.

Concur

GARLAND

OPINION OF HON. A.H. GARLAND

OPINION OF HON. A. H. GARLAND
DEPARTMENT OF JUSTICE
19 Op. Atty Gen. 219; 1889 U.S. AG LEXIS 80
SALARY OF MINISTER
January 12, 1889

Opinion

Opinion by: The SECRETARY OF STATE

By act of July 11, 1888, chapter 614, the office of charge d'affaires to Paraguay and Uruguay, the salary of which was $5,000 per annum, was abolished, and provision made for representing the United States there by a minister at $7,500 a year. B., who at that time held the former office, was on the 11th of August, 1888, appointed minister. He received his commission at his place of duty on the 3d of October, 1888, and on the latter date took the official oath and entered upon the duties of his office as minister: *Advised* that B. is entitled to draw his salary as minister from the 3d of October, 1888, the date on which he qualified for the office and entered upon its duties, and not from the date of his appointment (Aug. 11, 1888).

Concur

GARLAND

OPINION OF HON. RICHARD OLNEY

OPINION OF HON. RICHARD OLNEY
DEPARTMENT OF JUSTICE
20 Op. Atty Gen. 590; 1893 U.S. AG LEXIS 56
CRIMES IN FOREIGN COUNTRIES
May 8, 1893

Opinion

Opinion by: The SECRETARY OF STATE

No Federal court has jurisdiction to try persons whether or not claiming to be American citizens for crimes committed in foreign countries.

There are no common law offenses against the United States.

Concur

OLNEY

Dissent

SIR: I am in receipt of your communication of March 17, in relation to the case of James S. Proctor.

I am informed that said Proctor, claiming to be a citizen of the United States, is charged with murdering a native upon land in one of the New Hebrides Islands; that said islands are under the domain of no civilized power, except that Great Britain exercises some jurisdiction over them through a high commissioner, who, however, declines to exercise jurisdiction over this case; and that the islands are not within the jurisdiction of any consular officer of this Government.

My official opinion is asked as to whether any Federal court would have jurisdiction to try Proctor upon this charge if he should be brought before it under section 730 of the Revised Statutes, which provides that --

"The trial of all offenses committed upon the high seas *or elsewhere* out of the jurisdiction of any particular State or district shall be in the district where the offender is found, or into which he is first brought."

But the word "offenses" means "offenses against the United States." There are no common law offenses against the United States and Congress has not placed wrongs done upon foreign soil in this category.

I am obliged to answer the question in the negative.

Very respectfully,

RICHARD OLNEY.

JOINT RESOLUTION

"Joint Resolution

To assure uniform value to the coins and currencies of the United States.

Whereas the holding of or dealing in gold affect the public interest, and are therefore subject to proper regulation and restriction; and

Whereas the existing emergency has disclosed that provisions of obligations which purport to give the obligee a right to require payment in gold or a particular kind of coin or currency of the United States, or in an amount in money of the United States measured thereby, obstruct the power of the Congress to regulate the value of the money of the United States, and are inconsistent with the declared policy of the Congress to maintain at all times the equal power of every dollar, coined or issued by the United States, in the markets and in the payment of debts. Now, therefore, be it

Resolved by the Senate and House of Representatives of the United States of America in Congress assembled, That (a) every provision contained in or made with respect to any obligation which purports to give the obligee a right to require payment in gold or a particular kind of coin or currency, or in an amount in money of the United States measured thereby, is declared to be against public policy; and no such provision shall be contained in or made with respect to any obligation hereafter incurred. Every obligation, heretofore or hereafter incurred, whether or not any such provision is contained therein or made with respect thereto, shall be discharged upon payment, dollar for dollar, in any coin or currency which at the time of payment is legal tender for public and private debts. Any such provision contained in any law authorizing obligations to be issued by or under authority of the United States, is hereby repealed, but the repeal of any such provision shall not invalidate any other provision or authority contained in such law.

(b) As used in this resolution, the term 'obligation' means an obligation (including every obligation of and to the United States, excepting currency) payable in money of the United States; and the term 'coin or currency' means coin or currency of the United States, including Federal Reserve notes and circulating notes of Federal Reserve banks and national banking associations.

Sec. 2. The last sentence of paragraph (1) of subsection (b) of § 43 of the Act entitled 'An Act to relieve the existing national economic emergency by increasing agricultural purchasing power, to raise revenue for extraordinary expenses incurred by reason of such emergency, to provide emergency relief with respect to agricultural indebtedness, to provide for the orderly liquidation of joint-stock land banks, and for other purposes,' approved May 12, 1933, is amended to read as follows:

'All coins and currencies of the United States (including Federal Reserve notes and circulating notes of Federal Reserve banks and national banking associations) heretofore or hereafter coined or issued, shall be legal tender for all debts, public and private, public charges, taxes, duties, and dues, except that gold coins, when below the standard weight and limit of tolerance provided by law for the single piece, shall be legal tender only at valuation in proportion to their actual weight.'

Approved, June 5, 1933, 4.40 p. m."

Federal register / Vol. 80, No. 45 / Monday, March 9, 2015 /

Notices

on February 3, 2014, based on a complaint filed on behalf of Macronix International Co., Ltd. of Hsin-chu, Taiwan and Macronix America, Inc. of Milpitas, California, 79 FR 6227–28. The complaint, as amended, alleges violations of section 337 of the Tariff Act of 1930, as amended, 19 U.S.C. 1337, in the importation into the United States, the sale for importation, and the sale within the United States after importation of certain non-volatile memory devices and products containing the same by reason of infringement of certain claims of U.S. Patent Nos. 6,552,360; 6,100,557; and 6,002,630. The complaint further alleges a domestic industry exists or is in the process of being established. The Commission's notice of investigation, as amended, named the following respondents: Spansion, Inc., Spansion LLC, and Ruckus Wireless, Inc., all of Sunnyvale, California; Spansion (Thailand) Ltd. of Nonthaburi, Thailand; Tellabs Operations, Inc. and Tellabs North America, Inc., both of Naperville, Illinois (collectively, "the Tellabs respondents"); Beats Electronics LLC of Santa Monica, California; Delphi Automotive PLC of Kent, United Kingdom; Delphi Automotive Systems, LLC of Troy, Michigan; Harman International Industries, Inc. of Stamford, Connecticut; Harman Becker Automotive Systems, Inc. of Farmington Hills, Michigan; and Harman Becker Automotive Systems GmbH of Karlsbad, Germany. The Office of Unfair Import Investigations participated in the investigation.

On September 4, 2014, the Commission issued notice of its determination not to review the ALJ's ID (Order No. 15) terminating the investigation as to original respondent Tellabs, Inc. of Naperville, Illinois, and amending the complaint and notice of investigation to substitute the Tellabs respondents for Tellabs, Inc.

On January 29, 2015, complainants and all respondents jointly moved to terminate the investigation with respect to all respondents based on a settlement agreement. The Commission investigative attorney filed a response supporting the motion.

On January 30, 2015, the ALJ issued the subject ID (Order No. 23) granting the joint motion for termination of the investigation as to all respondents. He found that the motion satisfies Commission rules 210.21(a)(2), (b)(1). No party petitioned for review of the ID.

The Commission has determined not to review the subject ID, and has terminated the investigation.

The authority for the Commission's determination is contained in section 337 of the Tariff Act of 1930, as amended, 19 U.S.C. 1337, and in Part 210 of the Commission's Rules of Practice and Procedure, 19 CFR part 210.

By order of the Commission.

Issued: March 4, 2015.

Lisa R. Barton,
Secretary to the Commission.
[FR Doc. 2015–05424 Filed 3–6–15; 8:45 am]
BILLING CODE 7020–02–P

DEPARTMENT OF JUSTICE

Bureau of Prisons

Annual Determination of Average Cost of Incarceration

AGENCY: Bureau of Prisons, Justice.

ACTION: Notice.

SUMMARY: The fee to cover the average cost of incarceration for Federal inmates in Fiscal Year 2014 was $30,619.85 ($83.89 per day). (Please note: There were 365 days in FY 2014.) The average annual cost to confine an inmate in a Residential Re-entry Center for Fiscal Year 2014 was $28,999.25 ($79.45 per day).

DATES: *Effective Date:* March 10, 2015.

ADDRESSES: Office of General Counsel, Federal Bureau of Prisons, 320 First St. NW., Washington, DC 20534.

FOR FURTHER INFORMATION CONTACT: Sarah Qureshi, (202) 307–2105.

SUPPLEMENTARY INFORMATION: 28 CFR part 505 allows for assessment and collection of a fee to cover the average cost of incarceration for Federal inmates. We calculate this fee by dividing the number representing Bureau of Prisons facilities' monetary obligation (excluding activation costs) by the number of inmate-days incurred for the preceding fiscal year, and then by multiplying the quotient by 365. Under § 505.2, the Director of the Bureau of Prisons determined that, based upon fiscal year 2014 data, the fee to cover the average cost of incarceration for Federal inmates in Fiscal Year 2014 was $30,619.85 ($83.89 per day). (Please note: There were 365 days in FY 2014.) The average annual cost to confine an inmate in a Residential Re-entry Center for Fiscal Year 2014 was $28,999.25 ($79.45 per day).

Charles E. Samuels, Jr.,
Director, Bureau of Prisons.
[FR Doc. 2015–05437 Filed 3–6–15; 8:45 am]
BILLING CODE 4410–05–P

DEPARTMENT OF LABOR

Office of the Secretary

Bureau of International Labor Affairs National Advisory Committee for Labor Provisions of U.S. Free Trade Agreements

AGENCY: Bureau of International Labor Affairs, Department of Labor.

ACTION: Notice of Charter Renewal.

SUMMARY: Pursuant to the Federal Advisory Committee Act (FACA), as amended (5 U.S.C. App. 2), the North American Agreement on Labor Cooperation (NAALC), and the Labor Chapters of U.S. Free Trade Agreements (FTAs), the Secretary of Labor has determined that the renewal of the charter of the National Advisory Committee for Labor Provisions of U.S. Free Trade Agreements (NAC) is necessary and in the public interest and will provide information that cannot be obtained from other sources. The committee shall provide its views to the Secretary of Labor through the Bureau of International Labor Affairs of the U.S. Department of Labor, which is the point of contact for the NAALC and the Labor Chapters of U.S. FTAs. The committee shall comprise twelve members, four representing the labor community, four representing the business community, and four representing the public.

Purpose: In accordance with the provisions of the FACA, Article 17 of the NAALC, Article 17.4 of the United States-Singapore Free Trade Agreement, Article 18.4 of the United States-Chile Free Trade Agreement, Article 18.4 of the United States-Australia Free Trade Agreement, Article 16.4 of the United States-Morocco Free Trade Agreement, Article 16.4 of the Central America-Dominican Republic-United States Free Trade Agreement (CAFTA–DR), Article 15.4 of the United States-Bahrain Free Trade Agreement, Article 16.4 of the United States-Oman Free Trade Agreement, Article 17.5 of the United States-Peru Trade Promotion Agreement, Article 17.5 of the United States-Colombia Trade Promotion Agreement, Article 19.5 of the United States-Korea Free Trade Agreement, and Article 16.5 of the United States-Panama Trade Promotion Agreement, the Secretary of Labor has determined that the renewal of the charter of the NAC is necessary and in the public interest and will provide information that cannot be obtained from other sources.

The Bureau of International Labor Affairs of the U.S. Department of Labor serves as the U.S. point of contact under the FTAs listed above. The committee